ROBERT FULTON

Books by Cynthia Owen Philip

Robert Fulton: *A Biography*
Imprisoned in America: *Communications From Prison 1776 Through Attica*

Cynthia Owen Philip

ROBERT FULTON

A BIOGRAPHY

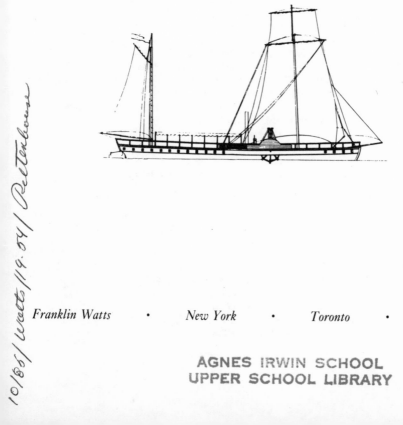

Franklin Watts • *New York* • *Toronto* • *1985*

Library of Congress Cataloging in Publication Data

Philip, Cynthia Owen.
Robert Fulton, a biography.

Bibliography: p.
Includes index.
1. Fulton, Robert, 1765–1815. 2. Marine Engineers
—United States—Biography. 3. Inventors—
United States—Biography. 4. Technology—
United States—History—18th century. 5. Technology
—United States—History—19th century. I. Title.
VM140.F9P45   1985   623.82'4'0924   [B]   85-3324
ISBN 0-531-09756-0

CONTENTS

Contents

"As the component parts of all
new machines may be said to be old . . .
the mechanic should sit down among
levers, screws, wedges, wheels, etc.
like a poet among the letters of
the alphabet, considering them as
the exhibition of his thoughts;
in which a new arrangement transmits
a new idea to the world."

Robert Fulton

To N. W. P.

· A C K N O W L E D G M E N T S ·

The recapturing of Robert Fulton's extraordinarily variegated life has been a great adventure, for the letters, diaries, business records, drawings, and paintings on which this biography is based are scattered in public and private collections in the United States, Great Britain, and France. My first thanks go to the many curators of documents and artworks for their unfailingly inventive and generous help. I am especially grateful to Thomas J. Dunnings, Jr., curator of manuscripts of the New-York Historical Society, whose cheerful interest has sustained me from the beginning of my research. Sara Dunlap Jackson, archivist of the National Historical Publications and Records Commission, John C. Dann, director of the William L. Clements Library, the University of Michigan, and John Bidwell, reference-acquisitions librarian of the William Andrews Clark Memorial Library, University of California, Los Angeles, led me to material I would not have found on my own. Jacques Payen of the Centre de Documentation d'Histoire des Techniques painstakingly explained the wonders of early French industrialization to me. Sheryl Gold, regional historic preservation supervisor, New York State Office of Parks, Recreation and Historic Preservation, and Bruce E. Naramore, historic site manager, Clermont State Historic Park, gave me the great joy of working with an abundance of rich materials in surroundings that Fulton knew well. Lillian Miller, editor of the Charles Willson Peale Papers, opened that invaluable collection to me when it was still in the process of being assembled. Charles M. Harris, Jr., editor of the William Thornton Papers, freely offered the fruits of his extensive labors, even though Robert Fulton and William Thornton were archenemies. Alan Frazer, curator/registrar of the New Jersey Historical Society, instructed me patiently in the wonders of the Alofsen-Stoudinger collection of engineering drawings. Richard Wiles, Professor of Economics, Bard College, illuminated important aspects of the financial background. The John Ross Delafield Foundation was exceptionally generous in allowing me to examine many of its fine documents.

Without the companionship of friends who read, encouraged, and criticized, this adventure would have been a weary trek. Norman MacKenzie, Scott Mykel, John Winthrop Aldrich, Richard Faust, Frank Jacobi, and Martica Sawin each provided special support. Patricia Owen Steiner and Nicholas Philip gracefully applied their rigorous intellects to criticizing the penultimate draft of my manuscript. Rafael Villier helped me organize and understand the myriad graphic materials. Finally, I thank the Rockefeller Foundation at whose Bellagio Study and Conference Center I enjoyed a delightfully resuscitating month of scholarly fellowship.

Pennsylvania Roots

❖

It was a hero's burial. On Saturday, February 25, 1815, as the last rays of the afternoon sun spilled across the New Jersey meadows reddening the great ice-filled Hudson River, knots of men wearing badges of mourning trudged through the freezing slush of lower Manhattan to pay their last respects to the inventor and entrepreneur Robert Fulton.

Reverently, Fulton was pronounced a national benefactor. The steamboat network he had established on the Hudson and Mississippi rivers was unique in the world, and his recently launched steam frigate, *Fulton I*, promised to make the United States equal to any nation in naval power. In the eight short years since his return from Europe, he had become a symbol of the country's dream of leading the technological revolution. "His is the only loss for which the public has no indemnity," the *New-York Evening Post*'s obituary proclaimed. "Politicians, historians, Poets etc. are found throughout the United States, and readily succeed to each other, but there is no person who will succeed to Mr. Fulton's genius as a mechanic, or be capable of prosecuting those schemes which he left in an unfinished state."

Fulton died of pneumonia on February 23. The following day, the newspapers announced his death in notices bordered with heavy black ink. In hurriedly called meetings, the cultural and trade associations to which he belonged—the New-York Historical Society, the Literary and

Philosophical Society, the Academy of Arts, and the General Society of Mechanics and Tradesmen—declared that, as a special tribute, they would join his cortege in membership groups. Thus the mourners came at this bleak hour not only from the handsome residences of nearby Wall Street, State Street, and Broadway but also from the workmen's neighborhoods north of City Hall and from the wharves of the East and Hudson rivers. Their mood was fittingly somber, for Fulton's death had been sudden, and in the fine mansion on the corner of Marketfield and State streets, just across the bowling green, were his grieving young widow and their four children, the eldest a boy only six years old.

Still, the event was suffused with an excitement that could not be entirely suppressed. The Treaty of Ghent ending the War of 1812 had been ratified the previous Saturday. All week long the city had been preparing a victory celebration of fireworks and light shows that would take place in two days. The Old Government House where the procession now assembled had already been transformed with transparent paper hangings into a "Temple of Peace." The air was electric with the challenges of a new era, of which Fulton, even in death, was a part.

Shortly after half-past four, the simple mahogany coffin with its small metal plaque engraved "Robert Fulton, age 49" was carried down the front steps of his home into the street. To the dull beat of guns fired from the West Battery and from the *Fulton I*, the marchers, led by all the federal, state, and city officials then in town, moved slowly up Broadway to Trinity Church where, to the ancient cadences, "ashes to ashes, dust to dust," Fulton's body was interred in the vault owned by his wife's family.

No New Yorker had ever been accorded so splendid a funeral. Yet dispersed through the crowd were scornful detractors who murmured that the much vaunted Fulton had callously used his rich, politically well-connected partners as a ladder to success. In his relentless quest for personal "fame and emolument," they complained, he had stolen the inventions of less ruthless and grasping predecessors. To defend his steamboat empire, he had committed perjury and perhaps even fraud.

This bitter carping was provoked by envy, for Fulton was believed to have reaped immense profits from his enterprises. It was magnified by his fierce pride and his vision. Like many bold imaginers, Fulton excited controversy. The perplexing contradictions of his character were, however, a source as well as a manifestation of his creative genius.

Robert Fulton was born on November 14, 1765, on a farm in Little Britain Township, Pennsylvania. Both his mother and father were Scotch-Irish immigrants. Robert Fulton, Senior, came from Kilkenny, Ireland, as a young man. By 1735 he had taken up the trade of tailor in Lancaster, Pennsylvania, a newly established frontier settlement, soon to become the largest inland town in America. Not until he was well into his forties did Fulton senior marry. His bride, Mary Smith, was from an educated family that must have been comparatively well off, for her father bequeathed her five pounds in his will and her brother was a promising minister in the church. For a small down payment and a large mortgage, the newly married couple bought a modest house on Lancaster's Central Square. They soon produced three daughters.

A gregarious man, Fulton senior was secretary of the volunteer fire company, an association almost as important for its convivial and political functions as for its utilitarian services. He was a charter member of the Juliana Library, the third oldest library in the country, and a founder and dedicated chorister of the First Presbyterian Church whose congregation included many of the prominent families of Lancaster. For a brief period he was the assistant burgess of the borough. He augmented his earnings as a tailor by trading in staples, including rum.

Mary Smith Fulton seems to have been a prudent woman, a steadfast helpmate, and a much needed balance wheel to her husband. Fragmentary evidence gleaned from later correspondence suggests that her primary concerns were the care of her little girls and the maintenance of close relations with her own family. Her most cherished hobby was gardening.

In February 1765 Robert and Mary Fulton sold their house and with the proceeds bought at auction a large farm on Conowingo Creek in Little Britain Township, a predominantly Presbyterian settlement thirty miles to the south of Lancaster. The property comprised 394 acres in two parcels, and a trim two-story house, solidly constructed of gray and brown stone. All of it was heavily mortgaged. The move from Lancaster constituted a significant uprooting for Fulton senior, who obviously enjoyed the ready sociability of town living. Perhaps Mary persuaded him that the country was a better place to bring up their daughters than Lancaster, which then supported thirty-two taverns.

Little more than nine months later, Mary Fulton gave birth to their first son. A handsome, brown-eyed baby, he was named Robert Fulton for his father.

There is no record of Robert's early years, but for his father, they were far from idyllic. Limestone fertilizer, which later increased the grain yields in that section of Pennsylvania, had not yet come into use, and although much of the soil was moderately productive, it needed an experienced hand as well as luck with the weather to make it pay. Somehow Fulton senior survived the unruly growing season of 1768, during which the hailstorms were so fierce that crops were flattened, fruit trees debarked, poultry decapitated, and windows shattered. In 1771 he paid the substantial tax of 1£2s6p on an establishment that boasted four head of cattle, two "prize" horses, one common horse, and one servant. The prosperity implied by that inventory was an illusion, however. He was, in fact, overwhelmed by debt.

In the grim January of 1772, Fulton senior was forced to sell his house, as he had bought it seven years earlier, at a sherriff's sale. Even the beds and kitchen utensils were auctioned, "only our Clothing was Excepted," he wrote the two mortgage holders who had taken steps to dispose of the remaining land. Hoping his good intentions would save him, he begged them to sell only the best meadows and orchards on which he claimed to have made improvements that doubled their value, and to permit him to continue farming the rest. "Y have Nothing to By Land Back Nor money to settup with in town Besides it is verrey Desegreable to my wife and Family to go Back," he wrote, "if you would be so good to sell only 200 acckr . . . with that Land & my head y Could Bring up my Family."[1] The mortgagors did not respond kindly to his plea and Fulton senior had no choice but to take his family—now increased by the birth of a second son—to Lancaster and resume the business of tailoring. Two years later, in 1774, Fulton senior died. In all probability his death was unexpected, for he had recently taken on an apprentice, and in an era when even the poor formally bequeathed such items as petticoats and tankards, he left no will.

The immediate effect on the six-year-old Robert of the humiliating sale of his home, followed so swiftly by the loss of his father, can only be imagined. In the many letters that have been preserved, Fulton never directly mentions his father. The single faint allusion to his death seems to deny him. When Fulton was twenty-three years old and living in London, he wrote to a Lancaster friend that he hoped the ailing King George would not die, because it would put him to the expense of buying mourning clothes. "As I never was in mourning for any of my own Family," he explained, "I think it hard to begin with People I have not the pleasure to be acquainted with."[2]

Unquestionably, Fulton felt the burden of being the eldest male in the family, more keenly perhaps because he bore the same name as his father. Despite years of separation he was always solicitous toward his mother and his sisters and helped them financially whenever he could. Yet his few existing letters to them, especially those to his mother, have a stilted quality that indicates a deep unhealed hurt.

Catastrophe, however, sometimes has a redeeming aspect. For young Fulton the return to Lancaster was a godsend. It was an exciting town. In addition to proliferating taverns, it had at least five hundred houses and over four thousand people. Connected to High Street in Philadelphia by the Kings Highway, to the western wilderness by the great Conestoga Road, and to the inland South by ancient Indian trails, it mingled the sophistication of a city with the turmoil of a crossroads and the individualism of the frontier. The first Lancastrians were real-estate speculators of English origin, but almost immediately the population was diversified by an influx of Swiss Mennonites, German Lutherans and Moravians, Jewish fur traders, French Huguenots, a few freed blacks and some slaves, and the strong Scotch-Irish Presbyterian group to which Fulton belonged. However, Lancaster made no attempt to become a melting pot. Each ethnic group retained its language and customs. The Huguenots persisted in speaking French. The Germans maintained German schools and newspapers. The Irish celebrated St. Patrick's Day, and until the Revolutionary War was declared, the English marked the king's birthday with stately dinners. Fourteen separate religious denominations claimed worshipers.

Most of the inhabitants were artisans and mechanics, attracted by cheap land. The gunsmiths were the elite craftsmen, but the builders of of the sturdy Conestoga wagons were also justly renowned. There were flourishing weaving, leather, and printing industries. Tradesmen, many with Philadelphia connections, prospered by serving the inhabitants' daily needs and by provisioning pioneers bound for the West. In the outlying areas, along with the productive farms, were a glassworks and a foundry that manufactured stoves. Ink, sheet music, and organs were produced by the Moravian community at nearby Lititz.

The widow Fulton managed well after her husband's death, probably with the help of relatives. The family was poor, but not impoverished. There were warm fires in which to roast chestnuts, books to read aloud, and the company of affectionate friends. Fulton indulged in the usual sibling contests, especially with his sisters; he seems to have dealt with his younger brother by ignoring him. In a sentimental, but probably reasonably accurate recollection to Betsy, the eldest, he wrote:

> I remember when we all lived in Lancaster opposite Irving *Beefs* and when you and Bell were good industrious girls. I was a stripling of a boy about 12 years old. Our mother being at Mr. Craig's in the country I had a battle against the two Sisters. You and Bell had turned me and the cat out of the truckle bed. It was of a winters evening about 8 o'clock. I instantly flew to the tongs and, as I stood in my shirt with uplifted arms ready to knock all your brains out, you were so much astonished at my resolute manner and wickedness as you supposed, that you began to cry and said you were sure I should some day be hanged. . . . I was instantly disarmed and throwing down the tongs I went up to you, took you by the hand and said no Betsy I shall live to be the protector of you and the family.[3]

Fulton received his earliest education from his mother. Then she placed him under the tutelage of one Caleb Johnson, a colorful Tory Quaker and a jack-of-all-trades. In addition to being a schoolmaster, Johnson was the building contractor for the workhouse and prison and a shopkeeper. From 1770 to 1776, he was clerk of the county commissioners. In 1777, he was incarcerated for aiding a notorious libeler of the revolutionary government escape jail. There is no record of how extensive a curriculum Johnson attempted; evidently he was an education in himself. Moreover, the town was small enough so that to an adventurous spirit, such as Fulton possessed, opportunities for learning by observing and questioning were always near at hand.

The legends describing Fulton's early creative genius probably contain some germ of truth. He is said to have invented a Roman candle, an air gun, a lead pencil, and a fishing boat with mechanical paddles, to have made so many experiments with mercury that he was known as "Quicksilver Bob," to have designed arabesques for gun barrels, and to have been a remarkable watercolorist. The story that Fulton was a dreamer with no taste for book learning seems highly unlikely. One of the traits that later distinguished him from rival experimenters was that he was not a tinkerer. He was able to use, and enjoy, printed material.

He evidently prized his own copy of Euclid's *Elements*, for on its flyleaf is the following verse, signed with a still immature hand:

> I write my name for to Betray
> Those that do Steal this Book away
> Steal not this Book for fear of Shame
> For here you see the owners name.[4]

Since his father had been a founding member, Fulton undoubtedly had access to the Juliana Library, which offered such delights as *Tom Jones*, *The Gentleman's Magazine*, and *London and Its Environs Described* as well as useful volumes such as *Ward's Young Mathematicians Guide*, *Mott's Treatise on Mechanical Powers*, and assorted works by Locke, Montesquieu, Addison, Newton, and Franklin. The library was kept by the scientist-mechanic William Henry, whose house was the intellectual center of Lancaster. A gifted eclectic, Henry had been Commander Edward Braddock's armorer during the French and Indian War. As surveyor general he had laid out a route for a canal between the Susquehanna and Lehigh rivers. More recently, he had invented a screw augur and built a model of a vessel propelled by steam. In addition to books, his rooms displayed such interesting items as an ostrich egg, an artificial magnet, an electric machine, a globe, various astronomical instruments, and a fine canvas entitled *The Death of Socrates* by a local artist named Benjamin West who had gone on to achieve fame, first in Italy and then in England. So lively a setting could not have failed to mold and inspire the young Fulton.

However, it was probably the Revolutionary War that made the most lasting impression on Fulton. It began when he was ten years old. No battles or even skirmishes were fought in Lancaster, and it is doubtful that Fulton ever felt personally threatened, but the focus of life was suddenly enlarged beyond local concerns to include the entire new nation and Europe as well. From the outset, the Lancastrians were zealous patriots; the Scotch-Irish were especially fervent revolutionaries. In 1777, the town was designated the supply center for the Continental Army. In addition to guns and wagons, it provided food, clothing, and horses and was a way station for American troops on the march. British and Hessian prisoners, as many as a thousand at a time, together with their wives, children and hangers-on, were encamped there. The townspeople complained about the malignant fevers that started in the prison compounds, but, because labor was in short supply, they were allowed to work as gunsmiths, weavers, wheelwrights, skin dressers, shoemakers and farm hands.

When the British occupied Philadelphia, refugees flooded into Lancaster. Thomas Paine was one of the early arrivals. He moved in with an eminent citizen named Caleb Cope and published the fifth number of the *American Crisis* series while there. William Henry gave shelter to David Rittenhouse, the brillant self-taught clockmaker and astronomer. The state government was briefly shifted to Lancaster, and the Continental Congress stopped by on its progress to York, gracing the town with the presence of Samuel and John Adams, John Hancock, and Charles Carroll.

Still, life went on with its customary demonstrations of good and evil. Weddings were performed, even for Anglicans whose church was boarded up because of its political affiliation. Horse thieves were hanged, whipped, or pilloried, depending on the enormity of their offense and the extent of their influence. There was hoarding, price gouging, and rampant inflation, and many basic necessities, such as pocket knives and frying pans, were impossible to obtain. At the same time, French fripperies abounded in the shops, especially after the Philadelphian infiltration. Season subscriptions to the dancing assemblies cost $300 and were in short supply. Christopher Marshall, a prominent Quaker apothecary who supplied medicine to troops and also speculated in sugar and whiskey, complained that due to lack of workmen he was forced to patch his own outhouse. "This is a strange age & place in which I dwell," he noted in his diary, "because nothing can be had cheap but lies, falsehood, & slanderous accusations."[5] Fulton's lifelong rage against the effects of war on the civilian population undoubtedly took root during these years.

When he was about fifteen years old, Fulton was apprenticed to a silversmith in Philadelphia, much against his inclinations, he later told a close friend. Even so, his years there must have been a great adventure. Despite the ravages of the war in the outlying districts, Philadelphia had weathered the British occupation well and was a handsome, cosmopolitan city. With a population of nearly forty thousand, it was the preeminent city of the new Republic, its center of painting, invention, philosophical and political thought, publishing, and shipping and commerce. Next to London, it was the most exciting English-speaking city in the world. The wide, paved streets, laid out on a grid, were provided with lights, brick walkways, and at frequent intervals, public water pumps. The uniform houses bespoke an understated opulence. Many of the "best" citizens had benefited from the war.

"Philadelphia," an acerbic French observer commented, "is the great sink wherein all the speculation of America terminates and mingles."[6] Yet, beneath its sophisticated exterior, the city's spirit was truly revolutionary. A German traveler reported less distinction in rank among its inhabitants than could be found in any other city in the world. Philadelphians were known for their charitable institutions. The prison reform and abolitionist movements were already strong.

No sure clue exists as to who Fulton's master was, but silversmiths were highly regarded. Most of them were patrons of civic and religious life and, because of the role of silver as specie, functioned as bankers. During his apprenticeship, Fulton must have learned something of design, metalworking, and money management—skills that would serve him in later life—but he liked neither the craft nor his subordinate position. Somehow, he obtained the means to buy back his indenture and set himself up as a miniaturist in a building owned by an engraver named James Trench. The location was excellent—on the corner of Second and Walnut streets, opposite the London Coffee House, Philadelphia's temple of gossip, news, commerce, and ticket sales.

In addition to portraiture Fulton offered hairworking—the making of meticulously executed pictures from human hair, usually intended as gifts. Dr. Benjamin Rush's description of the hairpiece he had made for an English friend in 1785 explains the elaborate detail involved. The memento, he wrote the recipient, was set on the reverse of a miniature portrait of Mrs. Rush and represented "your ladyship as having arrived in America and visiting your brother's tomb. A gentleman is pointing to the monument on which the words are inscribed 'Wm. Leslie ob. January 3rd, age 26.' Near your ladyship's lips is placed the following exclamation: 'Ah Willie.' Above the urn which stands on the monument are these words: 'My Redeemer liveth.' Over the whole device is thrown a large weeping willow. The figures of the monument, the urn, the lady, the willow and all the letters are composed of your ladyship's hair; the figure of the gentleman is composed of mine."[7] Both miniature painting and hairworking required formidable manual dexterity and patience. To undertake such painstaking work, Fulton must have possessed these characteristics innately. Later, he would exercise the same care in developing his engineering designs.

William Dunlap, in *A History of the Rise and Progress of the Arts of Design in the United States*, published nineteen years after Fulton's death, stated that Fulton probably received instruction in painting from the artist and showman Charles Willson Peale. The ingenious Peale, who had studied in London with Benjamin West, was so ubiquitous a public figure that Fulton must have been at least acquainted with him. Robert Edge Pine, who arrived from England in 1784 with a large collection of paintings and drawings, may also have given him some help. However, these men, and many others of lesser rank, would have provided strong competition as well. Still Fulton attracted enough clients to give him encouragement and a decent income.

Eight miniatures, two large oil portraits, and two landscapes have been attributed to his brush during this period. The style of several miniatures is forced, and the landscapes—a romantic river scene and the idyllic *La Blanchisseuse* (The Washerwoman)—were probably copied from engravings. Fulton's miniature of a young man named John Brown, set into the lid of a small box, conveys an extraordinarily vivid presence, however, and the large portrait of his friend, Joseph Bringhurst, is arresting for the attempt to manipulate light and shadow, a technique Fulton would later use to stunning advantage in renderings of wheels, shafts, and gears.

Nonetheless, it is difficult to believe that Fulton supported himself entirely from painting and hairworking. The prices the trades commanded were low, painting materials were expensive, and most artists were forced to supplement their incomes. Peale, for instance, maintained a portrait gallery of famous Americans to which he charged admission. He also presented moving picture shows—entertainments two hours long with sound effects and up to five changes of scene. Other artists designed shop signs and ornamented fire engines and carriages. Fulton probably continued his silverworking, for he is said to have been associated with Jeremiah Andrews, a jeweler who also had a Walnut Street shop.

There is no evidence that Fulton participated in the vigorous scientific life of Philadelphia, although it would not be surprising if he had. His age, background, and pocketbook would not have been obstacles, for science brought together men of all stations. The membership of the flourishing American Philosophical Society comprised merchants and ironmongers as well as clockmakers, physicians, and internationally celebrated figures. So avid was the general population for scientific mate-

Pennsylvania Roots

rial that articles were printed in newspapers before they were available in pamphlet form. Christopher Colles, an English immigrant who in 1771 had built the first American steam engine, made a good living by teaching night classes for mechanics. The subjects he advertised were "hydraulics, hydrostatics and pneumatics and the application of these sciences to the construction of water works, docks, bridges, locks, sluices and aqueducts for inland navigation and engines for abridging the labour of men."[8]

Benjamin Franklin's return from Europe in the autumn of 1785, celebrated with a delirium of brass bands and flying flags, pushed the scientific fever still higher. His house became a mecca for inventors. Thomas Paine first exhibited the model of his cast-iron bridge there. John Fitch later wrote that Franklin had spoken highly of the stern-paddle steamboat he was trying to build, although Franklin went on record in favor of a system of propulsion that drew water into a pipe at the bow and forced it out through the stern. Fulton's primary interest was still painting, but he could not have failed to absorb the scientific ferment.

It is disappointing that there are so few clues to Fulton's social life in Philadelphia. Brief references in later correspondence give the impression that he had many close men friends. Over six feet tall, with thick, curly brown hair, dark, intense eyes, strong, regular features, and full, finely shaped lips, he must have already developed the "vivacity, activity, comprehension and clearness of intellect"[9] that would always draw people to him.

Early in 1786, Fulton was taken ill with a blood-spitting inflammation of the lungs, probably tuberculosis, a common Philadelphia scourge. Contemporary cures for consumption included blisters, purges, prunes, salt in large doses, laudanum, clear mountain air, and exercise. *Poor Richard's Almanack* advocated a concoction of red roses and niter to be taken by the teaspoonful four to eight times a day depending on the urgency of the case. Fulton chose to visit the Warm Springs at Bath, Virginia. "Ye Famed Warm Springs," as George Washington called it when he visited as a young surveyor in 1748, had developed into a rustic but fashionable resort. In addition to a high elevation, from which the upper Potomac could be viewed, and its healthful waters—hot enough to boil an egg—it offered dancing, gambling, theatricals, horseracing, and a chance to rub shoulders with such luminaries as the Fairfaxes, the Carters, and the Washingtons.

Among the local residents of Bath was an innkeeper and carpenter named James Rumsey. After having entrusted him with the building of his house at the spa, Washington was so impressed with his abilities that he sponsored his appointment as the chief engineer of the canal that was to bypass the Great Falls of the Potomac River. At the same time, Rumsey was secretly working on a boat that would be capable of ascending a river using the current as a propelling force. A catamaran, it had a paddle wheel in the center that activated long poles by means of which the boat "walked" up stream. Rumsey had demonstrated his invention privately for Washington in September 1784, and Washington was convinced the machinery was so easy to build, it would be a great boon to inland navigation.

In 1785 or 1786, Rumsey began thinking about applying steam as a means of propulsion; the exact year was later a matter of fierce debate between him and Fitch. However, he had made virtually no progress, for he was preoccupied with the recalcitrant engineering problems presented by the Potomac canal. Because of Rumsey's penchant for secrecy, it is highly unlikely Fulton heard about his work with steam at that time, even as gossip.

Fulton returned to Philadelphia in splendid health and moved his shop to a more peripheral location, Front Street above Pine. He was not to reside there long, however, for within a few months he was making plans to study painting in London. He had acquired a letter of introduction, said to be from Benjamin Franklin to Benjamin West who, as the official history painter for George III, was one of the leaders of the London art world. Generous with his talent and his time, West had long served as the mentor of aspiring American artists who sought the instruction abroad that they could not find at home. In addition to the letter, Fulton had a purse of forty guineas, enough, he optimistically thought, to last him at least a year.

In May 1786 Fulton bought his mother a small, manageable farm in Hopewell Township, Pennsylvania. Her older brother, the Reverend Joseph Smith, had moved there the previous year as minister to the Presbyterian congregation, and the land was part of the property on which he settled. In September, Fulton also acquired three building lots as an investment in Washington, Pennsylvania, not far from his mother's farm. Where Fulton found the eight pounds for the down payment on the farm and the five pounds for the lots as well as the forty guineas for his trip to England is puzzling. Philadelphia was suffering from the extended financial crisis that gripped the country as a postlude to the Revolutionary War. Bartering was prevalent, and it was exceedingly difficult for anyone, let alone a young artist, to accumulate hard money. The most realistic explanation for Fulton's prosperity is that he found a patron, perhaps one of the rich frequenters of Bath. Joseph Delapaine, in his early nineteenth-century work on distinguished Americans, points to one Samuel Scorbitt. This may have been a misreading of Samuel Turbitt, Fulton's boyhood companion who, from later correspondence, seems an unlikely candidate. Always proud to announce that from the beginning he had made his own way, Fulton never spoke of an American patron, even to his closest friends.

Whatever the source of his good fortune, Fulton took himself down to the thronged wharves of Philadelphia and, from among the multitude of captains, chose the one who would carry him to the Old World and to an extraordinarily varied and productive new life.

Many, Many a Silant Solitary Hour

❖

Under the best of circumstances, conditions aboard transatlantic ships were oppressive in the late eighteenth century, for cargo always took precedence over human beings. Passengers slept in curtained bunks lining the common cabin in which they also cooked, ate, washed, and in barely recessed alcoves vomited and relieved themselves. If the weather was fair, they usually had access to the decks, but from October throughout the winter, when it could be expected to be foul, they were confined to their airless, reeking quarters.

The duration of the voyage was always uncertain: it could last forty, sixty, ninety, or over a hundred days. Ships frequently ran off their courses in storms and fogs. Quite as often they were becalmed. American captains, proud of their ability to improvise, were notorious for not laying in extra sails or even materials to mend torn sails. Food and water were too often carelessly stowed. It was not unheard of for rations to be reduced, while the ship was still far from land, to spoiled onions flavored with a hint of salt beef and moistened with a thimbleful of water. Prudent travelers brought their own live chickens as well as a supply of rhubarb, castor oil, and cream of tartar for constipation, soda water and tea for diarrhea, and Peruvian bark, wine, and cordials for strength. They had no defense at all against the bedbugs.

Yet—as often happens when risk and discomfort are shared in confined quarters—an air of sociability, even intimacy, prevailed. Passengers played endless games of cards and backgammon, exchanged gossip about the captain and crew, traded reading matter, and exclaimed over the astonishing beauty of the moonlight on the icebergs and the phosphorescence that "turned each wave into a shower of fire."[1] Fulton may very well have amused his companions by sketching their portraits.

There is no record of what ship Fulton took or at what port he disembarked. It could have been Falmouth, Plymouth, or Liverpool, from where, at some expense, he would have had to take a stage or mail coach to London. Most immediately satisfying, however, would have been to sail up the winding Thames to Gravesend, close to the great capital itself.

London in the late 1780s was a bustling metropolis of some 700,000 inhabitants—over fifteen times the size of Philadelphia. A contemporary guide called *The Ambulator or the Stranger's Companion* boasted that London possessed one cathedral, two collegiate churches, three choirs of music, 146 parishes and three synagogues, four pest houses, thirteen hospitals, fifteen inns of court, and twenty-seven public prisons. George III and his large family occupied three palaces, persons of rank lived in mansions on elegant squares, and tradesmen inhabited neat rows of yellow brick houses. They bought their provisions at the fifteen flesh, two herb, and forty-seven miscellaneous markets and twenty-four fairs. Potable water was piped in from the upper Thames. Because wood was so expensive, coal was used for heating, and throughout the winter, the city was shrouded in smoke.

The Thames was of virtually no planned scenic or recreational value to ordinary Londoners. Only Lambeth Palace, Somerset House, and the Temple had gardens overhanging its banks. But it was the world's greatest transportation artery. Up to the three bridges, oceangoing vessels lay tight-packed at anchor. Above them was a perpetual scurry of barges, wherries, and rowboats.

Walking was still the primary means of getting about. Among the useful information dispensed by a rival of the *Ambulator* was a long list of warnings for pedestrians: "Keep to the wall side, but don't dispute a cart or a carriage. . . . Do not walk under a penthouse lest perfors watering flower-pots, or other slops, should drop on your head. . . . When you walk with an umbrella, and meet a similar machine, lower yours in time, lest you either break it, or get entangled with the other. . . . Never stop in a crowd or look at the windows of a print shop or showglass, if you would not have your pockets picked."[2]

Like other newcomers, Fulton probably took a one-shilling room in a coffee house when he first arrived. Then, impatient to get on with his new life, he made his way to 14 Newman Street, the residence, gallery, and atelier of Benjamin West—a handsome edifice tangibly radiating the worldly success Fulton so hoped to emulate. If he arrived in the morning, he must have encountered other nascent painters, canvases in hand, eager for the criticism and encouragement West offered free of charge both as a moral obligation and for personal satisfaction. If he arrived in the afternoon, he would have been led by a liveried servant through a long gallery, hung with the fine collection of old masters West had bought or copied as well as with his own paintings. Beyond the gallery was the studio in which West was working on the series of thirty-five biblical scenes the king had commissioned for the Royal Chapel at Windsor. For Fulton, who in America had never had the opportunity to see works approaching this quality, it must have been a stunning rite of passage.

West appeared, a lady diarist noted, "a very pleasing man, simple, soft-mannered cheerful and serene."[3] It is easy to imagine him putting Fulton at ease by inquiring with genuine warmth about the health and latest projects of his friends Benjamin Franklin, William Henry, and Charles Willson Peale.

No indication exists of how West gauged Fulton's artistic potential on this first meeting or, in fact, at any other time in their long, close association. It can be assumed, however, that West offered the advice he never tired of repeating: "Give your heart and soul wholly to art, turn aside neither to the right nor to the left, but consider that hour lost in which a line has not been drawn, nor a masterpiece studied. . . . Don't shut yourself up from visitors when engaged in any great work. Hear their remarks and encourage their criticisms."[4]

West did not invite Fulton to live at 14 Newman Street, nor did he take him into his studio. But he did help him to find a convenient place to stay, a second-story workroom and furnished bedchamber in the house of the painter Robert Davy at 84 Charlotte Street. Room, board, fire, and candles cost one guinea a week—a good deal more than coffee house lodgings, but Fulton accepted, undoubtedly hoping he would be able to afford it before too many weeks had passed.

Davy, West knew, would be a useful contact. He could tell Fulton which of the St. Martin's Lane shops near Charlotte Street sold painting supplies most cheaply and how to avoid dealers who adulterated pigments with impure oils. Davy could also teach Fulton to set a palette in the Italian manner, as he had taught his previous tenant, the American William Dunlap.

Where Fulton found ongoing instruction is a matter of conjecture. The only serious school was connected to the Royal Academy. Tuition for six years was free, and the entrance policy was democratic—except that no women were admitted—but teaching was confined to drawing. Classes were held in the evening, because it was thought more demanding to draw by candlelight and because it left students free to work under the guidance of practicing oil painters during the day. Fulton did not enroll in the Royal Academy Schools immediately; perhaps West advised him he was not advanced enough to gain entrance.

Apprenticeship was considered risky, for to serve their own interests, masters were known to withhold both information and encouragement. His experience as a silversmith would have made Fulton wary of this alternative. Probably, except for criticism from West, he worked on his own, using his friends as models and studying old and contemporary masters. London was rich in private collections open to the public. The Queen's Gallery extracted an entrance fee of half a guinea, which made visits a luxury, but others could be enjoyed by giving the porter a tip. Most prominent contemporary artists maintained galleries similar to West's. Sir Joshua Reynolds, for instance, was known for his collection of drawings, which included an array of superlative works by Correggio, Michelangelo, Raphael, and Leonardo da Vinci. In addition, both bogus and genuine art of all periods could be viewed in West End auction rooms. Christie's, even then, was a haven for connoisseurs, artists, and rich idlers.

The most prestigious social event of the art year was the spring exhibition at the Royal Academy. Fulton would have arrived in time for the 1787 display. *The Gentleman's Magazine* complained of the artists' "unwillingness to submit their best drawings to the vulgar taste."[5] Nevertheless, rows of paintings crammed the walls from eye level up to the ceiling. Romney, Raeburn, Reynolds, and Gainsborough were the great presences in large-scale portraiture, and Cosway held sway in the field of miniatures. West led the Americans, the most prominent of whom were Stuart, Trumbull, and Mather Brown. Copley did not exhibit at the Royal Academy; he commanded a strong enough following to risk a one-man show, the profits of which would be his own. The realization that he would have to rival so much talent in order to make even a bare living from painting could only have been a sobering experience for Fulton.

"Many, many a Silant Solitary hour have I spent in the most unnerved Studdy Axiously pondering how to make funds to Support me till the fruits of my labours should be sufficient to pay them," Fulton wrote to his mother.[6] He changed lodgings often, was obliged to borrow money, and undoubtedly frequented the knot of cheap eating houses around St. Martin's Lane called Porridge Island. Yet he was, by his own account, never actually in want. Quite possibly he resorted to his old trade and, as Peale had done with West's encouragement, painted miniatures in a cooperative arrangement with a silversmith.

There is no question Fulton's austere existence was relieved by friends. He was, he said, "happily beloved by them." The most important to him was West. Although West probably did not help him financially—though liberal with hospitality, he was close with money—Fulton was a constant visitor to his home, and his deepening intimacy with the entire family did much to sustain him. Benjamin's wife, Elizabeth, an intelligent and enterprising woman, was especially drawn to Fulton. Later she would refer to him as her "favorite son," and Fulton would address her as his "petite Maman." Raphael Lamar West, the elder of their two boys, was Fulton's age and a competent if uncommitted painter. He would have been a guide to the best entertainments in town. It was, however, with Benjamin West himself that Fulton formed the strongest tie. Transcending their vocation as artists, their relationship was based on compatibility of temperament and on deep emotional need.

West was a far more complicated man than he at first appeared. It had taken courage to lay before the antiquities-loving British public a historical painting in which their heroes were garbed in contemporary dress rather than in Roman togas, as he had done with his *Death of General Wolfe* in 1771. Despite his assertion that the principles of art could be reduced to a set of rules, he was possessed by a streak of rampant fantasy. His apocalyptic *Death on a Pale Horse*, the first version of which he finished in 1783 but which obsessed him throughout his life, placed him in the vanguard of the romantic movement.

West was, moreover, frankly entrepreneurial. "There are but two ways of working successfully, that is lastingly for an artist," he delighted in saying, "the one is to paint for the king; the other is to mediate a scheme of your own."[7] From the engravings of *The Death of General Wolfe*, he was reputed to have reaped a small fortune. He earned still more as an appraiser, dealer, and restorer of old masters. He was not above making designs for ladies' fans or decorations for royal banquets.

Then, too, West was unabashedly vain. One sharp-tongued anecdote described him as standing before his *Saint Paul Shaking off the Viper* and remarking: "A little burst of genius, sir."[8]

West's vanity did not disturb Fulton. Praise, he thought, was West's due, earned by his willingness to work hard in order to excel. West's romanticism struck a resonant chord with Fulton's own questing spirit, and he certainly shared West's drive for wealth and fame. In return, West savored Fulton's adulation. Their relationship would go through many subtle permutations, but its essence, established at this time, would remain constant throughout Fulton's life. Of all his friendships, West's was the most durable and comforting.

Despite his quasi-adoption of and by the Wests, Fulton was often beset by uncertainty. Becoming a credible artist was far more difficult than he had imagined. He was intermittently seized by depression, which was aggravated by the fact that he did not hear from his family for two years. Not until November 1788 did he receive his first packet of mail. None of these letters from his family or his responses to them have been preserved, but his reply to Samuel Turbitt, a Lancaster friend whose letter he received at that time, is suffused with nostalgia for home and a latent sense of guilt for having so decisively separated himself from his mother and his sisters.

> do you know there is scarcely twenty four hours passes me without my Ideas dancing about Lancaster like an Invisible fairy? I fancy I See see [sic] and hear every thing, and this makes me anxious to know them in reality. I want I[n] particular to hear that all the Miss Fultons are Maried and to Men who have sense enough to see their worth. I am Sure the[y] have hearts Calculated to soothe Sorrow, banish Coroding Melancholy and render lifes rugged pathe smoothe and pleasant. We are told Mariages are made in heaven, be it So. I most sincerely Wish I was prime Minister at that divine Court for the sake of those Ladies. . . . But you may tell [t]hem for me I would make use of all my influence to get them just such husbands a[s] the[y] Could wish. By my honor it would be a plea-

sure to be their guardian angel for the Sake of protecting So much Virtue.

Well my dear little humble and happy family Altho the Ocean Separates us I am in the Midst of you at this moment. It is just now 9 O'clock at Night all is Silant as Solitude herself. Yes. there you are sitting in the back room one Candle and a fire bright as Countenances that Suround it. . . . I See you all Sitting round one table. there stands the Work Basket on one side and on the other the Cat. . . . There sits Turbitt, god Bless me Turbitt I beg your pardon I was led into a Small Soliloque and almost forgot I was Writing to you. . . . I am prosecuting my Studies as ardently as posible And I believe make some progress. I shall be happy when I return to shake friendship by the hand or Crack an evening Joke. . . . I am in good health and high Spirits. London has become a[s] familear to me as Phila. I[n] short there is nothing but what will loose its novelty. . . . now honest Turbitt I wish you a good night. I am most Confounded Sleepy. Please delive[r] the Inclosed letter to my Sister and you will oblige your most sincere R. Fulton.[9]

Fulton's correspondence with America picked up after this initial hiatus, but the mail was expensive and went by a circuitous route. His letters to his family took up to six months, even when carried across the ocean by a friend or a chance acquaintance to either Baltimore or Philadelphia, from where they went to Lancaster to Turbitt who sent them on to western Pennsylvania. The return was equally tedious. The recipient had to pay postage, and Fulton, who was counting every farthing, was obliged to admonish his mother "to write small and close" and to buy thin stationery. "We pay according to the weight and not the size," he told her, "so if you can send me a pound of news upon an ounce of paper I shall save almost a guinea by it."[10]

Only five letters, all from Fulton, remain. As in the letter to Turbitt, he visualizes daily life at home so intensely that he seems almost to participate in it. To his mother he wrote:

> I can easy conceive your garden to be the best in Washington, my ideas often hover around the little spot. I think I see it improved by your Industrious hand whilst the flowers of Spring lend their aid to beautify the scene; but chief of all I think I see you on a Sunday evening contemplatively walking on the grounds and with Silent pleasure viewing the labours of the week. . . . Here I could enter into a Chain of those Ideas which Crowd upon a heart sen-

sible of the feelings of a fond mother and the affection due from a child, but I must be silent and only answer your letter.[11]

In contrast to this sentimental outpouring, Fulton offered remarkably little information about his own social, professional, or emotional life. He assured his mother that the climate agreed with his health and that he expected his exertions as an artist would "have a good tendency." Despite his anxiety that "some unforeseen stroke" might separate them forever, he was glad she did not wish him to hurry home. "Indeed," he confessed, "it is of so much importance my gaining all possible knowledge that should I now return I might have it to repent of ever after."[12]

As the months went by, Fulton remained a doggedly persistent painter. He began to try larger canvases. A self-portrait he eventually sent to his mother shows a round-faced, pink cheeked, brown-eyed earnest young man whose curly hair is already beginning to thin at the temples. Its most interesting feature is that the thumb of the right hand, from which dangles a watch fob, has the concave arch that palmists associate with creativity.

In 1789, Fulton was at last able to tell his mother that his pictures had been "admitted into the Royal Academy And I hope this year to be a proficient in the Art."[13] By this he meant that the Royal Academy Schools had accepted his entrance submissions. This was an extraordinary opportunity as well as a vindication of his long struggle to become an artist, for the schools would provide instruction, criticism, and companionship in a structured environment, which he badly needed. Among his colleagues would be J. M. W. Turner, Thomas Lawrence, and James Earl, another of West's American protégés.

It is astonishing, therefore, that Fulton put off entering the Royal Academy Schools. Instead, he went to France for a tour of at least three months. Since he had so little money, the likelihood is that he found a benefactor and believed that a chance to study French painting was not to be missed. Later he recalled having inspected the steam-driven water pumps at Dunkirk, but in a letter to his mother all he said about the interlude was that it "proved very agreeable and was of some service to me in as much as I saw the works of some of the notable masters in the arts, which much improved my eye and taste."[14]

At least in the short run, Fulton may have made the right decision. The period following his trip to the Continent was highly productive.

In the spring of 1791, he was one of the 672 exhibitors at the Royal Academy where he hung two paintings. Four paintings were accepted by the less prestigious but respected Society of Artists. Only the catalogue listings survive. The paintings he sent to the Royal Academy were portraits of two young gentlemen, unfortunately unnamed. The Society of Artists hung *Elisha Raising the Widow's Son*, a theme previously treated by West; *Priscilla and Alladine*, inspired by Spenser's *Faerie Queene;* and two additional portraits of young gentlemen, also unnamed. Although his work "Rec'd every possible mark of Approbation," there was "no profit arising from it." His exertions were "all for honour," he wrote home, and "to Create a name that may hereafter produce business."[15]

The hoped-for business came immediately. In June, Fulton received an invitation from Viscount William Courtenay to visit Powderham Castle, his country seat in Devonshire, to paint his portrait. For Fulton, the commission was a long awaited entrée into the remunerative world of titled patrons, saving him, he later extravagantly declared, from being "Crushed by Poverties, Cold wind and Freezing Rain."[16] The twenty-three-year-old Courtenay, having recently succeeded to his title, had the fortune to indulge his artistic interests on a handsome scale.

Fulton packed his palette, pencils, and canvases and booked a seat—probably on the weekly "balloon coach" that traveled the dusty turnpike from London to Exeter, where the Courtenays maintained a small town house. From there it was only ten miles along the River Exe to Powderham. Had Fulton expected the castle to be a moated and turreted citadel, he would have been disappointed. It was an enlarged medieval manor house, a long, low parallelogram with six evenly spaced square towers, situated on a flat marsh facing the estuary of the Exe. The park surrounding it was nine miles in circumference, but, unlike the owners of other great houses of the day, the Courtenays had taken few pains with landscaping.

The interior, in contrast, was splendid. Recently subjected to extensive refurbishing, the rooms were elegant, comfortable, and, as expensive remodeling so often is, entertaining. The old chapel had been made into a library, the old granery into a chapel. Bow windows had been installed on either side of the central tower. The enormous dining hall had been divided in half by a grand staircase, richly decorated with elaborate Italianate plasterwork. Fulton would make Powderham his home for at least the next year and a half.

Unhappily, the portrait Fulton painted of Lord Courtenay has disappeared, and the only reference to his stay at Powderham is in a stilted letter to his mother written in January 1792. The painting "gave his lordship so much pleasure," he told her, "that he has introduced me to all his friends . . . and I am beginning to get a little money and pay some debt I was obliged to Contract . . . so I hope in about six months to be clear with the world or in other words out of debt and then start fair to Make all I Can." He mentioned, too, that he had been "doing some business for Lord Courtenay," but, tantalizingly, he did not specify what that was.[17]

In this case there was perhaps good cause for Fulton's reticence, for young Courtenay was a notorious homosexual, famous for having been seduced at sixteen by William Beckford, a collector of old masters and armorial bearings who was equally renowned for keeping a French dwarf as a valet and for fancying very young boys. His corruption of Courtenay was England's most gossiped-about sodomy case, scandalous not because pederasty was unusual at the time—quite the contrary—but because the particulars were made known by Courtenay's own family. An only son with eleven older and three younger sisters, Courtenay had a position to maintain.

Although Beckford's sequestered Gothic folly, Fonthill Abbey, was within easy traveling distance of Powderham, visiting back and forth was probably limited, for Beckford had soon tired of Courtenay, viciously snapping, "il se pare comme une poupée et se farde comme une p——." (He decks himself out like a doll and paints his face like a p[rostitute].)[18]

That Fulton accepted a flagrant homosexual as a patron was not in itself surprising. William Beckford's exotic reputation did not keep the Royal Academicians from vying for his commissions. West helped Beckford amass his art collections and soon would accept an annuity for a series of paintings based on the Book of Revelations. Indeed, it may well have been West who introduced Fulton to Courtenay. The unusual aspect of Fulton's residence at Powderham was its long duration. There is no evidence that Fulton was ever a homosexual, but, twenty-five years old, he had as yet formed no close romantic attachments with women. Shortly after he left Powderham, he received a letter from his sisters complaining that while he praised matrimony for them, he resisted it for himself. He sent back a sharp retort through Polly's husband whom he was congratulating on the birth of a son: "I am not old enough to grow musty and possibly I may one day like it. But at present, there is not the most distant prospect."[19] Even had he so desired, it is difficult to believe that Fulton could have remained detached from the life-style of Courtenay and his friends, on whom he was financially dependent.

Whatever its social content, the time spent at Powderham was fertile artistically, for the Royal Academy hung four of Fulton's paintings in the 1793 exhibition, which celebrated its twenty-fifth anniversary. One was a portrait of a Mrs. Murray, whose identity has not been established, and three were historical subjects, a new departure for Fulton. They formed a royal incarceration and death series. *Louis XVI in Prison Taking Leave of His Family*, the centerpiece, was sensationally topical, for the French king had been executed only a few months previously. *Mary Queen of Scots under Confinement* and *Lady Jane Grey the Night before Her Execution* were its companion pieces. What historical comment, if any, Fulton intended by these scenes of political executions is uncertain, but the theme was clearly the sublimity of the noble spirit in the face of death, an accepted and much depicted theme at that period and one especially favored by Benjamin West. Like the paintings executed at Powderham, these canvases have vanished. The Mary Queen of Scots and Lady Jane Grey paintings, however, are known from contemporary mezzotints engraved by John Ward, undoubtedly as a moneymaking scheme. Without the color and the subtle shadings, it is impossible to tell their true quality, and Ward, an accomplished artist, may have altered them substantially, despite Fulton's close supervision or perhaps even with his consent. In the mezzotints, the detail is meticulous, the light strongly focused, and the pathos of the subjects highly idealized. Each presents only one figure. Evidently, Fulton did not yet feel confident enough of his technique to attempt a more complex composition. The lost picture of Louis XVI and his family seems to have been the sole exception.

During this brief stay in London, Fulton lodged at 18 Newman Street, a few doors from the Wests. Benjamin West was now president of the Royal Academy, an extraordinary achievement for an American. On the death of Sir Joshua Reynolds the previous year, he had been elected by a vote of twenty-nine to one; Copley, who had had the bad taste to nominate himself for the presidency, was the lone dissenter. West's strength lay in his personal intimacy with the king. He seemed a safe compromise among the jealous, squabbling, and too often spiteful members. With the exception of a year's interlude, he would remain the Royal Academy's leader for the next twenty-eight years.

Fulton basked in West's glory and drew inspiration from it. To David Morris, West's nephew who had recently married Fulton's youngest sister Polly, he wrote: "Your uncle is a great genius and merits all the honor he has obtained—he has steadily pursued his Course, and Step by Step at length Reached the Summit where he now looks Round on the beauties of his Industry An Ornament to Society and Stimulus to young Men."[20]

Fulton's pride in his relationship with West and his enjoyment of the other pleasures of city life were not enough to keep him in London, however. Immediately after the exhibition, he journeyed again to Devonshire where he stayed, not at Powderham Castle, but in the nearby village of Torquay which, because of its romantic situation, convenient bathing, and extraordinarily sunny weather was becoming known as "a fit residence for those suffering from an irritable digestion, catarral affections and dry asthma."[21] Despite his enthusiastic reports about the London climate, the coal smoke and fog may well have revived his earlier respiratory ailment. On the other hand, he may just as easily have gone there to meet friends outside of, but near to, Courtenay's jurisdiction.

It was, in any case, a time of transition for Fulton. He enjoyed the sun, painted a portrait of the local magnate Sir Robert Palk, and made several watercolor landscapes. One was of Tor Bay, which that summer was filled with frigates and merchantmen, for the sheltered anchorage had been designated a rendezvous for the navy and for commercial convoys in March 1793, when the hostilities against France that would eventually become the Napoleonic Wars began. Fulton also sketched villagers, trudging beside their sturdy pack ponies, and he drew at least one cartoon. It shows a potbellied, bespurred man with a monocle examining a bald-headed cherub smoking a long clay pipe.

None of these was a serious work. None required more than desultory effort. The small progress Fulton had made, measured by the standards set by the major exhibitors at the Royal Academy, seems to have deadened his desire to persevere as a professional painter. Seeking a change that would refresh, challenge, and perhaps pay him, he looked to the local craft industry. Using the beautifully veined red, green, brown, gray, and blue marble quarried in the area, artisans fashioned intricate inlaid objects such as clocks, tables, and urns. Resurrecting talents he had not used since he was a silversmith's apprentice, and applying mechanical techniques he remembered from his boyhood in Lancaster, Fulton designed a better cutting and polishing instrument. It was so well executed that when he submitted a model to the Society for the Encouragement of Arts, Commerce and Manufactures the following year, it won a coveted silver medal.

This was not such a radical departure from painting as it might seem, for mechanical invention requires an ability to think spatially—"a mind practiced in forming and reforming multiple elements in varying ways."[22] Machines, like paintings, are artificial constructs resulting from a precise balancing of tensions. Facility in drawing is, in fact, crucial to invention, for through graphic representation ideas can be tested and developed without the expenditure of time and money for working models, vastly increasing the inventor's perceptual span. Fulton's artistic training would be of great advantage to him. It set him above the many inventors who, still bound by the trial-and-error craft approach, were unable to design by drawing. Nevertheless, Fulton's decision to divert his creative energies from painting to engineering was a radical change of direction.

Encouraged by his success with the marble cutting machine, Fulton undertook next to improve the deplorable transportation system of Devonshire and Cornwall. Hardly better than rutted tracks, the roads were so steep and narrow that virtually all goods were carried on the backs of ponies. Landowners and speculators were fully aware that poor transportation was as much a cause of rural poverty as poor soil, and for some time, prospectuses for canals that might bring the prosperity of the central and midland regions of England to the depressed southwest had been front-page news in the Devonshire press. Lord Courtenay, for instance, was a major promoter of the Bude Canal that was to run from Budehaven in Cornwall through the lands Courtenay owned in the northwest of Devonshire and would carry Welsh coal and sea sand that was much needed for fertilizer. Because the terrain was exceptionally hilly and there was neither the money to build locks nor the water to fill them, few of the canals had been implemented.

Fulton's object was to devise substitutes for traditional locks. When, in late October 1793, the Bude Canal Committee printed their surveyors' report in the *Exeter Flying Post,* he had, he believed, made enough progress to offer its chairman, the Earl of Stanhope, a plan for a more efficient way to build the canal than the report described. That letter is lost, but it must have aroused Stanhope's interest. Although Fulton was an utter stranger with scant credentials, Lord Stanhope promptly replied. Within a few months Fulton was able to establish a relationship with him, which, though often erratic and mystifying, would be crucial to Fulton for the rest of his life.

A Prospect of
Considerable Profits

❖

Charles Mahon, third earl of Stanhope, in whom Fulton had such high hopes of finding a generous and supportive benefactor, was a fearless, indefatigable eccentric. Because he espoused such unpopular causes as electoral reform, home rule for Ireland, abolition of the slave trade and the French Revolution, his colleagues in the House of Lords struck him a medal that carried the motto "A Minority of One." His bald pate, bony limbs, and fiery oratory inspired the cartoonist Gillray to caricature him as "The Don Quixote of the Nation [who] Beats his Own Windmill in Gesticulation."

Even his peers were caustic about his style. Lord Henry Richard Holland wrote that although Stanhope was "not activated by avarice or emotion or pride or resentment, nor deficient in vigour, spirit and effect," he was "inelegant and coarse, even to buffoonery. . . . His manner possessed a certain quaintness that added poignancy to his remarks," Holland observed, but his close, scholastic logic was "neither practical nor convincing."[1]

In playing out his convictions, the earl spared neither his family nor himself. Even the nobly born should have a useful trade, he believed. One son was trained to be a blacksmith, another a shoemaker, and his daughter, Lady Hester Stanhope, learned to keep turkeys—or so she wrote when she was an old woman. To imitate French republicans, Stanhope wore plain clothes and refused to powder his hair, and he ordered the coronets over his iron gates taken down and the armorial insignia struck from his carriages and silver. His ideas about health were idiosyncratic. He slept, Lady Hester said, with twelve blankets, no nightcap, and the window open. At daybreak he would "get out of bed and put on a thin dressing gown, with a pair of silk breeches that he had worn overnight and with slippers and no stockings and then he would sit in a part of the room which had no carpet, and take his tea with a bit of brown bread."[2] He gave up sugar in 1791 for dietary reasons and also to protest Britain's exploitation of the West Indies and her involvement in the slave trade. Although he was respected for his awesome moral consistency, it was said that Stanhope loved and was loved by no one but his mother.

The mainspring of Stanhope's life was not politics or family, however, but applied science. He was an ingenious experimenter. Among his inventions were a calculator, a system of shorthand, a fever thermometer, a cotter pin, fireproof building materials, and a system for preventing the counterfeiting of gold coins. He had corresponded with Benjamin Franklin on the subject of electricity and under his auspices had been elected a member of the American Philosophical Society. He was a member of the distinguished association of scientists, the Royal Society, and a founding member and vice-president of the Society for the Improvement of Naval Architecture, which hoped to bring scientific theory to bear on the tradition-bound craft of shipbuilding.

The use of steam for transportation had long occupied his attention. In 1790 he tried to run a steam-powered vehicle between Calais and Boulogne but, according to Lord Holland, the extraordinary result was a carriage that ran uphill rapidly, got along on the plain ground with some difficulty, and came to a dead stop on every descent. He had also designed a steam vessel. Named the *Ambinavigator* since she was double-ended so as to go forward or backward, she was intended to carry coals from Newcastle to London. The public joke that the boat would consume her cargo before reaching her destination did not faze Stanhope. He believed her capable of providing swift trans-Channel service that would so cement the interests of England and France that the two nations would never again war against each other. However, Boulton and Watt had politely declined to fabricate the engine he had designed. Thus far his experiments had been made with a model on the great pond at Chevening, his country seat at Sevenoaks in Kent. One gardener who was conscripted to tow it into motion later declared: "When his Lordship thought she was going all right, he would cut the rope without warning and let us all down."[3]

Nevertheless, because his idea was timely and because he had good connections—he was a brother-in-law of William Pitt and was twice related to the powerful Grenville family—Stanhope was able to persuade the Navy Board to build a full-scale ship for further trials. Launched in the spring of 1793 at the Admiralty's Deptford Dock, her slender hull was 55 feet long and just over 6 feet wide.

Stanhope was preparing to test the seaworthiness of the *Ambinavigator* under sail when Fulton wrote to him in November 1793. His first letter may have contained descriptions and drawings of two mechanisms, a steam-activated stern paddle that imitated the spring of a salmon's tail, and a three-bladed side wheel also powered by a steam engine, for many years later in an acrimonious lawsuit, Fulton produced a copy of a draft of such a letter, dated November 4, 1793. However, Fulton's initial letter and Stanhope's reply are lost. The first extant letter is dated November 27, 1793. It was inspired by the report of John and George Nuttals's plan for the construction of the Bude Canal that was published in the *Exeter Flying Post* on November 21. The canal they had laid out was to be 75 miles long and rise to a summit of 484 feet. To avoid using locks the Nuttals proposed substituting three segments of railroad over which their small 2-ton boats, suspended between a pair of wheels 6 feet in diameter, would be drawn by horses.

The "original thoughts," complete with drawings and cost estimates, that Fulton offered as a substitute for the locks and the Nuttals's railroads consisted of two devices he called "lock carriages." Sea sand would be the major cargo on the canal. To haul it from the beach where it was mined up a steep bank to the first level of the canal, Fulton designed a wheeled box that could be loaded onto a boat or towed like a barge. Instead of horses, water power would be used to lift the boxed sand up the slope. Water would be run into a parallel box on rails until it was just heavier than the box filled with sand. As the water-filled box descended on its rails, it would, by a series of pulleys, raise the cargo box up parallel rails. "[N]othing can be more simple," he told Stanhope, "than to exchange a Box of Water for a Box of sand or other Articles." His second device worked on the same principle of counterbalancing weights, but, instead of a box on wheels, Fulton envisioned an enormous wheeled carriage in which entire cargo-laden boats could be floated.

A Prospect of Considerable Profits

Unlike traditional locks, which used up to 125 cubic feet of water for a rise of only 12 or 13 feet, the water demand was so "trifling," Fulton claimed, it could be supplied by a 1½- to 2-inch tube and, if necessary, stored in reservoirs. The advantages of these lock carriages were that they would make canals feasible in areas blessed only with small streams, and they would eliminate the need for the four hundred horses at a cost of at least 7,700 pounds per annum the Nuttals's plan would require. Moreover, he said, his method was faster. By comparing the money, manpower, and time needed for operation and maintenance, he projected a savings of 5,500 pounds. This did not include the side benefits of releasing for the cultivation of wheat and barley the almost ten acres of fertile land it took to keep each horse in feed for a year—nearly two times the amount needed to maintain a laborer's family.

Crude as it was, Fulton had "little doubt of the Apperatus Working. . . . If ever Practice Could be expected From theory," he rhapsodized, "it is to be hoped for from those Simple Ideas—And I have not the least Doubt butt it may be found Usefull throughout the whole Canal Navigation of England and Scotland."[4]

Fulton was so entranced by his mechanisms that in his cover letter dated November 30 he suggested he would be willing to form a partnership with Stanhope to implement the scheme not only on the Bude Canal and wherever geographical conditions made it the only feasible method, but for any extension of the British canal system:

My Lord
    This moment I had the honour of yours, And would not loose an instant in giving your Lordship the earliest inteligence of my plan, for which purpose I am necessitated to inclose My first drawings and Estimate on the Subject. As I have not had time to make one more *Accurat* they will at least *Exhibit the Simplicity of the Lock Carriage*—With the Probility of the imense Saving of *5500 per Annum*. . . . Your Lordship will find that if the weights are Small it is so much the better. I only mentioned 50 tons to Show that Such a weight Could be Raised if necsure, but Small weights will be excessively Simple by this means. I must beg leave to Add that Should your Lordship think of applying this apperatus I have a Proposition to make to your Lordship which may be *very Productive* . . . which I will imediately state on Receiving your Lordships *Opinion* of the Plan, And for which purpose I think it prudent to keep this Idea Silent, until I Can Regulate a [model] in

Practice for your Lordship and Self. It will Give me Infinite Pleasure Should your Lordship Concur in my opinion on the [question] of Simplicity, as five or ten tons can thereby be Raised to any highth from 200 to 800 feet. I shall wait with anxiety for your Lordships Answer as this thought has for the Present arrested my Cornish Expedition. I return my Sincere thanks for the favour of the Speady Answer paid to former letters—And am with all
Possible Respect your Lordships most obedient and obliged
Robert Fulton[5]

Considering Stanhope's rank and reputation and the fact that they had never met, Fulton's presentation is remarkable for its familiarity, scope, and—despite the elegant flourish under the signature—careless penmanship and spelling. Unlike those letters to his mother in which he reported his progress in painting, it spills over with unbridled enthusiasm. It is as if his energy had been released from a great constraint. Yet, underpinning the exuberant tone is a solid core of determination and conviction. Fulton's sudden involvement with engineering was as emotionally charged as love at first sight. The new vistas that it opened so excited him that, godlike, he believed there was nothing he could not accomplish. Although all he could offer was an array of undigested theory, he did not limit himself to a plea for research money, but proposed to Stanhope that they enter into a working relationship as virtual equals.

Lord Stanhope's curiosity was aroused. He wasted no time in digesting Fulton's "ingenious Plan," and on December 6 he sent back a forceful, illustrated critique in which he told Fulton there was infinitely more to be considered than he appeared to be aware of. Rather than a "trifling" amount of water, Fulton's plan would require an immense quantity, for which numerous mill owners would have to be compensated annually. More water would be lost from the descending container at its terminus on the beach or, because of hydraulic pressure, at its junction with the upper canal pond. Furthermore, the slopes over which the canal must pass were not uniform. In the flat places, however short, the descending container would lose its pulling force, and many slopes required the rails to curve while ascending, a situation for which Fulton had not made and could not make adequate provision. In addition, one slope was over 2 miles long. No rope would maintain its effective pulling power for that distance. Finally, Fulton's plan would require two sets of rails rather than the one set called for by the Nuttals.

A Prospect of Considerable Profits

In fact, Stanhope pointed out, there was only one location along the route where Fulton's device—which he referred to as a "double inclined plane"—could be used. The experienced Nuttals had already proposed one for that place. Their method would be much faster. If Fulton would recalculate the time necessary to pass 2-ton containers along his inclined plane, he would find "there would not be *minutes enough* in the whole year" to handle the number of boats required to render his system feasible.[6]

The idea of a carriage or box riding on an inclined railed plane was not even novel, Stanhope continued. Nor was Fulton's plan for using water in a descending container as a raising power. Both had been suggested years before by a Mr. Leach. Besides, there was a better, lighter, and cheaper way to solve these problems, particularly the lack of uniformity of the terrain, and that was one of his own design. Coyly, Stanhope went only so far as to tell Fulton he had made a drawing of this invention, but he did not deign to describe it. The sole encouraging sentence in this missive was Stanhope's casual remark that after Parliament passed the enabling act for the Bude Canal, at least two sessions hence, he would again be in Devonshire and they might then meet.

Excited by his own optimism, Fulton chose to interpret the fact that Stanhope had replied at such length as a sure sign of interest and answered immediately that the Nuttal route should be reexamined. Further study had convinced him that even if he was required to use six inclined planes, he would need to hire only forty-eight men to operate them. The labor cost would be only 1 pound 6 shillings a day, or 721 pounds per annum. Thus, the savings over horses would still be at least 4,000 pounds. Moreover, the Nuttals's double inclined plane could be used only after the canal reached the summit, while his own lock carriages were effective from the very beginning on the beach. And, once loaded, they could descend slopes 1,000 feet long with almost as much ease as those of 50 feet without requiring a drop more water. The water, he stated, could be delivered through a pipe 4 inches in diameter—double, he failed to note, his former estimate—not enough to supply the smallest mill. If that was too much, he could devise catches and sluices to prevent the loss of more than one gallon per operation.

With equal certitude, he insisted his idea must be original. Mr. Leach's design must have been deficient, he said, or it would have already been in use throughout the kingdom. Anxious that his exertions would make "some Atonement" for the trouble he gave his lordship and sensible that his love of science would urge him to give his plan a "candid tryal," Fulton proposed that Stanhope recommend him to Mssrs. Nuttal so that he could "review the ground on the spot" and, in conjunction with them, "ascertain the facts."[7]

This was a presumptuous letter. Worse, it missed a crucial point: Stanhope was also working on a lifting device in which he took great pride and which, perhaps, was not very different from the lock carriage. Entranced by his own solutions and the profits they might yield, Fulton was so in need of outside validation for his scheme that he did not pause to contemplate the personal investment Stanhope might have in the development of the Bude Canal. The very next day he sent Stanhope a perspective view and short description of a gargantuan lock carriage that would be capable of raising at one time ten or fifteen boats of any size. It could perform sixty operations a day, up to 30 tons each.

This grandiose contrivance drew two smart letters from Stanhope. In his calculations, Fulton had falsely presumed that the Nuttals's railroads would pass only one boat at a time, whereas, like a turnpike, they could actually pass five, or twenty, or one hundred at one time. Stanhope acknowledged that using a water-powered inclined plane to reach the summit was a sensible idea, but since the horses' work in the mining operation could be accomplished in the morning, they would be available at no extra cost to work the railroads the rest of the day. There were yet a thousand things Fulton had not considered, Stanhope scolded, because he had "never made any Experiment on this, or any like Subject." A single stone, for instance, could stop his carriages. As incontrovertible proof he cited his own experiments in which he had pulled a full-scale boat up an inclined plane with his own muscle power. There was no need to trouble the Nuttals for another survey since "for seven weeks I was out almost every day, and all day long, *with my Theodolite, myself; & I Know* all the Levels Valleys, Hills, etc. for miles round Bude. . . . Your Principle (which is the same as Mr. Leach's) is a *good one* in favourable Cases; such you Perhaps may find in Wales, & in the North of England. But in *all* cases there is a better *mode* of Executing it, than the specifick mode you mention: so I said in my last. You see I tell you my thoughts freely, which is the best way for a man to be of Use to another Person."[8]

Stanhope's evaluation of the multi-boat carriage was justifiably more scathing: "The fifteen Boats on one Carriage *will not do. The Ropes must*

A Prospect of Considerable Profits

be Ship Cables or sink it in places, or wear it too much. It can never answer. . . . Your plan will not do for the Bude Canal."[9]

Even before he received these criticisms, Fulton had sent diagrams and a description of a variation of the lock carriage: a double inclined plane for crossing valleys that would take the place of the expensive and often monumental aqueducts that were built in the traditional lock system. Stanhope answered this package with sterner admonitions. He rehearsed his former arguments, laying unmistakably proud stress on his own fieldwork. The line he and the Nuttals had laid out was the right one. Still, Stanhope called Fulton an "ingenious man" and wished him success.

So intoxicated was Fulton by this attention that he ignored Stanhope's sharp criticism, deluding himself that Stanhope would "sanction" his work. Erroneously assuming that the earl's main interest was financial and that he was capable of paternal solicitude as well as susceptible to flattery, he composed a very neatly written letter begging for his "protection":

> As there Certainly Is a Prospect of Considerable profits Arising from this machine, If Introduced with proper Support, I propose to deliver to your Lordship *one half of my Gains* on this work until your Lordship *Shall Receve two hundred Pounds Per annum,* Provided your Lordship will be so good as to Protect this Enterprise with a Sum not *Exceeding five hundred Pounds,* but Probably much less. I will Candidly Acknowledge that the tide of misfortune has Run hard Against me in Spite of every Caution Which has much Embarrised my Circumstances and Retarded my Progress. While my Friends will not listen to my Mechanical Pursuits, But Insist that I Should Adhear to my *Portrait Pencil.* Thus your Lordship is the only one I have the honour to Communicate with who can Judge of my Mechanical thoughts and See their Utility or defects. I have therefor offered up my Ideas at the Shrine of Experience hoping to find that Protection In a Liberal and Penetrating Stranger which I Could not obtain of a friend. . . . Should your Lordship be so kind as to favour me, One hundred Pounds would Put me in Motion, As It is necessary to make a tour through Canal Countries to See for Situations where it might be Applied to advantage.

Signing with an ornate arabesque, he closed with a poetical flash of virtue, "My Lord I Submit with all diffidence to your Lordships Superior Judgment, But hope if there is one Spark in me which may Give the least Light to Society that your Lordships Infinate Goodness will Nourish it into a flame and believe me I Shall feel the warmth of Gratitude."[10]

Lord Stanhope was enticed neither by Fulton's "diffidence" nor by his plight. The financial proposition especially offended him. Although Stanhope filed notices at the patent office to protect his fame, he did not usually take out patents since he scorned charging fees for the use of his inventions. He viewed himself as a scientist and a benefactor of humanity: the status of entrepreneur was distasteful to him. Answering from London on December 27, he put an end to Fulton's hopes for his patronage in a surprisingly kindly manner. "I doubt whether you will do well to pursue Mechaniks *at present* as a Profession," he advised. "It is a wide Road but has been much trodden, and oftentimes, by able men, unsuccessfully. If, however, by pursuing the Portrait Pencil, or any other Life that leaves *leasure hours*, you should employ those leasure hours in your favorite pursuit and studying first Principles and the Applications of ditto, it is likely, that you may *hereafter* turn Mechanicks to advantage. I am sorry it will not be convenient to me to afford you at present the pecuniary assistance you mention in your Letter."[11]

Because it was a marginal project, few subscribers for the Bude Canal could be found, and it was held in abeyance for the course of the long war with France. Construction was finally commenced in the early 1820s, after both Fulton and Stanhope had died. The canal was not on the Nuttals's plan, but on an evolved form of Fulton's. It had six water-powered inclined planes, more than any other canal in Britain before or since.

Stanhope's unmistakable dismissal did nothing to slow Fulton's momentum. His self-generated optimism was impervious to criticism. On January 23, 1794, he placed an advertisement in the *Exeter Flying Post* addressed: "To Engineers and Canal Adventurers," in which he announced he had "constructed a simple Machine by which Four Men may with ease raise a Boat of 30 tons to the heighth of 500 feet in Fifteen Minutes." He claimed his plan would use less than one-tenth of the water required by locks and invited those who required proof through "Occular Demonstration" to view his model at Mr. Burrington Carter's Hotel in Exeter. He would charge no user's fee until the lift was in operation, and then the cost would be "only one half the evident savings which it might produce"—a standard form of payment at that time, but a substantial percentage.

Whether Fulton roused any interest in his invention is doubtful. It was unorthodox and unproven, and he had no patron to give it the stamp of reliability. Moreover, because of the recent failure of several canal schemes and the financial crisis caused by the war with France, the mania for canal building had lost its impetus. Nevertheless, confident that the low operating costs of his device would make it attractive to investors, he applied for a patent for his machine, a complicated, time-consuming process costing over 100 pounds. As he later said he owned thirty of thirty-two shares in the patent, he may have raised the money by selling a one-sixteenth interest to an indulgent, risk-taking friend.

The machinery Fulton attested he had developed "by long study and application, and after much trouble, labour and expence,"[12] was a refinement of the wheeled lock carriage he had first offered Stanhope. It consisted of a stone ramp, inclined at any angle from 20 to 90 degrees on which were placed two sets of timber or cast-iron rails, one for an ascending, the other for a descending carriage. These carriages could hold cargo-laden boats up to 50 tons. They were constructed with four, six, or eight wheels. The hind wheels were large enough in diameter to maintain the counterbalancing carriage in a horizontal position. To accommodate a one-way trade, the carriages were to be large enough to contain sufficient water to perform the operation without the weight of a boat. Smooth movement up and down the inclined plane was to be achieved by a system of rope pulleys attached to a strong wooden framework located over the upper canal terminus and by a friction brake.

For especially steep slopes, Fulton described a perpendicular lift— a brick-lined vertical shaft, long enough and wide enough to allow two lock carriages to pass side by side. These carriages also worked on the preponderating principle, but had no wheels. Access to and from the lower canal pond was through a short tunnel.

Fulton appended to the specifications thirteen pen and watercolor figures showing the component parts of the mechanism. Three of them are elevations with little touches of surrounding landscape. All are well drawn, for to augment his training as an artist, Fulton had been studying perspective drawing on his own and had already begun to evolve an original method of presentation that used a calculated distortion of perspective outstanding for its clarity. Even at this early stage in his engineering career, Fulton grasped the then novel idea that precise drawings easily read by fabricators were essential to successful implementation. His drawings as well as his verbal descriptions convey an impression that his machines were already in operation.

When the patent giving him exclusive rights for fourteen years was accorded the king's seal on June 3, 1794—a feat in itself since an average of only sixty-five patents a year were issued during that period—Fulton had at least an impressive document to give his invention substance. He then set forth on the tour to look for situations where his invention might be applied of which he had spoken to Stanhope. Sometime in the late summer or early fall of 1794, he went to Manchester. The city was the hub of England's canal network and, because primary materials and finished products could be so easily transported, the center of the country's burgeoning industrialization. Where Fulton got the money for this expedition is a mystery, for he still had no assured source of income.

Fulton left no diary of his journey north, but it is reasonable to assume that he traveled west to Shropshire to inspect the only inclined planes then in operation in Great Britain. In 1789 to supply his ironworks at Ketley with coal, William Reynolds had built a 66-foot inclined plane. Obviating the need for seven or eight locks, it was designed for a descending trade only, the loaded 5- and 8-ton boats providing the force to draw up the empty ones. The water supply was managed by a steam engine that pumped it from the lower to the upper pond as needed, an economical solution only because the coal was on hand. Nearby at Coalbrookdale, three inclined planes negotiated a 457-foot rise within a 7.5-mile stretch of the Shropshire Canal. Again the machinery was steam operated. On a branch of the canal, a perpendicular shaft 10 feet in diameter and 120 feet deep had been built so that boats would be lowered from the waterway to the railways that led to the Coalbrookdale ironworks and the Severn River.

Fulton undoubtedly also visited the Duke of Bridgewater's canal outside of Manchester, for it had initiated England's transportation revolution. With its efficient locks, steam-operated cranes, and monumental three-arch aqueduct over the River Irwell, it was the engineering marvel of the age. It was also highly profitable; in 1792 the canal earned Bridgewater at least 80,000 pounds. One late nineteenth-century writer stated that Fulton actually worked for the Duke of Bridgewater, but there is no evidence that they even met. However, Fulton must have been forcibly impressed by the many manifestations of prosperity in the Midlands that were directly attributable to the bold application of new technology.

When Fulton reached Manchester, he immediately contacted the Peak Forest Company, for he had heard that as soon as the corn harvest was in and laborers were available, the company would start digging a canal to connect the lime quarries and kilns of the area southeast of Manchester with the Midlands system of waterways. His inclined planes and perpendicular lift were ideally suited to the mountainous terrain through which the canal would pass. His presentation must have impressed the canal directors, for although he did not persuade the company to try his lock carriages, he did obtain a contract to cut a section of the canal in partnership with a local neophyte engineer, Charles McNiven. As Fulton had no construction experience whatever, this good fortune raises the question of whether he had found a patron on the Peak Forest Board. Indeed, the appointment turned out to be in the nature of a consultancy, and he was able to spend most of his time in Manchester rather than at Marple or Whaley Bridge, the termini of the proposed canal.

Manchester was a particularly congenial city for Americans. As importers of cotton and iron ore, Mancunians had long maintained commercial ties with the United States. As champions of political and social reform, they had forged strong emotional bonds. In fact, Mancunians were continually emigrating to the United States.

Although Fulton sometimes wrote letters from the fashionable Bridgewater Arms where the Peak Forest canal committee often held meetings, he stayed at a boardinghouse at 8 Brazenose Street. Robert Owen, the utopian industrialist, also lodged there, and it was not long before the two men struck up a friendship that would be extraordinarily advantageous to Fulton. Then only twenty-three years old, Owen was already the foremost cotton spinner in England. Largely self-educated, he came from a working-class family. His father was a saddler and an ironmonger, and Owen's first job had been in a draper's shop. Yet he was a natural manager and entrepreneur, and at nineteen was running a cotton mill that employed five hundred workers. He was skilled at implementing labor-saving devices and was the first weaver in England to use American-raised long-staple cotton to produce high-quality cloth. Already concerned with the social impact of large-scale manufacturing, he had begun instituting reforms to enhance the quality of life of his workers, for which he would become famous.

Entirely comfortable with Owen's idealism, stimulated by his achievement, and sharing a similar background, Fulton enjoyed Owen's company. Owen, who later described Fulton in his memoirs as a man of genius, enterprise, and great buoyancy of spirit, reciprocated by introducing him to his friends, a circle of remarkably versatile Englishmen who met frequently to discuss whatever topic struck their fancy. Erasmus Darwin was the wise elder of the group. A practicing physician and a poet, he nevertheless took time to pursue mechanics. Though his enthusiasm seldom carried through to implementation, he had experimented with windmills, speaking machines, seed drills, telescopic candlesticks, oxygen motors, and flush toilets, one of which he had installed in his own carriage. In 1765, he had worked up a design for a "firey chariot" to be moved by twin steam cylinders. In 1777, as an investor in the Grand Trunk Canal, he had proposed using a preponderating canal lift. In one of his long poems that took the world for its subject matter, he envisioned boats driven by steam. Since even in England the experimental scientific community was small, he corresponded with Stanhope.

John Dalton, a year younger than Fulton, was already launched on his distinguished career as a chemist and atomic physicist. He had published his *Meteorological Observations and Essays* and had recently delivered a paper before the Manchester Literary and Philosophical Society on his investigation of color blindness, a malady with which he was himself afflicted. A Quaker of artisan background, like Fulton he was largely self-taught.

The magnetic twenty-two-year-old poet Samuel Taylor Coleridge was at that time rushing about the countryside seeking converts for the communistic settlement he intended to establish on the banks of the Susquehanna River in Pennsylvania with the poet Robert Southey. He was only an occasional visitor, but Fulton may have met him earlier, for Coleridge had spent the summer of 1793 spouting republicanism in Exeter.

Fulton's questing intelligence and multiple creative talents were attractive to these men. As a painter turned engineer, he embodied a unity of interests that they considered not only highly desirable but wholly logical. His enthusiasm for new ideas, his ability to play with them and to develop them theoretically and concretely, was akin to their own. His independence and his boundless energy corroborated their notion of what an American should be.

For Fulton, this group was an exciting advance over the society he had enjoyed at Powderham and even during his painting years in London. It presented opportunities for patronage and assistance without the heavy homosexual overtones inherent in his relationship with Courtenay and without the potential rivalry of his relationship with Stanhope. With the exception of Darwin, the men were all slightly younger than Fulton. Able, ambitious, and productive, they offered much needed companionship and stimulus. To be befriended by men with such fertile, subtle minds gave Fulton a strong endorsement for the new direction he had taken. That this interlude in Manchester was an extraordinarily liberating experience, psychologically, is apparent in the gaiety of Fulton's letters to Owen. They have a sparkle that is entirely absent in his previous correspondence.

It is not surprising that, for a fleeting moment that winter, Fulton allowed his attention to be diverted from canals to steamboats. He was, perhaps, encouraged by Darwin's interest and by the fact that about that time one John Smith ran a boat briefly on the Bridgewater Canal at a speed of two miles an hour using an outmoded atmospheric engine. On November 4, 1794, ten days before his twenty-ninth birthday, Fulton wrote Boulton and Watt asking how much a three- or four-horsepower engine with a rotative movement designed to be placed in a boat would cost. His inquiry was little more than a request for free engineering advice, however, for he begged the company to specify what size boat it would require, how much coal it would consume in twelve hours, and "what Quantity of purchase" they allowed for each unit of horsepower. ("Purchase" is the pull on the water. In swimming, for instance, the movement of an extended arm with cupped hand is a means of gaining purchase on the water.) All Fulton was certain of was that the engine should occupy as little space as possible. Although they dutifully filed his letter, Boulton and Watt did not feel compelled to answer it, and Fulton, having the wisdom not to divide his creative energies at this stage, again focused his attention on canal building, which offered better prospects for immediate returns.

To cut labor costs and speed construction, he designed a canal-digging machine. Drawn by four horses, the shoveling device was attached to and powered by the rear axle of a four-wheeled frame. It scooped earth into a curved container from which it was thrown off to the embankment by a four-bladed fly, also powered by the rear axle. Although cumbersome, for its time it was an advanced attempt to cut labor costs by mechanizing excavation. Fulton claimed it could remove a cubic yard of dirt faster than a man and at one-third the expense. It was a salable idea.

As Fulton had exhausted whatever money he received for his Peak Forest contract, he applied to Owen for a loan to cover the expense of a patent for this machine. It was not suitable for the rugged Peak Forest country, he conceded, but he was confident he could obtain work excavating a portion of the canal that had been proposed to connect Gloucester with the Bristol Channel, and thus establish the profitability of his invention. Although Owen later wrote he thought the contrivance was "very problematical," he regarded the "little aid" he gave Fulton as money most fortunately expended in view of Fulton's ultimate contribution to his country. On December 17, 1794, Owen signed a detailed agreement in which he was to advance up to 400 pounds. When the digger showed a profit, Fulton would repay Owen and make him a partner in both the inclined plane and the digging machine patents. Owen gave him 60 pounds for current expenses, and Fulton promised to spend all of his time putting the machine into operation.

Soon afterward, Fulton made an exploratory trip to Gloucester, but he soon discovered that his chance of finding work there was slim. The Gloucester & Berkeley Canal Committee was having difficulty raising capital; there was little chance the project would actually get under way. Nevertheless, Fulton submitted a proposal for cutting the canal, and, not wishing to lose his prospective partner, he wrote Owen a spate of letters with new calculations, and various sketches of new machines, and improvements. In February, Fulton learned his bid had been turned down. This left him in desperate financial straits. "When the Rhino is gone," he told Owen, referring in slang to his pressing debts, "I will write you."[11]

Fulton's protracted absence caused a falling out with McNiven. On Owen's advice, he returned to Manchester to deal with the situation in person. Not only did Fulton succeed in persuading the Peak Forest Company to allow him to take over the contract himself, at six pence per yard to be paid fortnightly, but he also extracted another loan of 80 pounds from Owen "to make a fair experiment on the earth removing apperatus."[12]

At the same time Fulton worked on designs for prefabricated iron bridges and aqueducts that would bring down costs and make canals faster to build and more flexible. The idea was not new. William Reynolds and Benjamin Franklin Outram, both engineers and ironmongers, were recommending short span iron structures. Thomas Paine had been promoting the system he exhibited in Philadelphia and patented in England. However, the method of trussing Fulton advanced was lighter and stronger and the Peak Forest committee was so impressed that, although they had already commissioned a stone aqueduct for the river crossing at Marple, they asked Fulton to produce a model of an iron aqueduct 90 feet high and 300 feet long. The Committee also sent Outram, their chief engineer, with two other engineers, to inspect the small boats and inclined plane at Coalbrookdale.

In the end, the Peak Forest Canal used neither the aqueduct nor inclined planes and small boats, although Outram's report was favorable. However, the aqueduct on the Ellesmere canal at Pontcysyllte was built using Fulton's system. Completed in 1805, it has an iron trough with masonry piers and is 125 feet high and 1007 feet long. It is the world's loftiest and perhaps most beautiful aqueduct.

For his many drawings and plans for the improvement of the Peak Forest canal and the proposed aqueduct bridge, the committee presented Fulton with an award of 100 guineas. This windfall gave him an opportunity to ruminate about the broader implications of canal navigation, to view it not merely as a segmented moneymaking enterprise, but as a system of national transportation. Until this time, canals in England had been developed haphazardly, with little regard to the establishment of a uniform countrywide network. The variations in canal width and lock size from one territorial stretch to another often made transshipment of cargo necessary, resulting in loss, theft, breakage, and added charges. Large users were currently exerting pressure to have existing canals broadened to 72 feet so that all would be capable of carrying boats of at least 30 tons.

Fulton realized that this approach would not solve the problem of bringing easy transportation to areas that had little water, hilly terrain, or a small volume of trade and advocated that small canals, such as those used in Shropshire, be adopted as the norm. These narrow waterways accommodating 5- by 20-foot container boats could be connected into a vast system that would leave no area of the kingdom without service. They would be easier to finance than large canals as building, operation, and maintenance would be far cheaper and the risk would be more widely spread. So convinced was Fulton of the superiority of small canals that he abandoned his own solution of transferring boats to lock carriages as a waste of time and concentrated on perfecting a system using small boats of 2 to 5 tons for transporting both passengers and cargo.

The Peak Forest Committee liked these ideas and asked Fulton to publish them. They agreed to pay the cost of printing two hundred copies, with the stipulation that one copy be given to each of their investors. In this decisive support, Fulton at last had the encouragement he needed to persist as an engineer. The *Treatise on the Improvement of Canal Navigation*, which the Committee's liberal funding made possible, would become the cornerstone of a lifelong career.

An Adventurer
Armed with Fortitude

❖

When Fulton threw himself into writing about why small canals were preferable to large canals, he had acquired enough experience to realize that the publication presented a golden opportunity; it would provide him with lasting, distributable credentials. Almost thirty years old and still uncertain whether his engineering efforts would be rewarded with the success that had eluded him as a painter, he had need of public recognition, emotionally as well as professionally.

To give advance notice of the book and to blunt criticism from established canal builders, he composed an article for a popular newspaper in which, after briefly describing his system, he boldly called for comments from practicing engineers so that he could answer them in his work. Then he devoted all his time to writing the text and drawing pictures and diagrams of the machinery to illustrate it. In the course of the eight months this took, he constantly enlarged the scope until the final 160 pages of text encompassed philosophical, social and economic theory, comments on the patent law, cost-benefit comparisons, and a plan for a network of canals covering the state of Pennsylvania. Unlike the hit-or-miss cleverness of the tinkerer-mechanic addressing an isolated problem, Fulton's genius, which he was himself just beginning to grasp, was that he was able, indeed compelled, to envision an idea as a complex of many parts, to ferret out the social, economic and physical ramifications, and to integrate them into a continuously expanding system. The depth and breadth of his approach was unique in his day. The book is not only a personal testament, it is a model of comprehensive regional development planning.

Published on March 1, 1796, its full title was *A Treatise on the Improvement of Canal Navigation, exhibiting the numerous advantages to be derived from small canals and boats of two to five feet wide, containing from two to five tons burthen with a description of the Machinery for facilitating Conveyance by Water through the most Mountainous Countries, independent of Locks and Aqueducts including Observations on the great Importance of Water Communications, with Thoughts on, and Designs for, Aqueducts and Bridges of Iron and Wood.* The authorship was more succinct—simply R. Fulton, Civil Engineer.

The highly respected I. and J. Taylor of the Architectural Press were the printers. Fulton must have visited their workshop constantly to encourage and supervise, for the book is visually handsome—far more so than other works published by the Taylors in the same field. The typeface is elegant and the seventeen pages of engravings, executed from Fulton's carefully prepared pen and ink and watercolor drawings, have verve and grace. Many show his inventions in delightful rural settings, with people and animals as well as machines. The writing is forceful, concrete, and often eloquent. Fulton's transference of his first energies from painting to mechanics had obviously not dulled his aesthetic impulse. Rather it had been vitally extended. For Fulton, as for most of his contemporaries reared in the eighteenth-century "renaissance" ethos, there was no conflict between the verbal and the visual disciplines. They were but alternative means of conveying ideas to a broad audience.

It is not surprising, therefore—though it certainly was unusual in such a book—that after reminding the prestigious Board of Agriculture that it had found his model "deserving the attention of those who are engaged in the business of forming Inland navigation," Fulton used his Preface to examine the problem of the creative process in mechanics. He began with an analysis of the psychological plight of the inventor forced to combat the antagonism of vested interest. This passage is so emotionally charged that it could only have been drawn from his immediate experience. He then presented the powerful definition of invention as a discovery of relationships that he would repeat with messianic consistency throughout his life:

An Adventurer Armed with Fortitude

The fear of meeting the opposition of envy, or the illiberality of ignorance, is, no doubt, the frequent cause of preventing many ingenious men ushering opinions into the world, which may deviate from the common practice. Hence, for want of energy, the young idea is shackled with timidity, and a useful thought is buried in the impenetrable gloom of eternal oblivion. . . . The adventurer must therefore arm himself with fortitude to meet the attacks of illiberality and prejudice, determined to yield to nothing but superior reason. . . .

There is also a secret pride which urges many to conceal their speculative enquiries, rather than meet criticism, or not be thought the first in their favorite pursuit; ever anxious to claim the merit of invention, they cannot brook the idea of having their work dissected and the minute parts attributed to the genius of other men. But in mechanics, I conceive, we should rather consider them improvements than inventions . . . as the component parts of all new machines may be said to be old; but it is nice discriminating judgment, which discovers that a particular arrangement will produce a new and desired effect . . . [and] is usually dignified with the term Genius. Therefore, the mechanic should sit down among levers, screws, wedges, wheels etc. like a poet among the letters of the alphabet, considering them as the exhibition of his thoughts; in which a new arrangement transmits a new idea to the world."[1]

On the surface, this concept of invention was self-serving, his answer to Stanhope's—and undoubtedly other engineers'—accusations that his ideas were not entirely new. It is, however, far more than a personal defense. Fulton perceived that inventions rarely spring full-blown from the brain of a single individual in a kind of divine illumination but, on the contrary, are a societal event, the result of decades, even centuries, of accumulated information and techniques. An invention was for him the product of a long process of knowledge gathering, culminating in special insight. The wide community of scientists and mechanics provided the basic materials; the creative role of the individual was to improve on them by discovering new and useful relationships among them.

This was not a popularly accepted theory of mechanical invention. Despite the rationalist orientation of that period, the law embraced the popular image of invention as a semi-mystical event visited upon an individual with the sudden force of revelation. The invention must be practicable, but, more important, it must be unique. A new combination of known elements was not patentable. Nonetheless, Fulton's definition of "the curious fabric in which genius resides" was then, as now, true in practice. In mechanical invention, even the most talented individual must work within the existing body of theoretical and technical expertise, modifying it in ways that will in turn be changed and developed. Future rivals would take every opportunity to discredit this perception of invention, but Fulton would never deviate from it.

Fulton's use of a literary rather than a fine arts simile also seems at first surprising. He might have been expected to say "as a painter among his oils and brushes," instead of "as a poet among the letters of the alphabet," especially since his mentor West so strongly believed that artistic invention consisted of combining existing knowledge and materials by means of principles discovered by experiment. He chose well, however, for both in England and in America works of fine art were considered inherently unpatentable because they could not be duplicated even by the artist who executed them. In contrast, written works, like mechanical inventions, existed in order to be copied. The 1790 U.S. Patent law, which Fulton must have been acquainted with, links the two. Its basis was Article 1 Section 8 of the Constitution which gives Congress the power "to promote the progress of science and useful arts by securing for limited times to authors and inventors the exclusive right to their respective writings and discoveries."

The Introduction that followed this idea-filled Preface was equally personal. In it, Fulton briefly described his stumbling on the newspaper account of the Bude Canal and his initial interchange with Stanhope on the problems of the Nuttals's plan. This took place, he wrote in a startling non sequitur, which he underlined, at a time when he was "having some communication with his Lordship *on the practicality of navigating by steam.*"[2] Perhaps because his advances had been spurned, he did not elaborate but immediately went on to describe his subsequent experiments with canal devices, four variations of single and double inclined planes that he claimed worked with ease and certainty and that he said Stanhope had been pleased to compliment him on. To forestall the accusation he was ignorantly copying other men's ideas, he had the good sense to pay tribute to William Reynolds to whose genius, he said, "every future improver will feel infinitely indebted . . . however greatly his machine may be improved or varied in its operation."[3]

These prefatory remarks occupied sixteen pages, but, entranced by broad vistas, Fulton still was not ready to get down to specifics. In his first chapter, he presented a world history of canals, which he found "an inexhaustible fund of amusement" and which he hoped would "teach us the absurdity of presuming perfection." This essay required little research, for the Architectural Press had published John Phillips' *History of Canals* in 1792. Fulton inserted the history only to cast light on the universe within which he conceived his inventions.

Even this exercise did not exhaust Fulton's desire to place his invention in the great stream of human progress. In the second chapter he looked to the future, painting a noble picture of the close-knit, productive society that would be brought about by the excellent communications his system of small canals would provide: "[A]griculture and commerce will improve, and happiness spread in proportion as the facility of conveyance increases." People mingling in commercial intercourse with their neighbors would "imperceptibly lose their local prejudices." Their spirit of enterprise would be stimulated. "Small societies would become large and socially compact, bringing their various improvements into one common stock: a knowledge of mechanics would spread, and greater comforts would result from less labour."[4] Fulton already sensed the transforming effect of industrialization, still only in an infant stage, and he placed himself in its vanguard, for he realized that free circulation of goods and people was essential to it.

Equally important, small canals were an instrument for increasing productivity. Like the looms of the draper or hosier, they reduced labor costs while multiplying the work performed. "The produce of labour is the real wealth of a country," he stated, "the more the labour will produce so much more the nation improves."[5]

His system, moreover, would increase competition, which was in the best interest of society as well as of the individual. Unlike monopoly, which grabbed as much profit as it could, competition took as little profit as it could afford, he wrote. It furnished "the true polish of society." Because small canals were cheap to build and could service a far wider area, his system would generate competition among owners. Because they were simple to operate, the canals would permit competition among workers. Since one man, a boy, and a draft animal only were required to draw ten concatenated boats along the canal, any man who owned a horse, a mule, or even an ass could set himself up in business, acting as agent and toll collector as well as boatman. The resulting competition for the franchises would "not only produce attention and civility, but also moderate charges and new modes." Ideally, each boatman would work a specified stretch of canal that could be covered within one day so that he would "ever be in the neighborhood of his habitation." In contrast to the noisy, rough, drifting pool of laborers who worked the large canals, his boatmen would take a proprietary interest in the smooth operation of their territories. The work would be reduced to a system, rendering every man by habit familiar with his part and producing a chain of self interest," which was, Fulton believed, "the most prevailing stimulus to urge men to be active."[6]

For these concepts of productivity and competition Fulton owed a debt to Adam Smith, which he freely acknowledged early in the *Treatise* with a long quotation from *The Wealth of Nations*. In fact, the *Treatise* was a concrete application of Smith's concept that productivity and social improvement were dependent on wide communication of goods and ideas, which, in 1776 when *The Wealth of Nations* was published and in 1796 as well, meant increasing water carriage.

Almost as a second thought Fulton presented the mechanical details of his system. Woven into the philosophizing are descriptions of the wheeled passenger and cargo boats, double and single inclined planes for ascending short slopes, long inclined planes for crossing deep valleys, horizontal planes for crossing rivers, and the gears, chains, pulleys, cast-off hooks, and governors of which all his devices were composed. These descriptions are presented in vivid language and illustrated by seventeen pages of charming renderings and precise engineering drawings, proudly signed "R. Fulton inven. et delin."—inventor and delineator.

Although most of his ideas had already been tried, that of fixing wheels to the bottom of the boat instead of relying on rollers attached to the inclined plane was new. The first plate shows a "Market or Passage Boat" and a "Dispatch Boat" speeding down the canal loaded with people and goods. Designed with traditional curved hulls these vessels were to be used for fast service over relatively short distances. There is also a drawing of a "Common four-ton Boat," an oblong box 20 feet long and 4 feet wide. Because they were square-ended, these boats could be easily joined together to form trains of ten or twenty boats, which could be used to haul heavy merchandise over longer distances.

The tub-in-well, a further development of the mechanism he had patented, was also original. Used later on the Bude Canal and acknowledged to have been a workable design, it was unique in the legal sense of the word. It consisted of a covered metal bucket 9 feet in diameter to be filled with water then dropped into a vertical shaft, providing the force to raise boats on inclined planes when they could not be paired with descending boats. Just before it reached the bottom, the tub automatically braked, opened, released its water, then rose to the top by means of a counterweight. Theoretically all the water was conserved, at least to the canal system. Because it was largely automated, only one man was needed to operate it. Where the ascent was too steep to use an inclined plane, the boat could be hooked to a crane and dropped down or pulled up through a shaft, which was parallel to the tub-in-well. The tub-in-well was superior to other methods, Fulton asserted, because its perpendicular plunge gave it a raising power equal to its whole weight, friction excepted. Because it was adaptable to vertical ascents, it eliminated, in many cases, the need for tunnels.

As in his letters to Stanhope, Fulton numerically compared the time and costs of the whole and the parts of his system to the large canals with locks then in operation and showed them to be much more economical in capital, materials, and men. Pointing out that new methods of financing would be required to implement a truly integrated canal network, he proposed a "progressive" or "creative" plan. This proposal is one of the most innovative contributions of the *Treatise*. Probably because he realized it would be very difficult to change the entrenched pattern of individual subscribers in England, he presented this scheme as a coda to the main body of the text. It is in the form of a letter, addressed to Governor Mifflin of Pennsylvania who the previous year had addressed his constituents on the subject of a canal to unite the Delaware and Raritan rivers.

The canal Fulton envisioned would connect Philadelphia to Fort Pitt, 350 miles to the west. Because investment capital was scarce and because it was in the national interest to bring the produce of the interior to the markets on the coast, he suggested that the federal government provide seed money by subsidizing the first 60 or 70 miles. The cost would be about $150,000. Tolls from the first segment would be used to pay for subsequent segments until the network was complete. If work did not progress fast enough, the state could add its own money. Proprietors, whose land stood to increase in value as soon as the canal system reached it, might also be prevailed upon to contribute. Fulton believed the return of wealth from this small capital investment would have immense national significance. "Canals will pass through every vale, meander round each hill, and bind the whole country in bonds of social intercourse," he predicted; "hence population will be increased; each acre of land will become valuable, industry will be stimulated and the nation gaining in strength will rise to unparalleled importance, by virtue of so powerful an ally as canals."[7]

With this important achievement to offer his country, Fulton was again thinking of returning to the United States. He had good reason to believe that his ideas would be well received there, for even before the Revolutionary War Americans had been infected with canal fever. Numerous public-spirited and enterprising men had journeyed to England specifically to interview Bridgewater and inspect his canal. Although by the 1790s only one small canal on the Mohawk River in New York State was in operation, many had been projected. The frontier settlements were steadily growing, and New Yorkers, Pennsylvanians, Marylanders, and Virginians were vying for the best way of cornering western trade. Financing by the federal government had few supporters, but both the Federalist and Republican parties were keenly aware of the country's great need for improved transportation.

The optimism that pervades the *Treatise* is infectious. Fulton's arguments are entirely convincing. Yet, it is studded with outbursts of strident pride that suggest profound emotional uncertainty. All too often the voice in which Fulton proclaims his virtues as he parades his frustrations rises to a shrill pitch of insolence. His frequent calls for "candid investigation" to correct his "numerous errors" are frequently mere excuses to declare his own superiority: "As I venerate liberality and the light of reason I despise the pusillanimity of the individual, who, like a dark lantern, conceals the light he receives."[8]

While he declares with false modesty that he does not arrogate to himself "a great deal of that ingredient called genius," he taunts would-be detractors: "I here call on engineers and others, who think proper to answer the arguments in their favour . . . if they cannot do this I hold myself perfectly justifiable in criticizing the works of those men, who may hereafter either willfully, or ignorantly, prosecute the lock principle and draw their employers into the consequent errors."[9] Angrily and with more than a touch of self-pity, he repeatedly denounces the persecution visited on inventors: "[M]any a man of worthy demeanor is tormented by the criticism of ignorant insignificance, for men of the least genius are ever the first to depreciate, and the last to commend; and for an obvious reason, they have not sense to know the produce of genius when they see it. . . . If the old systems were invariably to be continued," he asserted, "there would be no more scientific improvement than in a bed of oysters."[10]

This, of course, has ever been the cry of inventors who, because they perceive in a new way, are set apart from their contemporaries; yet, to implement their ideas, they are necessarily dependent on them. Fulton's turbulence had a specific cause as well. The 200 guineas from the Peak Forest Company carried no assurance that his system of wheeled boats and inclined planes would be adopted. It was not. The Peak Forest canal, though narrow, was built with traditional locks throughout. Some personal power struggle may have been involved, for Fulton expresses no gratitude whatever in the *Treatise* for the committee's financial support. In fact, although many of the canal drawings depict settings strongly reminiscent of the Peak Forest country, Fulton makes no mention of the canal in the entire text. The sour, self-indulgent passages that permeate the *Treatise* may well have been generated by disappointing negotiations with the Peak Forest Company. At the same time they express the dark, egocentric side of Fulton's personality. Entwined with his optimism was a strand of self-destructive violence that he was never entirely able to suppress. Arrogant combativeness was, in fact, one source of his creative energy. "Friction," he wrote in a sudden flash of self-understanding, "brings forth the sparks of latent fire. . . . It is only illuminated particles which can give lustre."[11]

Despite its hubris, the *Treatise* was well received. Fulton's system of small canals was logical, his cornucopia of ideas provocative. His emphasis on the systematic integration of design, construction, operation, and financing into a comprehensive plan was conceptually brilliant. The popular *Monthly Review* devoted five pages to the *Treatise* in early 1797. The author of the article liked Fulton's theory; "whether or not it may conduce to his own emolument," he wrote, "there can be no doubt of its beneficial tendency in respect to the public." The "elegantly designed" plates impressed him as well. As late as 1810 the same magazine extended its praise. "His ideas," it said, "ought not to be hastily rejected."[12]

William Chapman, a prominent canal engineer whose evaluation Fulton had specifically sought, published a rebuttal in 1797, but, aside from disparaging Fulton's "warm imagination," all he could find to criticize was that the small wheels affixed to the underside of the boats might be injured by friction and by "their inability to surmount any casual obstacle." [13] He also thought that the dimensions of the boats were too narrow for coal, and too susceptible to tipping, and that the canals were too deep to be crossed without bridges, but he did not back up his criticisms with concrete details.

Stanhope's reaction was especially satisfying. Echoing—probably inadvertently—the fire metaphor Fulton had used in his unsuccessful begging letter almost three years earlier, he wrote, "Your book about Canals, has set me, you see, *on fire*. . . . So I hope that at last, I shall *burn* to some purpose, provided you keep *on blowing the Fire, as you have done*." [14] Even more flattering, he sent Fulton a stream of letters asking for help with his pendanter, the lifting device to which he had alluded, but had not described, in his 1793 correspondence.

Fulton was at Stockport, between Manchester and the Marple end of the Peak Forest canal, when he received the first of these inquiries at the end of April 1796. Tempting as it must have been to throw back Stanhope's "I tell you it will not do . . . it will not answer," Fulton refrained. His long, calculation-filled response began with the deferential observation that it gave him great pleasure to find His Lordship's mind so intent on improving navigation by canals and that he would feel particularly happy if His Lordship would reciprocate by assisting him to investigate his own new ideas. Unquestionably, Fulton still prized his connection with Stanhope and hoped for his patronage on the Bude Canal.

Nevertheless, when it came to examining Stanhope's invention, he did not mince words and threw in a few barbs as well. Mimicking Stanhope's early letters, he told him that his lifting device was too expensive, awkward, and leaky. Fulton himself had experimented with a similar idea and had found it extremely troublesome. Besides, the idea had already been patented. He even gave Stanhope the citation so that he could look it up. Fulton was more encouraging about Stanhope's variations on the inclined plane, though he was frank in stating he thought his own tub-in-well was a better solution to powering the mechanism, because it was more certain, cheaper, and easier to operate. "In this," he confided engagingly, "perhaps I am like a fond father who is pleased with the genius of his friend's children, yet his affections adhear to his own."

Fulton then put forward his own latest idea—the use of windmills to pump water to reservoirs from which it could be released as needed for power. For maximum efficiency, he had invented a method of using the wind to change the size of the sails to suit the force of the wind. He had also devised a tail that could turn the sails so as to catch the wind.

"Windmills have the virtue of being perpetual," he pointed out. "Night or Day without attendance the mill performs, while the Wind Blows and Deposits a power to be used at pleasure. . . . A hurricane Could do no harm and the least Breeze would be of service."

He also sent Stanhope a drawing of a small bascule bridge, a fine example of his careful attention to mechanical detail and to the needs of ordinary country people. The canal "cannot be less than two feet deep in many instances," he explained. "People will not like to wade through to fetch their Sheep, Cows, Produce, etc. particularly in Winter or in Case of Ice."[15] The idea was not entirely new, of course, but Fulton had greatly simplified it, bringing the average cost down to fourteen pounds. Such bridges are still in use today.

Stanhope, characteristically, was undismayed and protested that his pendanter saved all of the water required for locking while Fulton's inclined plane saved only half. They should compare costs. Fulton dispatched a sketch-filled reply. Confident that his own inventions were superior, he described Stanhope's designs as beautiful and charming, but puzzling. Then he dashed off a paean to America, which he called "a digression." Although he did not say it outright, he obviously fantasized being asked to implement his universal canal system there. "Perhaps there never was a Combination of Circumstances *except in Egypt* So favourable to the adoption of a Regular System of Canals," he wrote. "First the Country Comparetively is but Commencing Cultivation; the Public Roads are not even formed. The people have Spirit and are open to Conviction." In his mind's eye he saw his canal system spreading "through the States like the Love of Liberty. . . . Can there be anything more delightful than the prospect of opening easy Communication Into every Core of that Vast Continent. And Give the hand of Cultivation to every Acre? . . . For I will even say that Canals will have a direct tendency to eluminate the mind of America. In a Country where Liberty is equal, where Property Secure And the Land fertile with an easy means of Reaching the Market, Riches will be the Result. And Riches give ease, And time with the means of Improving the Mental Faculties."[16]

Stanhope was full of compliments for this American dream, giving Fulton "a pleasure nearly allied to Vanity,"[17] but he was stubborn about his pendanter. Throughout the spring he persisted in throwing out new solutions, which Fulton had the great satisfaction of countering. Although Stanhope acknowledged the benefit of sparring with Fulton— obviously he quite relished it, even extending an invitation to visit

Chevening—he never yielded to Fulton. His last letter that season announced triumphantly that he had discovered "a most simple Method of *saving* Water, by means of a double inclined Plane, in about *the same admirable* degree, in which it is saved by means of my *Pendanter.*"[18]

It is curious, particularly in view of Fulton's reference to their previous discussions about steam navigation in the *Treatise*, that during this period Stanhope did not ask for his advice about the *Ambinavigator*, which he was feverishly readying for tests. He had used Colonel Mark Beaufoy's tables of resistances and velocities in the design of the hull, yet he still had nothing but a series of embarrassing failures to show for his efforts. Not only had he failed to master "the ABC of the Science," he wrote an old mentor, but he had "not even arrived at the letter A."[19] Exasperated by his slow pace, the Admiralty had threatened to terminate the experiment. Stanhope's sole reference to the *Ambinavigator* was to tell Fulton he was aboard the ship, and the only assistance Fulton volunteered was in a brief postscript: "P.S. Has your Lordship heard of a Gent^m at Mr. Roundtree's factory, Blackfryar's Road who has constructed an engine acting by the expansion of air or Inflamible air Created by Spirits of tar. The Ambinavigator had just put me in mind of it."[20] Perhaps they saw each other in London or at Chevening and talked about it then.

When, in the middle of May, Fulton still had no work at hand, he left Stockport for Askham near York on undisclosed business. By July, if not before, he was back in London once more seeking productive employment. This time he stayed in Soho, but as usual he saw a good deal of the Wests.

West's life was in shambles. He had received the commission from William Beckford to paint the Book of Revelations series, but that did not compensate for his distressing loss of favor with the king. His more kindly colleagues attributed the fact that he was not invited to Windsor Castle as often as usual to his democratic leanings, which had become increasingly unpopular during the protracted war with France. West, however, pompously explained that the king wished "to prevent that envy which arose from seeing him there so often and so noticed."[21] Although he continued to be reelected president of the Royal Academy, many of the irascible members openly criticized his habitual pushing of his own work and derided what they considered his old-fashioned and self-serving thesis that only a virtuous man could be a great artist. He exposed himself to more deserved ridicule when he allowed himself to become the dupe of a father-and-daughter swindling team selling a method of enhancing color, which they claimed was similar to that used by Titian. West investigated it on behalf of the Royal Academy, but before reporting on his findings, he used the process on several of his own paintings. Jealous colleagues accused him of trying to monopolize this "Venetian Secret," and when it turned out to be a fraud, he became a bitter laughingstock.

Fulton's loyalty was unshakable, however. The incident cast no shadow on his warm appreciation of West's character and his achievement. Fulton's steadfastness was based on a natural desire to emulate this adopted father. On an even deeper level, he was fascinated by West's concept of fine art as a manifestation of personal virtue. To perceive himself and to have others perceive him as virtuous as well as clever was becoming exceedingly important to Fulton. This followed the tradition of the great Americans for whom to be "panting after Glory," as Jefferson so crisply put it, was an expected and entirely laudatory trait. However, Fulton's belief in "the Spark in me which may Give the least Light to Society" was obsessive. He increasingly used this vision of himself as a benign hero-benefactor as a stimulus to his creativity and also as a justification for his ambition.

At this time, however, Fulton had no opportunities for realizing such productive virtue; he was suffering through a baneful hiatus between projects, during which he could only mark time. Despite his patent, his *Treatise,* and several influential friends, he still had no active patron, no gripping project, no income-producing work. He was depressed. The English engineers with whom he must compete systematically ignored or denigrated his ideas. The war with France, then in its third year, and the financial dislocations it caused also worked to solidify the antagonism of entrenched interests. No other canal companies sought his services, except the Cornish Heyl and Helford Canal Company for which he did a quick survey. Pleading that because the corn was still unharvested, he could not examine the topography with any accuracy, he submitted a short report that is far stronger on promise and philosophy than on practical detail.

During this fallow period Fulton drew sketches of his canal-digging machine which he sent to Stanhope, and he made more canal drawings. Some hardly differ from those published in the *Treatise*. Others, though they depict only wheels and gears, are tinted with subtle pastel washes and have the eerie beauty of surrealist paintings. However, Fulton was not tempted to return to his easel. When he confessed to his brother-in-law David Morris that he had not had an oil brush in his hand for over two years, he did not seem to regret it.

Fulton could not have found much to celebrate on his thirty-second birthday or during the Christmas season, for on December 28, 1796, he wrote a poignant letter to Stanhope who suspected him of sacrificing "Public Good for private gain." Fulton pointed out that the licensing fee he proposed was a mere one penny halfpenny per ton per mile, far less than the general run of "ungenerous and rapacious" subscribers usually took. Maintaining this valiant approach for several pages, he finally got down to the real purpose of the letter—another half-plaintive, half-defiant request for money:

> [F]or unless I can acquire a Comfortable Mentainance and am Rather Independent, It will be almost Impossible for me to devote sufficient time to Combatt prejudices And Introduce the Creative System. Works of this kind Require much time, Patience and application. And till they are Brought About, Penury frequently Presses hard on the Projector; And this My Lord is so much my Case at this Moment, That I am now Sitting Reduced to half a Crown, Without knowing Where to obtain a shilling for some months. This my Lord is an awkward sensation to a feeling Mind, which would devote every minuet to Increase the Comforts of Mankind, And Who on Looking Round Sees thousands nursed in the Lap of fortune, grown to maturity, And now Spending their time In the endless Maze of Idle dissipation. Thus Circumstanced My Lord, would it be an Intrusion of your goodness and Philanthrophy to Request the Loan of 20 guineas Which I will Return as Soon as possible. . . . Requesting a favour of your Lordship . . . Realy gives me pain but my Lord Men of fortune Can have no Idea of the Cries of necessity—and I must Rely on you Lordship's Goodness.[22]

Stanhope, as Fulton should have anticipated, was not in the least moved by this pathetic plea. Although he perfectly well understood the plight of underfinanced inventors and occasionally gave support to promising countrymen, Stanhope's largess did not extend to an American who had not been willing or able to solve the problems of his pendanter. He did not give Fulton the modest sum he asked.

Thus rejected on every side, Fulton concluded that England held nothing but slights and unrewarded drudgery and began making preparations for ending his self-imposed exile of over ten years. There was no question in his mind that Americans recognized their desperate need for a better transportation system. He even viewed the Whiskey Rebellion as caused by lack of easy transport. "I have thought much and every deliberation has excited Sorrow for the Situation of that Country which is necessitated to distill their produce In order to Render it Portable and bring it to Market," Fulton observed to David Morris. "This I conceive to be your Case for had It been in the power of the western people to Convey their produce of Wheat, Rye etc., etc. to the ports of Phila or Baltimore or any other Mart of trade, it is more than Probable the System of distilation would be much diminished And Agriculture Infinitely Increased."[23]

In an attempt to secure George Washington's patronage Fulton had sent him a copy of his *Treatise*, with a cover letter hoping "his excellencie's sanction would awaken Public attention to the Subject."[24] The president, Fulton knew, was well acquainted with the benefits of canal communication, for he had ardently supported the Potomac canal as a link to the Ohio River, and during his presidency had promoted improved transportation as a bulwark against the "geographical discriminations" that threatened the solidarity of the Union. This was, in fact, a major theme of the Farewell Address he had published that fall.

In February 1797, Fulton received an official answer thanking him for his book but saying merely: "in the midst of preparatory scenes for Congress,I have not had leisure yet to give it the perusal which the importance of such a work would merit."[25] Fulton enthusiastically took this as an indication of Washington's interest and replied immediately with a new approach to financing. "Perhaps an Incorporated Company of Subscribers, who should be bound to apply half or a part of their profits to extension would be the best mode," he wrote, "as it would then be their interest to Promote the work *And guard their emoluments*." He predicted that, if each state were to commence such a plan, the creative system would "in Less than a Century bring Water Carriage within the easy Cartage of every Acre of the American States—conveying the Surplus Labours of one hundred Millions of Men."[26] Ignoring Washington's interest in the Potomac canal, Fulton described a canal from Philadelphia to Lake Erie that, within seventy years, would generate enough tolls to finance a national network of canals 9,000 miles long.

Washington did not answer, but warmed by this vision, Fulton put together a lively package for Pennsylvania legislators entitled "Thoughts on the Delaware and Raritan Canal Act." Headed by a watercolor view of a canal gently curving through clusters of greenery, the document is a delightful blend of visualization and implementation. It comprises three English canal acts, useful for their handling of safeguards and recompense to landowners and benefits to the public, and an idyllic description of how the canal should be built so as to combine convenience and beauty. The waterway, he wrote, should be lined with trees "of a picturesque kind—a Beech, Buttonwood, Ash, Poplar, Willow, Weeping Willow or others equally ornamental planted In rows . . . to Create a Shade from one extremity of the Canal to the other." A special fund should be set up to maintain and replace them. "This Clause on planting may a[t] first sight appear trivial And of little Importance or a thing to be Left to the option of the Committee," Fulton added apologetically, "But I see the propriety of ever uniting ornament to utility, Particularly when Such ornaments will pay their own expense."

No buildings or fences or other works were to be built within forty feet of the canal, except warehouses, cranes, or other works belonging to the company which would be grouped in designated areas. So that they could also be used as roads, the horse paths were to be at least twenty-four feet wide. "The advantage arising from this Union of Roads and Canals," Fulton explained, "Is that they will draw population to their Boarders In consequences of the Combined Convenience and Beauty of the object." [27]

Fulton's nostalgia for home was undeniably real. But beyond that, America was becoming to him a promised land where, untrammeled by the constraints of established tradition, he would be able to realize both his personal and his worldly ambitions. Anxious about what would happen when he did actually return, he romantically elevated the country to a paradisiacal frontier. There was truth in this dream, but like many expatriots, he was compelled to exaggerate it for his psychological survival.

The one saving grace of Fulton's day-to-day existence in London at this juncture was that he had become acquainted with the Reverend Edmund Cartwright, a poet, inventor, and reformer "whose house was a resort for projectors of various merits and pretensions." Cartwright had taken out several patents for power looms and tried to implement them in model factories, but, afraid the improvements would put them out of work, the mill hands had burned them. When Fulton met him, Cartwright was working on an alcohol-fueled steam engine; he may well have been the person Fulton referred to in his letter to Stanhope about the engine for his *Ambinavigator*, although Cartwright was by no means the only mechanic trying to solve that problem.

Fulton was a frequent and welcome guest, enjoyed, according to Cartwright's daughter, for his unusual "vivacity of character and original way of thinking."[28] Her father and Fulton constructed a windup steamboat model she later remembered, but it must have been only a passing fancy, for Fulton and Cartwright gave the model to the children of the household as a toy. Perhaps because of Cartwright's even disposition, they were able to admire each other's multifaceted abilities. For several years they took pleasure in helping each other.

Fulton required an active project and financial support as well as interesting talk, however, and as the months went by, he continued to seek out investors for his American canal venture. He endeavored to lure Benjamin West and through him his patron, William Beckford, into backing it. For his presentation he prepared a formal prospectus that contained the interesting suggestion that the patentee might bargain with potential subscribers for shares. The work, he promised, would "Reflect a lasting honor on the Promoters and Entail fortunes on the successors of all Concerned." Not only would it "Give the country the most Brilliant Polish," but unlike "the India or Guinea Company or other Associations of men who Blindly extirpate one half of the human race to Enrich the other," it would do so "without commiting one depredation on humanity."[29]

England was in the throes of a severe financial crisis, and neither West nor Beckford, whose fortune came from Jamaican sugar plantations, bought shares. In mid-April, however, Fulton sold one-fourth of his American canal prospects to the speculator John Barker Church who was about to return to the United States where, as the brother-in-law of Alexander Hamilton, he had excellent connections. The contract was a windfall. It specified that Fulton would receive 1,500 pounds—500 on April 17, another 500 six months later, and the final 500 when he arrived in America, sometime in June 1798. Meanwhile Fulton was to go to France, take out a patent, and exploit it.

To his erstwhile patron Robert Owen, with whom he had kept up a genial correspondence, he wrote, *"Thank heavens* (some men would say *please the pigs*) I have succeeded." And he sent him 60 pounds, promising to pay the rest of his debt when he returned to England around Christmastime. The following April he intended to sail for America, he told Owen, "where I have the most flattering field of invention before me, having already converted the first characters in that country to my small system of canals"[30]—a gross overstatement of his prospects to say the least.

When Fulton embarked at Dover for Calais in June 1797, he expected to stay in Paris for six months. He would remain there for seven extraordinary years.

A Curious Machine for Mending Politics

❖

Once Fulton made up his mind to leave England, he was in such a hurry he did not wait to get a passport for France. In this he was taking considerable risk, for no one was allowed into the interior of the country without one. Port officials were on watch for smugglers and illegally returning emigrés. In the summer of 1797, Americans traveling from England to France were subject to special harassment. French resentment of Jay's Treaty, by which the United States gave trading advantages to Great Britain, had brought diplomatic relations between France and America to the breaking point. The ruling Directory refused to receive the U.S. Minister and, to prevent commerce with the enemy, had authorized French naval vessels and privateers to seize neutral ships that had any intercourse whatever with the English. What American historians later called the Quasi-War with France had already begun.

Fulton had applied for the required French documents while in London, but was offered only the promise that they would be waiting for him at Calais. When he landed, the immigration officers knew nothing about them—hardly an auspicious beginning to this new phase of his life.

Having no choice but to remain at the port, Fulton took a room at Mme. Grandsire's Hotel in the hope that his papers would soon arrive. Calais was not without diversions for an engineer. He would have found it worth his while to investigate the ancient fortifications, the elaborate commercial quays and especially the great Canal of Calais which, built in 1685, was the mainstem of a network of inland waterways that eventually joined the sprawling Belgian and Dutch canal complex.

Vastly more amusing, however, was the friendship he struck up with Marie Josephine Louise de Montaut de Navailles, Duchesse de Gontaut-Biron, an exiled aristocrat who was attempting to reenter France disguised as Madame François, a bourgeois lace merchant. The duchesse was young, gay, valiant, and intelligent. To earn money in England, she had painted miniatures for sale in charity bazaars. She, too, was staying at Mme. Grandsire's.

Fulton, the duchesse recalled in her *Mémoires*, made her acquaintance by asking her to interpret for him on board ship. When he found she was being held under house arrest for having false papers, he took it upon himself to entertain her, inventing day after day a thousand ways for her to escape. His crowning scheme was that she should marry him. The duchesse was charmed, but she refused. She was already the happy wife of the Duc de Gontaut-Biron in whose behalf she had undertaken this perilous journey.

Either disappointed by the failure of his flirtation or, more likely, true to his notion of himself as "an adventurer armed with fortitude," Fulton left Calais after three weeks, still without a passport. He made "a wide circuit of three hundred miles," stopping to examine the steam engines at the collieries near Valenciennes.[1] Along the way he was impressed, as were most foreign visitors, by the excellent cultivation of the fields, the robust health and good humor of the peasants, the frightful condition of the roads, the great expense of transportation, and the plentitude of English contraband in all the towns and villages.

Somehow he passed through the *barrières* that guarded every entrance to the city and arrived at last in hot, vibrant Paris. Its beauty was, as always, astonishing. The seemingly endless white stone facades caught every modulation of light. The great monuments of the past rose high above the cobbled squares, giving dignity to the narrow dirt streets and the motley crowds passing through them. The most populous city on the Continent, Paris was surprisingly green with orchards and gardens in every quarter. Some were public parks, but many were attached to the handsome estates that still existed throughout the city. The grand Boulevard was elegantly planted with four rows of huge poplars. The Champs-Élysées was a sylvan retreat.

Despite its fast-moving current, the shimmering Seine bound rather than divided the city, giving it focus and an elemental vitality. Its wide stone bridges were busy centers of gossip and commerce as well as convenient crossings from one bank to the other. The Pont St. Michel was lined with a tumble of houses from which projected long poles festooned with drying clothes. The quays were used for swimming schools, bathhouses, laundries, and open air stalls for bootblacks, dog clippers, and nightingale vendors. Too shallow to be navigated by seafaring vessels, the Seine at Paris—unlike the Thames at London and the Delaware at Philadelphia—was decidedly domestic in character.

Although the memory of the Terror's mass executions had not been obliterated, the city exuded a sense of well-being. Good harvests had brought down the price of bread. The new rich spent freely. The great citizen army, having annexed the lands west of the Rhine and established "sister republics" in Belgium, Holland, and Savoy, were triumphantly occupying northern Italy. Momentary political stability masked the fact that the Revolution was inexorably headed toward military dictatorship.

Fulton had visited Paris in 1790, and probably knew his way around. Tracking down his passport was his first priority. He found it had reached Calais after he left. With his customary resilience, he took this as a good omen. "There's every symptom of my remaining here in peace," he wrote Cartwright, "although Americans are by no means well received or suffered to rest in quiet."[2] He was lucky, too, in the lodgings he found. There was a vacancy in a Left Bank pension, Madame Hillaire's at 555 rue de Bacq. It was not the best address for foreigners—that was on the Right Bank in the neighborhood of "that great vortex of dissipation, the Palais Royal"—but it was good enough, and it was within easy walking distance of almost anyplace business or entertainment would take him.

Madame Hillaire's was a convivial establishment. Noted for her strong Republican sympathies, she attracted patrons with similar views. At that particular time she was favored with a concentration of Americans. William Lee, a Boston merchant, was the American consul at Bordeaux. Samuel Miles Hopkins, whom Fulton may have met the previous year in London where Hopkins had vainly sought English buyers for his land in western New York State, was visiting Paris, "to enlarge his knowledge of men and things."[3] Ruth Barlow, a witty woman of great charm, was waiting for her husband, Joel Barlow, to return from

Algiers, where as U.S. minister plenipotentiary he was negotiating for the release of American sailors imprisoned by the Barbary pirates. Although Hopkins soon decided to live with a French family because too little French was spoken at Madame Hillaire's, this little group provided an instant social setting for Fulton. They remained lifelong friends.

"Paris," Fulton wrote Cartwright, "is all gay and joyous as if there were no war at all."[4] The focus of life was pleasure. Festival days were celebrated with processions, fireworks, chariot races, and rowing matches. For everyday amusement there was battledore and shuttlecock in the Tivoli Gardens, secluded walks in the Frascati, and street performances along the Boulevard. Everyone who could scrape together the admission frequented the theaters and the opera. And everywhere there was dancing. The waltz, with the novel requirement that partners put their arms around each other, was the latest rage.

"There are at Paris upwards of 30 places of Public Amusements such as theatres & the grandest of which is the Opera. The machinery, musick, acting & dancing are perfection, the dancers are almost naked when they represent Nymphs which might shock the modesty of Americans though it is not noticed for the dress here is very licentious . . . nothing else but the Greek customs or dress will take place in some time here for the Coiffure a la Grecq (for men & women) is all the mode & it is certainly very handsome & picturesque. . . . The Parisians are a tasty and agreeable people." So wrote the painter John Vanderlyn, who arrived in Paris a few weeks after Fulton, to his brother in Esopus, as Kingston, New York, was then called.[5]

Even art was part public entertainment. The collections of France's despoiled aristocrats were displayed as the property of the people in the refurbished corridors of the Louvre. To them were added the treasures extorted from conquered countries. These, when they reached Paris, were paraded through the streets, as royal captives had been in Roman times. The masterpieces from the Low Countries had already arrived. The Michelangelos, da Vincis, and other treasures confiscated during the Italian campaign were daily expected. "The collection of Paintings here is a superb one; already they fill a gallery as long as your Esopus Main Street, which is about the length of the Louvre," the ecstatic Vanderlyn wrote. "The paintings consist of all the different schools, the Italian, Flemish, & French . . . one is in raptures in gazing upon the works of a Raphail, a Corragio, Charicci, Titian, Rubins, Poussin, etc. Certainly one does not want opportunities for improvement here."[6]

Of more immediate importance to Fulton was that experimental science was fashionable. The respectability it enjoyed under the old regime had been increased by strong support from the revolutionary government. Eminent savants gave free lectures and were personally accessible in their "cabinets" and at open houses. The National Institute offered quarterly lectures in every branch of the sciences and humanities. The public could attend courses at state institutions of higher learning. Practice as well as theory was valued. The bridge engineer and hydrologist Gaspard Prony, for instance, took his students from the elite School of Bridges and Roads to examine the workshops of the Périer brothers, France's most distinguished manufacturers of machines. The National Conservatory of Arts and Trades had recently been installed in the church and refectory of St.-Martin-des-Champs, where it is still located. Its public galleries displayed models of inventions and prized scientific instruments, many of them the bounty of war. Ship models could be seen at the Louvre, and those emanating from the Public Works Department were exhibited in the Rue Grenelle, not far from where Fulton lived.

Yet despite the government's efforts to promote applied science, France's technological capability lagged far behind England's. French craftsmen were adept at making *objets de luxe* and mechanical gadgets for public spectacles, but there were, for instance, no more than a dozen steam engines in operation in the entire country, and most of them were obsolete atmospheric engines used to pump water rather than to drive machinery. For a nascent engineer the field was wide open. It is, indeed, difficult to imagine a situation in which person, time, and place were so well matched as were Fulton, the year 1797, and France. Fulton was aware of his opportunities. "When peace returns," he optimistically wrote Edmund Cartwright in November, "I conceive every encouragement will be given to the arts, and France will rise like a phoenix from the ashes of war."[7]

As he had promised his new partner Church, Fulton spent the autumn making friends for small canals. He had good reason to believe his system would be well received. Canals were France's primary means of transport for commodities and bulk goods, but for the past decade political turmoil, war, and inflation had reduced work on them to mere necessary maintenance. New canals were urgently needed throughout the country. Existing canals were generally 40 to 50 feet wide and 5 to 6 feet deep. Finding enough water to fill them was a serious problem, and the strongest argument for small canals was that they used comparatively little. Fulton's creative system of financing tied to a master plan of development was also attractive. Traditionally paid for by the government, canal building in France lacked the impetus provided by private capital in Britain.

While proselytizing for small canals, Fulton began his patent application. The underlying premise of the French law, passed on January 7, 1791, and based in part on the American law of 1790, was that every discovery in the mechanical arts was literally the property of its creator. As its champion stated: "If a man possesses any true property it is his thought. . . . It is personal, it is independent, it precedes all other transactions. The idea that is born in a man's mind belongs as incontestably to him as the tree that springs up in his field."[8] The machine or process to be patented must be new and workable, but to speed industrialization, France granted patents of importation to devices patented in other countries. No preliminary examination of either original or importation patents was required; it was thought undemocratic. Disputes about priority were settled in court. The term "novelty" was loosely interpreted.

Primarily to protect himself, but also as a service to other patentees, Fulton included a clarification of the concept "novelty" in his application. He brought out the "poet among the letters of the alphabet" argument he had enunciated in his *Treatise on Canals*—that, if the combination of elements was original, an invention was new even if all the parts had been used previously in other machines. For more complete protection he refined his argument by stipulating that neither a change nor a transposition of the parts nor an addition or removal of any of the parts would weaken the patent. In addition, he asserted that a rival could not patent improvements without the consent of the owner of the primary patent; reciprocally, improvements could not be used by a primary owner without the permission of the improver. Fulton worked these ideas into a preface to his patent application, an unusual procedure, but, because there was no standard format, one he thought would be accepted.

Embroidering on the patent law was not enough to satisfy Fulton's penchant for hortatory writing, however. Gripped by his dream of a new world order based on easy transportation of goods, capital, and people, Fulton envisioned himself its prime architect. To carry his ideas forward, he composed, in late October, a twenty-two-page monograph entitled "Thoughts on Free Trade with Reasons Why Foreign Possessions And all duties on Importation is Injurious to Nations."[9] Expanding the concept of productivity—"the fountain of riches and the cause of wealth"—introduced in the *Treatise*, it preached the necessity of removing all barriers to trade. Branding colonialism "a Monster of Ignorance, the dark, the dreadful enemy of mankind," Fulton declared that to monopolize foreign lands was "as false as to monopolize the sun's rays." Imposing duties on imports to encourage domestic manufacturers was absurd since the cost was passed on to the people. Only by stimulating domestic industries and bartering their products with other countries could a nation prosper. England was rich, he argued, not because of its colonies, the acquisition and control of which loaded its people with taxes, but because it had "more better machinery," which increased productivity. England's commodities and manufactures were so cheap and superior in quality that they were always in demand even when the price was increased by the cost of smuggling.

This monograph was intended for the directors of France for whom he grandiloquently "reserved the eternal honor of Removing the obstacles between man and Happiness." Pointing out that France could not maintain a fleet sufficient to prevent England from trading with all other countries, he exhorted the directors to promote a balance of trade by cultivating industries that would use France's natural advantages to produce "goods other people want," such as wine, brandy, oil, fine cambric, and lace. "Thus equal rights being established we should in the Spirit of Liberty and Philanthropy rejoice to See Each nation peaceably enjoy the Fruits of their Virtuous Industry."

To bring this ideal state into being, Fulton advised setting up an "Assisting Fund" to provide developing industries with capital. This was a remarkably farsighted substitute for the traditional monopolies and protective tariffs. "[T]o Introduce a new Manufacture or Multiply those which are useful, the Fund should advance half the money" for three years after which the enterprise would begin repayment at 5 percent interest. Fulton estimated that with an investment capital of 12 million livres, 300 such factories could be introduced each year. An additional 12 million livres, distributed to "Ingenius natives or Foreigners . . . In Weekly assistance Money or Bounties" would induce workmen to immigrate to France and improve the quality of its products. Such encouragement would generate 1,800 factories employing 3,600 workmen within six years. As the grants were repaid, the money would be used to fund still more manufacturers, many financed by private investors who would by then have the confidence to back new industries.

Ambitious as this program was, it need not increase the national budget, Fulton argued. Seed money for a modest beginning would be made available when restrictions on trade were abolished and the anti-smuggling force of 20,000 men was no longer needed. The savings would amount to 24,000 livres a year, Fulton calculated—12,000 in salaries and another 12,000 because those same men, instead of pursuing smugglers, would be engaged in productive labor.

Fulton had this document translated into French, but there is no record of how the directors responded. These ideas would not have been easy for them to accept. France was primarily an agricultural nation and wished to remain so. Even if France had adopted Fulton's novel financing scheme, the banking structure was too feeble to support the capital formation necessary for full-scale industrialization. Property was valued far above money. Bankers and financiers were distrusted. The strong movement for free trade was considered anti-English rather than pro-industrialization. France had no intention of giving up its sugar-producing West Indies voluntarily. The contest for colonies was, in fact, a major cause of the present war with England.

Fulton almost certainly composed "To the Friends of Mankind," an undated fifty-six-page manuscript, at the same time, for it expands the theme of "Thoughts on Free Trade" and expresses the same global idealism. In "To the Friends of Mankind," Fulton condemns war—an inevitable result of colonizing—as wasteful and unproductive. Soldiers, he noted, were rank consumers who were supported by the productive work of others. War created still another mass of nonproducers: "the Constructors of fortifications, the manufacturers of cannon, Muskets, Swords, Bayonets, Powder, ball and Soldiers apparel, the manufacturers of the numerous materials of Camp equipage, the Builders of Ships of War and all their Complicated arrangements through their various departments with their agents, Clarks and commissioners." Even more pernicious, preparations for war subverted the three cardinal principles on which a flourishing society must be based: attention to education; a strict attention to home improvements; and free circulation and exchange of the produce of genius and labor.

To make clear his deep personal commitment to these concepts,

A Curious Machine for Mending Politics

Fulton appended to the essay what he called "The Republican Creed." Composed of nine articles of faith, each followed by his rationale, it seems, at first glance, a non sequitur. On closer examination it is a moving exposition of the impulse behind the preceding anti-war statement. It is a strong declaration of his commitment to high republican principles which, while recognizing the place of tradition, exalts the free individual's capacity for self-improvement through education and work. The "Creed" takes its inspiration, of course, from Fulton's American experience, reinforced by his contact with Stanhope and the Manchester liberals. It is a strong protest against Britain's laws prohibiting the emigration of skilled craftsmen and against the repressive measures—the suspension of habeas corpus and the right to congregate—the British government had instituted to root out republicanism.

At once a statement of democratic faith and a vision of a new world order, the genius of "The Republican Creed" is that it places eighteenth-century idealism in the context of the needs of the industrial revolution.

On a personal level, the declaration is a remarkable exercise in self-exploration, a projection of Fulton's image of himself as a virtuous benefactor of humanity. In brief form, it is as follows.

1. I believe the inhabitants of all countries receive their Ideas and prejudices from the established customs which surround them in youth which customs plunge them into vice or lead them on to Virtue. . . .
2. I believe that, in consequence of men being governed by opinion, Society may be improved even to the establishment of perpetual peace by investigating and explaining the errors which misguide the mind and teaching the Youth just Ideas of honor and of Individual and national rights. . . .
3. I believe there should be no hereditary Legislators. Wisdom is the friend of man, hence genius should have an equal Clame to rise to the seat of power where Talents might exert their full force for the good of the Citizens. . . .
4. I believe there is no honor to be acquired but in following such pursuits as tend to harmonize Men and nations and Multiply the necessary and rational enjoyments of Life. . . .
5. I believe every man has a right to enjoy his own opinion of Re-

ligion. . . . Teach Industry and be industrious yourselves, love one another and do Justice is all the religion which is necessary for man to follow. . . .

6. I believe that industry applied to useful works is the source of all the conveniences of society. It is national riches and the Path to honour. . . .

7. I believe it is the true interest of Society that every person should be at liberty to move to any Country he thinks proper and take with him his property. He has a right to apply his talents to everything which does not Injure society and he has a right to Sell or exchange the produce of his Inquiry in any Country without any Restriction whatever. . . .

8. I believe that every nation Island and district should allow to every nation island and district a tranquil profession of their property and a free circulation of the whole produce of Industry. This is the true Rights of nation. . . .

9. I believe the whole Interior arrangements of Governments should be to promote *education and Industry.* Their whole exterior negotiations Should be to establish a Social intercourse with each other and give a free circulation to the whole produce of Virtuous industry . . . education without labour cannot produce the necessaries of Life. . . .[10]

Although Fulton's actions would often betray it, this egalitarian testament would serve as the integrating force of his thought, work, and dreams. His most cherished project, on which he had been secretly working and which he was about to unveil, was at least initially inspired by it.

During these first months in France, Fulton kept up a vigorous exchange of ideas with Cartwright. He mentioned that he was trying to design a rope-making machine, a project Cartwright was also working on, and that he was thinking about using steam to cut canals and to power boats. He sent Cartwright rough sketches of a mode of propulsion that used a fly of four parts—that is, a primitive screw propeller with blades similar to those used on windmills.

But what must have been the focus of Fulton's energies during the fall of 1797 was a project he whimsically described as "the contriving of a curious machine for mending the system of politics and applying manual labor to advantage."[11] It was a submarine.

There is, astonishingly, no record of how or when Fulton was seized by this idea. It was so well developed when he made it public that it must have been gestating for a long period, beginning perhaps in 1793 when he witnessed the massing of British warships in Tor Bay at the outset of the war with France and gaining in urgency as the war took its toll on commerce, industry, and civil liberties. Although they were much more, his monographs on free trade and the evils of war were also justifications of his submarine, for he believed it would provide a cheap, efficient, and sure means of eradicating not only maritime conflicts but all war.

On December 13, 1797, without prior written warning, Fulton submitted to the Executive Directory of France the precise terms under which he would sell his system of submarine warfare. To save the government the trouble and expense of developing it themselves he had, he said, put together a company that would bear the cost of building "a Mechanical Nautulus" [*sic*] on the following conditions:

First

That the Government of France Contract to pay the Nautulus Company 4000 Livers [*sic*] per Gun for each British Ship over 40 Guns which they may destroy; and 2000 Livers per Gun for All vessels of war under 40 tons which they destroy, that the sum be paid in Specie within six months after the destruction of Each Vessel.

Second

That all prizes of British Vessels and Cargoes taken by the Nautulus Company shall be the Property of the Company; nor meet with any interruption from the Agents of Government further than to Ascertain that they are British Property.

Third

That the Government Give to the Nautulus Company the exclusive Right to Use this Invention from all the Ports of France; Except when it is the desire of Government to Construct Such Vessels to Act against the Enemies of the Republic. In Such Case the Government to be at Liberty to Build and Multiply the Mechanical Nautulus on paying to the Company One hundred thousand Livers for Each Nautulus which they may Construct or use in the Service of the Republic.

Fourth

As a citizen of the American States I hope it may be Stipulated that this Invention, or Any Similar Invention, shall not be used by the Government of France Against the American States, Unless the Government of America First apply the Invention Against France.

Fifth

That if Peace is Concluded with England within three Months from the date hereof Government will pay to the Nautulus Company the Amount of the expenses which they may have Incurred In the experiments, Such payment to be made within three Months after the declaration of Peace.

Sixth

And whereas fire Ships or other unusual means of destroying Navies are Considered Contrary to the Laws of war, And persons taken in Such enterprise are Liable to Suffer death, it will be an object of Safety if the Directory give the Nautulus Company Commissions Specifying that all persons taken in the *Nautulus or Submarine expedition* Shall be treated as Prisoners of War, And in Case of Violence being offered the Government will Retaliate on the British Prisoners in a four fold degree.[12]

In a cover letter, Fulton claimed unequivocally that his engines could "annihilate the British navy" and achieve liberty of the seas. Since Bonaparte, just returned from his first triumphs in Italy, had been commissioned to invade the British Isles, Fulton urged the Directory to make a swift decision on his invention so that "the terror of it may spread before the descent on England, and that it may be brought into use to facilitate that descent."

The violence of Fulton's animosity toward England, where he had lived productively for over ten years, would seem to make him at best an opportunistic ingrate, and to a certain extent he was. However, Fulton messianically believed that the obliteration of maritime warfare and the advent of universal free trade would benefit England as well as the rest of humanity. Like many other fervent republicans in England and America, Fulton believed that with help from France a strong nucleus of Britons would support a democratic revolution. The mutiny of British seamen at Spithead and the Nore, earlier in 1797, seemed ample evidence for this view. Moreover, Fulton was convinced that free trade was in the best interests of France and that the Marine Ministry would sup-

A Curious Machine for Mending Politics

port him, since the motto "Freedom of the Seas" was embossed on the ministry's stationery.

So enthralled was Fulton by his new invention that he did not pause to consider that the submarine would be as effective against merchant vessels as against warships and could therefore be used as a powerful instrument in curtailing free trade. Nor did he carefully examine the possibility that France might use the submarine against the United States. Overlooking the fact that a declared maritime war between the two countries was imminent, he persuaded himself that France and America were inextricably united by their mutual republicanism and their desire to end Britain's domination of the seas. It is not to Fulton's credit that Clause 4 of his proposal was so weak as to be useless.

Fulton's chief worry at this time, and throughout the long negotiations, was personal. He realized that the submarine would be considered an illegal weapon and that if he or any of his crew were taken prisoner by the British, they would be executed as common criminals. The objection to submarine warfare was not that blood would be shed—the carnage caused by the traditional tactics of broadside and boarding was considered inevitable and even glorious—but that the submarine would attack with unscrupulous stealth. Seamen would be ignominiously drowned instead of being slaughtered in open conflict. Envisioning it as a heroic weapon, superior in power and prowess to all existing ships of war and capable of bringing about a millennium of peace and prosperity, Fulton did not intend to be branded an outlaw. It was absurd to ask the French government to "Retaliate on British prisoners" if he and his crew met with violence, but he desperately wanted this protection. For two years, both the Marine Ministry and the Directory found it impossible to comply with this clause. Yet, it was so crucial to Fulton that he never stopped pressing for it.

Fulton's proposal was a masterpiece of entrepreneurship. In addition to fame, Fulton expected his submarine to bring him a fortune. This was not an unusual notion. A major attraction of a naval career, for officers and seamen alike, had always been the anticipation of sizable rewards for captured ships and prisoners. Moreover, to augment their navies, governments also gave cash bounties to merchant ships for capturing or sinking enemy vessels. Both England and France were using this policy against American shipping at that very time. The remarkable ingredient of Fulton's scheme was, as Fulton himself put it, "the Magnitude of the Object." By means of his *Nautilus* he intended to transform the world. What Fulton recognized, but refused to face, was the inherent conflict between his quest for fame and his craving for fortune.

Aside from these essential moral issues, Fulton's proposal was sound. It accurately reflected France's maritime needs. Victorious in its continental land wars, it had been unable to diminish Britain's control of the sea. Although its elegant ships were faster, handled better, and carried heavier armament than English ships, because of the ravages of the Revolution they were poorly maintained, manned, commanded, and provisioned. Between 1793 and 1796, France had lost thirty-three ships of the line, each of which carried at least 72 guns.

But the real charm of Fulton's proposal was that, since his company would be paid only if the submarine succeeded, it would cost the government nothing to initiate. Even with the bounties, the cost would be no more than a tenth the price of rebuilding the navy to a strength at which France might consider challenging Britain's maritime supremacy. Moreover, it would require far less scarce materials and labor. Fulton was correct in assuming that his *Nautilus* would be tempting to the French government.

Fulton gave no description of the submarine or its method of attack in this extraordinary proposal. In a letter to the current president of the Directory, Louis Marie Larevellière-Lépeaux, he stated that the *Nautilus*, as he now spelled it, was "too difficult for any but a mechanical man to understand," but would be happy to explain it to the marine minister or to General Bonaparte who, he had been told, was "a good engineer."[13] Bonaparte was secretly planning to conquer Egypt and then, in the manner of Alexander the Great, move on to India. Nevertheless, he had ordered large-scale preparations for the invasion of Great Britain, and Fulton, with the general populace, believed he intended to carry it through. Fulton's high opinion of Bonaparte was further enhanced by the fact that the general was a member of the mathematical section of the prestigious National Institute. Sensing Bonaparte was the man of the future as well as of the hour, Fulton envisioned him as a kindred spirit and a potential sponsor. In this last he was misguided. Although Bonaparte's strength lay in his ability to innovate, he never displayed more than a fitful interest in the submarine.

The Marine Ministry, however, was intrigued by Fulton's proposal. The minister, Georges René Pleville-le-Pelley, was old and sick, but he was imaginative and experienced. He immediately grasped the lethal potential of the *Nautilus* and the competence of its inventor. In an early office memo he described Fulton as "an Anglo-American who appears to merit distinction from the great number of others who under pretext of public interest care only for pecuniary advancement."[14]

Pleville-le-Pelley was familiar with the notion of underwater navigation. A centuries-old dream with roots in the myth of the sea god Poseidon, it had long attracted French inventors. In 1780 one Beaugenet, observing that "La ruse vaut mieux que la force dans la guerre"—Ruse is better than force in war—had projected a vessel armed with cannons and carrying five or six men, that could sail like a regular boat, submerge when necessary, navigate underwater, and ascend to discharge its cannons. He intended to penetrate London harbor with it. In the same year Sillon de Valmer published a pamphlet describing an underwater craft propelled by goosefoot oars. A monstrous vessel 50 feet long, 15 feet wide, and 12 feet high, it was equipped with a windowed conning tower, sails, and air pumps. Fixed to the exterior were crampons, chains, and claws for grasping and raising objects. Divers operating outside the boat could draw air from the interior through special valves.

In 1795 Armand Maizière, a self-styled "friend of humanity" proposed an underwater vessel powered by "boiling water." Outfitted with devices on the exterior, he claimed it could attach large powder cases to the sides of ships, which when exploded would "create such havoc that the Patrie and all humanity would finally be avenged." The following year Jules Fabre offered a submarine shaped like a peach stone and carrying a barrel of powder—an infallible means, he asserted, of annihilating the British fleet. At the same time Louis Castera presented a design for a submarine that he anticipated could navigate to a depth of 10 meters drawing war machines behind it. Armed, it was probably intended as a method of transporting ordnance to England. Castera, like Maizière, believed that his machine would cause such panic during battle that the enemy would disperse or be easily captured.

All these projects displayed marvelous creative fancy, but none could be implemented. The only submarine design in the world that had approached practicality was David Bushnell's *American Turtle*, built in New Haven in 1776. Pleville-le-Pelley and other members of the French navy could well have heard about it while they were on duty in the United States during the Revolutionary War. Made of wood covered with tar and reinforced with iron bands, the *Turtle* was 7½ feet long and 6 feet high. It contained enough air for one man to remain submerged for thirty minutes. The operator navigated the boat with two hand-cranked Archimedes' screws, the first use of this method of propulsion. One screw was mounted horizontally on the foresection of the vessel and one mounted vertically on the inward curve above it. The *Turtle* was steered with an aft rudder also moved by hand. A foot pump admitted water into a bottom tank for descent and evacuated it for ascent. The primitive conning tower had windows and three air tubes. Affixed above the rudder was a time-lock activated bomb containing 150 pounds of powder, which Bushnell once called a "torpedo." The operator was to approach an enemy ship at night with only the conning tower and air vents projecting above the surface of the water. When close he would submerge and quickly drive the augur, to which a line to the explosive was attached, into the ship's underbelly. As the *Turtle* pulled away, the bomb would be drawn into contact with the ship, the timing mechanism would set it off, and the ship would be blown to bits.

Three such attacks had been attempted during the Revolution, but none was successful. The *Turtle* was not maneuverable underwater, and it was difficult to place the augur in total darkness. Poor health prevented Bushnell from manning an expedition himself. The substitutes he trained never achieved sufficient command of the multiple motions required to give the vessel a fair test. The *Turtle* was finally sunk while being carried back to port aboard another vessel. Bushnell salvaged it but had neither the strength nor the money to repair it. He did, however, launch contact mines from an ordinary whaleboat, using the tide and current to push them against enemy ships. When this mode proved unsuccessful, he gave up further experimentation and eventually moved to Georgia where he practiced medicine under an assumed name.

Fulton's *Nautilus* incorporated many of the *Turtle*'s features. Whether he borrowed them from Bushnell or discovered them himself is a moot point. The American Philosophical Society did not publish its article on the *Turtle* until 1799. None of the voluminous Fulton documents of this period relating to the *Nautilus* refer to either Bushnell or the *Turtle* by name. Fulton claimed the invention as his own and, according to his definition of invention, it was. He had sat down among the rudders, pumps, water tanks, conning towers, and gunpowder and had arranged them in a new way that had new meaning—a way that worked. Fulton undoubtedly built on ideas gleaned from previous inventors, including Bushnell. His design, however, was far more viable than those of his predecessors.

A Curious Machine for Mending Politics

Fulton first planned a submarine large enough for a crew of three. An imperfect ellipsoid 21 feet 3 inches long and 6 feet 5 inches in its extreme beam, its conning tower doubled as an entry hatch. Beneath the ellipsoid was an iron tank into which ballast had been added to reduce the quantity of water needed for submersion. To descend, the crew would pump water in by means of a hand crank. To ascend, they would evacuate the water.

When below the surface the *Nautilus* would be moved forward by means of a hand-cranked propeller with four slightly inclined blades. It would be capable of 240 revolutions a minute at full speed and 120 a minute during sustained movement. On the surface, it was propelled either by cranks or by sail like a normal boat. Its mast could be raised or lowered in a matter of minutes.

Passing through the center of the conning tower was what Fulton called the horn of the *Nautilus*—an augur to which a copper barrel containing a quintal of powder was attached by a long line. The strategy was identical to Bushnell's. The crew would maneuver the submarine beneath an enemy ship, implant the augur, and while retreating, draw the bomb into contact with the enemy ship. The superiority of the *Nautilus* was that it was large enough for the crew to share the work, it could stay submerged for three hours even when lighted by oxygen-consuming candles, and it would steer well both on the surface and beneath the water.

Pleville-le-Pelley studied Fulton's proposal with great care and essentially approved it. However, after conferring with his colleagues, he recommended that the bounties be cut in half and that no reimbursement be made if peace was declared. Still, Fulton would be paid for prizes—subject to a very small levy for the benefit of the marine hospital—and he could construct as many submarines as he wished as long as he built them away from the large ports. Only the retaliation clause, which Pleville-le-Pelley believed useless in any event, was unacceptable.

On January 13, Pleville-le-Pelley advised Fulton of the changes the ministry would require and urged him to reply as soon as possible. After a week's reflection, Fulton accepted the reduced bounties on behalf of the Nautilus Company and set a maximum of 25,000 francs reimbursement should peace be declared in three months. In a compromise on the retaliation provision he suggested that, if he and his crew were given commissions in the French navy, he would be satisfied if the government promised merely to threaten the British with reprisal.

Robert Fulton

Despite the fact that, to legitimize depredations against American merchant ships, the Directory decreed on January 18 that France would seize any ship with English goods on board, including sextants, rum jugs, and uniform buttons, Fulton did nothing to strengthen the clause prohibiting the offensive use of the submarine against American vessels.

Pleville-le-Pelley kept meticulous track of these negotiations, recording what had been proposed and accepted or rejected in a large multicolumned ledger and, on February 4, he reported to the Directory that while the potential cost of the project was considerable, it should be supported. However, the commissions and the threat of reprisal were out of the question. A report, probably drafted by a subordinate, reasoned that the British would undoubtedly copy the *Nautilus*, since they were ingenious at making machines, and that persons using such an atrocious weapon deserved whatever punishment might be inflicted. Avoiding both the moral and political implications of the submarine, Pleville-le-Pelley modified this passage to read that neither commissions nor retaliatory measures were possible because the ministry feared reprisals on the many French prisoners in England.

It is almost certain that Fulton did not meet Pleville-le-Pelley during this period, although he induced one Monsieur Cottran, an enthusiastic supporter and perhaps a member of the always anonymous Nautilus Company, to attempt to arrange an appointment. Nevertheless, Fulton undoubtedly got word of Pleville-le-Pelley's favorable report and savored the first flush of success. His elation was short-lived. On February 5 he learned that the directors had refused to accept the Marine Ministry's recommendation.

Fulton could do nothing at this juncture but stifle his frustration, bide his time, and hope for some change of policy in the volatile government. Fortunately, he had his canal venture to fall back on. On February 4, the day before he received the Directory's rejection, he was granted a fifteen-year patent for his system of small canals. The application he finally submitted is a charming document, handwritten and sewn into a little booklet. It is profusely illustrated with black-ink sketches—idyllic renderings of passenger boats gliding through the hilly countryside and such details of the machinery as modes of attaching a cable to a boat, a wheel and stem for winding rope, and a large-wheeled chariot for carrying boats overland. With it he deposited mechanical and construction models at the Conservatory of Arts and Trades, then France's patent office.

Exhilarated at having passed this milestone, Fulton wrote Stanhope: "I have created a revolution in the minds of French engineers I have met with."[15] To a surprising degree that was true for shortly afterwards François de Récicourt, chief of works of the Sambre and Oise and a reputed author of works on canals and commerce, asked permission to translate the *Treatise* into French. Fulton, having a clear appreciation of the value of broad distribution—French was commonly understood by educated people throughout the Continent—was pleased and flattered. Indeed, immediately after publication the French edition was translated into Portuguese under the auspices of the Prince Regent who grasped its applicability to Brazil. In 1805, at the command of the czar, it was translated into Russian.

Even more gratifying, Bonaparte liked what he heard about the small canal system and asked for more information. Exploiting this opportunity to its fullest extent, Fulton sent him a copy of the English edition of the *Treatise* and two memoirs in French. The first, "Observations on the Advantages which France Will Enjoy in Adopting the System of Small Canals," demonstrated how a very large portion of the public revenue could be raised from canal tolls. The second, "On Freedom of Trade and Why Foreign Possessions and Duties on Imports, Far from Being Beneficial to Nations Are Prejudicial to Them," preached the necessity of an entire liberty of commerce. With the book and tracts, Fulton sent a flowery plea for patronage, hoping Bonaparte would use his influence to support small canals, "the execution of which would render happy millions of men. . . . Can there be for virtuous genius a more delicious reward?"[16] Bonaparte's unannounced departure for Egypt gave Fulton his only answer.

For a fleeting moment Fulton entertained the idea of leaving his canal patent in the hands of a company and returning to the United States as he had contracted with Church to do. In a sentimental letter to Cartwright offering to act as his agent there he wrote: "Hitherto I have been like a wanderer in life, but in America I hope to become reasonably stationary, where, assembling a few friends around me, I may pursue my plans of public improvement with patient industry. Works of magnitude, I find, cannot be hurried."[17]

Fulton's nostalgia for a life of orderly tranquillity was little more than a brief fantasy. He had not given up his hope of building a *Nautilus* with French support, for Pleville-le-Pelley had been replaced as marine minister by the younger and more elastic Eustace Bruix. An amateur alchemist and opera librettist, Bruix was an excellent strategist with a penchant for surprises. Prior to being appointed to the ministry, he had been a major general in command of the force designated to invade Ireland. He could be expected to take a keen interest in the submarine.

The political climate was also much improved. A coup on May 11 placed men in power who, Fulton thought, would favor his project. The French public was clamoring for the subjugation of "haughty Brittania." Propagandists spewed forth a spate of books with such titles as *Liberty of the Seas or the English Government Exposed* and *The Burning of Plymouth and Portsmouth.* Over fifty thousand invasion troops were concentrated at Rouen and Le Havre awaiting orders to embark.

Using a two-edged tactic of blandishment and insistence, Fulton resubmitted his proposals to Bruix on July 23. "A project of this nature will appear extraordinary no doubt, at first glance, to a Marine Ministry," he began, "but your love of liberty and humanity will make you weigh my presentation attentively."[18] He informed Bruix he had built a "beautiful model of the *Nautilus* five feet long complete in all its parts"— submerging tank, conning tower, windows, anchor, rudder, propeller, cranking device, folding sail, and air valves. Certain that a full-scale demonstration would conclusively banish all doubts of the submarine's practicability, he requested that members of the National Institute examine his plans and model.

Delighted by the prospect of so novel a performance, Bruix agreed. To view it with him, Bruix appointed a commission both knowledgeable about and sympathetic to Fulton's invention. The group's president was F. E. Rosily-Mesros, a noted cartographer who had entered the navy at the age of fourteen. As director of the Depot de la Marine he was currently working on a long-range development plan for the navy. Pierre Forfait, an inspector general of the invasion flotilla, was the author of a monograph on navigable canals and a treatise on a plunging machine for underwater exploration. He was a first-rate naval architect who had designed an elegant prototype vessel for packetboat service. Gaspard Prony, Director of the School of Bridges and Roads, who had just published his *Nouvelle Architecture Hydrologique,* was known for his contribution to

A Curious Machine for Mending Politics

engineering theory. Auguste Charles Périer was an expert founder and machinist. Pierre Auguste Adet, a distinguished chemist, had been minister to the United States. Deputy F. Gautier du Var was a political writer, and M. Cachin a canal and harbor engineer.

The commission met at Fulton's lodgings, 970 rue de Vaugirard, at eleven o'clock on the morning of August 7, 1798. Fulton first explained his invention and his strategy. Then he ran the spring-propelled model in a very large basin of water. He must have been a convincing showman—competent, confident, and passionately intense—for the commissioners were enchanted. In their long assessment, illustrated with drawings, they praised its elegance, solidity, and splendid performance. Joyfully comparing the *Nautilus* to a fish that promenades under the water with only its head breaking the surface, the commission reported: "It can do anything a fish can do with its tail and fins. It is also like a boat and can do what a boat can do. And then once again it becomes a fish."[19] They dubbed it a *bateau-poisson*—boat-fish—and conservatively estimated it could stay underwater for at least ten hours.

Not every detail pleased the commissioners, however, and they put forward several well-observed criticisms. The sails, they asserted, were so proportioned that "a baby's breath could scuttle the boat." The single propeller did not rotate rapidly enough; a second propeller with horizontal blades was needed to provide up-and-down motion. The air supply must be increased. More important, they had doubts as to the immediate effectiveness of the *Nautilus* as an offensive weapon. They thought "piercing the flank of an enemy vessel would prove difficult"; perfecting the operation was not, they said, "the affair of a day." Furthermore, they believed the British already knew about the submarine and would be resourceful enough to find means of protecting their ships against it, perhaps by festooning them with nets to catch the *Nautilus*'s propellers.

Nevertheless, the commission was so fascinated by the potential of the *bateau-poisson* and by Fulton's evident skill that the report ended with a recommendation that the government recompense him for his work to date and sponsor further experiments. "The arm conceived by Citizen Fulton is a terrible means of destruction, because it acts in silence and in a manner almost inevitable," the savants wrote. "It is particularly suitable to the French because, having a weaker navy . . . than their adversary, the entire destruction of both navies is of advantage to them." In conclusion, they recommended that experiments be conducted below

Robert Fulton

Rouen in a convenient location that would combine tranquil water with some current and that they be kept secret so as to give the Marine Ministry time to prepare the public which they believed would "necessarily lack confidence in so novel a weapon."

Fulton was not immediately apprised of their positive evaluation and on August 23 he complained about the delay to Forfait, who was headquartered at Rouen, the head of deep-water navigation on the Seine. Although he desired to, Forfait was unable to help him, for the report had not yet been circulated. Somehow Fulton laid his hands on a copy. Its contents led him to expect prompt action. When as weeks went by and none was taken, he felt he had been callously deceived.

By October 10 he was so distraught he wrote an angry note to Bruix, reminding him that the commission had reported the *Nautilus* "executable" a month previously. Since he offered the plan "with no other interest than to serve the cause of France," he deserved a prompt answer.[20] The following week he resubmitted his original contract with two modifications. As soon as the first submarine had destroyed or captured one enemy vessel he wanted 500,000 in French money to build a fleet of ten *Nautiluses*. For every pound of shot the ships he put out of service were capable of discharging, he expected 100 francs in specie. These disgruntled communications produced no results.

Frantic with impatience and disturbed by rumors that many highly placed officials objected to his invention as immoral, Fulton held back for ten days, then sent a letter to each member of the Directory summarizing the benefits of submarine warfare. Written in forceful French, it concludes: "If at first glance the means I propose seem revolting, it is only because they are unusual. Certainly it is the mildest and the least bloody that a philosopher could imagine to overturn the system of brigandage and perpetual war that has always vexed maritime nations."[21] As soon as the *Nautilus* was introduced, he anticipated that the English and Irish republicans would rise up against the monarchists and that freedom of the seas and perpetual peace would be ensured.

The directors, all good bureaucrats when it suited their purposes, disposed of this intrusion by forwarding the letters to the Marine Ministry, and that was an end of it—at least for a time. Fulton had stirred wide and influential interest in his submarine, but the hour clearly had not yet arrived for the French to adopt his "curious machine for mending politics."

Works of Genius
and Utility

❖

Fulton was fortunate he did not have to suffer the pendulum swings of the French government alone. Ruth and Joel Barlow were constantly by his side with advice, support, and love. In many ways they served as a replacement for the Wests. His relationship with them, however, had become far more intimate, for shortly after Barlow's return from Algiers in late September 1797 they left Madame Hillaire's pension together and shared first one, then another set of rented rooms on the Left Bank.

Twelve years Fulton's senior, Joel Barlow was an ebullient eclectic. Successively a preacher, lawyer, poet, and pamphleteer in America, he had come to France in 1788 as an agent for the Scioto Associates. His objective was to sell Ohio land options to French emigrants. When that venture turned out to be a fraud and a failure, from which he was some-how able to extricate himself honorably, he became a speculator in com-modities, ships, and currencies—interests he had not abandoned during his two year's mission to Algeria. By the time Fulton met him, Barlow had achieved a reputation as a successful diplomat, a comfortable inde-pendence, and, he wrote from quarantine in the lazaretto at Marseilles, "a pure and undivided taste for tranquility, study and doing good." He also boasted of a set of "large mustaches—long, beautiful and black (a little grey however). As I am a lamb at heart, it was necessary for me to conceal this character beneath the exterior of some other animal," he observed, "and my mustaches give me very nearly the air of a tiger."[1]

Like Fulton, Barlow was a free trader and violently opposed to standing armies. An ardent republican, his vigorous essay against monarchism, "Advice to the Privileged Orders," and its rhymed sequel, "The Conspiracy of Kings," had earned him international respect in liberal circles for their strong sentiments if not for their lofty cadences. Although many of his friends had met the guillotine, and Thomas Paine, as he was carried off to the Luxembourg prison, had thrust the manuscript of the *Age of Reason* into his hands, Barlow passed through the Terror unscathed. Indeed, for his advice to the National Convention in 1792, he had been made an honorary citizen of France.

Nonetheless, Barlow remained a passionate American. His life work was an epic celebrating its "discovery, settlement, and majestic future." First published in 1787 as *The Vision of Columbus*, it was hailed as a fine indigenous work. By European standards, however, it was distinctly sophomoric. His later vastly expanded version, with which Fulton was to be closely associated, would be called *The Columbiad*. Barlow was equally proud of his poem, "The Hasty Pudding," which in three cantos extolled American cooking.

Fancying himself a renaissance man, Barlow also liked to dabble in mechanics. When he passed through England on his way to France in 1788, he had taken the trouble to examine James Rumsey's steamboat. "I am fully confident," he noted in his diary, "it may and will be applied to oceanic as well as river navigation; that from this single improvement the commerce of the world will be carried on with one half of the expense & double the expedition that it now is."[2] Daniel Parker, a fellow promoter of the Scioto scheme, had introduced Barlow to the inventor and shortly after Rumsey's sudden death, Barlow obtained a French patent of importation for a multitubular boiler. Based on a crude variation of Rumsey's English patent, for which Parker must have had the specifications, he claimed it could be applied to a steamboat engine.

The fact that any subject aroused Barlow's curiosity made him good company. One of the most prominent men in the Paris expatriot community, his circle of friends included literati, scientists, financiers, and government officials. He was on easy speaking terms with Lafayette, von Humboldt, Kosciusko, Volney, the Montgolfiers, and Paine. He corresponded actively with Jefferson and Monroe. He was a frequent visitor at the home of his neighbor the Marquise Reine-Phieberte de Villette, Voltaire's "bonne et belle" and an intermediary for Talleyrand in the XYZ Affair. Helen Maria Williams and her paramour John Hurford Stone who founded The English Press in Paris operated out of 970 rue de Vaugirard during the period Fulton and the Barlows were domiciled there. Through his various business ventures Barlow was connected with the many Americans who, like him, were "anxiously watching the times in order to cut in and carry off a slice."[3]

Fulton quickly recognized Barlow as a man of the world who could help him. Barlow did not disappoint him. He not only looked after Fulton's living arrangements and introduced him to his friends but also lent him money and helped him speculate with it. Yet it was Barlow's great capacity for affection that drew Fulton to him. Having no children, Joel relished playing indulgent paterfamilias. He consulted, consoled, and instructed. He discussed mathematics with Fulton and procured a French tutor for him. Barlow's fondness even extended to encouraging the tender sympathy of his "precious wife." Indeed, for Fulton, Ruth's attention may well have been a stronger magnet than Barlow's.

Fulton and Ruth had the opportunity to become well acquainted in the weeks before Barlow returned from Algiers, when they were both living at Madame Hillaire's pension. An imaginative, intelligent, and playful conversationalist, Ruth Barlow was the mature *amie* so prized in French society. She liked to admire as well as to elicit admiration. Her Grecian profile, wide, sensitive mouth, and pretty fringe of ringlets contrasted charmingly with her prim New England manner and dress. Constantly beset by mild illnesses, she looked frail though she was not. She easily fitted the multiple roles of surrogate mother, sister, mistress, and perhaps even daughter.

It pleased Fulton to be pampered by both husband and wife. Well into his thirties, he as yet had formed no serious female attachment and had shown no inclination to take on the encumbrances of a household of his own. The Barlows' companionship was emotionally satisfying and, with little entertainments such as round-robin dinners, provided Fulton with domestic sociability without seriously impinging on his freedom.

Although Fulton lived frugally with the Barlows, within a year he was seriously in debt. Church had been "unfriendly" enough to pay in cash only 300 pounds of the agreed-upon 500-pound installment on the American rights to the canal invention. For the remainder he had given Fulton a note which the person it was drawn on refused. For the second payment, Fulton drew a bill on Church which he was able to get an old Philadelphia friend who was then in Paris to endorse, but he was afraid Church would not honor it. (This circuitous and disaster-fraught method of handling money transactions was typical of the times, especially in Paris where the Americans had no bank.) Fulton had sent Church the French patent and a power of attorney, but Church must have found out they were worthless in America because the United States did not issue patents for inventions already patented abroad.

No longer able to count on income from that quarter, Fulton cast about for alternative ways to "convert the overflowings of his mind to cash." While he was stymied in his submarine negotiations, he had been nurturing two ideas "to fill up hours he did not otherwise know how to spend," and they were, he thought, sufficiently developed to attract investors.[4] Fulton's first idea was a cordelier capable of twisting four strands of yarn into a rope 2 inches in diameter and 120 fathoms long. With it he claimed one man could produce 3 miles of cordage a day in a building no larger than 30 by 40 feet. Rope, at that time, was made entirely by hand. The laborers walked backwards, stretching as they twisted to maintain proper tension. The job was so strenuous that, at a time when 12-hour days were common, the men worked in 4-hour-shifts. The factories, called ropewalks, were often over 600 feet long. Because ships required a constant supply, rope-making was a major industry. A machine that could save time, labor, and space had an extraordinarily profitable future.

Fulton found a ready buyer for the continental rights to this device in Nathaniel Cutting, a former Boston tea merchant, who had toured London with Parker and Barlow in 1788. Although he was the U.S. consul at Le Havre, he had arranged his affairs so as to spend most of his time in Paris. Gullible and improvident, he was still casting about for a sure moneymaker with which to repair his dwindling fortunes. Fulton promised he would provide working drawings and a model and do the legwork necessary for the patent if Cutting would advance the development money: 2,400 francs on signing the contract, 2,400 francs one month later, 2,400 francs three months after the second payment, and 2,400 francs when the patent was actually conveyed. Cutting would also pay the patent fees, which Fulton estimated at not more than 1,440 francs. In return he would receive all the profits on the rights covering France and its territories and half the profits for other continental rights. If for any reason Fulton failed to get the patent, he would reimburse Cutting in full. For an additional 7,500 francs, Fulton offered to super-intend, direct, and construct the machines. Should they not work, he promised to return the cost of materials, construction, and patent, whereupon Cutting would restore the patent rights to Fulton.

This contract, involving little financial risk and no expenditure of energy on his part, appealed to Cutting. On September 1, 1798, he put down a binder, and on October 13 he signed a formal agreement that included his full services and began his payments as scheduled.

From the outset the project was beset with problems. When Fulton applied for a patent in the middle of January, he was informed he had numerous competitors, several of whom had already acquired patents. Certain that his invention was infinitely more workable than his rivals', Fulton retorted that precedence should be given to the "active genius" who could implement as well as imagine a useful machine. He was then advised he must pay fees for three patents because he had added a yarn-spinning machine with two variants to his application. Raising a defense based on system, he maintained that each of his devices was a necessary component of a single rope-making process and, like the multiple elements of his canal patent, formed a single entity bound by one principle. The administrators disagreed. A patent for the yarn spinner was denied on the grounds it was not a new invention. However, a patent was issued for the cordelier in both Fulton's and Cutting's names. Fulton then engaged Jacques Constintin Périer, Auguste-Charles Périer's brother and partner to construct the first machine.

Fulton had better luck with a Panorama for which he was granted a patent on April 26, 1799. It consisted of "a circular picture without boundaries and the method of painting all the countryside, all the towns and villages . . . and other objects which can be seen from the summit of a mountain or a tower or other eminence."[5] This idea was essentially that patented in England by Richard Barker. Fulton must have seen the popular "View of the British fleet between Portsmouth and the Isle of Wight," displayed in Leicester Square in 1792. He was later accused of claiming the Panorama as his original invention, but his application straightforwardly states: "It is already established in London and is admired as a work of genius and utility." What he sought and was granted was a patent of *importation et perfectionnement*.

Fulton's primary interest in the Panorama arose from the certainty that it would generate quick returns in novelty-loving Paris. But, typically, his application vaunted its great national importance. It would, he wrote, "offer students a stimulant which would excite their emulation and serve to perfect their taste in landscape painting" and thereby "throw light on the Beaux arts." Moreover, it would help all citizens, particularly scientists who often could not afford to travel, acquire familiarity with interesting towns and views, both at home and abroad.

Fulton's instructions for exhibiting the painting differed little from Barker's. The canvas was hung on the interior walls of a circular building. In the center was a viewing platform. Reached by a spiral stair from below so that no door would interrupt the scene, it placed the spectator at the level of the picture's horizon. But while Barker merely stated the drawing should be correct, "making a complete circle and ending where it began," Fulton perfected that idea by detailing a method for doing it. He directed the artist to view the scene through a small hole in a disk that was aligned with a frame divided into squares by threads. The artist then painted what he saw on squared paper. Having obtained the correct perspective by taking nine such views, following a circular pattern placed on the ground, the artist would transfer them to canvas in oil or watercolor, enlarged twelve times.

For his first spectacular, Fulton decided on a bird's-eye view of Paris and its environs and, with characteristic aplomb, wrote the keepers of the Tuileries Palace for permission to take the view from the terrace that circled the dome of the central pavilion. This he was quickly granted on the strength of his reputation as a scientist in the field of canal engineering. Fulton undoubtedly enjoyed the painting aspects of the projects and contributed to the overall design, but he did not paint it himself. Since he wanted the profits as soon as possible, he hired four artists to do the painting while he supervised the construction of the building.

The Panorama, located in the pleasure garden of Apollo next to the Théâtre Faydeau just off the Boulevard Montmartre, was open from eight in the morning until eight in the evening. Admission was one and a half francs. It fast became a popular attraction. A tourist guide of the time was ecstatic: "Patrons enter through a dark tunnel and when they reach the painting, lighted by a central clerestory window, become so absorbed in the nuances of the view that they forget it is a mere illusion. . . . A stranger greets it with a sigh and takes leave of it regretfully."[6] The single complaint was that on a cloudy or foggy day the light was not sufficiently strong to produce the full mesmerizing effect.

Fulton sold this patent eight months after he obtained it to a compatriot, James W. Thayer, and his French wife, retaining a percentage of the receipts. Happily for his pocketbook, the Panorama proved so profitable that they soon erected a second building which was joined to the first by an arcade that exists today as the charming Passage des Panoramas. The new scene, "The Evacuation of Toulouse by the British in 1793," made such an impression that the National Institute felt compelled to send a committee to report on it. It even inspired a street ballad.

Nathaniel Cutting was not amused by this diversion, for work on his rope-making factory had not progressed as either he or Fulton anticipated. In July he accused Fulton of diverting to the Panorama the money he had advanced for the cordelier. Fulton frankly admitted he had paid only 1,000 francs of Cutting's money to Périer and, confessing he used the balance to settle a long overdue debt that caused him "much shame," he insisted that according to the "superintend" clause of the contract he had a personal right to it. Cutting, also pressed for cash, was justifiably offended and made clear to Fulton how he felt. In an extraordinary exhibition of one-upmanship, which he should have realized might make him an enemy, Fulton replied by scolding Cutting for not paying enough attention to the business:

> If I am to be narrowly dealt with, why should I expend my time and considerable sums to perfect a spinning engine for which I am to have no Compensation . . . *this friend Cutting is not right*. It is not reasonable that I should wreck my imagination, run after workmen and take on myself the expense of improvements without being supported in the undertaking and ultimately receiving some reasonable compensation. . . . You may take the engines as they now are, try them and if you do not like them I will take them and return your money in 6 months as Per Contract—*this I can do*—or I will find funds to finish the engines and put them in motion. I will try the experiments for which you will find the hemp. . . . when they are ready to be judged, you Shall then have 10 days to determine whether I will keep them or not. If you do I think 300 sterling to me over and above the whole expense of the engines cannot be deemed unreasonable. The money to be paid in 30 days from the day I pronounce the engines fit for Judgment. But if you do not keep the engines I will take them and return your money in 6 months as per contract.[7]

Cutting had no competence whatever in dealing with machines, but he did not succumb to Fulton's crude tactics, for soon afterward Fulton wrote him in a less taunting tone that since they differed materially, Barlow and Richard Codman—the American money-man to whom Fulton had paid the long overdue debt—could arbitrate. The business was patched up well enough that Fulton and Cutting continued a fitful partnership, although without much improvement of their business or personal relationship.

Fulton then enlisted Périer's help in finding investors. He made a sketch of a 30- by 40-foot factory building with an oilcloth or canvas roof so it could be easily transported. Fulton wrote Samuel Miles Hopkins, who had already returned to America, that he was about to place the machine in a factory, and perhaps he carried out this intention. However, it seems improbable that the device was even moderately successful, since ropewalks were used into the twentieth century because the tension problem was not fully solved. Cutting never ceased to be angry about the manner in which Fulton had conducted the affair. He felt he had been tricked, and, in the acrimonious steamboat lawsuit that went to trial many years later, he would seek revenge by testifying that Fulton had stolen the cordelier invention from Cartwright. This was not exactly true, for, as he experimented with the machine, Fulton kept Cartwright informed of his progress and even sent him samples of rope to evaluate.

Preoccupation with the cordelier and the Panorama did not prevent Fulton from pursuing his work on canals. For Récicourt's translation of the *Treatise*, to be published in the spring of 1799, he made six pages of mechanical drawings with a total of seventy-six figures. All depicted the machinery; there was not one pleasant landscape. A description and map of a canal designed to serve the naval base projected for the Bay of Ambleteuse on the Channel near Boulogne was added by Récicourt together with a reworked version of the benefits-to-France memoir Fulton had sent to Bonaparte advancing a plan for raising the entire national revenue by means of a tax on canals. After the publication of the French version of the *Treatise*, Fulton was certain that no French engineer would think of constructing a large canal with locks. He was confident his system would be adopted as soon as peace was declared.

Peace, however, was not in sight, and despite his profits from the Panoramas, his optimism about small canals, and his burning desire to implement his system of submarine warfare, Fulton was discouraged about his prospects abroad. Resorting to his vision of America as the promised land, he confided to Hopkins that he was "sick of the blind wicked politics of Europe" and expected in a few months to return to "Young Vigorous and Virtuous America . . . to Multiply Manual Labour and to promote freedom of trade through the destruction of military navies which they shall be if I am so fortunate as to live a few years and meet the support of my countrymen."[8]

To his mother, whom he had not seen in thirteen years, Fulton was more ambivalent about his imminent return. She must have expressed worry that he might marry a Frenchwoman and remain abroad forever or that he was showing no inclination whatever to marry, for in the carefully contrived letter composed to amuse her, he devoted a good deal of space to his lack of romantic attachment, without yielding any solid information about it at all:

> My dear Mother,
>   Still Europe holds me, not by ties of affection but by the bonds of business with which I am ever so much engaged that I have not had time even to fall in love. And now having arrived at the age of thirty-two years the ladies of my acquaintance, who, good creatures, are much concerned for my future happiness and honour, begin to fear that I shall die an Old bachelor; hence with eyes full of regard and the sweetest arguments they persuade me to avoid so miserable an end: In my own mind I have determined to avoid it but it is my intention to reserve all my affections for some amiable American whose customs and manners I prefer to anything I have yet seen in Europe. You will now ask when shall this be—when shall I return. This I will no longer promise because having promised frequently without being able to perform there is not much reliance in them: But still I hope the time is not distant when I will step into your neat little room, in one corner of which perhaps you have my picture, the only donation which I then had in my power to present, because being my own work it was attended with very little expense. I am in excellent health, six feet high and thin; this being thin I think rather an advantage because it suffers a man to be active. I would not be loaded with the quantity of fat which some gentlemen are obliged to carry into company, not for their whole estate.[9]

With this letter, Fulton sent thirty-six French guineas "to take some weight of cares off her weight of years" and pledged to continue to help her "in proportion to his circumstances." It was a promise he could not fulfill, for the "unforseen Stroke" he had long dreaded fell. Mary Smith Fulton died that year and probably never received his letter.

Even as Fulton wrote these consciously wistful letters, he initiated a new campaign to prolong his residence abroad. On July 17, 1799, he sent a stern memorandum to the military committee of the Executive Directory reviewing the positive reception the *Nautilus* had received from the savants. Once again he offered his submarine "with all the zeal of a disinterested patriot, who asks neither for place nor money . . . or for any other compensation after more than 18 months of work, expense and entreaty than the happiness of having contributed to the re-establishment of peace, the freedom of the seas and of commerce, and to the consolidation of the Republic." [10]

Overlooking his pomposity, the committee was enthusiastic. "The inventor is no charlatan," they reported. "He proposes to captain his engine himself and thus gives his head as a hostage for his success." Nor was the committee restrained by moral considerations as Fulton had expected. "Philosophy would not reprove a means of destroying the destroyers of the liberty of the seas," [11] the committee commented, advocating that Fulton be granted permission to build and operate a *Nautilus*. Nonetheless, as in the past, nothing came of the recommendation.

Exasperated, Fulton wrote a strong letter to the marine minister reminding him that precious time had been lost since the Directory had delivered its encouraging report. To this letter he attached a long essay entitled "Observations on the Moral Effects of the *Nautilus* Should It Be Employed with Success." The document, which justifies the submarine's use, exudes suppressed rage and frustration at the government for not having accepted his magnanimous and humanitarian scheme immediately. Joining an awkward series of threats and enticements to his old ultimate-weapon theme, he warned the minister that Americans would perfect the submarine and that other small countries such as Sweden and Denmark would follow suit, for it would put them on an equal footing with the most powerful nations without the expense of building a navy. To prevent this Fulton urged France to seize the moment.

The objection that the English would develop their own *Nautilus* for use against the French he blithely dismissed as unimportant since France's commerce was tied to the continent and therefore not dependent on the sea. At any rate, he asserted, the nature of submarine warfare was such that "two armies of *Nautilii* could not fight against each other." Nor could pirates take advantage of the submarine. If they did, he contended, all nations would rise up against them, depriving them of markets for the goods and vessels they captured. Just as the invention of pistols had not multiplied thefts, he argued, so the invention of the *Nautilus* would not propagate piracy. On the contrary, the submarine would "prevent people from pillaging their neighbors." In this elaborate piece of propagandizing, Fulton went so far as to prophesy that, when at last the *Nautilus* was put into action, peace and republicanism would spread unchecked until even Ireland and England became "a millennium," eager to "suppress old hatreds and treat each other like Sisters."[12]

The charge that submarine warfare would present a moral dilemma angered Fulton. Clinging to his blind conviction that his submarine would render naval warfare obsolete, he refused to face the probability that, duplicated by others, his weapons would become a staple in the arms inventory of many nations. To Joshua Gilpin, an American friend who reported from London that many of his acquaintances were shocked by his attempt to sell the submarine to France, Fulton testily replied, "If I know myself, I believe I am much governed by my own Contemplations, which Contemplations I believe always tend to promote the Interests of Mankind."[13] To Hopkins he blithely described himself simply as a "mechanicien busy in raising myself and hoping to be of some use to my country."[14]

Although "Observations on the Moral Effects of the *Nautilus*" was intended to defend the submarine as a humane weapon and enhance his reputation as a humane inventor, Fulton could not restrain himself from concluding with a corrosive threat: "I sincerely hope for the honor of France that I will not encounter petty objections or intrigues that will make it necessary for me to publish the principles of the Nautilus and its happy consequences or to seek in Holland or America the encouragement that I would hope to find in France and which Liberty and Philosophy demand."

Naive and contemptible as this tactic was, it worked. Shaken from his lethargy by the scatterings of truth in the "Observations," the marine minister replied that he would like to examine the model of the *Nautilus* at Fulton's lodgings on the morning of October 10. Fulton must have been highly satisfied with the visit, for as soon as the minister left, he composed another set of proposals similar to his earlier ones but with a markedly more conversational cast. In his flush of good humor, he even lauded France as "blessed with a wise and good directory which will listen with attention to any plan which has for its object the cultivation of humanity."[15]

The minister reported to the Executive Directory that Fulton's scheme was indeed cheaper than building a fleet, and he dourly remarked on the French navy's recent lack of success against the British. However, he opposed the clauses demanding commissions and a threat of retaliation. These were, he said, necessary policies to which he believed Fulton had at last realized he must submit.

Political events were also working in Fulton's favor. On October 16, 1799, Bonaparte returned in triumph from Italy, and on November 9–10 the Directory was overthrown in the coup known as the 18 Brumaire. As the first of three consuls—in fact the dictator of France—Bonaparte appointed Pierre Forfait, who had served on the 1798 *Nautilus* commission, as his marine minister. Certain that France would at last adopt submarine warfare, Fulton contracted with Périer to build the first *Nautilus* at his own expense. There is no record of where he got the 28,000 francs it would cost. A fair assumption is that Barlow arranged financing and that Périer extended credit, perhaps with a promise of a percentage of the bounties.

Throughout the winter, Fulton stood by Périer's side, improving the design of the submarine as the work proceeded. In April, he was able to write Forfait that the *Nautilus* was almost finished. Deluded that he had "every reason to hope from Bonaparte the welcome, the encouragement that have been so long refused by the Directors and Ministers,"[16] he begged Forfait to place his proposal before the first consul. Bonaparte was occupied with pacifying Brittany and the Vendée, censoring the entertainments presented in the theaters, and organizing the Army of the Rhine. He left for Austria during the first week of May, having failed to respond to the proposal.

Forfait, while acknowledging that the *Nautilus* infringed on the laws of war, did not withdraw his support. Euphoric, Fulton decided it was time to present his invention to the scientific and naval establishment and the general public by mounting a full demonstration of the *Nautilus* on the Seine River in Paris. He sent invitations to savants and government officials and counted on ordinary adventure-seeking citizens to hear of the event by word of mouth. The show would take place on June 13 in the stretch of river below Périer's workshops near the Chaillot water pumps.

The location was an excellent one for a spectacle. The Cours de la Reine just upriver provided box seats; from its tree-shaded, ballustraded walk spectators could enjoy a sweeping view of the river. Opposite was the Hôtel des Invalides, its gilded, ribbed dome offering aesthetic diversion for intervals when there was no action. Below were the quays, which were dirty but closer to the boat. Working people, perhaps the men who had built the machine, undoubtedly felt privileged to be there. Additional spectators could find places on the low piece of land at the foot of the Champs-de-Mars. It had recently become the site of the *triperie*, where the innards of animals were prepared for the market, but that would not have discouraged eager sensation seekers. Even from the Pont de la Révolution—soon to be renamed the Pont de la Concorde—it was possible to follow the action.

Fulton had trained as his chief assistant Nathaniel Sargent, a compatriot of "good character" who, according to his friends, had been driven to this work only out of dire necessity; ships in which he had an interest had been captured by both the British and the French. Tension mounted as the two men lighted a candle, and with a last proud glance over the hushed crowd, disappeared down the conning tower of the *Nautilus*. Surely, but without oars, sail, or tow, the "curious machine" moved to the middle of the fast-moving river. Then it plunged. Eighteen, nineteen, twenty minutes were slowly counted. Then, suddenly the submarine rose a considerable distance from where it had been enveloped by water. It dived again and returned underwater to its starting point. The crowd was ecstatic. It demanded to see how the miraculous *bateau-poisson* would maneuver under sail. Fulton hesitated. The water depths and wind were unfavorable. Then, undoubtedly curious himself, the ordered Sargent to raise the mast and tack across the river. This, too, was accomplished with dispatch.

Without question, the demonstration was an extraordinary scientific and mechanical tour de force. The *Nautilus* performed on its first trial as Fulton had expected. Almost as triumphant as its inventor, Forfait reported to Bonaparte that "everything that could be desired was completely achieved. The boat submerged and rose again with great facility. The men who operated it remained inside the boat for forty-five minutes without renewing the air and when they disembarked no alterations could be seen in their faces."[17] He added that the *Nautilus* sailed well and that when the sails were made larger it would run at two leagues an hour in good weather even before the wind. "There, my general, is the status of the affair. It begins to generate some hope and in a month the *Nautilus* could be in the sea and ready to act."

In Forfait's judgment the only obstacle to putting the *Nautilus* in action within a month was finding a way to meet Fulton's personal demands. To get some return on the money spent building her, Fulton asked 6,000 francs for the loan of the boat and he continued to insist that he and his men be awarded naval commissions. Forfait tactfully suggested to Bonaparte that although paying rent was against regulations, perhaps a means could be devised "to assist" the operator "if the First Consul deemed it appropriate." The retaliation clause was, as always, impossible, but he believed that Bonaparte would know how to stimulate Fulton's zeal. Meanwhile, he would send the *Nautilus* to Rouen for further tests. These he thought so important that he urged Bonaparte and his fellow consuls to visit Rouen incognito to witness the submarine tests with their own eyes.

It is a measure of Forfait's enthusiasm that he enclosed with his own letter Fulton's special plea for reprisal. Flattering the first consul that his overt protection could determine the outcome of the operations by inspiring great confidence in his companions, Fulton supplied an official but passionately personal declaration of Napoleon's intention of protecting his enterprise. It was addressed to the king of England and the officers of the British navy and, in his manic state, Fulton expected Bonaparte to sign it.

Satisfied he could do no more, Fulton put his affairs in order. Among his pressing concerns was mollifying Cutting, who was incensed by Fulton's cavalier attitude toward the cordelier. Then, adhering to Forfait's schedule, Fulton left for Rouen in the middle of July.

The waters of the port of Rouen were over 30 feet deep, and twice a day the force of the tide balanced the flow of the river for over an hour. Approximately 71 miles inland by water and 55 miles by land, the port was sequestered from the prying eyes of the British fleet, though not, of course, from the British spies who must have abounded in the area, since Rouen was the headquarters for the Army of England.

As soon as he arrived at the port, Fulton pulled the *Nautilus* out of the water and added a deck to disguise it as an ordinary boat as well as to permit the crew to leave their confined quarters when navigating on the surface. When he launched the submarine again on July 24, he plunged twice and found that the deck was so well executed that it in no way impaired the vessel's ability to submerge and maneuver under the water. He discovered, however, that the current was difficult and requested permission to proceed to Le Havre where, as soon as he finished his experiments, he could commence an operation against the enemy. Asking Forfait to send 1,000 kilograms of powder for the "torpedoes" and a letter of protection from the first consul, he concluded in a burst of ebullient camaraderie: "Adieu, Patience and perseverance are the friends of science. Count on my zeal to render the *Nautilus* successful."[18]

The *Nautilus* left Rouen on the morning tide of July 31. Towed by two barges, it reached its destination four days later. Though not militarily as important as the ports of Brest or Boulogne, Le Havre had far better access to the English channel. Its extensive quays had been well and handsomely built by Louis XIV. Its basin was almost 600 feet long, and the interaction of the tide and the current of the Seine stabilized the water for three hours twice a day.

Without a break, Fulton resumed his experiments. His own description, preserved in a letter to an anonymous Frenchman—a "dear friend of the arts"—tells how he first used a stern-mounted Archimedes' screw to obtain forward motion, but finding that imperfect, tried a two-bladed propeller similar to the one he had designed in 1797 for the propulsion of a steam vessel. This device, he was pleased to discover, would propel the *Nautilus* on the surface almost twice as fast as two men rowing. He was also certain it was "perfectly calculated" to move the boat underwater.

To control the depth while the submarine moved forward, Fulton placed a horizontal propeller on the bow of the *Nautilus*. This, too, was a success, for he descended to 5 feet and ran forward 450 feet, maintaining a constant depth of 4 to 6 feet. At the same time, he proved that his compass would work underwater as well as on the surface. Then, in order to be able to observe the movements of enemy ships for long periods while hidden just beneath the surface even in the strongest currents and roughest seas, he placed a lead anchor under the hull. Shaped like a sugar loaf and weighing 360 pounds, it was attached to a line 130 feet long and could be raised and lowered from inside the submarine. Next he designed a revolving periscope 1½ inches in diameter and set with a mirror at a 45-degree angle. An air tube with automatic valves prevented water entering from waves or during a sudden descent.

At the same time he was making these substantial modifications, Fulton experimented with a new means of delivering the torpedoes. With a real attack imminent, he wanted a method that was safer, surer, and more versatile than screwing a bomb into the bottom of an enemy vessel. The alternative method he devised was similar to Bushnell's aborted floating bombs and bridled bombs, which Fulton may have read about if he was able to secure a copy of the American Philosophical Society's *Transactions* of 1799. He may even have witnessed a demonstration of those devices when he was living in Philadelphia. The strategy used a cylinder filled with 30 pounds of powder and fitted with a trigger that would cause it to explode on contact. He threw the bomb overboard from an ordinary rowboat, and as it floated on the current toward a barrel, anchored as a target, he maneuverered it by means of a long, thin rope so that it struck the barrel. The explosion forced a stupendous column of water and smoke 100 feet into the air. This method, Fulton confidently reported, could not fail from a distance of 200 feet against so large a target as a ship.

Feverish to set his submarine in operation, Fulton was highly annoyed that the government still showed no sign of meeting his demands for personal protection. Petulantly complaining to his "friend of the arts" that "so promising a child" was "so badly nourished" and that he himself was treated like "a corsair," he insisted that only the lack of commissions for himself and his crew prevented him from assaulting the British fleet. Finally, in desperation, Fulton wrote Barlow, who was in Paris, to intercede with Forfait.

Barlow bustled over to the ministry with a "concise and clear" explanation of the situation. He gave it to the porter, who returned with the information that when Forfait read it he "shrugged his shoulders and said 'je ne puis pas, je ne puis pas (I certainly cannot do it')." Barlow despaired. "I always doubted whether this govt would suffer your expedition to go into effect," he wrote Fulton. "It is possible they have reserved to themselves this method to prevent it, always in hopes before that your preparatory experiments would fail or that your funds & patience would be exhausted & that you would never push them to this point." Barlow must have been astonished when the afternoon of that same day he received word that orders had just been sent by post to the prefect of the marine at Le Havre to deliver to Fulton the commissions he required. "Thus," Barlow commented sourly to Fulton, "if you can rely on a class of men on whom I have learned long ago not to rely at all, the business is done and they have only had the pleasure of disappointing you for about a week."[19] The remarkable absence of delay suggests that the order originated with Bonaparte. Fulton received the commissions he had so long pursued. According to Sargent's friends, Fulton was named an admiral, Nathaniel Sargent a captain, and their companion Fleuret a lieutenent. This satisfied Fulton; he made no further mention of the retaliatory clause.

On September 12, 1800, the *Nautilus* set sail for the Cap de la Hogue—the peninsula on the Normandy coast closest to England and at least 70 miles from Le Havre. "In this little voyage," Fulton reported with pride, "my Nautilus sometimes did a league and a half per hour, and I had the pleasure of seeing it ride the waves like an ordinary boat."[20] Five days later he put in at Growan, a small harbor near Isigny, on the east side of the peninsula. The journey was in itself an extraordinary feat.

In the face of equinoctial gales, which began the next day and lasted for twenty-five days, Fulton tried twice to attack two English brigs anchored three leagues from Growan. During one of the assaults the submarine remained submerged for an entire tide, taking in air only at intervals through its small, nearly invisible tube. Both times, however, the English "set sail and were quickly at a distance," whether by accident or design Fulton was unable to ascertain.

With the winter approaching, Fulton decided on October 20 that, since the *Nautilus* had not been constructed strongly enough to resist heavy seas, he would lay it up for the season and return to Paris where he could place the results of his experiments before the government and seek further backing.

Fulton had not succeeded in destroying even one warship with his submarine. Nor had the *Nautilus*'s presence in the Channel caused panic in the British fleet. Nevertheless, he remained convinced the fortune and fame he craved were nearly within his grasp.

SEVEN

Wifey, Hub, and Toot

❖

Experiments in submarine warfare were not Fulton's only occupations in the summer of 1800. During virtually all his time at Le Havre he stayed at the Hôtel du Bienvenu as the companion of Ruth Barlow. The record of this aspect of his life is tantalizingly one-sided. It consists of a series of extravagant letters Barlow dispatched almost every other day to Ruth, whom he called Wifey, Ipey, Itten Onga, Pretty Charmer, and often simply It. All were intended to be shared by Fulton, whom Barlow called Toot or Toddre. Some letters contained sections specifically directed to Fulton, while in others the message is woven in: "Tell toot his letter is in the body of wifey's and he must try to pick it out."[1]

These letters, of course, reveal more about Barlow—he refers to himself as Hub—than they do about Fulton or Ruth. Yet although none of their replies has survived, both wrote frequently and both undoubtedly contributed to the astonishing character of the correspondence, which was, in essence, a manifestation of the complex relationship the three had developed in the course of the two and a half years they had lived together. If Fulton and Ruth did not favor the baby talk that characterized Barlow's style, their letters certainly must have conveyed a receptive tone by wordplay, anecdote, and innuendo.

Barlow was, in any case, pleased with the responses he received, for he replied, "Wifey's dear little letter of the 3d is a jewel. How happy it makes hub to have these dear little faithful messangers come every

day and tell that the life of my life and soul of my soul is happy. . . .
Well was pretty charming wifey to make toot fill up the letter. I oves to
have em come double so, itten from on an itten from toddre. Hub noes
bote ove hub and hub noves bote."[2]

Ruth's pretext for being at Le Havre was that the sea air and bathing might improve her chronically poor health. Barlow had taken her
there himself and then almost immediately hurried back to Paris. Her
holiday with Fulton had his blessing. In fact, he reveled in it. In his first
letter, he instructed Fulton to "Tate dood tare of nitten wifey—sant
tweeze too ard—jus ov properly."[3] And a few days later, some sort of
anniversary—perhaps a mock marriage—he wrote: "I don't know whether
yonga & toot have feasted this day, 30 Thermidor. If they have not tell
em when you see em they ought to be divorsed & never have another
wedding day in their lives. They know it gives me great pleasure to reflect on the happiness it procured them & I hope they have not forgot
it."[4]

When Fulton was not working on his submarine he took infinite care
to entertain Ruth, whose main diversions, according to Barlow, were
"invading the boisterous domains of amphitrite by diving into her bag-
noire every morning and then driving around the countryside with her
sweetheart."[5] Barlow had left them a pair of sparky white ponies and
an elegant little phaeton, and they must have taken rides through the
flax and clover fields to the lighthouses on the promontory outside town
and perhaps picnicked on the fine pebbled beaches. In quieter moments
they played cards and backgammon and read and answered Barlow's
letters as they gossiped about him over their breakfasts of coffee, boiled
milk, and rolls.

Barlow let them know that he, too, was in "good spirits." He dined
with friends, conducted a little business, collected Fulton's commissions
from the Panorama and went house hunting, pushed to it, he said, because of "the extreme and repeated difficulties we found about lodgings,
especially now we are three and must have so many rooms separate and
yet compact, adjoining each other so as to be convenient." Although he
told Ruth "how hub ants de big beautiful hard warm sweet moutens to
lie in lap. Never ll do away din an eve wipey so long," he seemed pleased
she had "run away from hub" to be with "toot."[6] In an affectedly light-
hearted and profoundly ambiguous passage he mused on this fact: "It
may seem strange, but I certainly never was so happy in any absence as
now, & I certainly never loved you better if so well. 'Tis because I think

wifey is happy. If she was alone or surrounded with only common friends, oh I should die with impatience to return. How account for this? But it is not difficult. I love you so much more than I do myself that I love your happiness before all things, *independent of the idea of its depending on me.*"[7]

The devotion Barlow expressed toward Fulton was equally enigmatic. He admonished Ruth "not to forget to tell the dear toot how hub loves him, I want to make him all that he wants to make himself great & good & happy."[8] Yet his letters displayed virtually no interest in the submarine venture. Rampantly egocentric, he mentioned it only to focus attention upon himself. In an early letter he wrote: "I'm glad to hear of toot's success in experiment. Always repeat to him how much I love him. You cannot tell him too much of it."[9] Later, when Fulton was risking his life pursuing British warships in the Channel, Barlow overtly tried to identify Fulton with himself:

[T]ell toot that every strain, and extraordinary exertion and cold & damp, and twisting & wrenching, and unnatural & strained position that our bodies are exposed to in middle life, tend to stiffen the nerves & joints & mussels, & to bring on old age prematurely, perhaps sickness or decripitude. . . . That the machine of his body is better & more worthy his attention than any other machine that he can make. That preservation is more useful than creation. Unless he could create me one exactly in the image of himself with the materials now in his power, he had better preserve his own automoton.[10]

Yet, he belittled the enterprise.

I have not believed of late that there was much danger in the expedition. . . . I have certainly seen the day when I would have undertaken it without fear, or apprehension of extraordinary risk. I can't say that I am now without uneasiness. I should probably have less if I was in the boat and without bodily pain. But there is really very little to fear. The weather is fine. They are only going along the coast. He is master of all his movements & it appears to me one of the safest of all hostile enterprises that you can imagine.[11]

Barlow disliked the submarine, not for moral reasons but because it placed a barrier between him and Fulton. Although Barlow did bestir himself to visit the Marine Ministry to expedite the commissions for Fulton and his crew, and although he wrote Thomas Jefferson about

Fulton's progress, he seems to have secretly hoped the experiments would be unsuccessful.

That at such a critical turning point Fulton accepted Barlow's confused devotion and also found the psychological energy to play the cavalier to Ruth suggests the depth of his attachment to them. Although the nature of his relationship with Barlow and with Ruth—both separately and as a married couple—remains clouded because so few of his letters to them were saved, it is clear that he was tied to them by bonds of affection that even the most trying circumstances could not break. Needing and loving them, Fulton continued to cherish them throughout his life. Since Fulton must have felt his own personality reflected in and enriched by the Barlows, clues to the nature of his relationship with them must be sought in their relationship with each other.

Joel and Ruth Barlow were married in 1782 shortly after he graduated from Yale College. Although Barlow had boarded with Ruth's family and was a close friend of her brother, he made Ruth keep their union a secret for more than a year. His reason was that her blacksmith father would not think he was rich enough to support her properly. Barlow's letters of that time make it clear, however, that he thoroughly enjoyed the role of clandestine lover. He was excited by the theatricality of pretending.

In the ensuing years, the marriage was marked by long separations. When Barlow went to Europe, Ruth stayed behind. It suited them both. He finally prevailed upon her to join him in England two years later, but he failed to meet her on her arrival as she had every right to expect. Pleading that business detained him in Paris, he left her in the care of friends who, after some delay, accompanied her to France. The next four years they lived a peripatetic life in Paris, London, and Hamburg while Barlow speculated in commodities. Again Ruth was often on her own. Barlow's absence of two years in Algiers was merely one of a series of partings.

During these separations Barlow wrote copiously. Most of his letters exhibit a similar labored sentimentality, but lack the erotic tenor for which the Le Havre letters are remarkable. His pomposity is evident in the letter describing his love that he addressed expressly to Ruth at the Hôtel du Bienvenu.

> Apropos of praise and flattery in the matrimonial state. It is always my opinion (I don't know how often I have told you of it) that it ought to be indulged & cultivated as far as possible. It has

a double good effect where hearts are well disposed. 1st it makes the party praised improve the mind and actions to deserve that praise, & second it helps the praising party to fix in his mind a sort of standard of sentiment to which he resorts under every different feeling. When he forgets the merits of his other *moitie* [half] & feels peevish he recollects himself & says—but I often tell her she possesses such & such good qualities. Surely I don't tell her lies. Well then she does possess them. Well then she merits my love—and its ten to one all his love returns with this single reflection.[12]

Hub, of course, is short for husband, but it also signifies the unifying center to which all things are drawn. Barlow's romantic outpourings reveal a desire to dominate Ruth, to make her so much a part of himself that she could no longer exist as an individual. "When I speak to you I speak to my own heart," he wrote her. "You are my flesh & my blood, my life and my soul . . . my food, my hope for the future, my actual joy." Yet he was happy to keep a psychological as well as a physical distance from her. He realized she was adept at eluding him and counted on her doing so. "The centripetal force of the pole which is hub," he observed, "and the centrifugal force of the torrid zone which is wife just balance each other."[13] Barlow's egocentricity possibly masked a deep-seated fear of Ruth. It is not surprising that he set her up so cozily at Le Havre with her "sweetheart."

Ruth Baldwin Barlow came from a middle-class New Haven family to whom education was important. She prided herself on her rigorous mind. Even Barlow admired her judgment in financial and other practical matters. Yet, in one of Ruth's few letters to Barlow that has been preserved—it was written in French at his insistence while he was in Algiers—she laments:

> Oh what a child I am in everything that affects my heart when in every other matter I am courageous and even a little philosophic. It is my misfortune that my weakest part is always most strongly attacked. Sometimes I wish I had no sensibility at all, that I could experience everything without being affected. Unhappily my character is too formed and will not change. What I am now I will always be, although I would wish to make myself more worthy of you the best of men and of lovers.[14]

Ruth's deplored romanticism had many facets. She savored it in herself, and she indulged it in Barlow. Stimulated by his fancies, she enjoyed being his *"trop sensible amie,"* his "naughty idler." But she also used her vagrant sensibility, as she used her precarious health, to prevent him from absorbing her into himself. Surrounding herself with friends and admirers, she suffered his absences well. Her behavior, like Barlow's, was often conspiratorial. In her letters she regaled him with all her "t[r]icks" and "how happy & how bad" she was. When they were together, she shared her conquests with him. Fulton was, in fact, the most beloved of a series of *"grand garçons"* mutually enjoyed by the Barlows. Once Joel met Fulton, however, no one superseded him. In addition to being exciting company and extraordinarily handsome, he served Ruth and Barlow as a safe means of communication with each other and, simultaneously, as a safe means of escape from each other. Each also loved Fulton for himself. Later Barlow referred to him as "the mediatorial part of the new and happy trinity."[15] Flattering as this analogy may have been, it is a measure of Fulton's emotional immaturity that he accepted that role so easily and from it derived such evident satisfaction.

The question of whether Barlow and Fulton were engaged in a homosexual relationship, as Barlow's letters imply, is a difficult one. Certainly, homosexuality was a recognized life-style in the *beau monde* of Paris, although it was not nearly as prevalent as marital infidelity. It is possible that Fulton and Barlow were lovers. Fulton's long residence at Powderham as the protégé of a transvestite suggests that, at the least, he had a propensity for bisexuality. The impression given by the correspondence, however, is that Barlow was a fantast who preferred talk to action. His tone is that of an impotent man. He seems incapable of loving anyone but himself. Indeed, his gift of Ruth to Fulton may be understood as a self-enhancing act.

It was, of course, with Ruth that Fulton enjoyed the greater opportunity for physical love. Their friendship probably began in a bantering vein, but although only one letter from Ruth to Fulton has survived and only two from Fulton to Ruth, all of a later period, it is clear that their mutual attraction soon developed an erotic strain. Fulton's later behavior indicates that he was fascinated by Ruth and cared for her passionately. It is difficult to believe they were not lovers, in spirit if not in flesh, by the time they took rooms together at the Hôtel du Bienvenu. Either way, such a liaison would have been thoroughly approved by the French, who believed that "marriage was the most odious of monopolies." It was the vogue in Directory Paris for husbands to be proud of their wives' paramours, to befriend them, to share their residence with them, and even to choose them. In some cases these extramarital relationships were consummated sexually. Madame de Staël's multiple lovers offer a prime example; Madame Récamier's "affairs of the mind" were no less fashionable.

An atmosphere of childish make-believe permeates the trio's complex interaction. They often seem more like playmates than mature adults. This may well have appealed to Fulton, whose fragmented life had left him, in certain respects, emotionally undeveloped. It enabled him to prolong his youth. Moreover, because Barlow was a dabbler and a poseur rather than a doer and a striver, Fulton may well have found his disposition calming. He may have sensed, if only subconsciously, that it functioned as a check on his own tendency toward compulsive activity. He could thus afford to be loving and even protective toward Barlow.

If the Barlows' love was as narcissistic, demanding, and puerile as Joel's letters suggest, there was, however, potential danger that Fulton would be imprisoned by it. His strongest shield against Joel's appetite to domineer and Ruth's demands for attention was his abundant energy and his ability to become utterly absorbed in great projects. The very breadth of his genius separated him from the Barlows. The great risk in Fulton's relationship with them was that if he suffered too many frustrations and failures in his professional life, he might seek in their possessive affection a plausible safe haven.

In 1798 John Vanderlyn made charcoal drawings of Barlow and Fulton. Only forty-four years old, Barlow resembles an aging satyr. Fulton, at first glance, seems vulnerable. But beneath the charming surface is a vibrant self-awareness that approaches hardness. It is the portrait of a man who leads a rich and determined interior life.

Ruth did not sit for Vanderlyn, but there is a watercolor of her said to have been painted at about the same time by Charles de Villette, the son of a neighbor. Her eyes, under thin gracefully curved brows, have a sad, caressing expression. Her lips are gentle and very fine. Yet hers is a strong face, endowed, despite perpetual illnesses and frail sensibilities, with self-confidence and a certain stately solidity.

Any apprehension that he might be stifled by too intimate an association with the Barlows could not have entered Fulton's mind when he hurried back to Paris from Normandy in late October, for he happily settled into the palatial mansion Barlow had bought that summer as a setting for their *ménage à trois*. Built in 1789 by an aristocrat who had been forced to flee before he could live in it, the Hôtel de Tremouillet at 50 rue de Vaugirard on the northwest corner of the Luxembourg Gardens was considered one of the handsomest houses in Paris. Its gate alone cost 4,000 livres. Beyond the service courtyard, through an arch in a formal terrace, was a second courtyard with an entrance to the elegant vestibule. The main facade, however, fronted on the large garden from which three grand flights of steps swept up to the magnificent principal floor. The grand salon had 17-foot ceilings. Behind it was the dining salon, and library, and side apartments of three rooms each. On the second story were twenty-two guest rooms, sixteen with chimneys. The cellars were capable of holding five hundred casks of wine.

Despite the Hôtel de Tremouillet's splendor, Barlow bought it cheaply. There were many more dwellings of the old rich for sale than there were new rich buyers. However, the interiors were unfinished. The walls needed papering, the public rooms lacked their huge gilt mirrors, there was no furniture, and it was far from the fashionable center of town.

Before Ruth's return to Paris, just ahead of Fulton, Barlow had bought her a bed, a few chairs, and a table and had hired two maids, a houseman, and a gardener, but reluctant to invest more money he never furnished more than four rooms comfortably. He and Ruth and Fulton simply camped out in the *hôtel* in what must have been very close quarters.

Despite the failure of his first campaign against the British, Fulton's confidence in his submarine was higher than it had ever been. By November 7, 1800, he sent a summary of what he accomplished during the summer months to Pierre Simon Laplace and Gaspard Monge, the eminent scientists who had been appointed by the National Institute to assess his progress. Once more he was extraordinarily fortunate in the caliber and dispositions of his evaluators. Laplace, a mathematician and astronomer, was unquestionably the country's most celebrated scientist. His mind was ardent, tenacious, and elegant. Though of peasant origin, he had enjoyed virtually uninterrupted prosperity. He was an active benefactor of the "adopted children of his thought." He had taught at the École Militaire and had been an examiner of the royal artillery. Politically ambitious, he was eager to please Napoleon.

Monge, the son of an itinerant knife grinder, commenced his diversified career as a draftsman, and in his leisure time developed a system of descriptive geometry that became the basis of modern engineering drawing. In 1792 and 1793, he served as the marine minister. He wrote about the fabrication of cannons and was a founder of the École Polytechnique. In 1796, Monge was sent to Italy to receive the art objects confiscated in the wake of French victories. There he became an intimate of Bonaparte who invited him to join the Egyptian campaign in order to make precise measurements of the ancient monuments. On his return to Paris, Monge served as president of the Egyptian Institute and continued to teach and develop his system of descriptive geometry. Acquainted for some time with Fulton's submarine project, Monge was excited by it.

The report Fulton sent to Laplace and Monge concluded optimistically that, although he was still working on new ideas, he considered "the most difficult part of the work as done." On its heels, he sent a list of questions to help them in their evaluation, including with it a cost estimate of 57,000 livres for building and testing a new submarine which was to be 30 feet long and 6 feet in diameter. He told them he would be willing to turn over the command of the *Nautilus* to the government and, reiterating that his objective was not to make a fortune but to secure the liberty of the seas, he offered to supervise the construction of submarines for whatever remuneration the government chose. "I have expended as much as my circumstances will permit," he asserted, "and more than one individual should do for an object of general interest." [16] For a brief moment, Fulton may have been seeking a salaried position.

Laplace and Monge were even more enthusiastic about Fulton's plans than the earlier commission had been. Describing Fulton as an inventor who "combines with great erudition in the mechanic arts, an excellent courage and other moral qualities necessary for such an enterprise," they submitted his report and cost estimates to Bonaparte and urged him to grant Fulton an interview. [17] As the committee had done in 1798, Monge and Laplace counseled that experiments be conducted without publicity, although how they could have expected to keep them secret after the thoroughly visible trials at Paris, Rouen, and Le Havre is hard to imagine.

Within the week Bonaparte consented to the meeting. No record survives of what transpired, but Fulton's admiration for the first consul and his satisfaction at having at last reached the seat of power must have enhanced his already well honed skills of presentation. He undoubtedly demonstrated the maneuverability of the submarine by running the model in a tank of water, as he had done for the commission's meeting, and exhibited roll upon roll of drawings and computations in answer to Bonaparte's questioning. The results were inconclusive, however. Bonaparte ordered Marine Minister Forfait to gather still more information.

Disappointed, Fulton called on Forfait on December 2. It was not a happy interview. Summarizing the encounter in an indignant letter in which he berated Forfait for preaching economy and for questioning the results of his experiments, Fulton reminded him that it cost 2 million francs to build a ship of the line that could perfectly well be captured on its first day out. He, in contrast, asked only 100,000 francs with every probability that his boat would be more useful. Included with the letter was a copy of the report of his summer's expedition and a fifth set of terms, virtually identical to his past proposals. These, he maintained, represented an economy to the government and "simple justice" to him and his company. There was no question the project would succeed, he assured Forfait, since he would put all his own physical and intellectual force behind it.

This letter prompted Forfait to write a frank opinion to Bonaparte. Had Fulton seen it, he would have been infuriated. Forfait pointed out that 20,000 francs should be added to the cost estimates for the "hulk" Fulton said he needed for his torpedo experiments. This would bring the expense to 80,000 francs, too high a price for what in a sudden change of heart he now believed to be "insignificant gains."

Forfait's chief objection was that Fulton had changed his mode of attack. According to the new plan, which Fulton must have discussed with him at the December 2 meeting, the *Nautilus* would serve only as a means of transporting to the general area of the enemy fleet the torpedoes and the men who would set the bombs using separate boats. Forfait did not describe how, but it must have been the same method of deploying explosives Fulton had tried in August and described in his reports. "I always have been the most ardent supporter of the submarine," Forfait insisted, "and it is painful to me to see it abandonned" as an attack vessel. He strongly favored putting the *Nautilus* in order and returning to Fulton's original scheme of screwing bombs into the bottoms of enemy ships. He suggested that if Fulton persisted in refusing to do so, the government should buy the *Nautilus* which he thought it could do cheaply because Fulton still owed 8,000 francs for it. Forfait capped his argument by stating that he "could never advise the government to throw 60 or 80,000 francs into the sea with as little hope of gain as the new plans the projector offered." [18]

Bonaparte may have agreed with Forfait, but Laplace and Monge supported Fulton's cause with renewed vigor. They prevailed in part, and on February 27, 1801, Forfait notified Fulton that the first consul had directed that 10,000 francs be placed at his immediate disposal. The money was to be used to repair the *Nautilus* and to build more torpedo bombs. Fulton would be required to transport the submarine at his own expense to Brest where facilities would be made available to him. His personal recompense would be related to enemy vessels destroyed: from 60,000 francs for a ship carrying ten guns to 400,000 francs for a ship with more than thirty guns. The government's immediate investment was minimal.

Fulton agreed to these terms. A formal statement was sent to him on March 28 and, on April 4, he was issued a passport of eight months' duration for the purpose of entering French channel ports or the ocean by land or by sea. However, no authorization was given to build the new 30-foot submarine he wanted so badly.

During the aggravating waiting period, Fulton continued to improve the design of the *Nautilus*. Eager to increase the supply of oxygen, he sought advice from Louis Bernard Guyton de Morveau, an experimental chemist and a member of the National Institute who had been in charge of developing military balloons and with whose wife Fulton enjoyed a lighthearted flirtation. A witness to the demonstration in the Seine the previous year, Guyton de Morveau calculated that in the volume of air contained by the boat—about 212 cubic feet—there would be sufficient oxygen to sustain four men and two small candles for three hours. This air, he suggested, could be increased by uncorking bottles of oxygen as needed or by precipitating carbonic acid with lime. Fulton thought that the bottles would take up too much room and that the chemical solution was inconvenient. Instead he adopted a device that had first occurred to him in 1799, a compressed air tank consisting of a simple copper sphere to which was joined a pneumatic pump capable of forcing 200 cubic feet of common air into it. To monitor output, the tank was outfitted with two valves calibrated to measure the oxygen as it was dispensed. The tank would double to at least six hours the length of time the submarine could remain submerged without resurfacing. Fulton ordered the tank in Paris, to be shipped to him at Brest as soon as it was finished.

Fulton also used this interlude to play with new designs for the Panoramas so as to permit longer viewing time and greater variety of fare and, thereby, he hoped, generate more profits. The improvements did not display much ingenuity, but Fulton was granted a patent for them on April 26.

Sometime in late April or early May, Fulton went to Growan where he had left the *Nautilus*. To his dismay, he found that during the winter the bolts and arbors had rusted badly. Somehow he got the vessel to the great naval port of Brest, probably aboard a barge. Workmen were hard to find, but after two months the submarine was in good enough condition to begin a series of experiments to render it more versatile. These, in large part, were a refinement of the series Fulton had conducted earlier. With three companions aboard, he plunged to 25 feet, the maximum depth he considered safe for the boat. They stayed underwater for one hour. Next, under sail, they tacked back and forth in a light breeze at 2 miles an hour. He dismantled the sails in two minutes and, submerged, ran at a controlled depth of 5 feet with the aid of a bathometer and a compass. Hoping to dispense with candles because of the oxygen they consumed, he installed a 1½-inch-diameter window with ¾-inch-thick glass near the bow of the boat and found that at 25 feet he had sufficient light to read his watch.

Fulton was gratified by his compressed air tank. It took two men only an hour to fill and enabled him to remain submerged with three companions at a depth of 5 feet for an hour and forty minutes "without experiencing any inconvenience." Although not as long as he had promised, it was an impressive achievement. He was satisfied the time could be easily extended.

While he was perfecting the *Nautilus*, Fulton was also developing his new schemes for delivering torpedoes without using the submarine. He persuaded Charles Caffarelli, the maritime prefect of Brest, to build him a boat 36 feet long propelled both by sails and by a crew of twenty-four hand-picked men turning four cranks, two on each side of the vessel. For his experiments he obtained the hulk of a small sloop, which he anchored in the harbor as a target. When his delivery boat was within 200 feet, he threw overboard a torpedo containing 20 pounds of powder. Moved by the wind, tide, and current, it struck the target. "The explosion took place and the sloop was torn into atoms," Fulton reported triumphantly, "in fact, nothing was left but the buoy and cable, and the concussion was so great that a column of water, Smoke and fibres of the Sloop were cast from 80 to 100 feet."[19]

Caffarelli was not impressed. In his report to Forfait, he noted correctly that neither the plunging boat nor the elaborate new mechanical boat was needed for the operation, simply one or two light boats would do: "I think Mr. Fulton had at one and the same time three ingenious ideas: that of a boat sailing without oars or sails; that of a plunging boat which directs itself and works at will and that of a bomb; he has wanted to bring them all together as if one alone would not occupy attention enough. The third by itself . . . will suffice for the success of his projects."[20] However, since the cost was negligible, he promised to keep Fulton informed about the position of English cruisers in the channel and to give him every facility for attack.

The reaction of Admiral Étienne Villaret de Joyeuse, commander of the squadron at Brest, was more personal. He described Fulton as "enveloping himself in a cloud of mystery yesterday by desiring to go alone in his boat, while today after much flattery he had asked me to give him boats and men."[21] Distrusting Fulton, Villaret de Joyeuse stated that he would not be convinced the scheme was sound unless Fulton could perform the experiment in his presence and from his own boat and put the bomb in place at a distance of 180 feet. The admiral accurately put his finger on the key flaw in the system. The stealth on which the operation depended was virtually impossible to obtain. Nevertheless, like Caffarelli, he ended on a positive note, declaring he was favorably disposed to the project and did not want to lose a moment in executing it.

By the first of August, Fulton was ready to begin his second assault against the British. This time he intended to demonstrate his new strategy. He did not think the repaired *Nautilus* was sound enough for the task, and the new delivery boat proved too slow, unwieldy, and noisy, so he used ordinary boats. After lying in wait during six days of foul weather at Pointe de Saint-Mathieu, seaward of the inner basin at Brest, he sighted two British frigates and two cutters cruising off the bay and six ships of the line at anchor. Such a formidable array caused him to have second thoughts about the hit-and-run operation he had planned, and to protect his retreat he demanded that Caffarelli send him six more boats each with one officer and twenty to twenty-four men to whom he would offer special awards to ensure their "hearty good will."

Caffarelli refused to deliver the six boats and ignored the plea for the submarine. He reminded Fulton that for a long time he had had two cutters and a pinnace, all well armed. In a frank letter to Forfait, he pointed out that Fulton had jeopardized the operation by not using the submarine and observed that this mode of making war was so reprehensible that anyone captured would be hanged, certainly not an appropriate death for naval men.

Fulton did not give up. He wrote the adjutant commandant at Brest, asking for eight boats with twelve to sixteen oars each and one gunboat. He planned to depart at two o'clock in the afternoon and return on the flood tide the next morning for five or six nights running in order to perfect and, if possible, to execute the operation. His persistence was to no avail, and on September 6 he informed Bonaparte, not entirely accurately, that the expedition against the British had failed because he had no submarine boat.

With his excuses he offered a still more advanced system of submarine warfare. Large plunging boats, each capable of carrying twenty or thirty torpedoes, would be used to mine Portsmouth, Plymouth, Tor Bay, and the Thames. Some bombs would be armed with clockwork detonating devices set to explode in four minutes to four hours; others would be equipped with contact triggers. In this manner the enemy's ports would be blockaded at little expense. British commerce would be destroyed. Liberty of the seas would be restored, and great splendor would be added to Bonaparte's name.

Having dispatched this confident message, Fulton returned to Paris. Immediately on his arrival, he submitted a long report to the faithful Monge and Laplace and to Constantin François de Chasseboeuf Volney, a linguist and a philosopher who had been added to the submarine commission. Like Monge and Laplace he was intimate with Bonaparte. He had recently returned to Paris from Philadelphia, having been forced to flee the United States because of the Alien and Sedition Acts. He was one of Barlow's good friends.

The highlight of Fulton's report was a vivid master plan of the strategy he had presented in brief in his memorandum to Bonaparte. To implement it he would need one or two submarines each 36 feet long and 12 feet wide, capable of carrying six men, air for eight hours and twenty-five to thirty bombs. Their cylinders would be brass and of sufficient strength to descend to 60 or 80 feet underwater. As speed on the surface was not an important consideration because submarines could escape from the enemy while hidden beneath the water, they need sail only 5 to 7 miles an hour.

> [L]et the business of the boats be to go with cargos of bombs, and let them loose with the current into the harbours of Portsmouth, Plymouth, Torquay or elsewhere. Those with their grapplings floating under water could not be perceived. Some would hook in the cables, bow or stern, or touch in their passage: many, no doubt, would miss but some would hit, go off and destroy the vessels they touched. One or more vessels destroyed in a Port by such invisible agents would render it too dangerous to admit of any vessel remaining.

Two or three hundred placed in the Thames, he insisted, would destroy the commerce of London: "No pilot could steer clear of such hidden dangers—no one dare to raise them even if hooked by grapplings, as they could not tell the moment they might touch the Secret Spring which would cause the explosion and destruction of everything around them. No vessel could pass without the utmost danger of running on one of them and Her instant destruction."[22]

The commission had a few minor questions about the expense, but were so pleased with Fulton's advances that they showed the report to the first consul at once. Fulton's scheme was, at last, grandiose enough to excite Bonaparte's imagination. He sent word to Fulton that he wished to see the *Nautilus*. Fulton's astounding reply was that, because the vessel "leaked very much" and he "did not think her further useful," he had taken the submarine to pieces, sold the ironwork, lead, and cylinders, and in the process broken most of the moving parts.

That Fulton carried out his secret work of destruction because the *Nautilus* was no longer seaworthy was merely a polite story. In fact, he was afraid the boat might be used as a model for other submarines without his consent and without payment. Baldly stating that he considered the invention his private property, he refused even to show any of his drawings to government engineers. "The first Consul is too just, and you know me too well," he explained, "to construe this into an avaricious disposition in me. I have now laboured 3 years and at considerable expense to prove my experiments, And I find that a man who wishes to cultivate the Useful Arts cannot make rapid Progress without sufficient

funds to put his succession of Ideas to immediate proof; and which suf-
ficiency I conceive this invention should secure to me."[23]

Fulton's behavior was reckless and self-defeating. It could not further his cause. Still he was so enthralled by his invention that he could
not restrain himself from playing the role of messiah to whom homage
must be paid. By destroying his boat, he was reasserting his power as
its creator—and his right to whatever "emoluments" it might bring.

The course of events and his own temperament were working against
Fulton that autumn. In October, Forfait, a constant friend of the submarine boat if not of mines, was replaced as marine minister by the far
more conservative Admiral Denis DeCres. On November 10, the Preliminary Peace of Amiens was signed, bringing a respite in the war between France and England. Coinciding with the second anniversary of
the ascension of Napoleon to the consulate, it was celebrated with fanfare throughout the city. The Tuileries, which Bonaparte had made his
official residence, the Louvre and the quays were festooned with oil lamps.
The statue depicting Liberty in the Place de la Révolution was replaced
by a Temple of Peace flanked by Temples of Art and Industry, and a
Temple of Commerce was floated on a barge in the Seine.

Fulton's reaction to peace must have been ambivalent. Although art,
industry, and commerce had long been his professed idols, his devotion
to them had gained him neither fame nor fortune. In fact, the only tangible results of his work in France were the Panoramas—a borrowed and
comparatively frivolous idea for which the rights had long been sold—
lavish praise for his engineering brilliance in the pages of the *Annales des
Arts et Manufactures,* and the French and Portuguese translations of his
Treatise.

Barlow saw his opportunity and, at this despondent juncture, stepped
in to redirect his friend's life. He had started writing an epic called "The
Canal: A Poem on the Application of Physical Science to Political Economy" and now expected Fulton would occupy himself by fleshing it out
with scientific detail. An embarrassing work, it began:

> Yes my dear Fulton let us seize the lyre,
> And Give to Science all the Muses' fire
> Mount on the boat as it glides along
> We'll cheer the long Canal with a Useful song.[24]

Then, he offered the Hôtel de Tremouillet for sale and investigated
suitable properties in Washington City, where he thought the three of

them would find agreeable friends and useful occupations. He wrote another letter to President Jefferson commending the system of small canals to his attention and suggesting that submarine warfare be developed for the defense of the country. Solicitous as always of Fulton's emotional well-being, he continued to encourage Ruth's attachment to him. Barlow had decided it was time for the "trinity" to return to America.

Steamboat Experiments

❖

The Parisian winter of 1802 was more dismal than usual. It drizzled and rained week after week. The wet, gray monotony was broken only by a heavy snowfall in early January followed by such a severe freeze that hardy pleasure seekers organized skating parties in the Champs-Élysées.

Despite traditional celebrations at New Year's and Epiphany and two weeks of masked balls at carnival, it was not a cheerful season. Cynics correctly predicted that the pending Peace of Amiens was a sham and that the Concordat would give Napoleon control of religious institutions. Steadfast republicans had lost their influence and were being systematically purged from the government. Though gaining in social power, the old aristocracy was impoverished and bewildered. The new bureaucratic aristocracy was insecure. In "the magic lantern city," it was a time of uneasy change.

The "trinity" at 50 rue de Vaugirard suffered from their own malaise of transition. They kept telling their friends they would return to America, but beyond occasionally inquiring of visiting countrymen about the comparative merits of living in New York, Philadelphia, or Washington, they took no positive action. Lord Nelson's mistress, Lady Emma Hamilton, to whom Barlow had hoped to sell the Hôtel de Tremouillet, showed no interest in it. No other buyers could be found. The three continued to huddle fecklessly, as transients, in their four furnished rooms.

Barlow was feeling old. His circle of influential friends was shrinking, and the thought of returning to America filled him with anxiety. He made fidgety revisions to his fourteen completed pages of "The Canal," but, as he could no longer arouse Fulton's interest, he did not compose any new lines. "Should I not live to finish the Poem, which is probable," he wrote in a cranky marginal note, "I desire that this may be presented as a fragment."[1] Ruth was unwell. This time her illness took the form of a proliferation of small tumors afflicting her buttocks and genitalia. "Those hard hearted imps of the devil that fastened on to its sweet lovely flesh" was Barlow's lyric description of the malady.[2] For distraction, he increased the household with a fluffy white poodle named Baron de Min.

Fulton was more dispirited than he had ever been. In despair over France's steady march away from true republicanism, he grumbled that "the ten years war . . . had not exactly obtained the liberal objects for which it was commenced."[3] He undoubtedly was discouraged that his ten years' work as an engineer had not produced the fame and fortune for which he yearned. Having no immediate mechanical project to galvanize his energies, he resorted to gathering material for an even more encyclopedic anti-war, anti-colonial, pro-national improvement tract. It never progressed beyond the planning stage; his heart was not in it.

In such a state of mind it would not have been surprising if Fulton had succumbed to the Barlows' style of life and, content with dreams, dissipated his creativity by tending their complex needs. But that was not his nature or his destiny. Sometime in February or early March he met Robert R. Livingston, the U.S. minister plenipotentiary to France. Though vastly different in background, temperament, and capability, they quickly found a common bond: it was steam navigation.

Livingston had arrived in France with his wife, their two daughters and sons-in-law in December 1801. A rich, landed New Yorker, he had behind him a distinguished career as a statesman. He had served in the Continental Congress and was a member of the committee that drafted the Declaration of Independence. As chancellor of New York State he had administered the oath of office to George Washington who chose him as the nation's first secretary of foreign affairs. In Paris his mission was to secure passage of U.S. ships past New Orleans, a job that, with persistence, vision, and luck, he parlayed in the ensuing months into the great Louisiana Purchase.

Paramount to Fulton, however, was that, in addition to being a man of stature, Livingston was an ardent amateur of mechanics. Blessed with an inherited fortune with which to indulge this "hobby horse," as he called it, Livingston was proud of his accomplishments in the useful arts. He was a founding member and president of the New York Society for the Promotion of Arts, Agriculture and Manufactures. He held U.S. patents for a "Means of Diminishing the Friction of Spindles" and for "Manufacturing Paper out of River Weeds." In connection with making his vast estates more productive, he had tried to improve the operation of millstones.

But the project that had most engaged Livingston's mechanical fancy for the past five years was the building of a steamboat to run from New York City to Albany. It aroused him intellectually, and he expected it would bring him lasting fame as a benefactor of society and add to his fortune as well. The design he had been working on was not exactly his own. In 1797 he had an idea for a vessel propelled by a horizontal wheel suspended beneath the keel. He intended the wheel to be driven by horses plodding in a circle on the deck. It was his wife's brother, the fecund, nimble-witted inventor and land developer John Stevens of New Jersey, who advised him to dispatch the horses and use steam instead. Too vain to take direction from Stevens, but not sufficiently motivated to immerse himself in the complex engineering problems steam posed, Livingston merely modified his horseboat on the basis of a few calculations and minor experiments with a crude model. Then he contracted with Nicholas Roosevelt, who owned the best foundry in America and had some experience with steam pumps, to make the machinery and the boat. Roosevelt, who possessed a strong sense of his own worth, wasted no time in advising Livingston that his horizontal wheel could not make efficient use of steam power. His own solution, vertical wheels on the sides of the hull, he said was infinitely better. Livingston clung to his horizontal wheel, and, since he had money to risk and Roosevelt had none, he ordered Roosevelt to follow his plan. As Roosevelt's chief engineer, Charles Staudinger, complained: "Everyone has a certain portion of philauty and rich people particularly. They are not used to hear the truth and their idear is exalted by flatterers even if they are quite indifferent."[4] The building of that steamboat was carried on by correspondence. The patrician Livingston stayed at his country seat on the Hudson River, 120 miles north of Manhattan on the east bank of the Hudson and sent down a succession of changes and modifications based on whims and theories. Only occasionally did he inconvenience himself by visiting the foundry in Belleville, New Jersey, to examine the engine. Quite possibly he realized he would expose his deficient knowledge of working mechanics if he did so. When the boat was finally tested—Livingston was not on hand for the trial—it moved briefly between 3 and 5 miles an hour. But the engine was so heavy and vibrated so violently that the pipes burst and the seams opened. The steamboat had to be abandoned.

Livingston stubbornly refused to be discouraged. Marshaling his considerable political influence—he was still chancellor of New York State and had relatives in every branch of government—he applied to the New York State Legislature to abrogate the fourteen-year monopoly on steam navigation awarded to John Fitch in 1787 and to bestow it on himself. Arguing that Fitch had done nothing to implement his privilege in New York State and was probably dead, Livingston insisted that he could not undertake such "uncertain, hazardous and expensive experiments" without the incentive of a monopoly. The Legislature, after indulging in the pleasure of ridiculing "the hot water bill," did as it was bid with the proviso that Livingston construct, within a year, a boat capable of making the trip from New York to Albany at a speed of 4 miles an hour.

Certain he could produce a boat that would go 8 miles an hour, Livingston renewed his exertions with double the ardor, but with even less system. One after another his ideas, including an engine that used mercury in the cylinder, proved unworkable. In the end, he was forced to rely on Stevens. Fond of Livingston because of their social connection, Stevens enjoyed the deference Livingston paid to his superior mechanical ability, and in February 1800 they entered into a formal partnership to build a new boat, sharing costs and profits for the next twenty years. They were both disenchanted with Roosevelt, who was always behind schedule because of other commitments—boring cannon for the frigate *Constitution*, building an engine for the Philadelphia waterworks, taking out a patent for a steam engine for raising water, rolling grist and sawing wood in his own name, and helping Staudinger with his patent on a mechanism for propelling vessels—but they asked him to join them anyway. He agreed, contributing labor instead of capital.

However, even with their combined inventive, manufacturing, and financial capabilities, they had no more success with the second boat than with the first. When Livingston left for France in the fall of 1801, all he had to show for three years and at least $10,000 expended in steamboat experiments was a two-year extension of the New York State monopoly, the partnership agreement with Stevens and Roosevelt, and an order with Staudinger to make a new model and more drawings.

Livingston's widespread reputation as "an incorrigible projector" of farfetched schemes must have preceded him to Paris, but whether Fulton deliberately arranged an encounter with him or whether it happened by chance is not recorded. Livingston was an inveterate sightseer and he was especially careful not to miss the mechanical exhibitions that were popular in Paris. Fulton may well have run into him at the demonstration of illuminating gas that so captivated Livingston or at a balloon ascension where their mutual friend Joseph Montgolfier might have introduced them, or they might have become acquainted at one of the innumerable private or public functions to which they both would have been invited. Most probably they were brought together by the rich and successful expatriot financier Daniel Parker. During the Revolutionary War Parker had been a supplier to the American army in partnership with Livingston's cousin, and he had a latent interest in steam navigation because of his connection with Rumsey. It seems certain that Barlow did not perform the introduction on his own, for he had no previous connection with Livingston.

However and wherever Fulton and Livingston met, they immediately realized that they could be useful to each other. Livingston was impressed by Fulton's work with the submarine and torpedoes. He admired Fulton's ability to combine theoretical knowledge with practical experience and by the speed and clarity with which he marshaled his thoughts. He felt sure Fulton was entirely capable of implementing his ideas. Livingston was aware of and possibly envied Fulton's familiarity with prominent French scientists. And, since outward appearances were important to Livingston, he would have noticed that, in spite of his obscure heritage, Fulton dressed well and had the manners of a gentleman. Moreover, since Fulton was twenty years younger, Livingston imagined he could treat him as a junior associate.

Although Fulton had not thought much about steamboats since early 1798 when he briefly experimented with using a four-bladed fly as a means of propulsion, he was more than ready to take on a major project. Unintimidated by Livingston's exalted position and aristocratic manner— his involvement with Stanhope and the higher echelons of the French government had inured him to pressures of that sort—he embraced Livingston as a valuable patron. Fulton soon discovered his grasp of mechanics was far better than Livingston's and he believed he could dominate him. That Livingston expected both fame and fortune from the enterprise meshed perfectly with Fulton's own hopes and gave a special luster to their prospective joint venture.

Needing each other, provisionally trusting each other, and excited by their mutual enthusiasm, Fulton and Livingston began at once to work together. Resisting the temptation of trying to develop and fabricate a steam engine on their own, they agreed to use an English engine, built to their specifications. This crucial decision was not merely prudent judgment based on Livingston's chastening experiences; it was sound analysis. Fulton was convinced that earlier steamboats had failed, not because available engines were not strong enough, but because their hulls were out of proportion to their propelling mechanisms. He realized that the British, who were far advanced in the engine-building arts, could produce an engine with more than sufficient power, liberating him to focus on the different problem of designing a propelling mechanism and a hull that would use the engine to its full advantage and provide maximum space for passengers and cargo. Ahead of his time, Fulton employed the doctrine of the division of labor among experts which Adam Smith preached, but few put into practice.

Since both Fulton and Livingston had written Boulton and Watt about engines to be used in boats—Livingston on November 4, 1789, and Fulton on November 4, 1794—and neither had received a reply, both were disenchanted with the company. Fulton, therefore, first contacted his friend Cartwright whose alcohol-fueled engine he hoped was sufficiently perfected for their needs. He was disappointed. But he did not give up. He sent Cartwright a host of suggestions for making his engine lighter and increasing its power.

The next task was to persuade the British government to grant an export license for the engine when they got it. Protective of its industrial superiority, England rarely allowed machines to be shipped abroad. Since his submarine had made him persona non grata there, Fulton counted on Livingston to exert influence through the U.S. minister to the Court of St. James's, New Yorker Rufus King. His hasty note instructing Livingston what to do indicates the extraordinary speed with which his mind was working and the familiarity with which he already felt free to deal with his potential benefactor:

Dear Sir,

Perhaps after our experiments, it may be found necessary to have one of Watts or Cartwrights engines constructed in the best manner, but as such engines cannot be exported from England without an order from the privy council, I think it will be well to make application through Mr. King for permission to send to New York two Engines of not more than 24 inch Cylinders. I say two because if one is found good another perhaps may be wanting and this will avoid the necessity of a Second application and as it will cost nothing to make such a demand yet be satisfying to know it can be granted. The sooner it is done the better, in order to save time in case such engines should be wanted. I therefore think it advisable to write to Mr. King immediately.[5]

Livingston must have been jarred by the commanding tone of this letter, and he may well have been alarmed that Fulton had already jumped the ante to two engines. But he had nowhere else to turn, and although he did not do as Fulton directed, shortly afterward they ordered the expert but high-priced Étienne Calla to make a model with which Fulton could conduct experiments.

This model, 3 feet long and 8 inches wide, drew an inch of water and was square at both ends. The power was provided by two clockwork springs. The means of propulsion was an endless chain with boards—a mechanism similar to tank treads. As a result of an exhaustive array of calculations that must have dazzled Livingston, Fulton found this to be a far more promising method than the oars and paddles favored by Fitch and Stanhope, the column of water forced through the stern used by Rumsey, and the primitive propeller advocated by Cartwright. The purpose of the model was to measure the resistance of the hull and the endless chains to the water and to use that information to determine what arrangement of paddleboards attached to the chains would thrust the boat ahead with the greatest speed.

Fulton had grasped the important principle that eluded other experimenters, that calculations of resistances must consider not only the friction of the hull and paddles against the water, but also the fact that water gives way when it is pushed against. (It requires more energy, for instance, to run on soft sand than on firm gravel.) His job was to find a propelling method that would have maximum thrusting capability and minimum resistance and match it with a hull that would also minimize resistance. He figured that if he could convert at least half the engine's power into actual forward movement, his steamboat could be made to run efficiently and profitably.

Fulton's grand plan, at this stage, was to do the theoretical work, conduct the experiments, and eventually supervise the construction of the boat and the engine while Livingston financed the project, used his political influence to deal with customs, patent, and monopoly problems, and performed supplementary experiments if he so desired. Fulton's euphoria was so great that he believed he could easily induce Livington to cooperate.

With this most satisfactory partnership burgeoning but still unsealed by either a gentleman's or a legal agreement, it is astonishing that, at the end of April, Fulton elected to escort Ruth Barlow to Plombières, a spa situated in the Vosges Mountains where she hoped to find a cure for her tumors. In a reminiscence written after Fulton's death, Ruth stated that her husband accompanied them, but that is not true. On a lovely spring day, she and Fulton jogged off in the phaeton they had so enjoyed at Le Havre, leaving Barlow in Paris to cultivate Livingston, badger Calla, "dine at good tables" six nights out of seven, supervise the gardener, and pet the poodle, Baron de Min. Barlow encouraged the excursion and delighted vicariously in it. He was content, as he had been in the summer of 1800, to have Ruth and Fulton out of the house, glad for a while to enjoy their company in his fertile imagination rather than as a day to day reality. "What you are about," he wrote in one of his effusive letters, "is a party of pleasure, a summer's recreation . . . turned out like a couple of colts to pasture, romping in the woods, dashing in the water, without a care, breathing the fragrance of spring and tasting the innocence of nature. . . . I rejoice every time it talks to me of the little pleasures it takes in walking, riding and fooling with toot. You must keep him there and not let him budge."[6]

Barlow knew, of course, that Plombières was far from innocent. Since the Middle Ages, it had been one of France's most fashionable resorts, as famous for its dancing, horseracing, gambling, promenades, and liaisons as for its warm radioactive springs, reputedly effective for healing genital disorders. Montaigne, Richelieu, the daughters of Louis XV, Voltaire, and Beaumarchais were among the great who had tried its curative powers. Joséphine and Hortense Bonaparte, Marshal Bernadotte, and Marshal Ney were its current illustrious patrons.

The setting was luxurious. There were antique Roman statues in the baths where the afflicted, clad in brief muslin shifts or loincloths, reclined on the ancient steps encircling the pools. Elegant eighteenth-century arcades, ideal for rendezvous, adorned the public buildings and, on the steep hillsides surrounding the town within a morning's pleasant drive were magnificent beech forests with pretty grottos, sparkling cascades, and charming views of the Alps and the Augronne valley.

Barlow's almost daily letters were even more highly flavored with his special brand of eroticism than those he sent to Le Havre. Commending Ruth for her courage and virtue in withstanding the painful regime ordered by her doctor—"throwing gaseous water onto and into the affected parts," douching, and soaking in the baths—he rhapsodized, "Praise it! I shall praise it and love it & adore it and flog it & kiss it & fold it up in my soul till it comes, and then in my arms. I shall tell toot to reward it for all its good deeds as it goes along. Then hub will pay you both."[7] He urged Ruth to "give the waters fair play, even to sitting on the *trou des capucines*," a spring especially recommended for inducing fertility. Named after the religious order that had formerly presided over its rites, there were many ribald stories attributing cures to the attentiveness of the monks rather than to the therapeutic waters. Barlow savored elaborating on those tales. Inserting Fulton into the Aesculapian role, he wrote, "I reckon all those fine ladies who come for the purpose of making babies may find the same instruction and spiritual edification from toot as they used to from the barefoot brothers of St. Francis."[8]

Few letters are without direct expressions of his love for "the much inventing, life-endearing toot"—always to be delivered by Ruth and related to Fulton's attentions to her. "What a charming toot it is; must always tell him how much hub nubs him & ipey muss nub him too. . . . Tell toot I love him more than ever man was loved by man. His goodness to little one will not be forgot. Perhaps I shall owe my wife to him at last."[9] In Barlow's fancy Fulton was "the *real presence*, the body and blood of the mediatorial part of the little holy trinity."[10]

In addition to writing extravagant letters, Barlow felt compelled to provide Ruth and Fulton with political histories and the Paris newspapers as well as sugar, coffee, tea, and forty-one bottles of wine. To "toot" especially he sent painting materials, for Fulton had returned to his easel; he found it gave him pleasure and filled the hours. One work of this period was an eerily charming watercolor portrait of Charlotte de Villette, the recently deceased daughter of their rue de Vaugirard neighbor. Fulton also painted a miniature of Ruth which he gave to Barlow. Unfortunately, it has not been found. However, the similarity of the portrait of Ruth, attributed to Charles de Villette, to Fulton's painting of Charlotte, suggests that Charles's drawing of Ruth may have been copied from one by Fulton.

When Barlow delivered the picture of Charlotte de Villette to her grieving mother, he could not resist adding a few verses of his own on the back, because, as he wrote Fulton, "I like to have your works and mine go together."[11] Inspired by this sentiment, he persuaded Fulton to suggest and sketch illustrations for a monumental expansion of *The Vision of Columbus*, which he now called *The Columbiad*. His dream was to publish it in a splendid edition written, illustrated, and printed entirely by Americans. "I wish this work to be done in the family," he wrote Fulton by way of enticement when he sent him eight subjects ranging from "Capac relieving his son Rocha from the burning pyre, having killed Zamor & routed the savages," to "Cornwallis Surrendering to Washington."[12]

In lighter moments, Fulton drew cartoons. Barlow was particularly enraptured by a caricature depicting Ruth's therapy. Entitled "The Douche and the Old Man's Lesson," it featured a *tuyau de cuir* (leather tube) which Barlow thought "beat the devil . . . a good thing and a very wholesome thing for the ladies whether the *cuir* be tanned or not."[13] Having second thoughts about the drawing's crudeness, Fulton ordered him to burn it. Instead, Barlow showed it to all their friends and reported exultantly how much it had enhanced "toot's" reputation. It was, he said, "the very image of itten ippey."

So content was Fulton vacationing with Ruth that he did not return to Paris but entrusted Barlow to oversee the steamboat venture. Charmed by the assignment, Barlow spent May "running, scolding, and arranging" with the perfectionist Calla who was insisting on important reworkings of the model. In the line of duty, he also visited the Conservatory of Arts and Trades. "There," he reported, "I saw a strange thing. It was no less than your very steamboat in all its parts & principles, in a very elegant model . . . the steam engine is in its place, all complete with a wooden boiler, cylinder placed horizontal." This was the invention of Desblancs and differed from Fulton's mainly in that the endless chains were supported from above by two additional wheels. Of this Barlow drew a rough sketch that looks like an aroused porcupine; the extra wheels caused the path of the chain to be semicircular rather than elliptical. Montgolfier, too, declared emphatically that it would not work. "None of it will do," he expostulated, ". . . if Mr. Fulton had spoken to me about it, I would have cured him of his steamboat madness."[14] Ridiculing the notion that a propelling mechanism could be devised that would use a steam engine's power efficiently, he insisted that common oars and all other modes of moving an object in water, by pushing against the water, lost 99 percent of their power.

Barlow promised Fulton with conspiratorial relish that he would say nothing to Livingston about Desblancs's model, although he hardly could have expected Livingston to miss it. Actually, Barlow had seen very little of him. When Livingston at last invited him to dinner—"the only American in a high flock of ambassadors"—they talked only about the submarine. The English guests asserted that no civilized nation would use it because "men, governments, and nations would fight & that it was better for the morals & general happiness of all people that the fighting should be done on the ocean than on the land." Livingston, according to Barlow, "defended the submarine with great dignity & energy, and observed that the greater part of modern wars were commercial wars & these were occasioned by navies, & that the system ought to be overturned."[15] In fact, Livingston was so convinced of the humanity of the submarine that he had urged the American government to adopt it as a general mode of coastal defense. This was bold support and, in view of his ambivalent feelings about the submarine and his incipient jealousy of Livingston, it was good of Barlow to pass it on. Fulton had by no means abandoned his passion for submarine warfare, and the fact that Livingston shared it could only strengthen the personal relationship that would be necessary if they were to become long-term partners.

It was not until the last week in May that Calla—that "puppy," "rascal," and "snake," as Barlow was pleased to call him—gave the steamboat model its final coats of paint and sent it off to Plombières. Fulton put aside all thoughts of painting and dancing and playing with Ruth and in a fit of activity concentrated solely on his experiments. He made a 66-foot still-water testing basin, a novel idea at that time, by stopping up one of the small streams that fed the Augronne River. His plan was to use the model to make a controlled set of experiments that would determine "the most Advantageous application of Power"—that is, how he must arrange his paddleboards and endless chains to achieve an efficiency of 50 percent, the amount he estimated necessary for a commercially viable steamboat. The model's engine was a 4-inch spring-driven cylinder that made seven revolutions.

In his hurried and fragmented report to Livingston, he said he attached one end of a line to his model and the other to a fixed plank in the canal. To find out how fast the model must go to save half the power, he placed the model at one end of his basin and tied the loose end of the cylinder line to a fixed plank. Then, with a watch that struck seconds, he timed its passage through the water. In the first trial "the machinery pulling on the line drew the boat 56 feet in 45 seconds; second trial 42 seconds; 3rd trial, 40 seconds, I therefore take 42 as the medium," he explained. He then dispensed with the anchored line and sent the model down his basin propelled by paddleboards of various arrangements. With 4 inches continually in the water, the boat moved 21 feet in 15 seconds; with 8 inches 31½ feet in 27 seconds; with about 29 inches he finally obtained 42 feet in 42 seconds. "This convinces me," he triumphantly declared, relying as much on his engineering intuition as on his calculations, "that the fault is not in the steam engine, but has been in the bad form of the boat and a bad purchase on the water."[16]

Despite the importance of the experiments, Fulton apparently used them as a public entertainment. Today's guidebooks state that Madame Bonaparte attended, and given Fulton's predilection for instructive demonstrations, it is entirely possible there was a chattering gaggle of spectators presided over by Ruth Barlow. Unlike other inventors, Fulton never made serious efforts to keep his ideas secret. Rather it would seem he sought the attention of the general public and of potential competitors as a stimulus to his creativity.

The results of the tests put Fulton in a state of manic excitement. On the evening of the experiments, he vividly described to Livingston a 90-foot-long, 6-foot-wide steamboat propelled by a 10-inch cylinder at 8 miles an hour, the speed Livingston had boasted he could attain with his own invention in 1799 and twice the speed required by the fulfillment clause of the New York State monopoly. Thus, the 140 miles[17] from New York to Albany would take only eighteen hours. Since the total expense in crew and coal—1½ tons—would not be more than $10 or $12, the profits, if the steamboat carried a full load of fifty passengers, would be at least $198 each trip. His intention, Fulton told Livingston, was "to go quick, carry cheap, and thus avoid the competition of boats with sails or carriages."

This letter was obviously designed to whet Livingston's appetite, and yet it ends with a proud, rude note that could only have wounded Livingston's vanity: "Having now finished my experiments I will thank you to let me know how you proceed with yours; I am sorry I cannot be in Paris to aid you, however, if you cannot succeed to your satisfaction, yet I believe she will go as I think is before demonstrated."[18]

Within the week Fulton had produced an even grander vision. The boat he now projected would be 120 feet long and 8 feet wide and would run at 12 miles an hour and carry 120 passengers at a cost of 25 cents each. He would order a Cartwright or Watt engine to be shipped to America in six months, and in about two months he would leave France "to proceed with the hull and other parts of the machinery." Livingston had merely to sign a formal agreement, "The leading principle of which," Fulton told him, "is that I estimate my time (*for it is my attentions which must carry it into effect*, And my knowledge of the Subject), as an equivalent to your money."[19] In short, Livingston would put up all the money, but receive only half the profits.

Soon afterward Fulton put his calculations into a little booklet, with a jaunty cartoon of a passenger-laden steamboat captioned "The Steamboat from New York to Albany in 12 hours" on the title page. His latest estimates increased the boat's potential speed to at least 16 miles an hour. Still relying on Barlow to act for him in Paris, he sent the calculations to him with Calla's model to be put in safekeeping and a draft of a partnership agreement with Livingston on which he wanted advice.

Barlow's reaction was explosive. "I see . . . that you are mad. 16 miles an hour for a steamboat! le pauvre homme!" he yelped.[20] Then he blithely set off for England on a business trip. While in London he talked with William Chapman about Chapman's method of reducing friction in steam engines, but otherwise Barlow did not concern himself with steamboat business. His letters characteristically dwelt on such events as "gay evenings in St. James Park & Green Park" where he was shocked to see that the ladies' dresses covered "all their bubbies & bosoms & necks & gorges, clear up to the chin" and shopping expeditions when he bought "some nice stockings for itten own and some half stockings, called Socks for toot, to make him wear his pantaloons without boots—boots are going out of style."[21]

Barlow was away for two weeks. On July 3 he dined again at Livingston's residence. The occasion was probably a formal gathering celebrating American Independence Day to which all Americans in Paris were traditionally invited. There would have been no chance to discuss Fulton's latest ideas, which was just as well because Barlow had not had time to familiarize himself with them. Over the next few days he studied them thoroughly with Parker. But when he had finally grasped the particulars, he was unable to present them because Livingston's newborn grandson was dying from "an attack of hives." It was not until July 13 that Barlow felt free to call on him. Finding Livingston "either out or invisible," he left Fulton's booklet with a note offering to show him the model and to meet him at his convenience for further explanations. July 14 was Bastille Day. Livingston attended "a most noble review of troops reviewed by the 1st consul at the palace" and the state dinner that followed it. Barlow probably joined his republican friends in the spectacularly illuminated city to reminisce about better times. When Livingston called at 50 rue de Vaugirard on July 15, Barlow was out. Livingston left a card setting "a rendezvous for the next day at his house," and finally they were able to get together. Two days later, Barlow sent his impressions of the meeting to Fulton:

> I had a great talk with Livingston. He says he is perfectly satisfied with your experiments & calculations but is always suspicious that the engine beating up & down will break the boat to pieces. He seems to be for trying the horizontal cylinder, or for recurring to his mercurial engine. I see his mind is not settled & he promised now to write to you, which he says he should have done long ago, but he thought you were to be back every fortnight. He thinks the scale you talk of going upon is much too large and especially that part of the scale that respects the money. You have converted him as to the preference of the wheels above all other modes but he says they cannot be patented in America, because a man (I forget his name) has proposed the same thing there.

Barlow had some doubts whether Livingston would "act roundly with respect to the money part." He seemed to favor forming a company. "I wish Parker or I had the money instead of him," Barlow wistfully observed, "tho his influence in the State of New York would be energetic."[22]

This letter was an accurate summary of the meeting. When Livingston's letter arrived shortly afterward—the critique of a wary projector careful of his pride, power, and purse, yet not entirely sure of him-self—Fulton was well prepared. Livingston made it clear he was irritated that Fulton had not returned to Paris to discuss his experiments in person. He agreed that the trials had been useful, but pointed out that they had not solved the real difficulty which confronted them, the weight of the engine and the up-and-down movement of the piston, which would soon break a light boat to pieces. He suggested returning to his horizontal wheel, but confessed that new experiments "at great and what is worse an incalculable expense" would be necessary and therefore dropped the issue as soon as he raised it. He thought the endless chains might eventually prove to be the best propelling mechanism, but warned Fulton that they were unpatentable because they had already been invented by an "excellent practical workman" whom he intended to engage for the American boat. This meant that they would have to rely for protection on the New York State monopoly, which Livingston had already expended considerable sums to obtain. "All these considerations," he told Fulton, "make the demand you make of half the profits without any risk upon an untried scheme, much too great a compensation for the labour & time it will cost you." He was not willing to undertake a large boat. Even for one carrying only thirty passengers he would need more partners, especially those with political influence and mechanical expertise. Having assuaged his ego by disparaging Fulton's contribution, he closed, "I am Dear Sir with much optimism, Your Most Humb. Servt."[23]

Fulton replied with equal force. First, he said he was pleased that Livingston was convinced of the superiority of endless chains, which he was now sure were capable of driving a boat 24 miles an hour. Then he demonstrated how he would prevent the weight and pounding of the engine from injuring the hull by mounting the cylinder, boiler, and all heavy parts in an oak frame that would distribute the weight along the gunwales. The power would be communicated to crank wheels mounted on each side of the cylinder instead of to a walking beam.

But over half of Fulton's letter was devoted to a long explanation of why he believed his steamboat design was patentable. Starting with the argument he had advanced in his *Treatise on Canals* and in the French inclined plane patent specifications—that inventions in mechanics are "nine times out of ten a combination of known materials to produce an unknown effect"—he gave it a twist that further reduced the need for pristine novelty. He insisted that merely having an idea was not invention, what was decisive was the proof of its workability. Therefore, even if others had tried endless chains before him, he claimed to be their inventor because he was the first to prove their superiority. Crankily reminding Livingston that he had expended 3,000 pounds and eight years' work to acquire the mechanical knowledge that would save them from wasting money, he insolently pointed out: "You were the enemy to the chains till you received my memoire of my experiments. Thus if with your activity of mind and facility to investigate you were pursuing an error which could only lead to expense, it is evident there could be no distinct ideas of the superiority of chains till my experiments were made. . . . I have no doubt but the patent in America can be made good, that is, if the patent law means to secure to a man a movement of mind or discovery which is commonly called Inventions."

Despite the heat of his argument, Fulton did have doubts about his position. The American law gave priority to the person who first had the idea for an invention even if the idea had not been developed into a workable design. He therefore proposed "recompensating the person in New York with a sum of Money" or "weaving him into the web," if no other means could be found to render the patent secure. Furthermore, although he had great objection to partners, he suggested that "Mr. Stevens ought not to be excluded from hope of gain if there are shares." Livingston, it seems, had not yet informed Fulton that he already had a contractual agreement, valid for eighteen more years, with Stevens and also with Roosevelt, who must have been the "excellent practical workman" to whom he had referred.

As a compromise Fulton urged they build a 22-ton demonstration boat to carry forty to seventy passengers. It would be powered by a Cartwright engine—"the best yet known for this undertaking. . . . Without vanity," he proudly asserted, "I think I am perfect master of the details and perfectly calculated to carry the work to effect. . . . I am, sir, with an ardent desire to see this work executed, your most obedient Robert Fulton."[24]

No further correspondence between Livingston and Fulton has survived from that summer, and perhaps there was none, since at this juncture they were behaving more like sparring rivals than partners embarking on a momentous enterprise. Despite his confident reply, Fulton was profoundly uneasy. However, he did not rush back to Paris as might have been wise. He merely wrote Barlow not to leave the booklet and model in Livingston's possession.

Livingston was willing to let the matter rest for the moment, for he

was fully occupied by his diplomatic duties and had little time to devote
to the steamboat. During this period he wrote the sophisticated paper,
"Is it advantageous to France to take possession of Louisiana?" which
laid the groundwork for France's sale of the vast lands west of the Mississippi to the United States. His formal presence at Napoleon's court
claimed much of his time. Though an Englishman named Bertie Good-
speed described him as a deaf old man who could not speak a word of
French, Livingston, who had never been to Europe before, relished being
caught up in the "whirling vortex of social dissipation and follies" and
attending great state functions adorned with his "bag, sword, and em-
broidery."

In his free time, Livingston shopped for copies of antique statues
for the school of fine arts he was helping to found in New York. Ap-
prehensive about how his friends at home would respond to the nudity
of the *Laocoön*, *Apollo*, and *Venus* he had purchased, he wrote his cousin
Gilbert: "Though these statues were viewed by the most delicate women
here without a blush, yet the modesty of our country women renders a
covering necessary and I beg that you may begin by preparing one before you suffer them to be exhibited. This is done with a small concave
shell or fig leaf which you paint white and hang with a small white thread
about the waist."[25]

Only occasionally was Barlow able to penetrate Livingston's full
schedule to discuss the steamboat agreement. His assessment of Livingston's mood was that although Livingston was disposed to be a little
tough, he had no desire to go forward without Fulton and would be
brought to a reasonable compromise when Fulton returned to Paris.
Should Livingston bow out, however, Barlow offered an alternative
scheme. Fulton was to go directly to England and make a small experiment "all quiet & quick." If successful, he was to take the machinery to
New York, secure a U.S. patent and build a boat. "I think I will find
you the funds without any noise for the first operation in England,"
Barlow wrote, "& if it promises well, you will get as many funds & friends
in America as you want. — I should be clear for a small operation first,
for several reasons. — it can be made without noise. — There must be
imperfections in the first trial which you can remedy without disgrace
if done without noise. There will be no time lost, but probably time
gained, by the small experiment, because it will take less time and vexation to find the errors & find the remedies."[26]

Fulton was not seduced by this special pleading which displayed a poor grasp of pragmatics as well as a withering lack of faith, and he let Barlow know that he preferred to hold on to Livingston, who, after all, already possessed the New York State monopoly.

Fulton threw himself with even more ardor into the social delights of the spa. Despite Ruth's strenuous regime, which gave her headaches, she and Fulton spent the days "dressing & dancing & horseracing and scouring the forests & mountains." If he followed Barlow's advice, Fulton offered Ruth twenty kisses at breakfast and read to her in the bath. They made many friends and, from Barlow's letters, it is apparent that they enjoyed entertaining him with little stories of Ruth's "growing more wicked" and Fulton's "playing the rogue." "Hub" longed to hear more about their wickedness—"can't tell how much it pleases hub." But while praising "toot's attention & goodness & good humor & judgements & talents & genius," he gave vent to the crude humor that apparently flourished among them, inelegantly threatening if he did not "haave better," to "sharpen up knife and tut tok off . . . smack smooth goes im toks."[27]

Fulton soon recovered from his irritation at Livingston's carping. He was uncommonly happy and relaxed. Removed from Barlow's physical presence, if not from his jocular missives, he and Ruth could play as they wished. His lightheartedness is reflected in the charming note he wrote Fulwar Skipwith, the U.S. commercial agent in Paris, on Skipwith's marriage to a very young Belgian girl. The cartoon he drew to accompany the note depicts Skipwith eight months hence supporting a greatly pregnant and bewildered bride:

> Dear Skipwith—
>   Distant from the conjugal joys which environ you, I can only congratulate you on your happy union with an amiable and excellent woman. This I do from my heart; be assured marriage is one of the most important negotiations of a man's life, and when his lot is fortunate, he ought to be one of the most happy of beings. This I hope and indeed have no doubt will be your case, and be your joys ever so great, they will not surpass the pleasure I wish you as I know it will add to your domestic endearments to add to the number of your name. I have this morning consulted the astrologer, and had the pleasure to find your destiny cast in Gemini. Here is the sketch which was only designed for your eyes. You must not show it to Mrs. S. or she will think me imprudent, but you may to Mr. Barlow, because it will make him smile, and it gives me pleasure to add smiles to his moments and yours.[28]

Ruth and Fulton felt so carefree they even considered crossing the border to Switzerland. Although at first Barlow seemed surprised, he gave them a great deal of tourist advice. They did not make that expedition, but they did linger blissfully at Plombières, impervious to Barlow's news that Livingston was "desirous of bringing the thing forward" and that the Wests were in Paris and *désolés* not to see "toot" and that the painter Henry Fuseli, also just arrived from London, was "swearing like a Swiss because he can't see my wife and have a little laugh & fun."[29] It was not until the season at Plombières drew to a close at the end of the summer that Fulton, having sent his dirty linen on ahead, pointed the white ponies toward Paris and, with Ruth beside him in the phaeton, made his way slowly back to Barlow and Livingston.

Un Succès Complet et Brillant

❖

When Fulton and Ruth arrived at 50 rue de Vaugirard in the autumn of 1802, the oppressive summer heat that extended into the first weeks of September had abated, and the evenings were cool. Paris was in a festive mood. It was New Year's according to the Revolutionary calendar, and there were fireworks, illuminations, parades, and pageants.

British tourists filled the city, taking advantage of the Peace of Amiens to taste the long-prohibited pleasures of Paris. The Wests had prolonged their visit to see Fulton, but for some unknown reason he did not attend their large "public breakfast" in honor of France's leading artists and museum officials—at least the sharp-nosed diarist Joseph Farington did not list him among the guests. Both the Barlows were there. "Mrs. Barlow appeared to be a quiet unassuming woman," Farington noted. "I was told she was an American by birth & had a good fortune. . . . The person of Joel Barlow is tall & boney. His countenance ill favoured, but his look thoughtful & shrewd. To reflect & to observe seems to be his habit & is expressed in his appearance. His head is shrunk between his shoulders, and constantly leans to one side; and one of his hands is invariably placed upon his breast, as it were to support his Chin."[1]

Livingston, who had made an excursion to Holland at the end of August, returned to Paris shortly after Fulton, who immediately sent him a new set of figures for a boat to be built in America. More conservative than those sent from Plombières, he expected her to carry sixty passengers and run at only 6 to 8 rather than 12 miles an hour. Including 300 pounds to compensate him for "travelling, attention etc. for one year," the cost would be 1350 pounds—"at least the mind should be extended to that sum," Fulton wrote. "If anything can be economized it will be to the interest of all parties."[2] In lieu of money, Fulton was willing to take 25 percent of the hundred shares, prudently halving what he had asked for in June.

Cheap as it was, Livingston balked at this arrangement. Despite Fulton's repeated assurances of success, his primary concern was to minimize losses. Fulton reduced his sites further, perhaps on Barlow's advice. On October 2, he sent Livingston a second plan, which involved building a boat in England and borrowing a cylinder, boiler, and working parts from Boulton and Watt. Under this plan Fulton cut his time to four or five months or 120 pounds. The risk would not exceed 300 pounds each, even with interest at 12 percent for eighteen months. "To attempt to Economize more than this will be imprudent and cause a loss of time worth infinitely more than the Interest," Fulton pointed out. The "best, quickest and most economic mode of proceeding" was to borrow 500 pounds immediately. "With funds prepared I shall feel myself on a solid foundation," he declared, ". . . which is of no little importance when the mind should be wholly occupied on the combinations and Success of the machine."[3]

This revised strategy did not win Livingston over. To emphasize the strength of his New York State monopoly as opposed to Fulton's precarious patent claims, he may have suggested that Desblancs's patent might invalidate his, for on October 4 Fulton wrote an account of the Desblancs model complete with pen and ink drawings of gear wheels, cylinder, and boat. Desblancs's mechanism was unworkable, he insisted, because "the artist did not know the correct proportions." Fulton was right. When the boat was tried on the Saône River that year, it failed.

On October 10 Livingston, tired of skirmishing and realizing that he might jeopardize his association with Fulton, agreed to a contract that fused the elements of Fulton's previous proposals. The preamble undoubtedly required concessions of pride by both Livingston and Fulton, for it put them on an equal footing as experimenters. Seven well thought out conditions followed. The first three described the boat they would "attempt" to put into useful operation and the preliminary work Fulton must do:

1. A steamboat would be constructed in New York for the purpose of navigating between New York and Albany. The vessel would not exceed 120 feet in length and 8 feet in width, and would draw no more than 15 inches of water. It would run 8 miles an hour in stagnant water and carry at least sixty passengers, allowing 200 pounds weight for each person.
2. Fulton would procure a U.S. patent for "a new Mechanical combination of a boat to navigate by the power of a Steam Engine." Shares in the patent would be divided equally between the partners.
3. Fulton would go immediately to England to build an experimental boat of approximately the same dimensions. The engine would be borrowed from Boulton and Watt. If the boat failed, Livingston would pay losses up to 500 pounds, half of which Fulton would reimburse with interest within two years. Should the experiment succeed, Fulton would be paid his reasonable expenses for supervision.

The next three conditions dealt with disposal of shares and duration of contract:

4. Each partner could sell forty of his fifty shares, but the purchasers would have no voice in the conduct of the business. Operating expenses and the cost of new boats would be paid out of profits. Shareholders would not be called on to make advances.
5. Livingston's and Fulton's partnership would last for fourteen years—the patent term—or for any greater period to which the monopoly was extended in any of the American States.
6. In case either partner died, each heir and assign holding twenty shares would be considered an active partner. Should two partners be thus introduced, the surviving original partner would have two votes to counterbalance them.
7. The last condition permitted Livingston to withdraw from the partnership at any time after they had spent 500 pounds for experiments.

This "memorandum of agreement," by which each partner risked 250 pounds and Fulton stood to lose his time as well, was signed on October 10, 1802, and was witnessed by Livingston's son-in-law Robert L. Livingston.[4]

The new partners went right to work. Livingston delivered 1,000 francs on October 13, another 1,000 on October 14, and a third 1,000 on November 9. By the end of the year he had paid in 8,000 francs. He also asked his brother-in-law Thomas Tillotson, who was a power in New York State politics, to obtain another two-year extension of his monopoly's fulfillment clause. After giving him news of the family and French politics, he wrote:

> I must charge you with a commission that may be of considerable importance to me, yet I fear that you will laugh at me when I mention it, but I give you leave so to do provided you by no means neglect to execute it at this session of the legislature through some of my friends. You know my passion for steamboats and the money I have expended on that subject. I am not yet discouraged—all my old partners have given up the pursuit. I have found a new one in Robert Fulton, a most ingenious young man, the inventor of the diving boat which made so much noise in Europe. We are now actually making experiments on a large scale upon the Seine. Should they succeed it would be mortifying to have any other competitor for the advantages.[5]

Thus Livingston brushed aside his two old partners, although his contract with them was still valid. John Stevens was, in fact, actively pursuing new steamboat designs; the following year he would patent an improved multitubular boiler for a steam engine. Satisfied he had discharged his obligations to the steamboat venture, Livingston was off again on a short trip through Normandy and Brittany. While at L'Orient he visited Aaron Vail, American consul at that port. He may have discussed steam navigation with him during this time, for Vail's daughter had been a legatee of John Fitch and Vail had taken out a French patent in Fitch's name for a steam vessel propelled by paddles in the stern.

Meantime Fulton heard from Boulton and Watt, as he well may have expected, that borrowing an engine was out of the question. Fortunately, Périer was willing to take a risk. Well acquainted with steam engines, he had bought a Watt engine for the Chaillot waterworks in Paris and had built and run the steam flour mill on the Ile des Cygnes. He visited the Boulton and Watt works in Birmingham several times and held a fifteen-year patent of *importation et perfectionnement* for a double-acting rotative engine.

In the mid-1770s Périer had tried building a steamboat of his own, but like Livingston, he was defeated by the engine's racking and weight.

He may have been inspired to attempt a steamboat by Joseph d'Auxiron whose 115-foot boat propelled by steam-driven paddle wheels sank before it could be tried; Périer, who had a reputation for craftiness, was accused of sabotaging it. In 1783 Périer headed the committee appointed by the Academy of Sciences to evaluate a steamboat built by Claude François de Jouffroy d'Abbans. He found it useless, which it was, and when Jouffroy d'Abbans asked him to build a new boat and engine for him, Périer refused. His work on the submarine gave him great confidence in Fulton's mechanical ability, however, and he agreed to build a cylinder and lend or rent it to the partners.

Calla, the model-maker, was engaged to execute the boiler and moving parts of the engine. Fulton took responsibility for providing the hull. Thus, the building of the steamboat was a collaboration of experts with the special advantage that they all could communicate their ideas by means of drawings, and through their prior associations, they were thoroughly familiar with one another's habits.

By the time this work began, Fulton had altered his original strong conclusions and decided that side paddle wheels were a far more effective means of propulsion than endless chains. This was an old idea dating back at least to the sixteenth century. In France they had been used on Jouffroy d'Abbans's ill-fated steamboat as well as on d'Auxiron's. Livingston had rejected side wheels out of hand when Roosevelt suggested them in 1798, but he found Fulton's careful calculations more persuasive and now approved them. Throughout the winter Fulton made further "exact experiments" using his model—this time at Périer's pond on the hill above the foundry. With the crucial exception that he replaced endless chains with paddle wheels, these were an extension of those he made in June.

Fulton also experimented with the shape of the hull. He pointed the bow and the stern so that they made angles of 55 degrees and then measured the reduced resistances and increased velocities this modification produced. As a basis for his calculations he used the results of Beaufoy's Deptford Dock research, finally completed in 1798, and to a lesser extent the studies undertaken in France by the mathematician Charles Bossut, whose current specialty was planetary motion, but whose earlier work on ship resistances was well known. Stanhope had, of course, applied Beaufoy's discoveries to his *Ambinavigator*, but he had never progressed far enough to integrate them with the design of the engine and the propelling mechanism. Fulton did just that. Confident he had discovered the fundamental relationships between engine power, means of propulsion, and hull proportions that would make his boats work when all others had failed, he deposited drawings at the Conservatory of Arts and Trades, "as a prevention," he told Livingston, "to any similar thing being received till our experiment is made and we think it proper to patent it or not."[6]

The drawings show a steamboat propelled by side wheels, each with ten arms terminating in rectangular paddles. The engine and its supporting framework are similar to those described by Fulton in his July 25, 1802, letter to Livingston. It is placed in the middle of the hull, directly on the planking, which is reinforced under the boiler and piston. Unlike Desblancs's engine, which filled the entire hull, Fulton's occupied less than half the interior space. The vertical piston is in the center. Behind it is a rectangular boiler and, in front, the condenser and the driving parts. The hull is flat-bottomed and without a keel. The plan and elevation show it to have a sharply tapered bow and stern and to be steered by a rudder and a tiller. Two more drawings depict the steamboat as a tug drawing four barges. The tug has a pointed bow and a concave stern. Each barge as a rounded bow that fits snugly into the inward curve of the preceding vessel's stern. Thus joined, the train of boats acts as a single unit, theoretically creating the resistance of only one boat and also making for ease in maneuvering. Fulton had begun developing this idea with his canal boats.

In a memorandum that is remarkable for its candor, Fulton explained the rationale behind his invention to the conservatory's three evaluators, one of whom was the doubting Montgolfier. He told them that his first aim in working on the steam boat was to operate it on the long rivers of America where roads suitable for haulage were not practicable, and where, consequently, the expense of steam navigation would be compared with the labor of men rather than of horses as in France. Fulton was, of course, referring to the Mississippi where, at that time, virtually all commercial vessels carried merchandise as their primary function. Irregular banks and the vagaries of the channel made it impossible to employ workhorses for most of its length. Laden boats were slowly and painfully dragged or pulled upriver by men. The development of transportation in the western territories, also an important aspect of his canal planning, was a farsighted but reasonable goal. The expansion of Western civilization across the North American continent was exciting to Europeans as well as to Americans. Still, it is astonishing that Fulton made no mention whatever of establishing steamboats on the Hudson River which, after all, was the objective of his contract with Livingston.

The paragraphs of the most far-reaching consequence in this document, however, were those in which Fulton stated categorically—and accurately—that waterwheels were not a new application. Later, to his near ruin, he would try to prove that he was the first inventor to have thought of them. "In these plans you will find nothing new since they are only waterwheels, a means which has often been tried but always abandoned because it was believed they gave disadvantageous purchase on the water," he explained. "But after the experiments I have already made, I am convinced that the fault has not been in the wheel but in ignorance of proportions, speeds, powers, and probably mechanical combinations . . . consequently, although the wheels are not a new application, if I combine them in such a way that a good half of the power of the engine acts to propel the boat as it would if the purchase were against solid ground, the combinations will be infinitely better than anything that has been attempted up to the present and is in fact a new discovery."[7]

With Calla and Périer as co-workers, the Paris steamboat proceeded with gratifying speed. To placate Livingston, who was always attempting to cut costs, they tried a wooden boiler. It was, of course, unusable. Fulton and Calla went on to build an internally fired flash-type boiler capable of 450 pounds pressure per square inch. There was as yet no metal that would bear the enormous strain, however, and the boiler disintegrated when it was first tried. Their second metal boiler—7 feet long, 5 feet wide, and 5 feet high, low pressure and externally fired—functioned well. It is said to have been based on the crude designs for which Barlow received a patent in 1793 and to have contained no less than 130 tubes through which the water passed and was heated to steam by the flames burning around them. The attraction of such a boiler was that, because so much water-bearing surface was exposed to the fire, much less water and fuel were needed to produce a given quantity of steam. For the power produced, it was light and efficient. However, even for a metal-working genius like Calla, such a boiler would have been an extraordinary engineering breakthrough. Since no similar boiler was made or used in France prior to this one attributed to Fulton, and none was built until many years later, the actual boiler was probably less complex.

The cylinder, made by Périer, is believed to have been 450 millimeters in diameter and capable of yielding 8 horsepower. The other working parts were probably very close to those shown in the drawings Fulton submitted to the conservatory. Unfortunately no plans or detailed descriptions of the Paris boat exist.

When the machinery was finished, sometime during May, it was placed in the hull Fulton had constructed. It was 56½ feet long and just over 10½ feet wide, far less slim than the 120- by 8-foot passenger boat Fulton had projected the previous year and with even chunkier proportions than his model. Tied up at the quay next to the Chaillot waterworks, as the submarine had been, it lay in full view of Parisian curiosity-seekers who were vastly entertained by its bizarre appearance. It looked like a floating furnace with two great Catherine wheels attached to the sides, a vehicle more appropriate for a fireworks display than for carrying flesh-and-blood passengers and valuable cargo.

The bargemen were not so amused. The perceptive ones were afraid of the competition. It may well have been at their instigation that, just before the first trials were to begin, the boat was damaged and sunk, for the journals of the day reported the disaster as the work of malefactors. A later story—that the hull was not strong enough to support the machinery in a heavy storm—seems unlikely, as Fulton had built the hull to withstand the pounding of the piston which, except in extraordinary circumstances, would have been far more traumatic than thunder, lightning, rain, and waves. It is entirely believable, however, that Fulton was roused from his bed with the bad tidings in the black of night and labored for over twenty-four hours without food or rest to retrieve the machinery.

Whatever the causes, the disaster did not hold Fulton back. He did save the machinery and soon had it installed in a new hull, built at his own expense, probably with money Barlow gave him for an interest in the venture. This one was 74½ feet long and just over 8 feet wide, considerably longer and narrower than the one it replaced. By the end of July it was ready to be demonstrated. The sweet, witty letter Fulton wrote to Fulwar Skipwith on July 24 inviting him and his ladies to a private exhibition conveys the trepidation and the elation he felt in anticipation of this event.

Robert Fulton

My dear friend,

You have experienced all the anxiety of a fond father on a child's coming into the world. So have I. The little cherub, now plump as a partridge, advances to the perfection of her nature and each day presents some new charm. I wish mine may do the same. Some weeks hence, when you will be sitting in one corner of the room and Mrs. Skipwith in the other, learning the little creature to walk, the first unsteady step will scarcely balance the tottering frame; but you will have the pleasing perspective of seeing it grow to a steady walk and then to dancing. I wish mine may do the same. My boy, who is all bones and corners just like his daddy, and whose birth has given me much uneasiness, or rather anxiety,—is just learning to walk and I hope in time he will be an active runner. I therefore have the honour to invite you and the ladies to see his first movements on Monday next from 6 till 9 in the evening between the Barrière des Bons Hommes and the steam engine. May our children, my friend, be an honour to their country and a comfort to the grey hairs of their doting parents.[8]

This demonstration was held either the next day—which seems unlikely, for even if the invitation were hand-delivered it would have arrived at the last minute—or the following Monday, August 1. The results must have shored up Fulton's confidence, for he asked the National Institute to send a delegation to examine and evaluate the boat at the public demonstration to be held on Tuesday, August 9. Like the private demonstration, it would take place at six in the evening between the Barrière des Bons Hommes, opposite the Ile des Cygnes, and the Chaillot waterworks, a distance of about a mile.

It is hoped that August 9 was a fine day and that the luminous late afternoon sun shimmered on the swiftly flowing Seine and the gilded dome of the Invalides. All the *beau monde* of Paris assembled, together with much of the riffraff. Many of them certainly recalled the submarine demonstration held just upstream over three years earlier and hoped for another good show—possibly climaxed by an explosion and a drowning.

Neither the smoke billowing from the chimney of the boiler nor the rhythmical thump of the piston would have surprised the spectators, for the steam engine at the Chaillot waterworks and the steam-powered flour mill on the Ile des Cygnes had long been tourist attractions. What was astonishing were the great side wheels scooping the water and surely pushing the boat with two tow boats behind it against the current without aid of sail, man, or horse. This, the crowd sensed, was not an ephemeral amusement, but a lasting phenomenon that would perhaps change their lives.

Fulton tended the engine himself, his lean, taut, six-foot frame standing well above his three helpers. Towing two boats behind, he guided the steamboat—she was given no name—upstream between the Barrière and the waterworks at an estimated speed of about 2$\frac{9}{10}$ miles an hour. Downstream she went more than twice as fast, or so an energetic journalist who raced along the quay testified. Her average speed, he guessed, was about 4½ miles an hour. To demonstrate maneuverability, Fulton turned the train of boats to the port and to the starboard, then came to anchor and started up again.

In the towed boats Fulton gave rides to the savants and government officials who came to enjoy themselves as well as to inspect his creation. Among them were the imperially slim Lazare Carnot, a staunch republican popularly called "l'Organisateur de la Victoire" for his work in administering France's armies in 1793, but also renowned as a geometrician; Louis de Bougainville, a sprightly seventy-four-year-old *bon vivant* who had navigated the globe in his youth and secured his place in posterity by giving his name to that prolific tropical plant, the bougainvillea; Gaspard Prony, the bridge engineer who served on one of Fulton's submarine committees and had just published a monograph on how to determine the quantity of water needed for navigable canals; Charles Bossut, whose ship design theories Fulton has used in his experiments and who long before had examined Jouffroy d'Abbans's steamboat; Auguste Charles Périer, Fulton's collaborator's brother and partner, or perhaps Périer himself (the records do not give the first name); and the ubiquitous Constantin Volney.

Fulton traversed the river four times. Then, for a grand finale, he proceeded upstream toward the Pont de la Concorde, past the swimming school and the public baths, causing rocking waves, which thrilled the patrons who had secured an excellent view of the exhibition from the promenade decks of the bathhouse. The steamboat operated, as the *Nautilus* had, without a breakdown or even a need for serious adjustment throughout its first public display.

The event was *"un succès complet et brillant,"* reported the official newspaper, the *Journal des Debats*, on August 11, 1803. Capable of bringing tows and barges from Nantes to Paris in ten to fifteen days instead of the four months then required, the "celebrated American's" invention would have "important consequences for the commerce and internal navigation of France."

Only one disappointment tarnished the occasion for Fulton. Neither Livingston nor Barlow was in Paris to witness his triumph. Livingston was in Lyons on his way to Geneva. The temperature in Paris, he complained in a letter to his sister, had been over 90 degrees for more than a week. It was as hot as New York, and, as he thought it unhealthy, he had taken his family for a little vacation "to breathe fresh air from the Lake and the Alps and pay a visit for our more effectual cooling to the Glaciers."[9] Since they left the afternoon of August 1, it is entirely possible he did not even witness the private demonstration. Perhaps he thought it beneath his dignity as the U.S. minister plenipotentiary to be connected with a commercial venture. More probably he was overcome by his fear the experiment would fail and preferred to hide his association with it. Even when casting about for news from Paris to send his sister he did not mention the steamboat, but confined himself to describing the physical beauties of the city and the guests who danced on the lawn of his residence until four o'clock in the morning at his July 4 celebration. Apparently, he did not even confide to his old friend Lafayette that he was Fulton's partner in a Hudson River venture, for shortly after the demonstration, Lafayette mentioned the steamboat only as an afterthought: "I have been very happy to hear of the successful Experiment of our friend Fulton," he wrote, "and its boat which come in so *a propos* for the Navigation of the Mississippi."[10]

It may well have been, in some measure, a relief to Fulton not to have Livingston on hand to interfere with the demonstration or to share in its immediate success, but Barlow's truancy during both the trials was painful to him. Barlow had been in England since March "striving to hold with fingers frail, the eel of fortune by the tail."[11] Partly, that may have had to do with establishing a claim on a captured ship called the *Neptune* from which Fulton would eventually get a 2,000-pound share. In the few letters preserved from this separation, Barlow mentioned the steamboat only briefly and without strong interest. Fulton may have complained of his indifference, for in late July Barlow wrote Ruth he had got "toot's" letters of July 18 and 20, "which cut me to the soul."[12]

There is no question that Fulton's partnership with Livingston intruded on his relationship with Barlow and that Barlow resented Livingston for providing Fulton with the real support in terms of experience, influence, ideas, and money that was beyond his capacity to give.

Un Succès Complet et Brillant

That Livingston, as a star in the diplomatic world, far outshown Barlow made him an even more bitter rival. Barlow's only means of combating Livingston was by deliberately ignoring the steamboat—the center of Livingston's sphere of influence with Fulton—as decisively as he could.

Although Ruth almost certainly attended the demonstration as one of Fulton's honored guests, her reaction to his *succès complet et brillant* and its implications for their continuing intimacy remains a mystery for lack of documents. Barlow's letters suggest that she was quite ill throughout this period. But he so enjoyed her frailties and she found them so useful that it is difficult to tell what the state of her health really was. Subsequent events, however, make it probable that Fulton's growing interdependence with Livingston brought him closer to Ruth. For Fulton, Ruth's love was less consuming and more rewarding than Barlow's. It was safer. Fulton may even have felt more tender toward Ruth because loving her would serve as a partial expiation for not fulfilling Barlow's personal expectations of him. This subtle recasting of their holy trinity placed Ruth in the role of mediator, a part she had long played but that they had chosen not to emphasize.

In retrospect, Fulton's brusque letters to Livingston and his long stay at Plombières, when he gave Barlow the power to act for him in crucial matters, seem evidence of Fulton's strong resistance to a close association with Livingston that could only wound Barlow. Fulton must have known at least subconsciously that if he was to survive as a creative person he could not allow Livingston to dominate him as Barlow tried to do; he would have to prevail over both these father-providers. Thus, the interlude at the spa was more than a cozy vacation with Ruth. It was also a moratorium during which he could prepare and, indeed, harden himself to the fact that he must stop seeking refuge in the ministrations of a surrogate parent. With Ruth to help him, he used Plombières to avoid Barlow as well as Livingston. Unfortunately, Fulton was never able to resolve his emotional dependence on the Barlows and, to a lesser extent, on Livingston. The tension created by his divided loyalty to each of them persisted as an undercurrent that never ceased to disturb him.

It was probably about this time that Fulton painted the most forceful, and the most disturbing, of his many self-portraits. His pale face contrasts sharply with the brilliant turquois Parisian sky and the more muted Hôtel des Invalides and Seine River on which there is a steamboat. The two halves of his face do not match. The right side is more open, the expression at once benign, aloof, and frightened. The left side is compressed, its expression controlled and crafty. The distortions are deliberate. It is a portrait of the inner man.

The reaction of the French government was another thorn in Fulton's flesh. Although the *Journal des Debats* article was reprinted in the influential *Recueil polytechnique des Ponts et Chausées*, the savants made no formal report because no committee was officially appointed to do so. At that time Bonaparte, who controlled the institute's every action, was uninterested in domestic improvements that did not also have a military application. With the breakdown of the fragile Peace of Amiens in May, the invasion of England had become his obsession. Had the steamboat been seaworthy, and therefore capable of transporting troops across the Channel, Bonaparte undoubtedly would have supported it. Instead he chose to ridicule Fulton's achievement. "There are in every European capital a crowd of adventurers and projectors who run about the world offering heads of government discoveries which exist only in their imaginations," Bonaparte is said to have proclaimed. "They are either charlatans or impostors who have no other goal than to grab money. This American is one of that number. Do not speak to me about him again."[13] Later, Charles de Villette wrote that after Fulton left the first consul he went to Charles's mother's house and wept in despair because Bonaparte, to whom he had offered his steamboats, did not understand the magnitude of his invention.

Nevertheless, Fulton could not have been entirely surprised by this reaction. Several days before the demonstration, he had ordered from Boulton and Watt a 24-horsepower double-acting engine with piston, rods, and air pumps made to his own specifications. Fulton assured the company he would be able to obtain the necessary export permit through the good offices of the new American minister, James Monroe—another of Barlow's friends—and he gave instructions that it be delivered to New York City in care of Henry Brockholst Livingston, Robert R. Livingston's cousin.

Because the war had made direct communication between France and England unreliable, Fulton sent duplicate copies via Frankfurt and Rotterdam. Boulton and Watt received the order, but not the export permit, and in October the company notified Fulton they could not make his engine. Fulton wrote two urgent letters to Monroe begging for help. Candid about the poor reputation his submarine assaults against the British fleet had earned, he brashly wrote: "It will be well to ask permission for yourself without mentioning my name as I have reason to believe the

Government will not be much disposed to favor any wish of mine."[14] Monroe did not deign to answer.

Livingston, who should have undertaken this task, was of no assistance at all. He was waging a disagreeable letter and word-of-mouth campaign against Monroe who, he believed, was trying to steal credit for the Louisiana Purchase. Monroe had arrived in Paris on the eve of the signing with more power and newer instructions than Livingston had, and Livingston was tormented with the notion that posterity would judge that he had not done his job properly and would attribute this, the "noblest work" of his life, to Monroe. Livingston's self-esteem was so threatened that he endeavored to alter the date on an official document to make it appear that he had concluded the agreement before Monroe reached Paris. Obviously, Livingston could not ask Monroe to do him a favor.

Once again at loose ends, Fulton took the opportunity to visit friends in Holland, which was then a satellite of France called the Batavian Republic. From Amsterdam he jovially wrote Parker: "After much twisting over roads which disgrace nations called civilized from Antwerp to Rotterdam, I have arrived by land and water to this famous city where many a canal bears on its sable bosom the ponderous merchandize—dats vat saves de pavements myneheer."[15]

Fulton revisited Holland briefly in December, but was back in Paris in time to spend Christmas with the Barlows. Infinitely weary of France, they were again making preparations to leave for the United States. As a parting gesture, Fulton and Barlow commissioned Jean Antoine Houdon, justly famous for his ability to penetrate the psychological essence of his subjects, to sculpt their busts. The portrait of Fulton is an arresting sculpture, not because Fulton was still superlatively handsome at thirty-nine but because of the presence it captures: heroic, elegant, willful, sensitive, yearning, and virile. In contrast to Fulton's self-portrait, Houdon's bust is of a man in full possession of his genius. The Barlow bust is, in comparison, utterly lacking in grace. Houdon shows him to be fleshy with age and sedentary habits. His face is self-consciously frozen in a truculent mask.

About this time Vanderlyn painted a large oil of Livingston. His prominent and shapely nose, massive but undershot chin, and steady gaze are softened and made enormously attractive by the amused expression of his wide mouth. He seems to be recalling an entertaining incident in which he displayed his talents to particular advantage. It is a beguiling portrait, but its great strength is that no one viewing it would care to see those same features set in anger.

In early April 1804, Fulton let it be known he must leave for England to supervise the building of the steam engine so that he could begin the American operation as soon as possible. Somehow he persuaded Livingston to importune Monroe to use his influence to obtain the export license. Surprisingly, Livingston characterized the engine as for use on the Mississippi, "an important national objective."[16] Perhaps he believed Monroe would be more likely to use his influence for a project that might benefit the entire country than for a Hudson River monopoly that would primarily benefit Livingston.

On April 27, Fulton settled financial accounts with Barlow, who still had much business to finish in Paris before departing for America. Barlow's memoranda book contains such items as : "lent Mr. Fulton for Perrier 500f 28 therm. 7 yr.; I owe Fulton 40 plus 7, pd in full; . . . paid towards the patent of perfectionnment Panorama 812 fr.; To Fulton for Thayer 1000; . . . ditto 500 Oct. 2, 120 for stockings." It would seem that Barlow acted as a banker for Fulton, making long-term loans, collecting the percentage of the Panorama receipts due from Thayer and the profits from the speculations he helped Fulton with, and dispensing cash or notes as Fulton needed them. Surprisingly, despite Barlow's continuous disbursements, Fulton ended well in advance. The account for these years concludes: "the above settled & acct rendered the 27 April 1804 by which I owe Fulton £1926.12."[17]

On April 29, Fulton departed for London. With him he carried a letter from Livingston to his brother Edward in New York, full of details about his mission in France and ending with a hasty and somewhat bland introduction of Fulton, which Fulton would have been astonished to learn made no mention whatever of the steamboat. "This will be delivered to you by Mr. Fulton," Livingston wrote, "a very estimable young gentleman and very distinguished for his treatis on canals & his diving boat & you will find him a man of science in every line, particularly in mathematics & in the fine arts. I recommend him to your particular attention."[18] Livingston also wrote his brother-in-law John Stevens. Without even an allusion to the contract they signed in 1800, he described Fulton as his "partner in an experiment made here on the steamboat" and, not actually breaking his connection with Stevens but warning him of potential conflicts, informed him his object was "to build one in the United States by way of experiment."[19]

Fulton also carried letters from Barlow to be delivered to President Jefferson. Fulton, it seems, had not been candid with either of his friends. He had no intention of returning to the United States soon, for he had private business in England that would keep him occupied for several months at least. As it turned out, it held him there for the next three and a half years.

Alias Robert Francis

❖

Robert Fulton arrived in London on May 15, 1804. His object was not to find a vessel that would take him and his steam engine to New York, but to sell his submarine inventions to the British government. Sometime in 1803 he had been approached by an agent of the secret service, whom he later identified only as an American named Smith. At a meeting in Paris, Smith told Fulton that the British were considering using his devices against the French and would pay him well for his plans. Fulton did not hesitate. The price he demanded for leaving France for England was 10,000 pounds, with 10,000 pounds more to build a submarine, if "occular proof" should be required.

Smith returned to England with these terms, promising to meet Fulton in Amsterdam with the government's answer. Undoubtedly this was the primary purpose of Fulton's trips to Holland the previous fall. The rendezvous did not take place either in October or December, allegedly because "adverse winds" prevented Smith from landing. It was not until March 1804 that Smith was able to reenter Paris to resume negotiations. He had been provided with 800 pounds "for expenses," but otherwise carried only a letter from Lord Hawkesbury, the minister of foreign affairs, offering "utmost liberality and Generosity" should Fulton agree to cross over. Fulton accepted.[1]

Since he first chased their ships with his *Nautilus* in 1800, the British had kept themselves apprised of Fulton's submarine activities. They knew about the explosion at Brest and his plan to mine the Channel ports and the Thames. Twice Stanhope had warned the House of Lords about the danger of Fulton's boat and bombs, once again making himself the butt of Gillray's satire. Perhaps because he was accused of being in league with Fulton, he told the peers, without any basis in fact, that Fulton had been forced to reveal his celebrated project to the French in order to save his life. Although highly placed authorities were undoubtedly aware that Fulton had not overtly worked on his system since the fall of 1801, they were alarmed by the potential of submarine warfare. The Admiralty Office issued a secret memorandum enjoining the Channel Fleet to take whatever measures it could to prevent France from deploying Fulton's bombs.

When, in the spring of 1803, the British were driven by Napoleon's duplicity to resume hostilities, what had been a maritime war for Britain threatened to become a land war. For the first time invasion was imminent. Throughout the long summer, from the villages along the coast, the British could see the campfires of the French army massing at Boulogne. Whipped to a fervor by the Emperor Napoleon, who boasted that if the French could master the Channel for six hours, he could conquer the world, the array awaited only the completion of the transport flotilla. By February 1804, 320 warships and 347 transport ships were ready; in late April, there were 390 warships and 914 transports together with fishing boats commandeered from Holland.

The extravagant cartoons these preparations inspired in the British press were vastly entertaining, but the sober reality was that Boulogne lay just over 20 miles southeast of Dover. England had as yet no allies, and Napoleon's Grand Army was the most skillful and experienced fighting force in Europe. With tension mounting, the prime minister and cabinet could no longer allow Fulton to remain in the employ of the enemy. In the face of opposition by most naval officers who disdained submarine warfare as cowardly, they determined to woo him to their side and to use his weapons in an offensive attack against the French navy as well as in defense of their shores.

That Fulton should defect to the British, whose infamous fleet he had promised the French he would annihilate, was in large part an unpleasant example of the maxim that every man has his price. Fulton's price was the British foreign minister's promise of "generosity." Regarding his inventions as "rich gems drawn from the mines of science," which he had a right to convert to his own advantage, Fulton went to England to make a fortune. He thought he was entitled to it. At the same time, Fulton was avid for fame. Clinging to the belief that his submarine system was capable of eliminating first war at sea and then all war forever, he expected this assignment to give him an opportunity to win worldwide acclaim.

To justify Fulton's changing sides, it might be argued that Napoleon's recent assumption of dictatorial power and imperial trappings made Fulton realize that democracy in France was dying. That is only marginally true. Like so many others, Fulton never entirely lost his fascination either for Bonaparte or for French republicanism. In essence, Fulton's motivation was personal. Rankled by what he considered France's "outrageous" behavior toward him, he eagerly embraced whatever patronage might help him develop his system of submarine warfare.

As when he contracted with the French, Fulton chose to believe the submarine would ultimately benefit America, that once the invention was recognized as effective, the natural result would be peace and free trade. He deceived himself. At that time, England was, in fact, an enemy of the United States. To enforce its control of trade with the West Indies and with the Continent, England had stepped up its restrictions on American shipping. Free trade was against its interest, for England was on the brink of realizing its centuries old ambition of dominating the seas.

Fulton's move into the British camp did not prove as simple or as rewarding as he so sanguinely expected. The next three and a half years constituted a rancid episode in his life. He would lay the foundation of the fortune that he so desired, but he would pay for it with his integrity.

Just before Fulton left France, the Addington government in England—with which he had made his initial arrangements—fell because of its ineptitude in pursuing the war against France. This might have made for complications, but the more able and steadfast William Pitt agreed to become prime minister again and, in the political merry-go-round that followed, he made Lord Hawkesbury the head of the Home Office. As a secret service operation, the submarine project fell under his jurisdiction. It was Hawkesbury who opened the next round of negotiations with a request for a written proposal on May 19.

Fulton had his terms ready. For revealing all the combinations and movements of the submarine vessel and bombs and for explaining his strategies of attack, he demanded 200 pounds a month for as long as it would take to implement his system. For personally directing an attack from aboard a ship of war, he demanded one-fourth the value of each vessel burned or destroyed. In addition, he required one good mechanic to execute the machinery, 40 tons of powder, and a naval officer to choose and command one hundred hardy seamen who were good swimmers. The cost of the expedition would be about 7,000 pounds, not including the explosives. With his proposal he sent a full set of carefully made drawings showing his latest improvements to the submarine boat and bombs as well as a brief description of the principles governing them— a proud and compulsive gesture, since he was revealing far more than necessary. Fulton signed the proposal "Robert Francis," the alias he would use in all his dealings with the government. This must have been at the behest of the British secret service, for Fulton so identified with his inventions that he detested using a pseudonym. Except for record-keeping purposes it was meaningless. Fulton was living at the popular Storey's Gate Coffee House, near the Admiralty, and he constantly saw many of his English friends. His submarine investigations had long reached the level of common gossip.

Eager to launch his first expedition during the calmer summer season, Fulton requested that a commission "composed of at least two able mechanicians and one Chymest" be formed at once to evaluate his plan.[2] Two slow weeks went by without response, and on June 6 Fulton wrote the prime minister asking for twenty minutes so that he might "trace over the political consequences" of his system.[3] Pitt did not reply. Fulton persisted, suggesting that the government appoint his friends Lord Stanhope and Edmund Cartwright to the commission, along with Sir John Sinclair, the president of the Board of Agriculture who had shown an interest in his canal system, and a Bishop Watson. This was no more effective in eliciting a response, and for the next fortnight Fulton had nothing better to do than write and rewrite some "Last and most perfect notes on the submarine."

Incensed that his treatment by the British was turning out to be no more than a dismal repetition of his experience with the French, Fulton fired off a peremptory letter to Hawkesbury's secretary.

> [H]aving been here 5 weeks in some degree like a prisoner, and at present as much in the dark as on the day of my arrival such a state of Suspence begins to grow extremely unpleasant. . . . The flattering and I believe candid promises of the late ministry induced me to come to this country and as yet I do not repent it,

Robert Fulton

but beg to be informed if the present ministry means to act up to the spirit of Lord Hawkesburies letter to me or what do they desire of me? . . . you will have the goodness to give me their ultimatum when I shall have the honor to see you on tuesday."[4]

Considering the recent upheaval in the government, such impatience was politically naive. It was, however, rewarded. Shortly afterward, a first-class reviewing commission was appointed. It comprised Sir Joseph Banks, the president of the Royal Society; Henry Cavendish, a distinguished chemist and physicist; Sir Home Popham, who developed the code of flag signals that would revolutionize British naval strategy; William Congreve, who was perfecting the rocket that would achieve lasting fame during the British assault on Baltimore harbor in 1812; and John Rennie, an irascible engineer experienced in port construction with whom Fulton had become professionally acquainted during his canal days.

The commission met without delay, but unlike its French counterpart, did not invite Fulton to present his invention in person. The members simply examined a packet of sealed papers and drawings from Robert Francis and on that basis alone recommended that the use of submarine bombs be further investigated and that the submarine vessel be abandoned. They gave no reasons for their decision, but they probably thought, as Fulton had at Brest, that the bombs could be delivered more cheaply and equally effectively by specially made small boats. Moreover, the odium of stealth would be at least partially removed if the submarine boat was excluded from the system.

Fulton was furious. Petulantly asserting that the commissioners disapproved of the *Nautilus* because they did not know the plans were those of the celebrated Robert Fulton, "therby leaving the government as much uninformed of the truth and probable consequences of Submarine navigation as though I had never arrived," he asked permission to meet Popham, Cavendish, and Congreve privately to explain the risk of adopting only a part of the system.[5] Pitt quietly sent word that he would offend Sir Joseph Banks and John Rennie if he did so.

The government took the committee's report under consideration, but still was not ready to accept even its limited recommendation. Perhaps to pacify Fulton, it granted him a permit to build a steam engine. During the first week in July he hurried off to Birmingham to confer with Boulton and Watt about its design and cost. The company's estimate came to 380 pounds for a common engine, and Fulton, with Livingston's money in hand and high hopes of rewards from his submarine, cheerfully guaranteed whatever extra would be needed to modify it for a steam vessel. To save the company from the difficulties of shipping to America, which required a special export permit, he offered to take delivery at their shops and arrange transportation himself.

Relieved to work on a project over which he had some measure of control, Fulton returned to London and made a new set of steam engine drawings incorporating several improvements that aimed "to keep everything trim and unencumbered."[6] He relocated the air pump between the floor timbers and squared the bottom of the cylinder so it could rest on the condensing vat. To connect the cylinder with the paddle wheels, he devised a bell-crank lever, a solution he ultimately developed into the bell-crank engine. Concerned that salt water would corrode his machinery, he ordered the air valve to be made of brass instead of iron, although it raised the price by more than a third, and he inquired about having the boiler made of copper.

Meanwhile, despite Fulton's angry presentiment that the submarine project would miscarry, the government was giving it priority attention. Pitt, who had both a strong visionary streak and a love of economy, became a strong supporter and—in a very fast action under the circumstances—instructed Sir Home Popham to work out a formal agreement with Fulton. Although no provision was made for building a submarine boat, the terms they finally arrived at were far more liberal than those Fulton had first proposed. He would be paid 200 pounds a month and expenses for superintending the execution of his plan. When, by blowing up a decked vessel, he demonstrated that his system was capable of destroying the enemy's fleet, he would be paid 40,000 pounds and thereafter one-half the value of all vessels destroyed, as long as he supervised the operation. If either he or the government desired to terminate his participation, he would thereafter receive a quarter of the value of vessels destroyed by his bombs for a period of fourteen years.

Suspicious that the government's real motive in buying his weapons was not to use them but to control and bury them, Fulton insisted that an arbitration clause be inserted that would protect him if the government decided for any reason to abandon the project. Two commissioners would be appointed by each party to examine his principles and try such experiments as they deemed proper. If the majority decided Fulton's plan was more effective than any then in practice, the government would pay him 40,000 pounds as a compensation for demonstrating the principles and revealing his plans.

In addition, Fulton bound himself to retrieve the submarine drawings he had deposited with a friend in Paris—probably either Barlow or Parker—and promised not to divulge any part of them to anyone for fourteen years.

In contrast to his French proposal, this contract contained no demand for commissions in the navy or reprisals against the enemy should he be captured. Politics and tradition would have made such a request even more unwelcome to the English than it was to the French. There was not even a weak clause discouraging Britain's use of submarine warfare against America. Since the United States possessed only a skeleton navy, this contract was tantamount to placing his country in Britain's thrall for at least fourteen years. If his system of submarine warfare developed as he dreamed, the British could use it not only to destroy America's shipping industry, but also to prostrate every city, town, and hamlet situated near navigable water. Fulton could no longer delude himself that his actions contained any element of patriotism.

On July 20, 1804, Fulton breakfasted with Pitt and Sir Home Popham at the prime minister's country house to present the agreement. Pitt told Fulton his system of submarine warfare was "an extraordinary invention which seemed to go to the destruction of all fleets." Gratified, Fulton replied that he had invented it with that view and added that submarine warfare would lead to the total annihilation of the existing system of naval war, including Britain's. Pitt disagreed. In its present state, he replied, "those who command the seas will be benefited by it while the minor maritime powers can draw no advantage from what is now known." Fulton saw fit to concede that, unless the submarine boat was used, that position was perhaps correct.[7]

Without further observation, Pitt signed the contract and asked Sir Home Popham to get the signature of Lord Melville, first lord of the Admiralty, who had been expected but had not arrived. Fulton promised to launch a submarine bomb attack on the French fleet at Boulogne as soon as the engines could be constructed and to meet Pitt at his house the following week to report on his progress.

Fulton's salary of 200 pounds a month started immediately. It made him a rich man. He went immediately to work with Sir Home Popham who was to supervise the project. A schemer and maverick adventurer, Popham had no position in either the government or the navy. His major current preoccupation was a protracted lawsuit in which the East India Company alleged he had infringed its monopoly by dealing in con-

Alias Robert Francis

traband in their waters. That event had cost him his captain's rating, but subsequently he became the Duke of York's protégé and served in Flanders as his superintendent of navigation. The duke's protection as well as the invaluable service Popham had rendered the navy with his "Marine Vocabulary"—though jealous detractors said it was a mere adaptation rather than an original creation—provided entrée into high-level marine circles. Considered one of the most scientific seamen of his day, he and Fulton had enough in common, at least at the start, to make their collaboration productive.

The "torpedoes" devised by Fulton and Sir Popham were oblong boxes lined with lead, covered with canvas and tar, and painted sea colors for camouflage. To increase their destructive power, the boxes were laden with tightly packed stones as well as with barrels of gunpowder. The detonating mechanism was a clockwork lock that could be set at varying times from ten minutes to six hours and was activated by the removal of a pin. Called carcasses, coffers, smacks, hogsheads, and occasionally torpedoes, the larger ones, weighing up to 2 tons, were designed to be towed into the midst of the enemy fleet by catamarans or plungers—rowboats made of two pieces of timber 9 feet long and slung so low in the water that they were virtually invisible on a moonlit night. The rower, clad in black waistcoat, trousers, guernsey sweater, and cap, sat on a crossbar and, when approaching the enemy, could lower himself so as to be almost flush with the water—a cold, wet, and dangerous maneuver. Small bombs could be carried in cutters and lifted overboard by one man. The bombs, with contact or time-lock detonators, would be awash on the tide until they came in contact with an enemy hull.

These devices were built at the Portmouth Navy Yard under Fulton's and Popham's joint supervision. They had difficulty finding competent workmen because of the novelty of these bombs, but on September 15 Popham was able to report that "the New Curiosities" would be finished the following week and preparations for the attack could begin.

Fulton moved to the naval installation at New Romney near Dover "to load, balance and arrange" the five large and five small coffers and ten hogsheads that would be used in the attack. On September 20, Admiral Keith, who was in charge of the operation, asked Fulton to come aboard his ship, which was cruising off Boulogne. Though flattered, Fulton put him off until September 23; he was still instructing the volunteer sailors whose taxing mission was to row amid the enemy ships, set and launch the bombs, and retreat if they could, with only the darkness of night to protect them, and a few boats nearby for picking up the wounded. Fulton's proposed schedule was to conduct a rehearsal on the night of September 24 and to attack the next night.

Foul weather intervened. The French ships retreated from the fog of the Channel to Boulogne's protected inner harbor. After a long week of waiting, the weather changed and on October 2, Lord Keith, having counted 150 vulnerable French ships, gave orders to commence the attack that night. First Lord of the Admiralty Melville went aboard Keith's ship. Popham joined them, but Fulton felt obliged to stay behind at New Romney to attend to last minute details. Pitt was able to watch the expedition's sortie from the comfort of Walmer Castle, his residence at nearby Deal.

The attack began at a quarter after nine. The night was unusually clear. An officer in charge of a crew raised from the H.M.S. *Leopard*, described the operation immediately afterward to Lord Keith:

> Sir, I proceeded with two casks in the *Leopard*'s long cutter, one in the bow, the other in the stern sheets; stood in shore and made the round battery to the southward. I dropped down until I could plainly see the flotilla, and driving directly for them by the tide, at the distance of about half a cable, I took the pin out of the machine on the aftermost cask. William Bailey, boatswain, laid hold of it after it was out. I put my ear to the machinery and heard it going, then ordered it to be thrown overboard and told Mr. Gilbert, Mid. with Wm. Rogers (whom I had stationed forward) to take the pin out of the cask in the bow. They answered it was out. I then ordered the cask to be thrown overboard. Mr. Gilbert reported to me that he heard the machinery going. I think they must have heard the splashing of the casks from the shore, as they commenced firing musketry immediately, the balls coming over the boats. This was the first firing that took place.[8]

The action lasted until four o'clock the next morning when a gale drove the squadron to the shelter of the Downs. All who witnessed the attack were certain the French were taken by surprise and that a number of carcasses had exploded. There was no consensus, however, as to how much damage had been done. Lord Melville, with whom Fulton dined at Walmer Castle the following evening, had nothing but hearty priase for the expedition. Keith conceded that the assault had caused considerable confusion, but was disappointed that, because the French vessels lay at great distances from one another, the injury inflicted was minimal. Nevertheless, he believed that a more extended effort might succeed. Popham confessed he was too exhausted to do more than count heads in a most cursory manner because he had been without sleep for two nights running and because, as a civilian, he had little familiarity with the fleet.

Fulton's sole existing account is extraordinarily subdued. To Elizabeth West, his "dear petite maman," he wrote, "In the gloom of Thursday night my first attack was made on 130 gunboats in the outer harbour of Boulogne, 25 disappeared. My opinion is that very few were destroyed and the others made their escape. . . . The secret may now be said to be blown."[9]

In subsequent weeks, a strong cadre of naval officers made their objections public. Some were afraid submarine warfare would deprive them of the bounties they expected from prisoners and prizes, others considered it cowardly, little different from the midnight attack of a burglar who robbed his sleeping victim of money and life.

Anti-government journalists were quick to pick up the dissension, but William Cobbett delighted detractors with a satirical little ballad that ended:

> Your project new? Jack Mutters
> Avast! 'tis very stale:
> 'Tis catching birds, landlubbers!
> By salt upon the tail.[10]

The violence of partisan opposition did not sway Pitt and Melville from their decision to adopt submarine warfare. They informed Keith he would be provided immediately with whatever he needed for a second expedition. Ambitious to be reinstated in the navy, Popham again offered his services. He was refused a commission, but as a compromise was given a ship for his own use. Although it put him in an awkward position—he was still outside the hierarchy and unable to subject his subordinates to binding orders—he returned to the project as a civilian volunteer.

Fulton found himself in an even worse situation. What meager close association he had enjoyed with those in command was rapidly dissolving. Popham, having mastered the operation of the machinery, had become so sure of himself that he persuaded Melville that he no longer needed Fulton for the attack on Boulogne. The inventor, he said, should be sent merely as a consultant to organize a secondary assault on Rochefort.

In the hope of restoring some measure of control over the implementation of his system, Fulton urged the formation of a special squadron, highly trained in submarine combat, that would have cruising orders to pick off enemy vessels one at a time instead of waiting for them to mass. Popham could command the men, and Fulton himself would supervise the mechanics.

This special strike force was too radical for Keith to accept. As a last resort, Fulton endeavored to persuade him to postpone all further operations until the spring when the weather would be more propitious. Melville, however, was determined "to keep up and increase the pannick" by mounting another assault on Boulogne's fortifications.[11] He also intended to use Fulton's torpedoes to destroy Fort Rouge near Calais.

On the night of December 3, Popham scurried across the Channel to Boulogne, but arrived too late to risk an attack. Better organized a week later, he set out with three carcasses. They were only partially effective. He placed one carcass against a pile supporting the battery, but it did not detonate. Luckily a brave volunteer rescued it as he was attempting to lash a second carcass to the structure. Only the third did its work, damaging the breastwork and the western side of the fort.

The poor results were exactly what the growing number of naval officers opposed to submarine warfare hoped for. They complained that the torpedoes were an unwarranted expense. Even Keith's advocacy was beginning to cool. Rough seas and the mire of intragovernmental maneuverings brought the battle season to a close. The lucrative bounties Fulton had anticipated were as remote as ever. He still collected his 200 pounds a month—a cause of envy among naval officers, most of whom earned far less—but he could do nothing to further torpedo warfare until spring.

With time on his hands, Fulton's social life took on more importance. The Barlows had arrived in November. They had stopped off in England on their way to America, ostensibly in the hope that English doctors would find a cure for Ruth's persistent illnesses. Since Fulton moved to 9 Bedford Square from Storey's Gate Tavern, it seems likely they resumed their *ménage à trois*.

Barlow was still laboring over his *Columbiad*. Fulton had not produced the promised illustrations, and with his concurrence, Barlow had engaged John Vanderlyn to do them. However, when Barlow received a bill of 100 louis for *The Massacre of Jane Macrae*, he paid Vanderlyn and hired Fulton's friend, the painter and book illustrator Robert Smirke, who agreed to do the work for half the price. Fulton would supervise the engraving. His principal artistic contribution to the volume was a portrait of Barlow, which he probably painted at this time and which was eventually used as the epic's frontispiece. A highly idealized work, it depicts Barlow as a benign elderly philosopher with only a hint of the romantic that Barlow so wished to project and Fulton had always been happy to foster. The preliminary oil sketch has far more life.

The portrait's aloofness may well have been a manifestation of the temporary but unpleasant rift that disturbed their relationship. Afraid that Fulton's collusion with the British would arouse animosity in America, Barlow was anxious to protect himself from being accused of supporting him. He composed a letter, which, while it purports to champion Fulton, makes amply clear his disapproval of his tactics. Barlow sent copies of this letter to influential American friends, including President Jefferson:

> I have nothing to do with my friend Fulton's European projects. He perseveres in the establishment of his principle under every circumstance with an energy equal to the grandeur of his conceptions. Convinced in himself that he is right, his mind has taken a strong hold of his subject and presses forward to the completion of his views, in whatever country he can find a footing for his machines, regardless of the momentary opinions of his friends or enemies; who may have drawn conclusions without having well considered the premises. Should he accomplish his object, it will be seen and confessed that there was a uniform greatness, far from inconsistency, in his mode of acting. It will be for dispassionate philosophy, not for vulgar prejudice to judge of him some years hence.
>
> His humane views, his facility in the useful arts, his attachment to the true republican interests of his country & his excellent moral character, would make few men, who should know him as I do, fear to be his friend, or apprehensive of suffering by his reputation.[12]

Chastened, perhaps, by Barlow's criticism, Fulton wrote a monograph, called "Observations on American Affairs." An attempt to recapture the lost innocence of his canal days and of the "Republican Creed" and to curry favor with Jeffersonians, he described America as a debt-free paradise dedicated to the cultivation of the agricultural arts rather than to war. National funds would be used to build roads and canals. Full employment would inevitably follow. Ambition would be allowed free rein. The monograph was in the form of a letter addressed to Lord Stanhope with whom he still wished to ingratiate himself and who he hoped would have it published. Fulton did not know, or chose to ignore, that Stanhope was working on his *Weatherer*, a fast, light mine-sweeper. Outfitted with "Protectors" hung from the anchor cable as well as the boat itself and "Straddlers," long, thin horizontal boards for cutting torpedo cables, Stanhope claimed one *Weatherer* could sweep up bombs as fast as they could be laid. Unmoved by Fulton's romantic longing for America and by his fine philosophical distinction between ambitions, he ignored Fulton's request.

When the spring of 1805 arrived, making trans-Channel excursions possible, Fulton begged for new opportunities to attack the French navy. His expectations were considerably lower than they had been during the previous year. Admitting that his torpedoes were far from perfect, he advised a foray against Fort Rouge. Its principal objective would be to measure the perpendicular action of powder exploded beneath the water. Keith replied that Fulton would probably find it difficult to get volunteers because no promotions or special pay had been awarded the sailors and officers who participated in previous expeditions. Moreover, he himself thought the catamaran was dangerously unseaworthy.

To make matters more difficult, Lord Melville was impeached for mismanagement of naval funds alleged to have taken place in 1792. Eighty-year-old Lord Barham, an avowed conservative, replaced him as first lord of the Admiralty. On all fronts enthusiasm for submarine warfare had soured. As the young American Benjamin Silliman noted in his diary after having taken tea with Fulton at the Barlows': "Mr. Fulton's project was at present the subject of some apprehension and of a good deal of asperity and ridicule in England."[13]

What seemed like a final blow came in July when Fulton learned that his bombs had been retired to a warehouse at the navy's depot at Portsmouth. Interpreting this as a personal affront, Fulton wrote an indignant letter to Pitt stating that he wished to settle his affairs with the government as he had "previous engagements of much magnitude which called for his attention" in America.[14] Again, on August 9, he rehearsed his grievance at having been falsely induced to come to England and subsequently cast aside. Reiterating the need for a systematic approach to submarine warfare based on a special squadron, he expressed his anger at having been deprived by Popham and Keith of the authority to implement his invention. "I conceive," Fulton wrote with some justification, "the inventor of a new mode of warfare ought to be considered the best judge of the mode of using his own engines to advantage. . . . I ought not to have more than one commander to consult, who should be a man of resource of mind and some enthusiasm."[15] Should that not be possible, he conceded, he was willing to let the idea lie dormant and retire—with proper payment, of course.

Pitt sent this message to Viscount Castlereagh, who was then secretary for war. As so often before, Fulton was able to exercise his magnetism at a crucial juncture, for in this dynamic pragmatist Fulton found a new and vigorous champion. Castlereagh was so attracted by the breadth of Fulton's approach that he ordered the stored carcasses sent to Dover and authorized Fulton to construct one hundred more of them. Sir Sidney Smith, operational commander of the Channel Fleet under Keith, was told to provide ten catamarans and nine galleys, each with twelve men. Castlereagh's hope was to destroy the inner basin at Boulogne without damaging the town. If that was not possible—and it was not because of the long, shallow approach and the tides—he wanted Fulton to repeat the previous year's strategy by attacking the French fleet the moment it ventured into the Channel. Fulton would have to share the glory, however, for, charmed by unorthodox methods of warfare, Castlereagh invited Congreve to join in the expedition with not less than five hundred of his newly invented artillery rockets.

Lord Barham, who hated novelty of any kind, opposed Castlereagh. "All these dilatory proceedings," he expostulated, "promise nothing to repay our expense."[16] The most he would authorize was a trial of rockets at Cádiz, where the fleet was assembling under Lord Horatio Nelson for a major assault on the combined French and Spanish flotillas. When Castlereagh approached Nelson directly with the suggestion that he use torpedoes as well as rockets, the admiral predictably retorted that he had little faith in Congreve's and less in Francis's instruments as a means of annihilating the enemy: "I depend more upon hunger for driving them out and upon the gallant officers and men under my command for their destruction."[17] Only out of duty did Nelson agree to cooperate.

Castlereagh, who was accustomed to getting his way, carried out the Boulogne expedition. Sir Sidney Smith, whom Barham derided as "wanting judgment," provided energetic leadership. On September 30, when thirty-two French ships sailed out of Boulogne harbor with all flags flying and to the accompaniment of a *feu de joie*, Keith ordered the mission to set forth from Dover. Fulton was accorded no active role. He was reduced to mingling with the crowd of "speculators and guessers" who came to Dover to enjoy the excitement. Lasting from just after midnight until two in the morning, the expedition was a dismal failure. The French captured two of the carcasses; one exploded, killing four sailors, the other they were able to preserve for close examination.

In a letter to West, Fulton ironically observed that the French were reported to have run about crying "the infernal machines are coming . . . which shews that they were much frightened or that the public must be amused with a long story." He had no such illusions. "The torpedoes," he confessed, "did not produce the desired effect, and I saw a great prejudice arise in the minds of the officers against them."[18]

Fulton's perception was accurate. Keith wrote to Barham: "As for attempting to burn a few vessels in that extensive road of Boulogne, it is nonsense."[19] And Barham wrote to Castlereagh: "To support this kind of warfare, after the experience we have had, will bring our judgment with the public into question and end in nothing but disgrace."[20]

Fulton was desperate. In order to give teeth to his contract, he realized it was crucial to prove conclusively that his bombs were effective. Drawing on his last shred of credibility with Pitt and Castlereagh, he extracted permission to exhibit before their eyes the true power of an underwater explosion. He acquired the *Dorothea*, a recently captured 200-ton Danish brig, put her in order, and sent her to Deal where she was anchored a half-mile from Walmer Castle.

Fulton spent the afternoon of October 14 and the morning of October 15 conducting practice runs. The beach between Deal and Walmer Castle was packed with onlookers, and although Pitt was called to London at the last moment, Keith, Smith, Congreve, and Popham's replacement, Owen, together with most of the officers of the Channel Fleet assembled at the castle. Jokes and scornful predictions ran rampant. One officer went so far as to boast that "if a Torpedo were placed under his cabin while he was at dinner, he should feel no concern for the consequence."[21]

At three o'clock in the afternoon Fulton strode onto the beach, loaded a bomb filled with 170 pounds of powder onto a long galley, set the clock for fifteen minutes and gave the order to attack. The galley, manned by a spirited lieutenant named Robinson, rushed forward and grappled the torpedo's line in the cable of the brig. The tide pressed the torpedo under the brig's hull, and fifteen minutes later it exploded.

In his report to Sir Sidney Smith which Smith passed on to Castlereagh, Owen wrote: "The starboard side of the vessel was lifted bodily; then went to pieces; she then appeared to break in two by her own weight . . . the masts, as she sunk, fell over, and crossed each other, in short, in less time than you have taken to read these six lines, they were, as it were, as two felled trees would appear on the axe cutting the last fibre that held them upright, and the whole disappeared a misshapen black mass floating on the surface."[22]

Even Fulton was stunned. He had imagined, but had never witnessed, the full destructive power of his submarine bombs when applied to a large ship. For a brief moment it made him ponder the implications of his invention. In an otherwise exuberant description of the event for West he wrote: "the experiment was the most complete that Could be desired but most tremendious and frightful and carries with it the reflection which gives me some pain that In vessels thus attacked it will be impossible to save the men—and many a worthy character must perish."[23]

Castlereagh had no such qualms. He immediately authorized payment to Fulton of 10,000 pounds, one-fourth the amount stipulated in his contract for destroying an enemy warship. Fulton was exultant at the money, but the government's concession that torpedo warfare was effective was far more important to him. After eight years of striving, he had succeeded magnificently. He was now certain the obstacles that had so long frustrated his attempts to perfect submarine warfare would dissolve at once.

In this exhilarating hour, Fulton thought not only of himself. One of his first actions after the destruction of the *Dorothea* was to share his joy with his sisters and his brother. Even though he had not seen them for almost twenty years, he still held them in affection and felt responsible for them. The day after the explosion he wrote his brother-in-law David Morris to give $300 to Betsy whose husband had become a drunk and a debtor, $300 to Belle who was a widow, $200 to Abraham who was a teacher, and $50 to Polly who was well provided for by Morris. In a burst of pedagogical concern, he also asked Morris to take $50 to buy each family a copy of Johnson's spelling dictionary, an arithmetic book, good copperplate examples of large and small script, and a set of the *Spectator*. He had, he said, observed much bad handwriting and spelling in the letters from his nieces and nephews and knew "that such errors might be corrected with a little industry and care on winter evenings."[24]

In addition, Fulton wrote to Mr. Hoge, who had acted in his behalf in connection with the Hopewell property. He now asked Hoge to make sure the deeds to his lots had been permanently made over to his sisters. He also requested Hoge's help in aiding them "according to their several necessities and merits." To this act of generosity he attached the following stern proviso, aimed undoubtedly at Betsy's husband:

> If there is intemperance in any one of them, I have only to say I cannot be that person's friend; for I feel a kind of contempt for the being who is so imprudent as to extinguish the little sense which falls to the lot of a man on the poisonous fumes of ardent liquors, such a person has not sense to be their own friend and does not merit the friendship of others. When a good woman is cursed with such a husband she is to be pitied and still merits our tenderness and aid.[25]

To mitigate this temper, Fulton took the trouble to send Betsy on the same day an amusing recollection of their childhood spats with assurances that he would always look after her.

Apparently the triumphant destruction of the *Dorothea* freed Fulton to replace the father who so long ago had failed them. Although it is doubtful Fulton identified with his father, who may very well have been a drunkard, he obviously cared about playing the role. Having deprived himself of natural fatherhood by not marrying, he sought an outlet for his paternal feelings in helping his sisters and brother and their children.

Although it was late in the season, Castlereagh pressed Fulton to try his torpedoes once again against the harbour at Boulogne, if only to show the extent to which he, rather than the first lord of the Admiralty, controlled war strategy. A small attack took place, and at least one bomb was delivered and exploded, but no ship was even slightly damaged. Castlereagh's enthusiasm was not dampened. He simply attributed the results to bad luck and rough weather. Believing southern waters would be more hospitable, he wrote Lord Nelson on October 27 to inform him that he was sending him Mr. Congreve and Mr. Francis with their respective inventions for his use at Cádiz. "Since your lordship sailed," he explained, "the power of Mr. Francis's instruments has been satisfactorily ascertained by an experiment upon a large vessel. . . . I am sure your Lordship will facilitate their application."[26]

Communication was painfully slow in those days. Castlereagh had not yet received word that the English had decimated the French and Spanish fleets at Trafalgar on October 21 and that Lord Nelson was dead.

Mine Is No Common Cause

❖

Victory at Trafalgar made Great Britain the undisputed ruler of the seas and secured the island kingdom from the threat of invasion. It also abruptly changed the government's attitude toward Fulton. His unorthodox weapons, still unproven in battle, were now superfluous. So that there would be no chance of his misunderstanding his position, the government stopped paying his monthly salary. The financial blow cut deep. Equally devastating was the humiliation he suffered when he learned that Congreve continued to receive support for his rockets and had been asked to bomb Boulogne at the end of November.

Unable to stay away from the scene of action, Fulton went to Dover to view the rockets' red glare from the shore. He was rewarded by witnessing a total disaster. To West he gleefully wrote: "behold there came on mighty winds and of 12 rocket boats sunk all save two and the men therein were saved; and the rest were happy to get off with whole bones and this project is ended for the season." [1]

Emboldened by Congreve's failure, Fulton wrote Castlereagh suggesting an assault on Brest for which he claimed to have Sir Sidney Smith's approval. With a hundred carcasses, fifty boats, and six hundred men—all to be carried in unarmed cargo vessels—he promised to annihilate the remnants of the French fleet. As might be expected, Castlereagh would have nothing to do with that scheme.

Mine Is No Common Cause

Fulton was enraged and mortified at being coldly rejected when he so recently expected to achieve his heart's desire. Unaware that Napoleon's defeat of the Austrians at Austerlitz and his subsequent annexation of conquered lands had almost paralyzed the British government with fear, Fulton was convinced he had been singled out for callous treatment. In mid-December, he wrote Castlereagh a defiant letter claiming that if he had been allowed to build a submarine boat, he would have "produced the most brilliant success and have acquired an immense fortune . . . more than a Million Sterling."[2] His current price, however, for guaranteeing never to use the submarine boat against the British was only 60,000 pounds, plus his current salary of 2,400 pounds a year for life—in all no more than the interest on 100,000 pounds. Should he break the agreement, he declared, he would forfeit the annuity but not the 60,000 pounds.

Impelled by his resentment to new heights of recklessness, Fulton sent this letter to Pitt on January 6, 1806, together with an explanatory note, the product of numerous drafts, in which he arrogantly stated his position.

> That you may have an opportunity before you come to Town, to judge of what I conceive my rights And the government Interest . . . . I will not disguise that I feel the power which I possess is no less than to be the means, if I think proper, of giving to the world a System which must from necessity sweep all military marines from the ocean by giving to the weaker maritime powers Advantages over the stronger which the Strong cannot prevent. . . . This is a power which is not possessed by even Bonapart. It is concentrated in me and two friends who are governed by my success in this country. . . . It must be observed I did not come here so much with a view to do you any material good as to Shew that I have the power and might in the exercise of my plan to acquire fortune, do you an Infinate Injury, which Ministers, if they thought proper, might prevent by an arrangement with me.[3]

The insolence of these letters amounted to blackmail, infinitely magnified because the body of Lord Nelson was lying in state at Greenwich, receiving the last tributes of an anguished public, and because Pitt was slowly succumbing to a mortal illness at Bath. Fulton, however, was so infuriated that he had been robbed again of his chance to play hero-benefactor to the world and to line his pockets with silver, that he re-

fused to realize the vehemence he turned on the British could only result in harm to himself.

Pitt died on January 23, 1806. His death and the subsequent political upheaval did not restrain Fulton. On February 7 he wrote Lord Earl
St. Vincent, who had resumed command of the Channel Fleet, criticizing the government's faithlessness and vaunting his own zeal. Then, on
February 22, the very day of Pitt's funeral, he wrote Charles Grey, the
new first lord of the Admiralty, that he wanted a committee, small in
number for secrecy, to assess his rights. With these letters he had the
temerity to send copies of his Pitt letters. Grey did not reply. Again, in
mid-March, Fulton importuned Grey for a prompt settlement. Nevertheless, unable to relinquish his hope for a successful strike with his torpedoes, he put forward in the same letter still another plan for an experimental expedition against the French.

Even Fulton must have been astonished when Grey agreed. He reacted with almost childish pleasure. However, his joy was short-lived.
Grey did nothing to implement the trials. His brief show of interest may
well have been a ploy to glean more information about the bombs and
submarine boat from Fulton before disposing of him for good.

Fulton believed he had been belittled and tricked. The modicum of
self-control he had preserved disintegrated. No longer able to avoid the
painful fact that the British had abandoned submarine warfare, he demanded arbitration in accordance with his contract. Fulton's harrowed
state of mind is evident in every sentence of the boasting, preaching,
lying, and menacing letter he sent to Alexander Davison, the government contractor and eager patron of the arts whom he had asked to serve
as arbitrator:

> I have the pleasure to inform you that the Project of my Steam
> Vessel to navigate the Mississippi succeeds beyond my expecta-
> tion. I have just received letters from my Friends informing me
> that 280,000 dollars, or about 60,000 pounds have been subscribed
> at New York to build 20 vessels, each of which according to the
> Calculations of the Committee will make a neat profit of upwards
> of £2000 per annum, so that it will be near Cent per Cent for the
> Capital advanced. The patent of this Invention has been secured
> to me for 14 years.

Not one word of this "report" was true. As to the settlement, he told
Davison in a bid for sympathy that disintegrated into an arrogant declaration of power:

I will depend on my own strength in mathematics and demonstration to convince you all of my natural rights and your policy to deal with me in the most liberal manner. Should you mistake the Nation's Interest, the Sin will lie at your own door, this you will perhaps think odd Language, but let any man place himself in my situation and then ask himself if he has not a right to convert his labours into fame and emolument, for what other objects do men labour? . . . I have now to confess to you as a Friend that I have for sometime felt myself awkward in this Country. I see a kind of suspicion attached to my character which I detest, and I am kept amused dancing after publick affairs as though I were asking Favours, whereas I who know my strength and resources came here by Invitation to grant Favours and not to ask them. . . . I will not fritter down my powers to a humble supplicant.[4]

Yet, obsessed by his invention, Fulton groveled before government officials. He begged Grey, now Lord Howick through the death of his father, to give him just five minutes to explain a new proving expedition, and he secured affidavits of the torpedo's worth from Captain Owen and Lieutenant Robinson. For the next month he bombarded the government with a steady stream of letters that could do no good.

When the government's imperturbability became unbearable, Fulton put his case before Lord Grenville, the new prime minister: "Mine is no common cause," he declared. "I never will abandon my private interest Till satisfied."[5]

For the remainder of the month, Fulton vented his spleen privately by writing and rewriting vain and menacing letters to a variety of officials for treating him "in a most ungentlemanlike manner, with a want of politeness and Injustice which I feel in the most sensible manner a degrading neglect."[6] Somehow he marshaled enough fortitude not to send them. However, in a frenetic lunge for recognition, he threatened Lord Grenville that unless the government acceded to his demands he would make public all their correspondence pertaining to the submarine project.

It was, perhaps, the thought that Fulton might be a madman that moved the government to appoint arbitrators to hear his case. Sir Charles Blagden and Captain Thomas Hamilton, both of whom considered any deviation from traditional forms of warfare unmanly, represented the government. Fulton persuaded Cartwright to serve with Davison in his behalf.

The arbitrators met on August 10. As his brief, Fulton submitted a set of twelve drawings, detailed verbal descriptions of his submarine boat and bombs and a long memorandum entitled "Motives for inventing submarine Navigation and attack, Statement of the causes which brought me to England, contract with Pitt and Melville, Statement of sums received and disbursed."[7] A long paean to the American form of government—"a system which should progress as near as man is capable, to the perfection of civilization"—the document's main purpose was to give Fulton an opportunity to announce that it was his desire to protect American democracy that first induced him to contemplate submarine warfare.

As if this assorted collection of materials were not enough, Fulton read aloud an agitated justification for the large settlement he demanded, warning the arbitrators that, if their award did not meet with his partners' (still unnamed) views of wealth, he would expose his invention to the whole world, concluding: "I never will consent to let these inventions lie dormant Should my Country at any time have need of them, Were you to grant me an Annuity of £120,000, I would sacrifice all to the safety & independence of my Country."[8]

Captain Hamilton suggested that Fulton's torpedoes were worthless because no volunteers would be found to deliver them since if caught they would be treated as criminals; that France would not mine the channel because it would cut off her trade; that the mines would not stay put in a storm; and that, in any case, vessels with cables could sweep the channel. This brought the hearings to a close. One hour after Fulton left the room, the arbitrators decided his system was "not so far novel, practicable, and effective as to entitle him to the terms of the original contract. Their award allowed him to keep the 10,000 pounds paid after the blow-up of the *Dorothea*. In addition, he would be given 1,000 pounds above the salary of 4,000 pounds he had already received, and 646 pounds, 12 shillings, 6 pence due on the balance of his accounts—1,000 pounds less than the invoice he submitted, for his arithmetic had been in error to that amount.

The arbitrators advised the government against bribing Fulton to prevent him from selling his inventions to other nations. France, the main enemy, already knew the principles. Since his pledge of secrecy would be impossible to monitor, the large recompense Fulton demanded would be a useless and immoral expenditure of public money.

Smoldering with wrath that his inventions and his reputation had been so disparaged, Fulton wrote Grenville two abusive letters demanding a full hearing before the cabinet or twelve "nautical gentlemen," and payment of an annuity as long as the engines were not used against England. Not trusting the letters to ordinary channels, Fulton carried them in person to 10 Downing Street. In a note scribbled on the copy he kept for his records, he described his humiliating encounter with the prime minister: "On the 3d of September 1806 I had an interview with Lord Grenville in Downing street. I entered his room about three oclock. He was alone, handed me a chair. I sat down near him and after a few words I read him the preceding letters, on which no comment whatever was made. His Lordship only observed that he could not then say anything on the Subject and I retired."[9]

Fulton's response to this aborted audience was to compose a series of reflections on his past and future intentions that had all the qualities of a gallows speech. To exonerate himself from not having first offered his inventions to the United States, he resorted to a cynical distortion of fact. He said he had offered them to President Jefferson, who did not respond. Therefore he did not know whether he would receive the least encouragement to systematize his plans in America. He even tried to make use of his commitment to the steamboat to cast his actions in a virtuous light. "I am," he said, "Bound in honor to Mr. Livingston to put my steamboat in practice and such an engine is of more immediate use to my country than submarine navigation."[10] Whatever annuity might be granted he vowed to use to further that invention.

On September 23 Fulton took his full correspondence with Grenville to a printer as he had threatened. He sent copies to influential men, including, he claimed, King George III and the Prince of Wales. While he set the date for his departure from England on October 5, he also offered to buy a sloop at his own expense and prove his torpedoes by blowing it up. Should he fail, he would forfeit 1,000 guineas. "If you shrink from this fair experiment, which brings the subject home to feelings," he ranted, "it is proof that you fear the engines."[11]

Next he sent a diatribe to Cartwright for distribution to the arbitrators, stating that unless he received justice he would take violent measures that would lead to the total subjugation of England. His current price was 40,000 pounds outright or an annuity of 3,000 pounds.

Cartwright had not lost his respect for Fulton's mechanical genius and for the essential soundness of his invention, despite his wild conduct. He informed Grenville that almost everyone who investigated Fulton's plans, Hamilton excepted, felt they could be implemented, and that if the French gained possession of them, British maritime supremacy would be ruined. Therefore, the total annihilation of Fulton's invention "could scarcely be purchased at too great a price." Since this might not be practicable, he advised buying Fulton off for his lifetime: "In this case there is a chance also that it might lie so long dormant as to die of itself and be forgotten . . . . the price, high as it is, and arrogantly as it is demanded, ought not, perhaps, in prudence be objected to." [12]

Cartwright's respected pleading bore no fruit, however. Fulton received only the 646 pounds agreed to at the August meeting.

It is extraordinary that Fulton's turbulent dealings with the government did not alienate his friends. But his personality was so protean that he spent a companionable autumn. He was as intimate as ever with West. The previous September he had bought two of his paintings, *King Lear* and *Ophelia*, when the Boydell Shakespeare Gallery's collection was put up for auction. As a parting gift, West painted a romantic portrait of Fulton. Curly haired with fiery eyes and a sphinxlike smile, Fulton is seated near a window through which is a view of an exploding warship. As a further testimony of his regard, West gave him a fascinating and unusual double portrait in which he depicted himself painting Mrs. West.

During this period Fulton also saw a good deal of Stanhope who was as ebulliently knee-deep in inventions as ever. In addition to his antitorpedo devices, he had contrived a tuning instrument and a mechanical method of musical notation for his recently acquired Bohemian mistress. To reduce the cost of printing, he had perfected a labor-saving cast-iron press that could print twelve pages at one pull and a roller for inking that would save 50 percent of the time and render more beautiful type than the current method of tamping ink on with a pad made of cotton waste to which a handle was attached. He had also developed a method of making stereoptic plates that was so efficient it promised to bring printed material within the purse of the working class. Willfully inept at business, Stanhope was having difficulty getting this process adopted and sought Fulton's advice. Tactlessly, Fulton replied that the machinery was too expensive and that his manager was too greedy. Stereotype printing would succeed, Fulton instructed Stanhope, only if it was "placed on the liberal footing of all other manufactures . . . free from restrictions, and the spirit of monopoly."[13] Despite the scolding, Stanhope remained friendly enough to allow Fulton to paint his portrait, holding a stereotype plate in his hand. A stately, idealized likeness, it is surprisingly far more expressive than Fulton's portrait of Barlow.

Fulton was still immersed in supervising the illustrations for Barlow's *Columbiad*. He and Smirke employed ten engravers. Fulton paid the entire cost out of his own pocket. Later he said it was his way of thanking the Barlows for their kindness to him in Paris. The bill was $5,000.

In a lighter vein, Fulton resumed his fleeting acquaintance with the Duchesse de Gontaut-Biron. They recognized each other at the opera, she wrote in her *Memoirs*, and subsequently saw each other often. She was amused that he had chosen the alias "Francis," an anglicization of the one she had assumed for her clandestine excursion into France in 1797.

Fulton even found time to court an English widow of fortune. Unfortunately all that is known about this romance is contained in a letter from Barlow—a long, shrieking lament in which he expressed his horror that Fulton could contemplate destroying the trinity's *"beau rêve"* of future happiness in America even for the "angelic being" he had described so lovingly. The marriage would rend the "mighty fabric" of their friendship, Barlow shuddered. Because the lady was by education, habits, feeling, character, and cast of mind English, they obviously could not live in America, and therefore Fulton would be unable to help him finish the canal epic. "Oh my inestimable friend, my younger self, my expansion & prolongation of existence!" he howled, ". . . your patriotism, your philosophy, your ideas of public improvement, your wishes to be a comfort to me and my wife in our declining years (if we should be so unfortunate as to have many of them) would tend to make you uneasy at such a distance from the theatre of so much good."[14]

Fulton did not marry the widow. Whatever the cause, the affair ended. Perhaps he was influenced by Barlow's excessive reaction, for there is no question he was still profoundly attached to both him and Ruth although he teased Ruth by advising her that while there was not much risk of his forming an alliance with an Englishwoman, were he to stay in England another winter he should certainly be "shaped up" by someone.

By the middle of October, Fulton conceded that haranguing the British government for more money was fruitless and began to think seriously of returning to America. He packed his extensive wardrobe, which, according to an April 1806 inventory included twenty-three fine shirts; fifty cravats; one red striped, one yellow, one black satin, and thirteen white waistcoasts; buckskin and cashmere breeches; blue, dark gray, and olive pantaloons; brown, blue, and black coats; five pairs of shoes; three pairs of half boots; three pairs of whole boots; nine pairs of white silk stockings; seven pairs of black stockings; lots of underclothes; and a swimming waistcoat and pantaloons.

In a final settlement of his financial affairs, Fulton asked Daniel Parker to send the funds Parker had invested for him to America, "as I and my friend will need all our means to settle down comfortable." Inviting Parker to join them, he wrote: "I love and esteem you . . . how much it would add to the pleasures of our Athenian garden to have you living on the margin of it." There was no chance of it, for Parker was well settled in France; he owned a fine *hôtel* in Paris and a splendid château in the countryside, and he had an elegant mistress to help him enjoy them. Probably as a joke, Fulton signed the letter with a new alias, "Robt. Ferguson." [15]

Fulton's parting with the Wests must have been an emotional wrench. However, he intended to promote West's work in the United States and undoubtedly expected that, since travel between London and the port cities of America was common, he would either see them there or return to England himself before much time elapsed.

Because it was more commodious and reliable than ordinary ships, Fulton booked passage on the *Windsor Castle*, the packet boat sailing from Falmouth. He arranged to ship his pictures, prints, and other important personal effects the following spring when there would be less risk of damage or loss due to storms. Unwilling to entrust "the produce of his studies and experience" to an ocean voyage, he sealed a complete set of drawings and descriptions of his system of submarine warfare in a tin cylinder and left them with the American consul with instructions not to open them unless he was lost at sea. With them he placed a last will and testament. Should he die, Barlow was to be provided with funds to publish the system in a handsome illustrated edition that would show how submarines and topedoes could bring about liberty of the seas.

Describing himself to Barlow as in "excellent health, never better, and in good spirits," Fulton truly looked forward to returning to Amer-

Robert Fulton in Paris.
Top: portrait of Robert Fulton
by John Vanderlyn, 1798;
bottom: self-portrait, 1803.

Robert Fulton. *Above:* portrait by Benjamin West, London, 1806;
opposite top: self-portrait, New York, c. 1812;
opposite bottom: by Charles Willson Peale, Philadelphia, 1807.

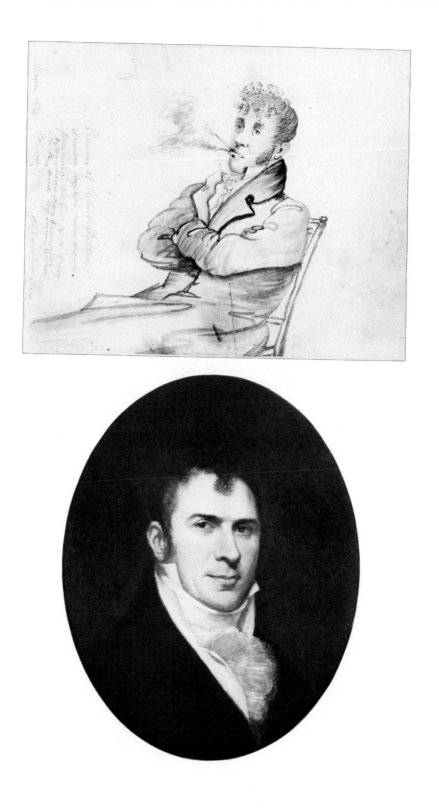

Top: Fulton's miniature of
his two oldest children,
Robert Barlow Fulton
and Julia Fulton, c. 1814;
bottom: miniature of his wife,
Harriet Livingston Fulton, c. 1810.

Top left: Joel Barlow by
Robert Fulton, London, 1805;
top right: Ruth Baldwin
Barlow, probably a copy
of lost portrait painted by
Fulton at Plombières, France,
1802; *right:* Benjamin West
self-portrait, painting his wife,
Elizabeth, London, 1806.

Top left: Robert R. Livingston by John Vanderlyn, Paris, 1804;
top right: Charles, 3rd Earl of Stanhope,
by Robert Fulton, London, 1806;
bottom left: William Thornton by Robert Field, 1800;
bottom right: Benjamin Henry Latrobe by Charles Willson Peale,
Philadelphia, 1804.

Top left: Edward Livingston by
John Trumbull, 1805;
top right: John Livingston by
Robert Fulton, c. 1812;
bottom: John Stevens, attributed
to John Trumbull, c. 1805.

Fulton's rendering of his perpendicular
lift, or "tub-in-well," published in
*A Treatise on the Improvement of
Canal Navigation*, London, 1796.

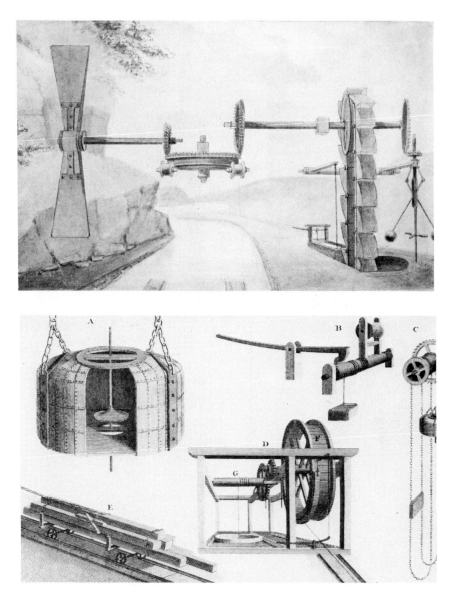

Details of inclined plane machinery by Fulton.
Top: landscape with fly wheel, gears, chain
bucket drive system and governor, London 1797;
bottom: illustration from *A Treatise on the
Improvement of Canal Navigation*, London, 1796;
A. water tub, B. stopper, C. balance chains,
D. apparatus to return empty boats,
E. mode for passing timber of any length.

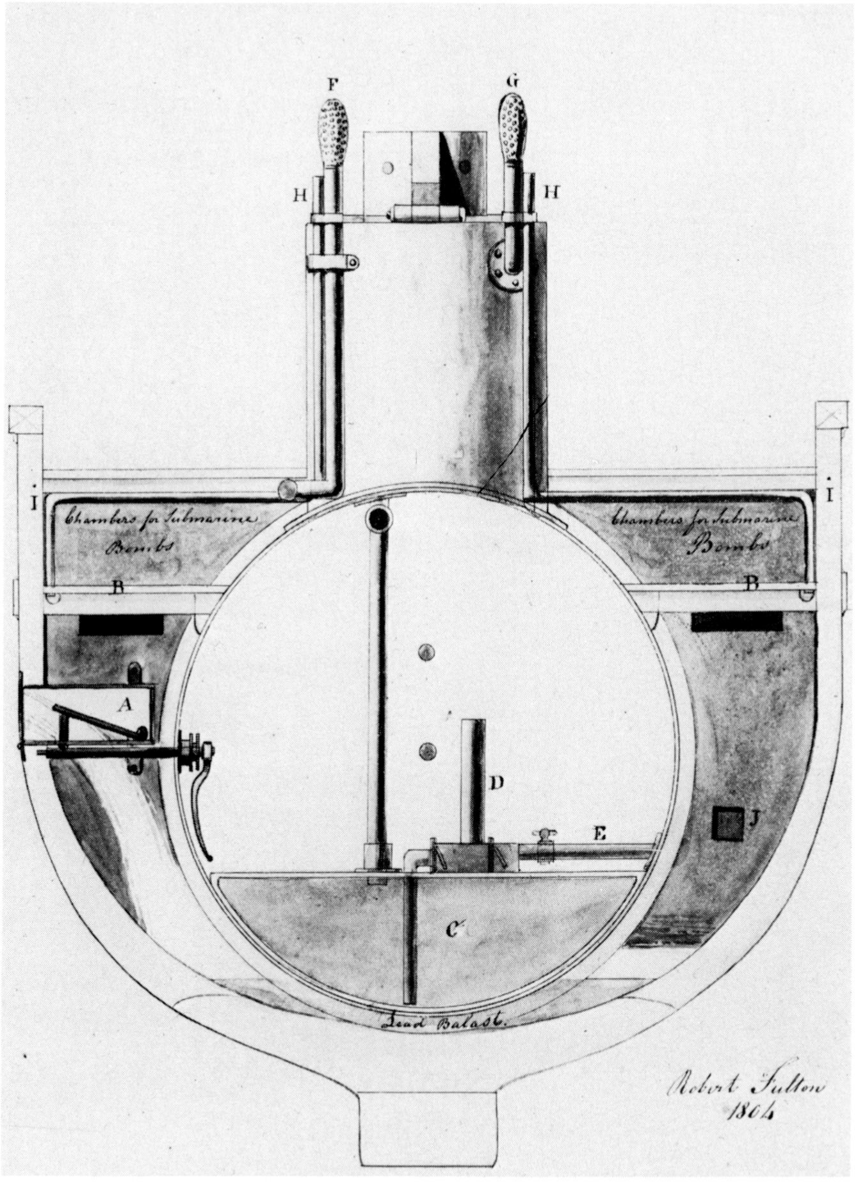
F
G
H
H
I
I
Chambers for Submarine Bombs
Chambers for Submarine Bombs
B
B
A
D
E
J
C
Lead Balast
Robert Fulton
1804

Fulton's drawings of his submarine boat, London, 1804. *Above:* transverse section—chambers for transporting bombs are above the water line; *opposite top:* self-portrait demonstrating periscope—Figure the Third is a bathometer; *opposite bottom:* longitudinal section—the mast and boom are to be tied to the deck before descent.

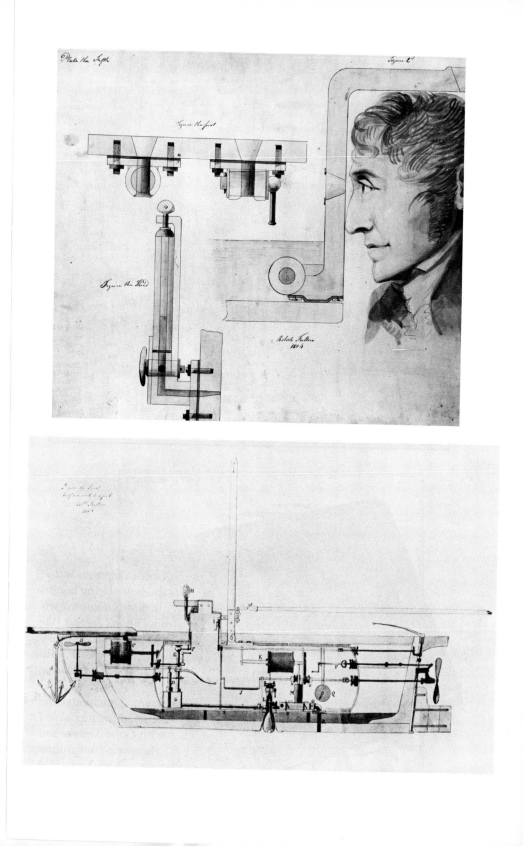

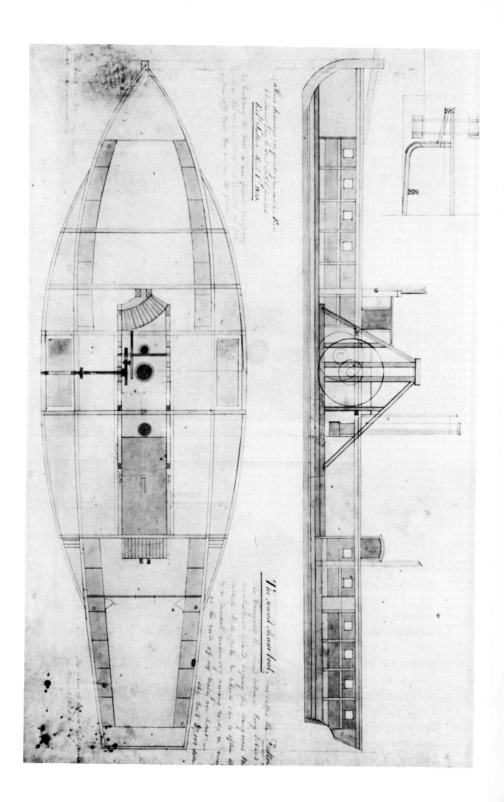

Opposite: drawings from the Long Island Sound
steamboat *Fulton*, New York, 1813;
top: sketch of the *North River* steamboat
from Fulton's notebook; *bottom:* drawing of
North River steamboat's machinery.

Top: design for row housing, London, c. 1806; *bottom:* cartoon enclosed in a letter congratulating Fulwar Skipwith on his marriage, 1802.

ica where he had two or three projects "of the first order of sublimity" to carry out. "My situation now is, my hands are free to burn, sink, and destroy whom I please," he confided. "I have or will have . . . 500 sterling a year, with a steam engine and pictures worth £2000. Therefore I am not in a state to be pitied."[16]

His steam engine awaited him in a warehouse in New York.

America

❖

The voyage across the bleak North Atlantic, including a layover in Halifax, took a long nine and a half weeks. Time, the cold salt air, and forced inactivity purged Fulton of the self-destructive spite that had gripped him during his final negotiations with the British government. When the *Windsor Castle* sailed into New York harbor on December 13, he was flush with confidence that his compatriots would offer his genius the sustained support he had not received in Europe.

Fulton came home at an opportune moment. With an exploding population and seemingly inexhaustible frontiers, the country was an entrepreneur's paradise. Even from the deck of the packet he could see that New York City, which had supplanted Philadelphia as the nation's commercial capital, was a boom town. The swirling waters of the East and Hudson rivers were alive with sail- and man-powered boats. The wharves were thick with the tall masts of merchant ships loading goods bound for ports throughout the world. Over five hundred vessels docked in the harbor that December. As a British observer wrote, "every thought, work, look, and action of the multitude seemed to be absorbed in commerce." [1]

New York's population had passed 80,000 and was increasing at a rate of 10 percent a year. To make room for northward expansion, the swales and swamps were being filled, rocky outcroppings leveled, and the woods cut down. New buildings were rising on every spare lot. More houses were under construction than ever before. The already half-completed City Hall was an elegant architectural jewel, a symbol of New Yorkers' conscious delight in their aspiring, free-wheeling way of life.

Only the presence of British warships aggressively cruising the coast and the increasingly frequent news that ships, cargoes, and seamen had been seized by the British threatened New York's spiralling prosperity. No one was deceived that the gunboats stationed at the Navy Yard could put up an adequate defense should the tenuous peace be broken. Beneath the bustling, striving, satisfied facade was a steady current of fear. Painfully recalling the city's occupation during the Revolutionary War, prominent citizens had formed a committee to solicit proposals for the defense of the harbor. Fulton had every reason to believe that both submarine warfare and steam navigation would find an enthusiastic reception.

As soon as Fulton touched shore, he wrote to Livingston, who had happily retired to his vast Hudson River estate, that he was "now ready to Carry Steam [to the o]ptimum of its powers."[2] Promising a boat that would run at least four miles an hour, Fulton questioned him about the tides and ice on the Hudson and about the volume of stagecoach passengers between New York and Albany. To enhance their social intimacy, he also declared his attachment to the Livingston family and his pride in being numbered among their friends.

Despite this effusion, it was not to Livingston at Clermont that Fulton sped, but to the Barlows who had been frantically awaiting his arrival in Philadelphia. Still undecided where to establish their Athenian Garden, they were temporarily settled in the former national capital where Ruth found the society had at least a modicum of *bon ton* and Barlow was able to pepper Conrad, the printer chosen to publish his *Columbiad*, with fussy last-minute changes in the text.

In an unusual departure from customary practice, the newspaper *Aurora* ran a glowing announcement of Fulton's return:

> In the British packet which arrived at New York last Saturday came passenger Robert Fulton, a native of Pennsylvania, author of various improvements in *civil engineering* and the *mechanical arts* which have secured him a lasting reputation in Europe, especially in France and England. His return will be an important acquisition to our country in the various branches of public improvement, of which it is so susceptible; and we cannot but hope that his system of *submarine navigation* may be advantageously united

with that of our *gun boats* to form the cheapest and surest defense of our harbours and coasts.[3]

Although the prominence accorded submarine warfare suggests Fulton was the main author, he must have been pleased to be heralded with so splendid a public welcome twenty years after his departure with little more than forty guineas, a budding artistic talent, and youth.

To be reunited with the Barlows was without question an immense joy. Still, Fulton worried that he had slighted Livingston. When he did not receive a quick reply to his homecoming letter, he wrote again to say that they must find a time and place where they might meet to decide whether the Hudson or the Mississippi would yield the most profits. For a basis of comparison, he told Livingston he would ask President Jefferson to order government agents stationed in the vicinity of the Mississippi to measure the river's velocity from station to station and from month to month during a year.

This was a shocking suggestion. Livingston's sole objective, as clearly stated in their partnership agreement, was to establish a steam passenger service on the Hudson River. His New York State monopoly required that they do this immediately. However, to Fulton the 150 miles from New York to Albany seemed puny indeed compared with the enormous potential of the Mississippi and its tributaries, where his boats would carry cargo as well as passengers.

Without waiting for an answer from Livingston, Fulton set off for Washington with Barlow. Visually they made a cartoonish pair—Fulton lean, honed, and fiercely ambitious for his inventions; paunchy Barlow playing at the soft roles of elder statesman and genial impresario. With Fulton's nation-building schemes and Barlow's good contacts, they were, in fact, an extraordinarily sharp team.

No longer a wilderness of shacks and ragged fields broken by a scattering of state buildings and rich men's houses, Washington, including the long settled port of Georgetown, boasted ten thousand inhabitants while Congress was in session. Most of the legislators lived simply in boardinghouses, and Pennsylvania Avenue was still a dirt road, alternately a dust bowl and a river of mud. But the walls of the handsome Capitol were steadily rising. The Senate was already housed in its south wing chamber, and the north wing with its columned oval hall for the House of Representatives would soon be completed. The foundations of the domed rotunda that would join them had been laid. At the President's Palace, as the White House was then familiarly called, extensive landscaping was at last under way. A decent stone wall had replaced the picket fence. The English gardens promised a stately setting. Perhaps more important, the new carriage road would do away with the disgraceful open sewer that ran past the main entrance.

The atmosphere of the Federal City was at the same time intimate and charged with vitality. The Jefferson administration eagerly embraced new ideas, and the opening of the West profoundly stirred the country's imagination. The town was currently celebrating the return of Meriwether Lewis from his historic expedition with news of a transcontinental route following the Mississippi, Missouri, and Columbia Rivers.

Fulton's request for a survey of the Mississippi could not have been better timed. Henry Dearborn, the secretary of war and one of Barlow's close friends, ordered it carried out. In the meantime, Daniel Clark, a Paris acquaintance who had become the congressional delegate from the Orleans Territory, provided enough general information about the currents of the river and the present volume of trade for Fulton to make projections of profits. These he sent to Livingston, pledging him to secrecy, lest competition be aroused.

Since the work of government blended happily in Washington with balls, dinners, theatricals, and general "racketting about," Fulton and Barlow made several new and influential friends. After leaving the great press of well-wishers and gawkers who thronged the President's New Year reception, they spent the evening with Samuel Harrison Smith, the publisher of the *National Intelligencer*. Smith had reprinted the *Aurora* notice under the caption "An American Genius" and, after their evening together, followed it up with a description of Fulton as "a man no less distinguished for science than beneficence, and from whom his country may expect to reap the fruits of an extensive observation and experience derived from a long residence in Europe."[4] His wife, Margaret Bayard Smith, an avid diarist, noted later that month that Barlow and Fulton were frequent visitors and afforded her "that gratification which is derived from the society of men of learning and genius. Both Mr. and Mrs. Barlow were very fond of chess," she wrote her sister, and Mr. Fulton expounded delightfully on philosophy and the fine arts.[5]

With little effort Fulton and Barlow also struck up a visiting relationship with William Thornton, the clerk—although he preferred to be called the superintendent—of the Patent Office. Born in Tortola in the West Indies and educated in Great Britain, Thornton prided himself on being a renaissance man, and he was. He possessed a degree as a physician, but finding the practice of medicine not to his liking quickly abandoned it. As a self-taught architect he won the competition for the designs of the Library Company of Philadelphia and of the national Capitol. On a smaller though not less elegant scale, he drew plans for the town houses of his friends. He was an excellent amateur artist and a passionate racehorse breeder. Under the clever management of his ambitious young wife, his drawing room was a meeting place for influential Washingtonians.

Thornton was also an amateur inventor. He had been a major shareholder and adviser in Fitch's steamboat venture and, although the first engine he developed "crumpled like an eggshell," Fitch used a later version in his successful boat. In gratitude for his support, Fitch left him an interest in his estate. In 1803 Thornton issued himself a patent for a boiler improvement, probably based on one projected by Fitch. Its principal application was for distilling rather than for steamboats; no one had seen fit to try it.

The week after they met, Thornton invited Fulton and Barlow to breakfast. To cement their relationship, Fulton left him some prints and had the pleasure of retrieving them the next day. It was probably through Thornton's good graces that Fulton was privileged to examine all the patents pertaining to steamboats, for Thornton usually refused access to specifications unless they were required in a lawsuit. Beginning with Rumsey's and Fitch's, twelve had been granted, "not one of which," Fulton reported to Livingston, "approaches to practicality."[6] Fulton and Thornton undoubtedly talked about the patent law, for Congress was debating a bill extending the life of patents. Proponents argued that, because the country was so sparsely settled, few patents were worth possessing unless the inventor was given at least twenty-eight years to realize a return on his time and investment.

Fulton's encounter with Thornton seemed to have all the earmarks of a pleasant and profitable association. However, beneath his urbane veneer, Thornton was jealous, avaricious, and unscrupulous. Of all the enemies Fulton would make in the course of establishing his steamboat empire, Thornton would be the most implacable.

Fulton stayed in Washington to attend the banquet honoring Meriwether Lewis. While Barlow was composing a nine-stanza poem for the occasion comparing the Potomac, Ohio, Missouri, and Columbia rivers to "a garland of flowers" that entwined "all our states in a band," Fulton drew a fine pencil portrait of Ruth's brother Abraham, then a senator from Georgia. Shortly afterward, Fulton departed for Lancaster by himself, perhaps to renew his friendship with Samuel Turbitt, but principally to call on the eminent surveyor Andrew Ellicott. In 1787, Ellicott had given Fitch a certificate attesting to the merits of his steamboat, but his chief interest for Fulton was that he had measured the current of the Mississippi from the Ohio to New Orleans and was able to corroborate Clark's information. As Fulton did not get back to Philadelphia until January 24, he may have traveled to western Pennsylvania to see his sisters and their children in whose education he had taken so strong an interest, and to visit his mother's grave. There is, however, no record that he did so.

In Philadelphia, Fulton joined the Barlows at Mrs. Wood's boardinghouse, 312 High Street. Despite the obvious fact that his center of activity would be in New York—a city that Barlow found uncongenial to his desire for a life of contemplative retirement—or in faraway New Orleans, they clung to the hope that they could reinstate their past intimacy. They had far from exhausted their emotional need for each other and made plans to set up a joint household in Washington.

Awaiting Fulton in Philadelphia was the long anticipated letter from Livingston. It must have contained a negative reaction to the proposal that they transfer their first efforts to the Mississippi River, for Fulton immediately dashed off twelve calculation-filled pages endeavoring to demonstrate that they could expect a far greater return on their investment from a western operation. Because their principal objective was to carry cargo, he described a boat drawing square-ended barges, similar to those he had exhibited in Paris. Such a train of boats would ascend the river three times faster than the usual hauling method, Fulton pointed out, and thus could make the 1,000-mile trip from New Orleans to the junction of the Ohio three times a year. At three dollars a hundredweight—a dollar less than the prevailing charge—and expenses conservatively estimated at $5,520, the profit, not including passenger fees and return trade, would be a handsome $48,480. Looking forward to the inevitable surge in population, he enthusiastically predicted that the volume of cargo would soon increase to 10,000 tons a year, requiring twelve sets of boats and netting $500,000 a year.

The expected profits on a Hudson River passenger line, Fulton hurriedly stated, were far lower. Taking advantage of the tide, which reached its height six hours later at Albany than at New York, he was certain he could achieve an average speed of at least 4½ miles an hour. With three hundred ice-free days and one trip every forty-eight hours, the profits at $3 a passenger would be $39,960. Astounded that this was only $8,500 less than the projected Mississippi profits, Fulton lamely pled: "This looks better on paper than I at first supposed, but I am afraid it will not all prove true. Either there are not so many passengers or they will not pay so much, or the tide will not favor us so much as here calculated."

Fulton was exasperated at having fallen into a trap of his own devising, but he was too excited to rewrite the letter. Instead he peevishly informed Livingston it would cost them $6,000 to set the operation on the Hudson in motion—"I mean 6000 in addition to my present advance which is 1150£ or 5111 dollars." As if to soften this sudden thrust at Livingston's pocketbook, Fulton concluded the letter with another gallantry which, had he paused to reflect, was sure to irritate the aristocratic Livingston: "I return my thanks to the Ladies for their goodness. And in gratitude kind souls I will make all their fortunes. Pin money shall be as abundant as the hearts most ample wish, but for this patience & faith are necessary."[7]

Livinston was not pleased by Fulton's stubborn predilection for the western waters. Despite his pride in the Louisiana Purchase, he was first and foremost a man of the Hudson River Valley. He was both too provincial and too advanced in years to contemplate directing his attention much beyond the Catskill Mountains, which he admired from his lawn. At Clermont he was fully engaged in establishing a prize flock of merino sheep and in managing his tenants and his extended family. Steam navigation was a passionate but somewhat embarrassing hobby, the cost of which he strenuously endeavored to hold in check. Still not fully convinced the steamboat would succeed, he even talked of selling a part of his interest. For Livingston, the Albany run was far less risky than the Mississippi project. The Hudson was familiar territory, over which he exercised great influence through his social and political connections. He was perfectly aware that the monopoly he had procured in 1798 and had extended several times, was his primary contribution to the partnership.

Livingston's disapproval of Fulton's Mississippi scheme took the form of a disagreeable contention about the substance of their agreement. It was his recollection, he told Fulton, that they had modified their 1802 contract during the Paris experiments to give him "one quarter of the first steam boat which shall be established on the Hudson River, *free of all expense.*"[8] Therefore, he was liable for only one-third of all expenses, but entitled to one-half of all profits. Unfortunately, he confessed, he could find no copy of this later agreement.

Fulton, recalling no change in the October 1802 contract, which clearly specified that Livingston would put up 500 pounds for the initial experiments in exchange for a half interest in the patent, denied that any had been made. But he, too, could offer no proof because a ship carrying several boxes of his European papers had sunk in New York harbor—or so he said. So sensitive a misunderstanding between the partners obviously could not be dispelled by mail. There was nothing Fulton could do but make the bone-jarring two- or three-day stagecoach journey to Clermont. It would be their first face-to-face meeting since Livingston left England in May 1804.

During his years in Europe, Fulton had learned to take fine surroundings in his stride. Still he must have been fascinated, if not initially overwhelmed, by the setting into which his partner had been born and which continued to mold his life and temperament. Clermont, the mansion Livingston had built for himself in 1793, stood high on a natural terrace looking across the broad Hudson River Valley to the timeworn Catskill Mountains, their rounded peaks silvery at that season with encrustations of ice and snow. The design of the house was highly personal. Extending from the two-story central section were four one-story pavilions—in plan like an H with the 104-foot-long sides squarely facing the river and the mountains beyond. Built of brick and local stone and covered with stucco, the most striking feature was the great multi-paned windows, which gave the exterior the airy elegance of a small French château and admitted to the interior abundant light. Much of the furniture and the wallpaper was imported from France. The library, of which Livingston was justly proud, contained over four thousand volumes. The greenhouse, with adjoining bathing rooms and offices that he had just added to the south wing, was innovative and pleasant.

Like the architecture, the domestic atmosphere Livingston established had the ingratiating characteristic of seeming casual while it was, indeed, luxurious. Slave children, dressed in green livery trimmed with red, were always at hand to fetch and carry and to summon their elders.

When not needed, they were allowed to tumble about on the carpets. For sociability Livingston could rely on his intelligent but retiring wife, Mary Stevens Livingston, and their two daughters, both of whom had quite properly married Livingston cousins. Elizabeth Stevens Livingston Livingston lived with her husband and children just below in the great house, also called Clermont, which Livingston had given them when his mother died. Margaret Maria Livingston Livingston divided her time between her father's Clermont and Teviotdale, her husband's family house in nearby Linlithgo. Fulton had met them all in Paris.

Livingston owned land much farther than the eye could see. But his own property comprised only a part of his patrimony. Through his blood relations, his sphere of influence ran thirteen miles along the river; its eastern border, nineteen miles distant on the Massachusetts line, ran for twenty miles. There were, in addition, immense holdings west of the Hudson. This great estate was sparsely settled, even where the soil was fertile, because the farmers who worked it lived as tenants of the Livingstons who would rent them land but would not sell it to them without retaining stringent control over land use and resale. The countryside surrounding Clermont was, indeed, a vast enclave of Livingston privilege and, despite bitter quarrels, the family lived as a clan. Robert R. Livingston, their preeminent member, was their head. It was well that Fulton had the opportunity to experience this source of Livingston's statewide power and of his self-esteem at first hand.

Whether feigned or real, Livingston's confusion about the terms of their contract was disquieting. The outcome of what only could have been trying negotiations was a strained compromise, in which the emphasis was on what would happen if the boat failed, probably an expression of Livingston's abiding anxiety. It stated that, if the contract were found, Livingston would pay, as asserted, one-third of all expenses for which he would be entitled to one-half of all the profits. Should the boat fail, the parts would be sold and Livingston would receive one-third of the proceeds and Fulton two-thirds. On the other hand, if the document did not turn up, Livingston would pay one-half of the expenses and enjoy one-half of the profits. In case of failure, the proceeds of the sale would be divided equally. No provision for expanding the enterprise to the Mississippi River was included. Like the 1802 agreement, this new document was witnessed by Livingston's son-in-law, Robert Livingston Livingston, who had been on hand to perform the same function in 1802.

This makeshift compromise concluded, it must have been with great relief that Fulton left the Livingston seigniory and returned to New York City where he had more complete command of his actions. As soon as he arrived, he contracted with Charles Browne, a skillful shipwright with workshops at Corlear's Hook on the East River, to build the hull for a Hudson River steamboat. She was to be 146 feet long—almost half again as long as Fulton's estimates—but still only 12 feet wide. Her depth at the gunwale was 5 feet, raised 2 feet over the cabin, giving an interior height of 6½ feet, "sufficient," Fulton said, "for a man with a hat on." To lessen resistance she was flat-bottomed and straight-sided. Browne promised "to give a fine form to her bow and stern" as Fulton directed and to deliver the vessel "strong and well built" in eight weeks. His price was $1,666 to be paid in four installments.[9]

That done, Fulton retrieved his steam engine from the warehouse where it had lain for over a year. Livingston had refused to pay the $654 in duties, and Barlow would not advance the money in Fulton's behalf because, he told Livingston, he had "no interest in all this business but the interest of friendship."[10] Fulton engaged the able Robert McQueen who had been trained by Nicholas Roosevelt to execute the ironwork for the paddle mechanism and a coppersmith named Marshall to make the boiler—apparently the one he had ordered in England had never been shipped. Reporting to Livingston in detail so there would be no question of their joint commitment, he estimated that, including carpentry and fittings, the cost would run no higher than $5,000—a thousand dollars less than he had anticipated but all of which Livingston would have to pay to balance the $5,111 Fulton had advanced while in Europe.

By the last week in March, Fulton judged the work progressing well enough to take time off for a visit with Ruth, who was mourning the sudden death of her brother Abraham. Barlow was in Washington arranging for his burial and, at the same time, searching for a mansion where he, Ruth, and Fulton could settle down.

While in Philadelphia Fulton had the pleasure of sitting for Charles Willson Peale, who desired his portrait for the gallery of praiseworthy Americans he lovingly called "the Temple of Wisdom." Despite his extraordinarily sweet nature, Peale had a sharp eye. Fulton's cheeks are slightly pinched, and his hairline is markedly receding. His tight, thin lips and glinty eye speak of intractable resolution. Although Peale would become an affectionate and helpful friend, he apparently perceived in Fulton at age forty-one nothing charismatic or even particularly affable.

During this interlude, Fulton received a request from President Jefferson to design a canal between the Mississippi River and Lake Pontchartrain as part of the defenses of New Orleans. Although Barlow urged him to delay answering until they could talk it over, Fulton refused outright. He simply used the occasion to spout his version of the nationally financed program of roads and canals Jefferson had advanced in his second inaugural address. Like Jefferson, he believed that even though the Treasury was running a surplus, taxes should be continued. In fact, he advocated increasing the taxes on liquor—the "poison of minds and morals"—and using the revenue to fund construction loans raised in Europe.

Fulton gave solace to the grieving Ruth for three weeks. Then, realizing he had too much at stake to leave his contractors without personal supervision, he pulled himself away and returned to New York. Thoroughly pleased with what had been accomplished in his absence, he wrote Livingston: "There is a large fortune lying within 4 miles [an hour] all additional Speed will be clear gain and real pleasure." At the same time Fulton went to great lengths to impress on Livingston that it was by his own "purse and perseverance" that the experiments in Paris had succeeded. The entries in the daybook he always kept with him proved that he had put 24,348 livres into the Paris boat not including six months' labor which he had freely contributed. "Having thus fairly met you if not exceeded you in the three important points of *disbursements, Labor* and Invention," he scolded, "Could it in reason be expected that I should to a certainty expend 2000£ Sterling In building a Boat at New York, take on myself the probable risk of expending a much larger sum, give my time and attention till arrived at perfection . . . and then give away one fourth?" The experiments Livingston had made in the 1790s could not be added in, he insisted, because they were essentially useless. At any rate, in the last twelve years he had laid out over 9,000 pounds, and "therefore the account is balanced."[11]

Livingston absorbed Fulton's deprecatory treatment as calmly as he had in France. Satisfied that the work was progressing extremely well without any real effort on his part, he merely sent Fulton mild warnings to take precautions against river hazards such as shoals, posts, and nets and, without argument, paid his half of current expenses including Fulton's lodging at Mrs. Loring's fashionable Broadway boardinghouse.

America

Under Fulton's experienced and meticulous supervision the progress on the boat was, indeed, phenomenal. Fulton inspired his workmen to perform well. Neither large problems nor trifles dampened his contagious enthusiasm. Despite his penchant for elegant clothes and his sometimes formal manner, he had not forgotten his artisan background. He understood and valued his workmen's skills and sought their advice. He gave clear orders and was able to lend a hand as well as to redesign details as the need arose. Probably at his happiest when he was solving problems on the site, he was remarkably patient. "I never heard him use ill words to any one of those employed under him no matter how strong the provocation might be—and I do know there was enough of that at times," his chief engineer later recalled.[12]

Fulton was not even troubled when John Stevens, Livingston's early partner, paid long visits looking for hints on how to improve the steamboat he was building in Hoboken, New Jersey, to run to Albany in defiance of the monopoly. Fulton had heard of his plan within days of his arrival in America and had prudently urged Livingston to give Stevens a share in their venture, "to save him the labor and expense of experiment."[13] Livingston had no desire to divide and, even if he made the offer, Stevens would have been too proud and stubborn to accept. Fulton gave Stevens the run of his works. He enjoyed having so imaginative an experimenter to talk with and was entirely confident that his own carefully worked out proportions and his strong Boulton and Watt engine were far superior to the conventional hull and the unproven engine Stevens had in mind.

By the last week in May Fulton's boat was ready for painting. He intended to have the machinery installed and running by July 10, and ready to make a test run up the river by July 20—"and thus run away from the yellow fevers." Addicted as he was to counting future profits, he sent off yet another set of figures to Livingston, more conservative than the last because he had reduced the running season by three weeks. With an average of fifty passengers on every trip, four trips a week, and forty weeks without ice, he expected an annual net profit of $32,000. "This beats the Story of Mareno Sheep and the Shaved Bear," he ebulliently joked to his partner, "as this calculation makes me feel warm and generous, please now to give my love to the Ladies."[14]

Fulton kept to schedule and on July 14 reported that the wheels moved admirably. With water in the boiler, cinders in the furnace, and 8 tons of coal stacked along the sides—sufficient for five trips of thirty-six hours each—the boat would draw only 18 inches of water. The adjustments to the levers, screws, bolts, pumps, and rods would be finished within the week. "I cannot say when I shall be with you," he told Livingston, "but the time I think cannot be distant perhaps In 10 or 16 days."[15]

Nowhere in this reassuring correspondence did Fulton mention to Livingston that while he was working on their steamboat, he was also building prototype torpedoes for a public demonstration of his system of submarine warfare. In late January he formally offered his bombs to Robert Smith, secretary of the navy, to protect American ports from the increasingly belligerent British navy. They would be far quicker and cheaper to install, he pointed out, than any of the alternatives under consideration. The scheme contemplated by New York, for instance, involved cordoning off the entrance to the harbor with iron chains, wooden booms, and great masonry obstructions. The obstructions would take a year to build; they would place the same constraints on domestic as on enemy shipping; and they would be difficult and expensive to remove once the threat of invasion was over; the estimated cost was one million dollars.

When on June 20, 1807, the H.M.S. *Leopard* fired on the U.S.S. *Chesapeake* and three American seamen were killed, eighteen wounded, and four kidnapped, a declaration of war was daily expected. Fulton was then given permission to mount an exhibition of his defense system in New York Harbor. It would take place on July 20—the day he had told Livingston he would test the steamboat. Fulton's elation at being able to prove to his countrymen the immense value of his submarine explosives must have been intense. For the first time, he would be acting as a patriot rather than as a foreign mercenary.

True to his instincts for showmanship and tutelage, Fulton invited the governor, mayor, and other New York dignitaries to attend a preparatory lecture explaining his "engines." This took place on July 18 at the fortification on Governors Island. Fulton spelled out his system's rationale and, with a diabolical flourish, pointed to a bomb loaded with 170 pounds of gunpowder and triggered by a clockwork detonator set for 15 minutes. He put it in motion by pulling the pin. Not until most of the terrified audience had fled did he stop the mechanism. One spectator later observed: "The apprehensions of the company surprised, but amused him, and he took the occasion to remark how true it was that fear frequently arose from ignorance." His own composure testified to his confidence in the system.[16]

Two days later, a crowd estimated at two thousand lined the tip of Manhattan for the show. The strategy was similar to that used for the destruction of the *Dorothea*. A derelict 200-ton brig was anchored between Governors and Ellis islands. Boatmen were to drop two bombs tied together by a 120-foot line so close to the brig's anchor cable that they would be swept under the keel by the tide and current. When they struck, the brig would be blown to atoms.

The first bombs were launched amid a shiver of expectations. They failed to explode. The detonating powder had fallen out of the pans. Fulton calmly adjusted the mechanism and launched them once again. This time they burst approximately 100 yards from the brig. Disappointed and disbelieving, most of the good New York burghers went home to dinner. Seemingly unruffled, Fulton persevered. On his third attempt he succeeded. At seven o'clock in the evening the ship "was rent in two and went to the bottom in 20 seconds. . . . Thus," Fulton triumphantly reported, "the practibility of destroying vessels by this means has been fully proved."[17]

In a letter addressed to the governor, mayor, and corporation of New York and published in the *New-York Spectator*, explaining away his "little difficulties and errors" as common in all new inventions, Fulton drew a vivid picture of how "the right application of one torpedo will annihilate a ship of the line nor leave a man to relate the dreadful catastrophe."[18]

The press was more judgmental. "No machinery like this which requires the manager to proceed in full view, within 30 or 50 yards of the vessel to be destroyed, can ever in any way succeed," the *Commercial Advertiser* editorialized. "A thousand of them with the managers and their boats could be blown from the surface of the water before they could approach so near as to do the least injury to a hostile fleet."[19] Washington Irving, using the pen name William Wizard, Esq., satirized this "dog-day whim-wham" in his new monthly *Salmagundi*:

> It may be readily supposed, that our citizens did not refuse the invitation . . . to the blow-up; it was the first naval action ever exhibited in our port, and the good people all crowded to see the British navy blown up in effigy. The young ladies were delighted with the novelty of the show, and declared that if war could be conducted in this manner it would become a fashionable amuse-

ment; and the destruction of a fleet be as pleasant as a ball or a tea-party. The old folks were equally pleased with the spectacle—because it cost them nothing. Dear souls, how hard was it they should be disappointed! The brig most obstinately refused to be decomposed; the dinners were cold, and the puddings were over boiled, throughout the renowned city of Gotham; . . . all returned home after having threatened to pull down the flag-staff by way of taking satisfaction for their disappointment.

Mr. Icabod Fungus informed him, Wizard continued, that after a world of maneuvering the bomb had finally gone off. It was, Fungus thought, "an excellent plan of defence; no need of batteries, forts, frigates, and gun-boats; observe sir, all that's necessary is that the ships must come to anchor in a convenient place; watch must be asleep, or so complacent as not to disturb any boats paddling about them—fair wind and tide—*no moonlight*—machines well directed—mustn't flash in the pan—bang's the word, and the vessel's blown up in a moment."

"Christopher Cockloft," Wizard's honest old mouthpiece, offered a more profound condemnation of this "attempt to introduce a dastardly and exterminating mode of warfare. . . . [W]ar is already invested with sufficient horrors and calamities," he lectured. "Let us not increase the catalogue; let us not, by these deadly artifices, provoke a system of insidious and indiscriminate hostility, that shall terminate in laying our cities desolate, and exposing our women, our children and our infirm to the sword of pitiless recrimination."[20]

Vice-Admiral George Berkeley, the British commander of naval forces in North America who had ordered the assault on the *Chesapeake*, was expecially delighted by "the wholesome stripes" Irving bestowed upon "the Folly of Gotham. The Scheme was scouted not perhaps so much from its failure," he commented from his station in Halifax, Nova Scotia, "as from the baseness of Cowardice of this species of warfare."[21]

Fulton retained his equilibrium. He coolly wrote President Jefferson that the people of New York seemed well pleased with the experiment, and he believed they would be happy to see it united with other modes of defense. Informing him that the flopping motion that caused both locks to misfire had been corrected, Fulton urged Jefferson to advocate that submarine warfare be organized into a general system for the national defense.

Fanatically committed to avoiding the expense of building and maintaining a conventional navy, Jefferson was ever on the lookout for cheap ways of supplementing the gunboat fleet he had caused to be built to defend American ports. Fulton's system of submarine warfare appealed to him. He wrote Fulton that he favored establishing a special submarine corps and would inquire if he had the authority to draw the men from the existing naval establishment. Putting his finger on the delivery problem, he particularly hoped Fulton had not abandoned the submarine boat as impracticable.

Despite his enthusiasm for submarine warfare, Jefferson had not given up hope that Fulton would undertake the New Orleans canal survey. Addressing him as Colonel Fulton, the President offered him that rank in the Flying Artillery if he would accept. Fulton was not to be tempted. His first wish, he replied, was to remain the master of his own movements.

Hudson River Triumphs

❖

Fulton did not allow himself to become depressed about his torpedoes' poor performance. He switched his attention to his steamboat, and in less than three weeks, she was ready to be launched. Tied up at Browne's wharf at Corlear's Hook, the 146-foot hull was sound. Flat-bottomed like a skiff and straight-sided like a scow, she had, nevertheless, the graceful bow and stern lines Fulton insisted on. Enough coal was stored below deck for 192 hours of running time. Although he did not intend to use it all on his initial trip, the vessel was outfitted with large square sails fore and aft. The exposed copper boiler was arched at the top. It rested on two rows of fire brick and had been made self-feeding by a mechanism similar to a float-operated toilet. Except for the wheel paddles whose ultimate size he was still not sure about, only small items such as boat hooks and water casks were lacking.

The day Fulton chose for the first trial was August 9, 1807, exactly four years to the day after his *succès brillant* on the Seine. But instead of offering a full public demonstration, he intended only to test the hull's maneuverability and to find out the most efficient dimensions for the paddleboards. It was a Sunday, however, and he knew that inquisitive spectators would congregate along the waterfront to see if his luck was as bad with his steamboat as it had been with his bombs.

By noon the steam pressure was strong enough to begin. He ran the boat one mile up the river—off what is now Houston Street—using paddleboards only 3 feet by 8 inches, but, he wrote Livingston, she "beat all the sloops that were endeavoring to stem the tide." He anchored, doubled the depth of the paddles by adding another board of the same size, and ran back to Browne's wharf at 4 miles an hour—3 derived from the power of the engine, the fourth from the outgoing tide.

The results of the experiment were gratifying. Despite her exceedingly long, thin proportions, she answered the helm "equal to anything that ever was built." The axles proved strong enough to run the engine at full power. Fulton could, therefore, make the paddleboards half again as large to achieve greater speed. He also decided to increase the size of the condenser's water pump. Otherwise, the engine needed only overhauling and new packing—hardly surprising since it was the first time the engine had been worked in a boat. Together with the final touches on the cabins, the changes could be made within the week. "Whatever may be the fate of steamboats for the Hudson," Fulton blithely informed Livingston, "my thing is completely proved for the Mississippi And the object is immense—please to forward to me 1000 or 1500 dollars as soon as possible." [1]

Livingston at last had faith. He did not go so far as to leave his comfortable domain—perhaps he wished to avoid the influenza epidemic that was raging through the city—but he was liberal with invitations for a "sail" on his steamboat. "Cousin Chancellor has a wonderful new boat which is to make the voyage up the Hudson some day soon," wrote young Helen Livingston to her mother. "It will hold a good many passengers and he has, with his usual kindness, invited us to be of the party. He says it will be something to remember all our lives. He says we need not trouble ourselves about provisions, as his men will see to all that." [2]

Fulton could not have enjoyed Livingston's sudden proprietary attitude. He perceived the maiden voyage as an experiment, not a gala. Still, he bought wine, sugar, brandy, and dishes for the trip to Albany. Then, to assert his independence, he granted an interview to the *American Citizen*, which stated that his "Ingenius Steamboat, invented with a view to the navigation of the Mississippi from New Orleans upward," would "certainly make an exceedingly valuable aquisition to the commerce of the Western States." [3]

On August 16, Fulton took the steamboat around the Battery to the dock on the North River near the State Prison in Greenwich Village. Again it was a Sunday with a built-in audience of promenaders along the route. Several gentlemen—all friends or relatives of Livingston—were intrepid enough to join him in this short but crucial run. U.S. Senator Samuel Latham Mitchill was the most eminent, a doctor, lawyer, naturalist, chemist, and politician who, as a New York State legislator, first introduced the much derided "hot-water bill" by which Livingston took over Fitch's monopoly. Fulton must have been acquainted with him, for he was the chairman of the Senate Defense Committee and was a prime mover in obtaining appropriations for the defense of New York Harbor. Dr. William McNiven and the dean of Ripon Cathedral, England, also risked the adventure. Representing the absent partner were his younger brother John R. Livingston, who never had anything agreeable to say about the venture, and his distant cousin John Swift Livingston.

The transfer to the new berth was accomplished without the slightest mishap. The steamboat, Mrs. Mitchill wrote to her sister, was a curious-looking thing that "rolled through the water by her two great arms, resembling the wheels of a Grist Mill," and would "frighten some of the Old Dutchmen half out of their wits. They will conclude the enemy is coming in earnest with a machine to blow them all up."[4] To Peale's son Rembrandt, she seemed like a huge paddling tortoise. Fulton thought she was quite perfect—the work of an inventive genius. Confident that she would perform well, he was determined to set forth for Albany the next day—Monday, August 17, 1807—when the almanacs told him high tide was at eight o'clock and would begin its flood again shortly before two in the afternoon. The sun would not set until 6:48, and the moon, rising at 4:38, would be full.

The dock was a good two miles north of City Hall, but everyone in the metropolis who could possibly do so paraded to the site. Few had any acquaintance with steam engines, and the notion that such a contraption could propel a boat was considered crackpot, irresponsible, or possibly suicidal. The enormous wheels and long, thin proportions were at best comical, for a proper Hudson River craft had an oversized gaff rig and was broad of beam. Dire predictions were interspersed with gleeful jests about "Fulton's Folly." When the chimney began to belch black smoke, bets were on that the entire absurdity would blow up or be claimed by the devil himself.

Fulton missed none of the jibes, but he did not allow them to distract him. In a clear, high voice that carried over the hubbub, he gave precise orders to his engineer, an Englishman named George Jackson for whom he had great respect, and to his captain, Davis Hunt, who was of more questionable character, but who at least had the courage to sign on.

It was one o'clock, almost an hour before the turn of the tide, when the "Folly" cast off from the wharf with only the inventor and his skeleton crew aboard. The breeze was against her, but it was light as she began her 150-mile journey. Without faltering, her splashing paddle wheels pushed against the down-flowing river. At first, her progress was slow, but as the tide changed, it visibly quickened and she "overtook many sloops and schooners beating to windward and passed them as if they had been at anchor."[5] Within two hours, the steamboat's distant form, dwarfed by the imperial Palisades, could be seen from the wharf only as a banner of black smoke. As night fell and the tide turned against her, she entered wide Haverstraw Bay. The luminous August moon was high as her vibrating, spark-throwing engines thrust her through the narrow waters of the Highlands, past the rugged promontory at West Point. Toward mid-morning on August 18, as the steamboat rounded the bend at Kingston, the hazy blue-green Catskills signaled her approach to Clermont. The tide was with her again, and at precisely one o'clock in the afternoon she faultlessly steamed up to Livingston's private landing and dropped anchor. "Time 24 hours, distance 110 miles," Fulton wrote in his remarkably laconic account for the press.[6] The steamboat had achieved just over 4½ miles an hour, powered only by her engines.

It has been said that Livingston arranged a splendid gathering "on this day of crowning glory" and prophesied that the name of the inventor would descend to posterity as a benefactor to the world. Celebration there must have been, for as the proprietor of so vast a domain, Livingston would have thought it fitting to share the culmination of his twenty-year dream with his clan and his neighbors and tenants. There is, however, no record of it. All that is known is that, despite the uninterrupted tension and labor of the previous days, Fulton put the engines in motion for the last 40 miles of the journey at 9:13 the following morning, August 19.

Livingston, accompanied by his son-in-law Edward and the English prelate, boarded for what was to him a delightful outing. Against a pleasant head of wind the steamboat churned through the ebb tide for 8 miles. She then took the flood tide, and just after five o'clock arrived at Albany. "Without any accident or interruption what ever," she achieved almost 5 miles an hour. "She is unquestionably the most pleasant boat

I ever went in," the dean of Ripon Cathedral reported to his compatriots. "In her the mind is free from suspense. Perpetual motion authorizes you to calculate on a certain time to land; her works move with all the facility of a clock; and the noise when on board is not greater than that of a vessel sailing with a good breeze."[7]

Led by the governor, an Albany contingent that had been no more credulous than the New Yorkers stood on the waterfront to greet the vessel propelled by steam. For them the anticipation of disaster was magnified, for that summer a ferry had sunk in the harbor and thirty passengers drowned. Astonishingly, there is no mention of the boat's arrival in the newspapers, but the sheer novelty of the event must have occasioned a fete for the heroes that evening.

Fulton was exhausted. The physical and emotional strain had so drained him that he could scarcely walk. It was, he later said, the turning point of his destiny, the first actual recognition of his usefulness to his fellow man.

At the moment, however, Fulton had no time for reflection or respite. The next morning he hung a placard on the side of the boat announcing the steamboat would start for New York the following day, fare $7.00—over twice as much as the sloops charged. His men laid in provisions—bread, sauce, fowls, liquor, a barrel of water, and a table. Ignoring Fulton's orders, Captain Hunt took gaping sightseers aboard at a shilling a head. But so great was the fear of the boiler exploding, that, in addition to Livingston and the dean, only two Frenchmen—the distinguished botanist François André Michaux and his companion, a French army officer named Parmentier—dared the trip.

The steamboat left Albany at nine o'clock on Thursday morning and arrived at Clermont at six in the evening. Again there was a light wind against her, but no waves. News traveled fast by word of mouth, and Livingston proudly wrote his son-in-law Robert: "at Hudson, & indeed at every publick landing the sight was amusing. All the people of the town were upon the hills that bound the river, upwards of twenty boats filled with men & women came to meet us having seen us at a great distance coming down. They all made the utmost efforts to keep up with us & thus there was in the number of five-oared barge double manned. They could not by all their efforts keep near us more than two minutes. She has exceeded Fulton's and justified my calculations."[8]

After a scant hour's layover, during which Livingston and the dean disembarked, Fulton started for New York. From the riverbanks along the way, excited citizens waved their handkerchiefs and cheered. At West Point the whole garrison turned out and sent up repeated huzzahs. Nonetheless, the ominous aspects of the invention did not escape notice. As one acute—though thrilled—witness wrote: "The whole country talked of nothing but the sea monster, belching forth fire and smoke. The fishermen became terrified, and rowed homewards, and they saw nothing but destruction of their fishing grounds, whilst the wreaths of black vapour, and rushing noise of the paddlewheels, foaming with the stirred up waters, produced great excitement amid the boatmen."[9]

Fulton guided his steamboat into her berth in New York City at four o'clock on Friday afternoon, August 21. Emotionally spent, he could no more than state for the *American Citizen:* "time 30 hours, space run through 150 miles, equal 5 miles an hour."[10] It was only for Livingston that Fulton revived his characteristic enthusiasm. In a hasty note he wrote: "funds and spirit are now only wanting to do the handsomest and lucrative things which has been performed for some years."[11]

The press ignored the momentous first trip of the steamboat, except for Fulton's laconic notice in the *Citizen* and the brief editorial that accompanied it: "We congratulate Mr. Fulton and the country on his success in the steamboat which cannot fail of being very advantageous. We understand that not the smallest inconvenience is felt in the boat, either from heat or smoke." At that time the newspapers were filled with detailed reports of the conspiracy trial of former vice-president Aaron Burr, who had allegedly raised a private army with the intention of forming the lands west of the Mississippi into a separate nation. Ironically, Fulton was left on his own to broadcast his vision of a great nation unified by strong bonds of communication. To Barlow who had not come to New York either to wish his beloved friend godspeed or to congratulate him on his brilliant achievement, he announced his dream of establishing steam navigation in the West in a letter that was intended for—and received—broad publication. Scornfully commenting on the sarcasm he had endured at the outset of his momentous voyage as the way "in which ignorant men compliment what they call philosophers and projectors," Fulton declared that steam would give cheap and quick access to merchandise on the Mississippi, Missouri, and other great rivers, thus "laying open their treasures to the enterprise of our countrymen." However, unable to resist the opportunity to proselytize once more for submarine warfare, which in his all-encompassing mind was inextricably bound with steamboats as a means of bringing about free trade, Fulton concluded:

> I will not admit that it [the steamboat] is half so important as the torpedo system of defense and attack; for out of this will grow the liberty of the seas; an object of infinite importance to the welfare of America and every civilized country. . . . [I]n case we have war and the enemy's ships come into our waters, if the government will give me reasonable means of action, I will soon convince the world that we have surer and cheaper modes of defense than they are aware of.[12]

The next day, Fulton plunged into the work of rendering his boat safer and more suitable for passengers, "boarding all the sides, decking over the boiler and works, finishing each cabin with twelve berths to make them comfortable, and strengthening many parts of the iron work."[13] It was probably at this time that he changed from coal to wood to fire his boilers. At that time there was no assured source of coal, and wood was still plentiful and relatively cheap.

Fulton's hope was to run a scheduled service for six weeks or two months, beginning on Wednesday, September 2. Incessant rain delayed the caulkers, but on that day Fulton placed an advertisement in the newspaper announcing that the steamboat would leave New York for Albany on Friday, September 4, at six o'clock in the evening and would arrive thirty-six hours later. He hired one Shoek Johnston as the assistant steward, waiter, and pilot at $18 a month, and a black man named Graft Griffin to be the cook and waiter at $15 a month. In anticipation of a good turnout of thirsty and hungry passengers they laid in more brandy and rum as well as bread and butter, beef, fowls, eggs, watermelon, and sugar.

On September 3, Fulton enrolled the boat at the port of New York as the *North River Steam Boat*. The name was derived from the Hudson, which as it passes Manhattan was called the North River. Fulton was listed as the sole owner, an arrangement that was agreeable to Livingston, because Fulton had advanced far more money than he to pay for her. She was certified to be 142 feet in length and 78⁷¹⁄₉₅ tons. Although this steamboat is virtually always referred to as the *Clermont*, after Livingston's country seat, she was never called by that name during Fulton's lifetime. In the beginning, she was simply called the *Steamboat*. There was, in the world, no other.

The first trip of the *Steamboat* as a commercial passenger boat was an unqualified success. That is not to say that most of the spectators who found places on the piers and rooftops to witness her departure were converts, but she left as scheduled from the more centrally located Powles Hook Ferry dock at the foot of Cortlandt Street with all berths taken. Twelve passengers booked through to Albany, one embarked for Tarrytown, one for Newburgh, and, together with Fulton, one other for Clermont. The vessel's progress was considered high theater. At every landing, craft of all kinds pulled alongside for a good view. The Fishkill ferry was commandeered especially for the ladies, to whom Fulton is said to have gallantly raised his hat and exclaimed, "That is the finest sight we have yet seen." [14] When a miller shouted he wanted to see where the grindstones were installed on this floating sawmill, Fulton took him aboard and gave him a thorough lecture on the mechanical arrangements.

The *Steamboat* arrived in Albany at 11:27 on September 5. Her running time was 28 hours, 45 minutes, an hour and a half faster than the initial northbound trip and 6 hours and 33 minutes ahead of schedule. An affidavit, signed by the passengers, one of whom was Selah Strong, the president of the New York City Council, stated that the "accommodations and conveniences on board exceeded their most sanguine expectations." [15]

In subsequent trips, Fulton was able to maintain this excellent speed. When the wind was favorable, the crew hoisted the sails to supplement the paddle wheels. The sloops sometimes outpaced her, but she was never becalmed. Riding the *Steamboat* became fashionable. Within a month she carried up to ninety passengers each trip, and it was suggested that the Postmaster General engage her to carry mail from New York City to Albany.

Fulton and Livingston had, without question, struck gold. However, it was not to be easily mined. Accidents, most of them deliberately inflicted by jealous sloop captains, were a constant worry. On her return from Albany in the second week of September, the sloop *Fox* rammed her wheels, then went about and hit her again, driving her on to a sand bank which broke her axle wheels. Fortunately, no one was hurt. The ladies "behaved like angels;" they regretted only having missed an agreeable voyage. The *Steamboat* did not resume her schedule until September 23. Ten days later she tangled with a sloop in a stiff wind.

This time she lost a paddle wheel and was forced to proceed with only one wheel operating which caused her to pitch dangerously.

Blaming these accidents on Captain Hunt's carelessness—he was later said to have been bribed by the sloop captains—Fulton immediately replaced him with Andrew Brink of Esopus. "You must insist on each one doing his duty or turn him on shore and put another in his place," he instructed Brink. "Everything must be kept in order, everything in its place, and all parts of the Boat scoured and clean. It is not sufficient to tell men to do a thing, but stand over them and make them do it. One pair of Quick and good eyes is worth six pair of hands in a commander." When overtaking sailing vessels, Brink must always run under their stern, unless it was certain he could clear their bow by 50 yards or more.[16]

Brink was no more satisfactory than Hunt, and within a few weeks he had been supplanted by Samuel Wiswall of Hudson who proved more faithful and energetic. Nevertheless, Fulton continued to complain to Livingston: "Our Hands are too numerous, their Wages too high, Our fuel more than half too dear and the quantity may be economized."[17]

These repetitive problems began to weary Fulton, who was eager to get on with his patent application and to lay the groundwork for new government-sponsored submarine experiments. By the end of October he was so restless he took the risk of leaving for Washington. The Barlows whom he had not seen for over six months were now living there.

Fulton broke his journey briefly in Philadelphia. He called on Peale who was in the throes of establishing America's first true art museum, the Pennsylvania Academy of the Fine Arts. It was Peale's dream that the proceeds from the exhibition would so increase the academy's income that he would be able to open a school for figure drawing and also a room for selling paintings by contemporary artists. Fulton fervently believed that an understanding of the fine arts was vital for a flourishing society and agreed to lend Peale his works by West and Smirkes as well as his copies of paintings by Rubens, Titian, and Poussin, all of which had been shipped from England in the spring. To help Fulton, Peale offered to shepherd his boxes through customs to prevent the officials from ransacking them and from charging overly high duties.

Fulton must also have called on Conrad, the printer, for Barlow's *Columbiad* was at last ready for publication. The engraving of his patriarchal portrait of Barlow, which was to be used as a frontispiece, and of the Smirke illustrations, for which he had paid $5,000 in England, was well executed and the typography was extraordinarily beautiful.

However, the volume cost $20 a copy and, though Fulton predicted the poetry would be quoted "forever," the style was pompous and vacuous. It was neither a critical nor a commercial success.

Only one couplet alludes to Fulton's genius, and that is lost in an elegy on the transformation of "earth's portless inland realms": "Canals curve thro them many a liquid line / Prune their wild streams, their lake and oceans join." It was in the emotional prose dedication that Barlow chose to celebrate their close relationship:

> This poem is your property. Our friendship has been uncommonly useful to us both. Yet in no instance has that delicious bond of union been more disinterested than between you and me . . . take it, as long as it is to live, a monument to our friendship; you cannot need it as a monument to your fame.
>
> Continue to be happy, my Fulton, as your various merit entitles you to be. Continue to enhance that merit by well directed labours for the good of mankind; and since this address will not outlast the poem to which it is prefixed, I leave you to take some other method to unite my memory more durably with your own.[18]

If Fulton was embarrassed by this effusion, he made no mention of it in writing. By November 1, he joined the Barlows in the stylish "Six Buildings" near Georgetown and on November 4 he described himself as busy getting them settled in their capital new house. With the understanding they would live together as they had in Paris, Barlow bought a large property on a high ridge near Rock Creek just outside the village of Georgetown—the estate Jefferson had written him about when Barlow first contemplated returning to the United States in 1802. Because it suffered the inconvenience of being three miles by way of a corrugated road from the capital, Barlow got the house and thirty acres for only $14,000. It had, he boasted, "one of the finest views in America." On the plain below were the President's house and the Capitol, beyond them the winding Potomac and Alexandria. The land was wooded and sloped down to a stream "so closely shut in by rocks and evergreens, that it might serve as a noonday bath for Diana and her nymphs." With the few improvements Fulton suggested and a change of name from the too common Belair to the Greek Kalorama, meaning "fine view," he was certain it would become "a little paradise."[19]

The fatigue that resulted from setting up her first serious household at the age of fifty had left Ruth exhausted, but with Fulton's arrival her strength returned. Being together again put them all "in good spirits."

They talked over plans for the remodeling, and Fulton corresponded with Peale about mangles and stoves to make housekeeping neat and modern. If he had any qualms about thus reinforcing his "delicious bond of union" with Barlow, Fulton was able to suppress them. Their *ménage à trois* was as necessary to him as it had been in Paris.

Having put himself at such a physical—and psychological—distance from Livingston, Fulton was careful to nurture their partnership through a vigorous correspondence. He wrote at length about current operations and future plans, joking that the postage for his letters, which sometimes ran well over ten pages, would have to come out of next year's profits. Because he regarded the *Steamboat*'s service that autumn as an "experiment under every disadvantage" and, in fact, admitted that the present boat was cranky and needed to be 3 or 4 feet wider for stability, he advocated scrapping everything except the engine and building a far larger and more luxurious vessel. Livingston considered that plan rash and told Fulton they would be better off, from a point of view of expense and of flexibility, with two moderate-sized boats. That did not suit Fulton, and he persuaded Livingston they should refurbish the *Steamboat* during the winter, run her all spring and summer, then apply the profits to building a sister ship to be launched in time for the 1809 season. This, he told Livingston, "will give us pleasure and time for arrangements. If we put ourselves in a situation to be pressed for money we shall have more Vexation than I would care to suffer for the [$]3000 which might arise from a new boat in one year to which there would be all the trouble and blunders which arise from hurry in Constructing her."[20]

Livingston advanced a flood of ill-conceived mechanical suggestions. For instance, to save money, he proposed a boiler made from wood and leather, lined with lead and covered with a paste, the principal ingredients of which were oxblood and eggwhites. Fulton genially but forcefully replied that no makeshift solutions would be safe.

Fulton and Livingston finally agreed that as soon as cold weather brought the season to a close they would take the *Steamboat* to Red Hook, a protected cove south of Clermont, where they would set up a workshop. Fulton could stay with Livingston and supervise the remodeling on a day-to-day basis. They would build a new hull for the engine, increasing the length to 150 feet and the width to 15 or 16 feet with a flare to 18 feet at the deck level. This would make the boat twice as stiff as before, Fulton said, and allow her to carry "a much greater quantity of sail." The carpenters could use timbers salvaged from the original hull. To accommodate the 4 additional feet in width, the new boiler would be made capable of raising steam to 5 pounds per square inch. The wheels would be enclosed by guards to prevent them from splashing water on the deck. Built into the exterior would be steps to facilitate boarding from rowboats. Inside, before the wheels, would be "commodities" for the men. Aft would be storage space for fuel and bins for fish, lobsters, and oysters, which they would sell in Albany. This was one of Livingston's few good suggestions; the profits, he figured, would cover the cost of firewood.

Fulton insisted that the appearance and comfort of the accommodations be outstanding:

> I have found it necessary to keep the Mens room and Berths the Stewards room and Berths the Kitchen and every thing below deck So that the deck and all the part 72 feet long and under the permanent Awning may be clear for passengers and their baggage. There the passengers will be sheltered from rain and Sunshine. There they can dine in fine weather and the place is so spacious it will be charming; by confining the kitchen men and Butlers rooms to the center of the Boat and round the Boiler and Works it keeps all dirt out of sight. The stewards room removes the after cabin from heat should there be any; the men's room removes the fore cabin from the noise of the works.[21]

The deck would be finished with one-inch boards and, because it was "almost impossible to make such a deck perfectly tight and handsome by means of Caulking," he intended to cover it, except where the parcels and trunks would be stowed, with light olive-colored oil cloth, "thick as pasteboard," and costing $1.25 for a 15-foot-wide yard. He had seen this treatment in John Stevens's dining room where, despite the wear caused by numerous children, it had been down sixteen years without getting a single hole in it. These alterations would cost two or three thousand dollars.

Leaping ahead to the operating schedule and prospective profits, Fulton wrote that he planned to run their boat up the river on Monday and Thursday mornings and down on Tuesday and Friday evenings. Sundays in New York would be used to clean the boiler and rest the men. "In this manner with a sound Strong Boat we Should make 120 voyages a year . . . which averaging 30 persons a Voyage or 3600 persons a year will clear us 12,000 dollars. . . . Nil deperandum."[22]

This was a happy period for Fulton. Almost every line of this correspondence is shot through with euphoria and pride. When Livingston suggested they might expand the ownership of the *Steamboat* because he wanted to give a percentage to each of his sons-in-law, Fulton answered: "I am so well pleased with her and my prospects In her that I have no desire to sell any of my Interest and should I you shall have the refusal. I have funds for my part and perhaps the prudent measure is for us to hold the North River to ourselves." Yet he made a great point of identifying himself with Livingston. "I am delighted that on all great points we not only agree but seem to anticipate each other's wishes, this makes business and partnership a real pleasure particularly when the prospect of emolument is 75 percent per annum upon the capital." And, reaching out to embrace the whole family as he so liked to do, he added, "Best respects to Mrs. Livingston. If I reside with you while the boat is repairing, I mean to paint her portrait to match in *Size* those of Stuart that is if I can get the canvas and paints. So Give my compliments to her and tell her to begin now to make her mouth and features up, for so noble and interesting a work."[23]

The only serious divergence of opinion between Fulton and Livingston that autumn concerned how they would protect their steamboat enterprise from competition. Still an adept lawyer, Livingston was worried that his state monopoly would be endangered if they applied for a U.S. patent, since by so doing they would acknowledge the supremacy of the federal patent law. The courts had not yet clarified the crucial question of whether the states ceded their right to grant exclusive privileges for useful improvements when the federal law was passed, and it was subject to varying interpretations.

Livingston believed that a state grant differed from a federal patent in that it was a contract to fulfill a service rather than a reward for making public a novel and useful mechanism. He argued that the possession of a state monopoly was, like personal property, under the jurisdiction of the state. Moreover, the state retained the right to restrain the use of patented articles within its borders. "Were a man to patent a new musical instrument would that give him the right to play in your garden and set your children dancing when you wished them to study," he queried.[24] Similarly, the state could prevent a mountebank from vending poisonous patent medicines, even though it permitted the sale of salubrious medicines.

Fulton did not agree. It had always been his private opinion, he

replied, that "The law of the United States Authorizes every inventor
to Use his invention throughout the whole of the states, and no particular state can prevent him. Hence if a steam boat which should be acknowledged New and different from ours were to appear on the North
River we could not prevent her." The patent protected only against im-
itators. Therefore, he insisted they secure their invention with a patent.
Seeking corroboration for his view, Fulton borrowed a copy of the patent law from William Thornton and discussed the problem briefly with
him. Thornton, he reported to Livingston, was adamant that the states
had no right to grant exclusive privileges to navigate their rivers. However, in case both his and Thornton's interpretations proved wrong, Fulton
promised he would say nothing about it in public "for I would not have
the idea circulated."

The best solution, Fulton thought, was that they take out a patent
in the usual form for as long as possible. Then in the spring when their
boat was running, he would personally examine the Mississippi. "If I
find it practicable and profitable for steam boats we could hold out a
bait to congress," he wrote Livingston, "let them give us the exclusive
right to the Hudson, Mississippi, Ohio and Missouri Or to the Hudson,
Mississippi and its waters for 25 or 30 years And we will make the nation a present of the Invention for all the other waters of America." Fulton's real hope was that, because the heavy expenses of building a boat
and the still uncertain profits would deter anyone from trying to pirate
their invention immediately, they would have about two years' head start,
enough time to firmly establish their hegemony in steam navigation.

Fulton's difficulty was that he still could not find the right words
and form of presentation that would establish the originality of his invention. Despite his constant past assertions that the "indispensable
principles" he had discovered did indeed constitute an original creation,
when confronted with the reality of the patent law, he was baffled about
how to express his claim. It would require some study, he confessed to
Livingston, to make drawings that would plainly show why he had succeeded where all others had failed, "for although the effect produced is
new, the whole is composed of old parts and looks as though different
persons who have attempted Steam boats had tried the whole of them.
You will therefore be so good As to aid me with your Ideas of the distinction which makes the novelty of this invention and renders it superior to all attempts of the kind which have been made."[25]

Livingston was unable or unwilling to advise him. His principal contribution to the enterprise was, after all, the possession of the New York State monopoly. In the end he succeeded in convincing Fulton, at least temporarily, that neither their New York monopoly nor their prospective patent was in jeopardy. Not daring to face the patent problem alone, Fulton postponed his plan to file an application until the following spring when he and Livingston would have had a chance to work on it together. Although he did not acknowledge it openly, he was unquestionably dependent on Livingston.

Meanwhile, reports of accidents to the *Steamboat* continued to flow in from Captain Wiswall. On November 11 when she was six miles out of Albany she was "designedly" run into by the sloop *Linnet* and was saved from great damage only by the exertions of the passengers. The following Friday one of her axles broke, and she was obliged to return to New York at a loss of fifty fares. Cold weather struck unusually early that year. The deck was iced over on the morning of November 16. Alarmed, Fulton ordered Livingston to get her into dock by the twentieth. "Present accidents are all trifles, only let not her be sunk," he nervously advised; "our improvements, economy, systems and profits will commence in March or April. . . . Next year we will carry all the passengers on the Hudson and starve the skippers of Albany."[26]

Fulton should have returned to New York long before, but he stayed on in Washington not only because he enjoyed the Barlows' company but also because he was strenuously seeking support for his system of submarine warfare. Tension between England and America had not subsided. As Stevens who was also devising harbor defenses put it: "A formidable British fleet is now hovering on our coast & like hungry Vultures are only waiting for orders to seize on their defenseless prey."[27] The Senate was engaged in passing a large appropriation for the national defense. Although in the short run Americans would suffer, Jefferson was convinced an embargo would force both England and France to stop using American merchant ships as pawns in their war. It was, he believed, a way of waging war using peaceable means. A strong faction in the country scorned the embargo as suicidal. It would be much better, these partisans thought, to build up the navy immediately and meet force with force. With a surplus in the Treasury and England fully occupied fighting France, they had no doubt the United States would prevail.

As a low-priced defensive weapon with potential for attack, Fulton's torpedoes offered an alternative to both extremes. In early December Fulton wrote the secretary of the navy that he desired to mount another demonstration and sent Jefferson estimates of the cost of experiments. Even if only a few out of two hundred bombs hit, he was certain his torpedoes could annihilate the British navy. The immense cost of building and maintaining a conventional fleet of warships would be avoided. "[A]ll courage is founded on the hope of success and calculations on superior advantages," he wrote the President, undoubtedly speaking of himself; "cowardice is forced upon the mind as soon as it feels its inferiority."[28]

To improve his delivery system, Fulton was experimenting with a harpoon gun, designed to shoot a bolt of iron 2 feet long into the hull of a ship. It had a barbed point at one end and an eye at the other through which was passed a 60-foot rope with a torpedo set with a time lock tied to its end. He tried shooting the harpoon out of a gun, and it penetrated 6 inches of oak at 40 feet.

Barlow, who perceived that none of his friends objected to the fact that Fulton had previously sold his torpedoes to both the French and the British, was at last a true convert. "If this man is supported," he wrote Jefferson, "he will give us the liberty of the seas and a system of interior public improvements superior to what has been seen in any country. His whole soul is in those two subjects . . . and his energy is equal to the task."[29] When Jefferson expressed his "great satisfaction" with Fulton's plans, Fulton was ecstatic; he had, he wrote Livingston, "blown the mind of the Executive" with his torpedoes.[30]

As winter drew near, Fulton saw no reason to hurry back to New York when there was still so much he could accomplish in Washington. He worked on a paper for Secretary of the Treasury Albert Gallatin's landmark "Report to the Senate on the Subject of Public Roads and Canals." This was Fulton's major American contribution to this field. A compendium of his European canal writings, it expressed his grand vision of the "general and mutual" benefits to be obtained from the opening of the western lands and is remarkable for the fund of detailed information he had mastered in the short, busy months he had been back in the country. Urging that the development be federally orchestrated, he argued:

> The lands sold by the United States in 1806, averaged about 2 dollars an acre, and certainly every acre accommodated with a canal, would produce 6 dollars; thus only 20 miles of canal each

year, running through national lands, would raise the value of 512,000 acres at least 4 dollars an acre, giving 2,048,000 to the treasury, a sum sufficient to make 136 miles of canal. Had an individual such a property, and funds to construct canals to its centre, he certainly would do it for his own interest. The nation has the property, and the nation possesses the ample funds for such undertakings. . . . The merchandise which can bear the expense of carriage on our present roads to Pittsburgh, Kentucky, Tennessee, or any other distance of 300 miles, and which for that distance pays 100 dollars a ton, could be boated on canals *ten thousand miles for that sum.*[31]

As had become his habit, Fulton took the opportunity to strike at the ever-flourishing liquor industry. Grain, he said, was the most important and abundant product of the interior. With a canal system such as he proposed it would no longer be necessary to distill it into brutalizing alcohol.

In a lighter vein, Fulton corresponded with Peale about the forthcoming Academy of Fine Arts exhibition. Peale had just uncrated Fulton's painting collection, and he wrote Fulton how much he admired it, especially West's *Ophelia* and his son Raphael's *Orlando*. Sticking varnish had caused some of the paint on the *King Lear* to pull away, he reported, but fortunately it had not affected the figures; his son Rembrandt could easily retouch it. Requesting Fulton's opinion, he sent him a labeled diagram of how he intended to hang them. In the center were the Wests and beneath them the Smirkes. Fulton, who was otherwise delighted with Peale's efforts, thought the Smirkes too delicate to be placed directly below the Wests and suggested hanging them by themselves at eye level with the inscription "Eleven pictures by R. Smirke, Esq from Mr. Barlows Columbiad."[32]

Nowhere in this correspondence is there a hint that Fulton wished to display his own work in the exhibition, although the portraits of Barlow and Stanhope were certainly of sufficiently high caliber. Perhaps they had not yet arrived, for neither Fulton nor Peale mentioned them or West's self-portrait or West's portrait of Fulton, which the public would have been eager to see. Considering his great personal pride, it is noteworthy that Fulton had no vanity about his ability as an artist. Painting had become a true recreation for him, one of his few, if not his only one. It satisfied his need for visual stimulation in a manner that designing steamboats and torpedo systems could not.

By the middle of December Fulton had his multiple affairs well enough in order to leave Washington for New York. Before he could get away, however, he received a disturbing letter from William Thornton. Putting at least some of his cards on the table, Thornton recited the history of his connection with John Fitch, stating that he had invented the boiler that made the Delaware River boat successful. He acknowledged that Fitch's patent had expired, but said he was prepared to take patents on his own inventions: "I wish to carry them extensively in[to] use, and therefore propose to you who are not only active in such affairs but scientific, that on [my] taking out a Patent you take one third, Mssrs Livingston, Clarke (or whoever may bear the original expenses, to be refunded from the first profits), another third, and that I retain the remaining third, and prosecute the Business extensively wherever the Profits will warrant it."[33] He claimed he had received an exclusive privilege for the Mississippi and its tributaries from the king of Spain. In fact, he had formed a company to capitalize on it and had been prevented from carrying the enterprise through only because, at a crucial moment, he had been required to visit his aging mother in the West Indies. While he was gone, his company had sold the only two boats they had built.

Whether Fulton regarded this as a request for a bribe or a serious threat of competition, he could not accept Thornton's interference and, ostrichlike, he avoided dealing with it by putting it out of his mind. Not honoring Thornton with a response, Fulton went off to New York.

Christmas was not celebrated as a festive holiday at that time, and Fulton spent the week doing errands connected with the remodeling of the *Steamboat*. Livingston, always looking for bargains, told him to find out if his erstwhile partner Nicholas Roosevelt would rent them the engine he had ordered before he left for Paris. Fulton discovered that the cylinder had not been cast and the boiler was unsuited for a boat, but, since Roosevelt had fallen on hard times he was able to buy a bellows and anvil and other tools for use at Red Hook. Fulton arranged with Charles Staudinger, at one time Roosevelt's foreman, to superintend Robert McQueen who would build the fittings and boiler in New York. He constructed a pasteboard model for them to follow. Prevailing over Livingston's thriftiness, Fulton ordered McQueen to make the boiler of copper. Fulton spent New Year's Day 1808 in New York City. Then, on January 5, he packed his bags and departed for Columbia County where he intended to pass the remainder of the winter. Traveling with him were John Cox Stevens, Livingston's nephew, and Walter and Harriet Livingston, his second cousins, whose country seat, Teviotdale, was only eight miles northeast of Clermont. The party went directly to Teviotdale, and on the evening of January 7, Harriet Livingston and Robert Fulton were married in the family parlor by the local Dutch Reform minister.

Virtually no warning had been given of this great event, even to close relations. Livingston knew only that the group were on their way from New York. Fulton made no reference to the impending nuptials in a friendly letter to him, written and mailed in New York on January 5. Nowhere in the many letters Fulton wrote during this period is there any mention whatever of the approaching wedding, unless the short note appended to a letter to Livingston early in November alludes to some phase of the courtship: "There is one passage in your letter at which I can only guess, but which I feel desirous to have clearly explained. 'I can tell you in confidence that B. has offered and been refused, to the great mortification of all H.'s friends and family.' Please to put the real names in these initials."[34]

Considering Fulton's frantic schedule, it is difficult to imagine when he found time to court Harriet. Since family tradition places the announcement of their engagement at the Clermont party celebrating the maiden voyage of the *Steamboat*, they may very well have first met then and renewed their acquaintance in New York City where Harriet would have been a welcome visitor in any one of the Livingston clan's town houses. But from the end of October to the middle of December, Fulton was in Washington, settling in very happily with the Barlows. His intimate involvement with Kalorama certainly suggests he intended to live there whenever he could get away from New York.

Like so many of his projects, Fulton must have approached his marriage with whirlwind intensity. Having made a success of steam navigation, he was at last ready to fall in love with "some amiable American." That this tie might also improve his social standing with Livingston could only have made it more attractive to him.

Harriet Livingston was well educated, an accomplished amateur painter and musician, a minor heiress, and just twenty-four years old. She was not pretty, but her admirable Livingston nose and strong chin gave her a decidedly patrician air. If Fulton's miniature portrait of her is reliable, she was endowed with a *belle poitrine* and chose gowns that displayed it to good advantage.

It was her pleasant lot to belong to a large and affectionate family. She had three older brothers and three older sisters and a younger sister and brother. Although her father died when she was fourteen, she was nurtured in ease. Teviotdale, situated on a gentle rise above the Roeleff Jansen Kill, consisted of almost 500 acres of the original Livingston grant. The house was not large, but its proportions were elegant and its furnishings carefully chosen.

Harriet's father, a lawyer of some repute, was also a speculator. He had been associated with Fulton's friend Daniel Parker in supplying provisions to the Revolutionary Army and then with the notorious financier William Duer in western land ventures. When these failed, he almost lost his property. However, he declared bankruptcy and arranged for his brothers to buy his house and land at the sheriff's sale, which they managed to ensure was poorly attended. As soon as the scandal blew over, he bought back the property—an illustration of the graceful power of the well-connected.

The social world in which Harriet grew up comprised Livingstons and Schuylers and the few families with whom they formed alliances through marriage, many of whom lived within a short carriage drive from Teviotdale. Her only departure from this protective milieu was to the Moravian Seminary at Bethlehem, Pennsylvania, which she attended as a boarding student for two years. It was an important departure, for it gave her a superior education that set her apart from most of her relatives and friends and some experience of the world outside the charmed family circle.

Although he was nineteen years older than she, Fulton must have seemed a marvelously romantic figure to Harriet. It is unlikely she had ever encountered anyone quite like him. His drawing room manners had a European polish, and he probably retained traces of an English accent. Yet, his success, as he gladly stated, was the result of his own active genius. He was an ambitious self-made man, unencumbered by inherited land and an extended family. His interests were urban and his vision global. He must have presented an exciting departure from her accustomed way of life.

There is no record of how Harriet's immediate family and the rest of the Livingstons felt about her marriage to an entrepreneur of undistinguished lineage. Her brother Robert, in Paris for his health, had no chance to voice objections, if he had any. Livingston simply wrote Robert, who was also his son-in-law: "I give you joy of the marriage of Harriet and Mr. Fulton." [35]

The new couple did not establish their own home. Since Fulton expected to return to New York as soon as the *Steamboat*'s reconstruction was well under way, they moved into Teviotdale with short visits to Clermont, which was closer to the workshop. Fulton's midwinter assessment was that "the honeymoon & Steamboat go on charmingly." [36] It was an idyllic interlude.

Monopolies Are Justly Held as Odious

❖

On January 7, 1808, the day Fulton married Harriet Livingston, John Stevens signed a contract to build a steamboat 100 feet long and 16 feet wide, to be "afloat in the water in a good and workmanlike manner" by April 1. Like the *Steamboat*, she would be propelled by side wheels, but Stevens counted on improvements he made in the steam engine to drive her faster—at least 6 miles an hour. She would ply the Hudson in defiance of Livingston's monopoly. Wryly Stevens called his boat the *Phoenix*.

Fulton and Livingston had known for some time what Stevens was up to, for just after Christmas Stevens discussed his plans with Fulton and wrote Livingston a letter that was informative, conciliatory, and at the same time contentious. He said that if his boat made better time than theirs, they would be imprudent to rely on their New York State monopoly to restrain his operation. He would obtain a federal coasting license, which was used to distinguish American vessels trading with home ports from those engaged in foreign trade, and run the *Phoenix* from Hoboken to Albany. "Will a New Jersey jury impose heavy damages for infringement; will a federal court find for a monopoly against the constitution?" He was confident they would not. Yet the desire "to avoid those collisions and interfering claims which must inevitably arise" were they to proceed separately led him to suggest they find some way of uniting their efforts. He could, for instance, make the machinery for their new boats. He hoped Fulton would not order another English engine until the *Phoenix* had been tried.[1]

Stevens was obviously testing Livingston and Fulton. He was ready to flout their state monopoly, although he was not entirely certain he could do so with impunity. He believed Fulton's "unique combinations" were unpatentable, but he was uneasy about an expensive and inconvenient court challenge. Since the application of the federal patent law was not clear, the outcome was unpredictable.

Fulton's response was pragmatic. As he liked Stevens, appreciated his ability as an engineer, and feared him as a competitor, he urged Livingston "to deal generously by him." It was understandable that Stevens felt "a kind of claim to the participation of profits of the North river," Fulton temporized, because he had already spent so much time and money experimenting. "As there are situations in America to occupy all his capital and ours, I wish to avoid all disputes with those who should be friends."[2]

Irritated by his brother-in-law's independence, Livingston was not disposed to be sympathetic. Stevens's attack on the monopoly was to him tantamount to an assault on his person. He put off replying until he had a chance to consult with Fulton at Clermont. Then, in the guise of a conciliatory offer made "out of mere friendship," he sent Stevens a twenty-one-page defense of the state grant. In a forceful mixture of legalistic argument and homely example, he told Stevens that neither he nor Fulton had the slightest apprehension about the strength of the New York State monopoly: "if we did, it would be madness in us to proceed on the extensive scale that we now do." The legislature, in giving them an exclusive privilege, was simply exercising the control it retained over the use of all property within its jurisdiction. The federal government had no constitutional authority to interfere with that right. States could control their waterways as they saw fit. Since rivers were not merely within the jurisdiction of the state, but were a part of its territorial rights, they might, if they pleased, keep out all vessels belonging to citizens of neighboring states. A state might even stop navigation altogether, Livingston maintained. "Would it not be very extraordinary if the state, which can give me the whole river if they chose, could not give me a privilege in it?" Moreover, the states had not been deprived by the federal patent law of the right to grant monopolies they had enjoyed under the colonial governments. Congress exercised its patent right, and the states exercised their monopoly rights concurrently.

His own imagination exhausted, Livingston resorted to Fulton's argument. He admitted that neither the length of the boat nor the use of wheels was the result of new reasoning, but like poets rearranging the letters of the alphabet, they had taken known materials and produced a new effect. They had been the first to make an efficient steamboat and the first to specify in their patent a precise table of proportions and velocities from which other steamboats could be built.

Reminding Stevens that his own engine, though ingenious, was also not original and that until the success of the *Steamboat* Stevens had disdained their long boat and wheels, he warned him that by adopting their "unique combinations" he encroached on their patent.

Having laid out the position from which he would never deviate, Livingston warned Stevens of the dire consequences of proceeding without his and Fulton's sanction:

> Your beginning a boat without . . . any previous arrangement with us may induce others to believe that we have no right . . . or have become indifferent as to protection. . . . If we were led to divide with you from the dread of competition, any other who imagined he had discovered an improvement in the Steam engine would reduce us to new divisions and thus, after having run all the risk of a new improvement and effected what had never before been effected, we should be compelled to abandon the profits to those who trod in our steps and made use of the most essential parts of our discovery—a long boat and wheels.

Strenuous as Livingston's presentation appeared, it was defensive. Its objective was to provide a persuasive setting for a compromise, probably drafted by Fulton. They would let Stevens use their principles and run the *Phoenix* from New York to New Brunswick and from Trenton to Philadelphia. All Stevens need do was provide a written acknowledgment that his boat was operated by their permission under their patent right. Although Fulton agreed to the content of this long letter and probably helped draft it, he was not on hand to sign it. In a postscript, Livingston hospitably opened the door to more moderate terms: "I think if you should upon a fair trial succeed so as to run a mile or two faster than we do, that we might make a better plan."[3]

Stevens was not in the least perturbed by this fragmented tirade. He retorted that although he found the "arguments very sprightly and ingenious," they were in reality "arrant nonsense, a waste of mental powers in a quixotic tilting at windmills." The idea of patenting proportions was ridiculous. Did they mean to say: "you shall not put your freight into two boats of 12 feet by 100 because it interferes with my patent, but you are perfectly at liberty to put the whole on board a boat of 23 by 100"?

In addition, the notion that the state had a right to grant an individual a whole river was too absurd to receive serious consideration. The state was not a private garden. Clearly, protection for inventions was vested in the federal government under the patent law. If states could limit that security, patents would "become nugatory . . . serving only to ensnare the unhappy wight whose folly should lead him to place confidence in his rights." Furthermore, should a monopolist in one state set himself against the monopolist of another, "the effect contemplated by the constitution of free and uninterrupted intercourse between states would be jeopardized." The duty of Congress to regulate the nation's commerce as set forth in the Constitution prevailed over state controls.

In short, Stevens scolded, "Monopolies are very justly held, in every free country, as odious. A monopoly gives an unlimited power to one man or set of men to lay heavy contributions on all the rest of the community."

As to his own case, Stevens proudly maintained he had steadily improved upon the Boulton and Watt engine by making it smaller, lighter, and capable of withstanding higher pressures. In fact, in 1794, long before Fulton thought about steamboats and four years before Livingston was awarded his exclusive privilege, Stevens had demonstrated his vessel on the waters of New York State. Moveover, because his twenty-year partnership agreement with Livingston was still in force, he could already claim clear title to one-third of the *Steamboat*'s earnings.

Having delivered himself of so spirited a reply, Stevens, like Livingston and Fulton, was eager to leave room for negotiations:

> You have as little confidence in my success this season, as I had in yours, last season. So be it. . . . As I have not the least doubt that both parties will ultimately find it to their interest to form a joint concern, I shall not attempt to say anything in answer to your very masterly defense of your rights under the law of the state. But do not mistake me. It is only because I consider it unnecessary . . . and not because I feel myself unable to make a vigourous attack.[4]

In 1808 there was merit to both Livingston's and Stevens's arguments. Each was well acquainted with the law as it stood, Livingston from having been chancellor of New York State and Stevens as one of the principal initiators of the federal patent law. In this exchange of concepts they were wrestling with unresolved states rights issues. The jurisdiction of the federal government over the navigable waters of the states had not yet been established. In fact, although they did not realize it, in defending their monopoly Livingston and Fulton were sowing the first controversial seeds of the landmark case that would have a thorny history in the state courts and, as *Gibbons* v. *Ogden*, go on to the U.S. Supreme Court. In 1824, Chief Justice John Marshall conceded that while states could regulate commerce wholly within their borders, "every species of commercial intercourse" between states fell under the jurisdiction of the federal government. Thus the New York State monopoly was finally broken. But by that time both Livingston and Fulton were dead.

As was typical of families in those days, the brothers-in-law maintained cordial relations on a social level despite their adversarial posture in business. Stevens and his son John visited Clermont at the end of January, and the three of them built an iceboat. Modeled on those Livingston had seen in Holland, its speed was 18 miles an hour. In February the Stevenses invited Livingston to an evening party in the city. In March, although Livingston was plagued with eye trouble, making it difficult for him to write, he sent Stevens lengthy advice about the education of his sons.

Fulton, who was supposedly honeymooning at Teviotdale, spent his days coordinating the rebuilding of the *Steamboat*, "scurrying backwards and forwards between his mother-in-law's and Red Hook," Stevens said.[5] The ice and cold wind, which provided Livingston with such fine recreation, offered nothing to Fulton but the constant worry that the workmen's stove would set the boat on fire.

When the ice roared out of the Hudson on March 10 and the river was again open to navigation, the rebuilding of the *Steamboat* was far from complete. Nonetheless, eager to reestablish his presence and reap the profits, Fulton brought her to New York for the final rush of supervising, coordinating, ordering, planning, paying, and cajoling. "I am working as hard as I can and at so many parts great and Small that I cannot detail them," he wrote Livingston who remained serenely at Clermont.[6] By April 5 the carpenters and joiners had finished the cabins, the roaster and boilers for the kitchen were within a day of completion, and work had begun on the wheel guards, stairs, and engine covering. Attaching the four lee boards and mounting the wheels would take another week. Twenty-three cords of wood—enough for six trips—were already stacked on the dock. Without fail, Fulton promised, they would leave for Albany on Monday, April 18.

Stevens had just launched his hull with great public fanfare, but he was having trouble with the boiler of the high-pressure engine in which he put so much faith. He came around to see what progress Fulton was making and, also, he was forced to confess, to avail himself of the "hints and improvements" Fulton's boat offered. After a barrage of friendly advice such as he could never resist offering, Fulton warned Stevens that, because his boat was so small, even if he removed all the machinery she would not be able to accommodate as many passengers as their refurbished boat. "I then mentioned that he was copying my wheels and proportions," Fulton reported to Livingston, "And if he thought himself Justified in so doing, then Dr. Thornton and every person who has attempted steamboats had an equal right . . . of course there would be an end to our exclusive right and his also. This argument . . . made him look grave. I think I can perceive that he is losing confidence in high steam, and that he will ultimately be willing to work under our patents."[7]

Stevens's situation was even more precarious than Fulton imagined, for he was deeply in debt to Livingston. Presuming upon his friendship and kinship, he had signed notes over to Livingston without asking his permission. Impervious to pledges of quick repayment and a good deal of abject flattery, Livingston refused to honor them. Not even a sly letter from Mrs. Stevens, who enjoyed a coquettish relationship with Livingston, swayed him. "I begin to suspect that Mr. Fulton is afraid we ladies shall steal some of his inventions for, by all account, there is no end to the contrivances & useful improvements on board," she wrote, while Stevens petulantly accused his brother-in-law of "hard and harsh" treatment.[8]

The *Steamboat* made her first trip up the Hudson on April 26, only eight days later than Fulton predicted. He was enormously proud of her. No exact drawings have been preserved, but from the many verbal descriptions and Fulton's ink sketches there is no question she was a handsome and convenient passenger boat. The deck was covered with the oilcloth he had so strongly recommended. Aft of the wheels was a permanent awning suspended from the rear mast by an ingenious network of tension cables; passengers who preferred to remain on deck for their meals were served at a pair of long tables sheltered beneath it. Below deck were three excellent cabins, one reserved for women and children. There were fifty-four sleeping accommodations—double tiers of berths along the sides, and sofas in rows on the floors. A shelf was provided above each berth for footgear and clothes. For privacy and coziness, the windows were framed with calico that Fulton himself selected. Adjacent to the engine were a steward's room, the prize kitchen, a larder, and a bar. The furnishings were of the first quality as the fine mahogany sideboard that was preserved by the family testifies.

When the wind and tide were fair, the *Steamboat* maintained 6 or 7 miles an hour, sometimes using sail to boost her speed. The foremast, which when not in use lay parallel to the deck and extended about the same distance as a bowsprit beyond it, had a weighted base so that, like the one Fulton designed for the *Nautilus*, it could be maneuvered into position in a few minutes. Because the hull was now wider, longer, and deeper, the average speed was one-half mile an hour less than that of the original boat, sometimes increasing the running time between New York and Albany to thirty-five hours. Nevertheless, passengers flocked aboard. Some complained of smoke and noise, the suffocating heat of the cabin, and the dirty, overcrowded inns and insolent innkeepers at the landing places, but these seemed minor inconveniences. The *Steamboat* generally met her schedule, and she was fashionable. By July she carried up to 140 passengers on a single trip and was clearing over $1,000 a week.

To advertise his steamboat Fulton published a flyer. It announced "For the Information of the Public" that the *Steamboat* would leave New York for Albany every Saturday afternoon at exactly five o'clock and leave Albany every Wednesday morning at exactly eight o'clock. Crisscrossing the river, she would take on and deposit passengers at the principal Hudson River settlements of West Point, Newburgh, Poughkeepsie, Esopus, Red Hook, Catskill, Hudson, and other points along the way if hailed. Because of varying winds and tides, passengers were enjoined to be "on the spot" an hour in advance. The price was $1.00 for every 20 miles, $7.00 for the full trip; the minimum fare was $2.00. Children and servants paid less. Above 60 pounds of baggage, the charge was three cents a pound. Because there were no onshore landings except at New York and Albany, the innkeepers and boatmen taking passengers to and from the boat were paid a shilling a passenger. Dinner was served at two o'clock, tea with meats at eight in the evening, and breakfast at nine o'clock. Each cost fifty cents. The berths, sofas, and lockers were assigned on a first-come, first-served basis.

A vivid picture of the public's traveling decorum, which had never been high aboard the sloops and undoubtedly deteriorated noticeably when waits at the landing taverns proved longer than expected, is provided by the long list of rules Fulton felt obliged to set down to maintain order, cleanliness, and propriety. Smoking was allowed only on the deck and in the cabin reserved for men. The penalties for breaking this rule were $1.50 plus a half-dollar for every half-hour the offense continued, the money to be spent on wine for the company. Passengers lying down with their boots or shoes on were subject to the same fines. All cards and games were to cease at ten o'clock in the evening in the ladies' cabin and in the great cabin so that sleepers would not be disturbed.

The *Steamboat*'s extraordinary success was clearly due to Fulton's careful planning and supervision. Livingston's important but not taxing contribution was to shepherd through the legislature "An Act for the Relief of Robert Fulton and Robert R. Livingston," extending their grant five years for each boat they put on the river, up to thirty years. It was passed on April 11, 1808. This time Livingston took care of the enrollment. Having paid Fulton the $10,000 he owed him, he could now officially list himself as co-owner. He gave the vessel's name as the *North River Steam Boat*, the hailing port as Clermont, and the master as Captain Samuel Wiswall. The boat measured 149 feet and 182⁴⁸⁄₉₅ tons, only 7 feet longer than the original boat but, because of her greater width, the tonnage, based on carrying capacity, was more than doubled.

Fulton had every reason to be elated by all he had accomplished since his return from Europe. In just over a year he had placed himself at the forefront of America's development. Even his work on canals was bearing fruit as a contribution to the welfare of the nation. The paper he had prepared for Albert Gallatin's report to the Senate on inland communications had just been published, prompting the government to survey what would eventually become the Erie Canal. Heady with the vision of a bright future for his own canal system, he wrote Samuel Miles Hopkins, who was practicing law in New York that, as soon as John Barker Church, to whom Fulton had sold an interest in his American canal prospects in 1797, came up with his second payment, he would take out a patent for small canals.

Yet Fulton was not content. Certain aspects of his marriage did not entirely satisfy him. Harriet had stayed throughout the spring with her mother at Teviotdale. She was pregnant and not well. Weary of living surrounded by so many Livingstons and of commuting between Columbia County and New York City, Fulton longed for the companionship of the Barlows of which he had been deprived for almost six months. As summer approached, he decided that he and Harriet would join them in Washington.

On June 5, during a sojourn at Teviotdale, he wrote an astonishing letter to "dear Barlow" which, after a few lines about the success of his steamboat, quickly drifted into what can only be called a love letter to Ruth:

> You have not told me Mrs. Barlow's plan for the Summer, whether to stay at Washington or to travel and where to or how. Will she wait until our arrival and then form a plan? Say how shall it be ruthlinda? . . . Shall we unite our fortunes to Make Kalorama the centre of taste, beauty, love and dearest friendship or by dividing Interests never arrive at that comfort, elegance or happiness for which our souls are formed. There Shall the Sage enjoying every blessing, prosecute with tranquil mind his literary pursuits, the artist his plans of Improvement. Ruthlinda, dear ruthlinda, heart of love, and Harriet, receiving Information by her example require all that is the most endearing. How much of this depends on you Ruthlinda!
>
> . . . P.S. Harriet sends Mr. Barlow and you her love and best wishes. She is very desirous to know whether I think you will love her and I always tell her that depends on how She behaves.[9]

This outpouring did not bode well for Harriet. But perhaps her curiousity to meet her husband's intimate friends outweighed any reluctance to pay them what could only be a protracted visit. Despite the unremitting heat and humidity and the sickly miasmas for which Washington was well known, Fulton set off for Kalorama with Harriet, who was by then five months pregnant.

They were at least a week on the road. When they at last arrived, Ruth was ill, probably as much by design as in fact. Mrs. Samuel Latham Mitchill, who visited her when she was recovering from this "singular" attack, commented: "She was confined to her room when I called. . . . However, she admitted us into her bedchamber, sat up in the easy chair, and conversed with so much sprightliness as a well person."[10]

Harriet, whose mere presence was obviously an intrusion on her husband's and the Barlows' cherished pattern of living, could not have enjoyed vying with Ruth as to the relative delicacy of her physical condition. To make matters worse, the house was in disarray because of remodeling, instigated and mostly paid for by Fulton. Benjamin Henry Latrobe, Barlow's friend and the architect for the renovation, described Harriet at that time as "a very learned lady, somewhat stricken . . . rich, elegant, spirited & able to manage any man."[11] But Ruth told Mrs. Harrison Smith that Harriet was so indisposed she seldom left her chamber. Barlow's departure for Monticello to visit Jefferson in September, made a new "trinity" at Kalorama. It could not have improved Harriet's position.

Fulton happily pursued his own affairs. He visited the navy yard where his former associate Nathaniel Cutting had managed to install a cordelier, and he exchanged ideas with President Jefferson about ways of making brick neatly and quickly. He must have decided to paint seriously again, for he asked Peale where to find the best canvas and oils. Along with detailed advice on methods of sizing, Peale sent Fulton a set of colors, a small marble slab on which to prepare his paints, gum mastic for making a special drying oil, and Fulton's old palette, which he had valiantly tried to clean.

Fulton thoroughly enjoyed this vacation from superintending the steamboat operation. Informing Livingston he saw no need to return to New York until the boat was laid up for the winter, he sent off a list of orders that has much the same domineering tone as some of his letters from Plombières: "Take care that She be neither burned nor sunk; That her decks be scoured and her inside clean; That her accounts shall be squared so as to know the *neat profits of each voyage to one dollar.*" Advising Livingston to give up his idea of installing a ventilating system operated by the wheels until the season ended as he did not wish the current schedule to be interrupted, he commanded, "Let what will do very well for the present alone."[12]

In fact, Fulton had left Livingston with a set of far-ranging problems, the most serious of which was competition. Not only were a group of Albany men putting together a rival company, but several Canadians had already started work on a Lake Champlain steamer that would connect with the stage running from Montreal to St. Jean in Canada, and from Whitehall to Troy in New York, enabling travelers to make the 150-mile journey in 24 hours. John Winants, a *Steamboat* workman Fulton had been obliged to fire, set up the company with his brother. To build the machinery, they engaged James Smallman, the English-trained mechanic, who had worked on Livingston's early engines with Charles Staudinger and, in 1798, had patented a steam engine with Nicholas Roosevelt. In addition, the *Experiment*, an elegantly outfitted passenger sloop from the city of Hudson, was attracting a good many customers. Although the trip generally took three days and Stevens thought the ladies' cabin so confined and cluttered as to afford neither room nor comfort, the fare was only three dollars, meals included.

Stevens, however, remained the greatest thorn in their flesh. He even went so far as to tease Livingston—from whom he was nonetheless still trying to borrow money—for having roused a host of competitors "besides your humb. svt.," and he was quietly pleased when Livingston's own brother, John R. Livingston, made confidential overtures toward helping him establish a rival Hudson River line based in Hoboken, New Jersey.

At first Livingston's letters to Stevens were temperate. "[I]t is not surprising," he wearily philosophized, "that the success that promises to crown our expenses and labour should awaken the cupidity of many."[13] But as the *Phoenix* neared completion his tone became more acrimonious. "You will recollect the penalty is forfeiture of the boat & engine & £100," he warned, "muchsoever I might be disposed to remit this I doubt whether the same disposition would be found in Mr. Fulton. . . . the world will judge of the justice or delicacy of your interference with us, particularly after our generous offer to you."[14]

Outraged that Stevens was copying his long narrow proportions, Fulton wrote Livingston that he would abide by the law whatever it might be, but he would never admit that Stevens had the right to use side wheels or build a steamboat whose length was more than five times her breadth. Stevens, to whom Livingston sent this letter, perhaps with Fulton's prior approval, testily replied that if they brought suit and failed, it would prove fatal to them.

United as never before by Stevens's stubborn resistance, Livingston and Fulton licensed John R. Livingston to establish lines from New York City to Staten Island and New Jersey, south of Powles Hook and north of Sandy Hook, the same area previously offered to Stevens. This was a potentially lucrative territory, for it offered swift transportation to Elizabeth Town Point, Perth and South Amboy and New Brunswick, where connections could be made with the stagecoach routes to Philadelphia and Washington. Although John R. was known to be devious and quarrelsome and had greeted the first boat with derision, Livingston believed—and Fulton concurred—they would be best served by keeping the enterprise close to the bosom of the family, a favored position for which Stevens clearly no longer qualified. John R. let contracts at once for the *Rariton*, which would run from Manhattan up the Raritan River to New Brunswick, New Jersey.

Stevens was too engrossed in his *Phoenix* to find out about this development. He was, at any rate, far ahead of John R. as an occupying force. On September 27 he took his boat on a trial run to Perth Amboy. He made the 30-mile return trip to Powles Hook in five hours and twenty-six minutes—or at a speed of over 5½ miles an hour, exactly as he had so confidently predicted. However, his boiler showed serious signs of strain, and—much to Fulton's and Livingston's satisfaction—he was forced to lay the boat up for repairs and improvements.

This persistent rivalry arose as much from compulsive optimism as from greed and vanity, for the times were not conducive to business expansion. In December 1807, Jefferson persuaded Congress to pass the Embargo Act. Although it had little effect on the British, it virtually destroyed the commerce of New York. "Not a box, bale, cask, barrel, or package was to be seen upon the wharfs," a British traveler noted. "The few solitary merchants, clerks, porters, and laborers that were to be seen, were walking about with their hands in their pockets . . . the coffee house was almost empty . . . grass grew on the wharfs."[15]

Fulton and Livingston were not dependent on cargo, but the decline of trade could only reduce the number of passengers. Nevertheless, to cement their control of steam navigation Fulton and Livingston began work on a second boat for the Hudson that would be even larger and more luxurious than the *Steamboat*. Her fanciful name was the *Car of Neptune*. Again Charles Browne was the builder. The contract was signed on October 9; Browne promised to deliver the hull in six months.

While Fulton was thus multiplying his passenger boats, Harriet was adding to their family. She gave birth to a boy on October 10, 1808. Instead of naming him Robert Livingston, which would have been a compliment to Harriet as well as a tribute to his patron and the partnership agreement they had signed exactly six years previously, Fulton named the baby Robert Barlow and called him Barlow.

Fulton's great joy at becoming a father radiates from a letter he wrote two weeks after the birth:

In February I hope to show you a boy as a pattern for works of this kind—every wheel, pinion, screw, bolt, lever and pin about him is of the best proportion size and strength. This has been a fair and successful experiment. My dear Harriet is Charming and charmingly up running about, pleased to the soul, gay as a lark, laughing, singing, dancing, playing and plaguing my soul out while I am making these long letters and calculations. She Sends you all kind love.[16]

Fulton might not have been so lighthearted, despite his fine son, if he had known William Thornton, Fitch's former associate, had begun a furtive campaign to destroy his steamboat enterprise. On October 11, under the pretext of asking advice about a faulty rowing machine, Thornton wrote John Stevens that he wished to join him. He described the perfect propelling mechanism he had developed with Fitch—"three paddles in the stern, moving by double levers, which carried them in a very beautiful elliptical manner." He boasted also of having invented a cheap, safe, efficient boiler. He had no doubt that, on the basis of his interest in Fitch's expired patent from the United States and his monopoly from the king of Spain—which Thornton now assumed as his own—he would be able to set aside Fulton's New York State monopoly and also oppose his application for the exclusive navigation of the Mississippi. "I do not wish to injure those whom I so much respect," he confided, "but I hope to have Boats on that river my self."[17]

Thornton pressed his offer again on November 2 and November 24, and urged Stevens to visit him in Washington. To exhibit his good faith, he revealed that Fulton had yet to deposit his patent application and promised to notify Stevens when Fulton did so. At the same time, Thornton wrote an influential acquaintance in New Orleans asking him to mount "a regular Protest" should Livingston and Fulton apply for a monopoly on the Mississippi since it had long been his own intention to establish steamboats there.

Fulton had no knowledge of Thornton's scheming. Still hoping to lure Stevens into the fold, Fulton offered him the route from Trenton to New Castle, Delaware. Tied in with John R.'s New Brunswick line, it would attract passengers bound for Wilmington, Baltimore, and Washington. Fulton promised to help him *gratis* and, as a further enticement, proffered a right to run ferries from Powles Hook and "elsewhere" in the North and East rivers. These would "almost equal a bridge," he said, and very much increase the value of Stevens's property in New Jersey. Nevertheless, Fulton refused to lower his price in terms of personal concessions: "[A]ll I shall ask," he wrote, "is an acknowledgment that you work under my patent." Lest Stevens think he acted out of weakness, he reiterated that he could never give up his priority on the use of wheels, for he was the first in the world to demonstrate their utility.[18]

Livingston also badgered Stevens. His approach was firm, friendly, and familial, but it met with even less success than Fulton's. Stevens was incensed by the slurring remarks Livingston had made in pseudonymous newspaper articles and by his continued refusal to lend him money. He would neither write nor speak to him. Injured, Livingston accused Stevens of "contemptuous neglect." Stevens was not moved.

It is a measure of Livingston's panic that he unchivalrously put his case before Stevens's wife, hoping that she would intervene because of their long-standing friendship. "The subject of this letter is one that might more properly perhaps have been addressed to Mr. Stevens," Livingston entreated, "but I cannot again submit to the indignity of writing to one who has treated for some time past my letters with the utmost contemptuous silence."[19] Through her he made one last offer. Stevens could have one of three exclusive routes: Long Island to New York, Trenton to Philadelphia, or Philadelphia to New Castle. So anxious was he for a swift reply that he arranged for his sons-in-law to carry any messages Stevens might have to Fulton, who was still in Washington. Stevens refused to break his silence.

Fulton then took his turn at beleaguering Stevens. Implying that he lacked the necessary understanding of hydraulics to design a successful steamboat, he challenged Stevens to calculate the resistance of a 100- by 15-foot boat running 1, 2, 3, 4, 5, or 6 miles an hour and the size of cylinder he would need to overcome the resistance. The solution should not take more than an hour, he taunted, but "I allow you 2 days to answer these in the *Citizen*. If the answer does not then Appear it is a fair inference that you are still in a state of experiment and working without any certain rule."[20]

Fulton was not, in fact, sure of himself, and he showed his anxiety by fretting nervously about the safety of his steamboat. "Not a moment should be lost in getting a good berth at New York," he wrote Livingston at the first breath of cold weather.[21] On November 14—his birthday—he heard from Captain Wiswall that freezing temperatures made the boat increasingly difficult to manage, although the last two trips had paid well. Fulton insisted they be content with a better season than they had expected. Nothing should induce them to run the *Steamboat* beyond November 24.

Fulton was tempted to go to New York. He was kept in Washington, however, not only by Harriet and the baby, but by his patent application. The novelty criterion was giving him trouble. To meet it—or perhaps to overwhelm it—he compiled an imposing document of over five thousand words together with diagrams, tables, calculations, and twelve plates. The overblown verbal description cost fifteen dollars just to have copied. Although his fundamental concepts dated from the "letters of the alphabet" passage in the *Treatise on Canals*, he had evolved no convincing way of articulating his conviction that invention consisted of a new combination of existing elements. The message he desperately hoped to convey was that, unlike other inventors of the time, he was not a tinkerer but a sophisticated, systematic experimenter using a comprehensive approach to bring theory into practice. This was indeed true, but the law was designed with discrete machines or processes in mind. Theories were not patentable, no matter how useful they might be.

Fulton's description of his invention began with the assertion that the successful construction of a steamboat did not depend on any new form of steam engine or boiler, but on his unique discovery of the principles governing the total steamboat design. By using his formula any intelligent artisan could determine the relationship of engine power, wheel size, and hull dimensions that would use steam most advantageously. Basically, a steamboat's bow should be pointed to at least 60 degrees, the length "such that her friction will equal her plus and minus pressure," and her bottom flat. Paddle wheels were preferable to endless chains or smoke jack flyers—that is, propellers.

To explain how he arrived at his method of finding minimum resistances and velocities, Fulton included the definitions and table evolved by Beaufoy from his experiments at Deptford Dock in the 1790s and published in 1802 in Charnock's *History of Naval Architecture*. In addition, he ran through an exhaustive series of calculations based on the dimensions and machinery of his steamboat, which he illustrated with fourteen figures, tables, and drawings. The first is a rendering of the

Steamboat passing through a dramatic section of the Highlands, included, perhaps, to satisfy his aesthetic sensibilities but also to remind Thornton his invention was a reality. Another drawing was of a boat breasting powerful rapids by means of a winch worked by her engine, a device he expected would be useful on the Mississippi.

In the course of his text, Fulton frankly admitted that a boat could be propelled by steam even though his exact proportions were not observed and that a stern wheel might be used instead of side wheels, but he insisted that his proportions were necessary to achieve the greatest speed with a given power. "Having been the first to discover and describe the exact principles and proportions on which steamboats should be built, and having given a mechanical combination, the utility of which is proved by practice," he concluded, "I shall consider every attempt to construct such vessels on those principles as an infringement on my rights."

Foolishly, Fulton did not trouble to sign the application, but asked one Fletcher, probably the person who copied it, to sign it for him. This legal irregularity would cause him serious embarrassment when, as was inevitable, his patent was challenged in court.

The application is dated January 1, 1809; so it must have been sometime during the first week in January that Fulton took his patent, neatly bound and protected by an expensive mahogany box, to the Patent Office. Thornton, who had just returned from several weeks' stay in the country to escape creditors, awarded himself patents on January 16 for propelling steamboats with a stern wheel and for a boiler in which the water completely surrounded the fire. Although he quickly denied it, Thornton must have read Fulton's application before he did so, for on January 17, he told Stevens he did not think Fulton's patent was as good as his own and warned that the moment Fulton's patent was issued, his New York State monopoly would be void. On January 23, Thornton wrote Stevens again to say he had only "slightly examined" Fulton's application, which he had not received until January 19. He thought Fulton must have made improvements in the engine, he added, but that would not matter because Fulton had already acknowledged his priority. Thornton was, of course, attempting to deny that he had used his position as clerk of the Patent Office to advance his own interests. His letters were also a thinly veiled attempt to seduce Stevens into joining him. No more willing to cede his independence to Thornton than to Livingston and Fulton, Stevens remained aloof.

All the Weight on One Fulcrum

❖

The domestic atmosphere in which Fulton labored to bring forth his patent document was not nearly as blissful as his October letter to Livingston suggested. For several weeks after the birth of the baby, Harriet was not well. Neither, of course, was Ruth. The household turned in on itself. Mrs. Samuel Harrison Smith gossiped that she had "not heard of a single creature asked to dine or spend the evening at Calorama, but Dearborn's family."[1]

Neither Barlow nor Fulton found that the Federal City lived up to their expectations. Barlow's longing to play the role of elder statesman had not been satisfied. Instead of finding "men who preferred talents to intrigue," he had "seen imbecility on stilts stride over genius." Fulton thought Georgetown "a country of inconveniences," and "wished to return to a city where everything being created and coming to market could be had for money without cares." Though important to him as the seat of government, Washington was simply too remote from the theater of his interests. He belonged in New York where he could supervise his steamboat enterprise more closely and told Barlow he intended to move there as soon as the weather and roads permitted.

Stricken, Barlow accused him of faithlessness, of succumbing to pressure from Harriet and his Livingston relations and partners. Fulton confessed that the experiment of two families living in the same establishment, each with different habits and "ideas of interior arrangements," had proved untenable.[2] Protesting that Barlow's ease and happiness and that of the dear and amicable Ruthlinda were as precious to him as his own, Fulton nevertheless resolved to leave them.

The prospect of release from Kalorama restored Harriet's health and spirits. On a cold and windy night in late December, the Fultons attended a splendid ball. Harriet was reported to be "the Lady most admired for her grace and fashionable air."[3]

In his professional life, Fulton was caught up in an entirely different kind of dance. The tune was set by Nicholas Roosevelt with orchestration by the architect, Benjamin Henry Latrobe. Roosevelt was badly in debt and being sued by the federal government for having misappropriated funds advanced to provide copper to the navy. Hoping the partnership agreement he had signed with Livingston and Stevens in 1800 offered a solution to his financial woes, he asked Latrobe what action to take. Latrobe, who too often joined Roosevelt in disastrous ventures, sensed that trouble lay ahead but, as Roosevelt had recently married his beloved sixteen-year-old daughter, he eagerly became involved. Latrobe sent Fulton a note informing him that Roosevelt was the true inventor of the steamboat and warning him that if he did not acknowledge Roosevelt's partnership with Livingston and Stevens, Roosevelt would be force to seek redress.

Fulton hastened to Latrobe's office. He asserted he knew nothing at all about the contract and denied he ever pretended to be the first inventor of the steamboat. "Hundreds have tried it and have failed," Fulton declared—or so Latrobe excitedly reported to Roosevelt:

> Neither do I pretend to an exclusive right to navigate steamboats except in New York. Mr. Stevens or any one else can build as many boats as they want, but I shall prevent their using my principles. . . . As to Mr. R. I think him a noble minded intelligent man and would do anything to serve him which I could. I cannot let him into any part of the interest of the New York boats. That is arranged and in such order that it cost me no trouble but to keep it a going in money and repairs.[4]

Intimating greater magnanimity in the future, Fulton went on to say that although the Mississippi project was still unripe, he might find a place for Roosevelt in that venture.

Latrobe wrote Roosevelt he was not afraid of Fulton's "principles," but since anything was better than a lawsuit, advised him to get concessions from Livingston before Fulton had a chance to talk to him. Incurably devious, Roosevelt approached Stevens instead, suggesting they build a large boat together. Rebuking him for being so foolish as to put himself in Stevens's power, Latrobe insisted the best strategy was to play Stevens off against Livingston.

Unaware that he had failed to placate Roosevelt and that both he and Thornton were endeavoring to capture Stevens, Fulton relegated steamboats to the back of his mind and devoted what little time he had left in Washington to promoting submarine warfare. The Navy Department received him with "coldness and procrastination," but Jefferson remained faithful to the cause, and through his intervention Fulton was allocated enough money to pay two workmen to assist him in performing new experiments.

On February 12, Fulton demonstrated his harpoon gun on the pond at Kalorama before Jefferson, President-elect Madison, key members of Congress, Thornton, and other government officials. Admitting his debt to the inventive genius of Bushnell, Fulton exhibited a model and drawings of his submarine boat and then casually stated that, because diving boats were so expensive to build and so hazardous to operate, he doubted they would be extensively used. Far more effective was his system of mining harbors with torpedoes, which he declared was so simple it would soon be adopted by other nations, enabling the weak to challenge the strong.

The naval establishment did not agree. It rejected his strategy, Fulton complained to Madison, "as a Pope would reject a profession of faith that might destroy his infallibility."[5] Suggesting that Barlow be named secretary of the navy, Fulton promised to defend the entire coast without warships or fortifications.

Madison was not as attracted by submarine warfare as Jefferson. Perhaps because he saw little hope of support from the American government, Fulton wrote François de Barbé-Marbois, the French minister of finance and a friend, who he thought would be less hostile to his proposal than the conservative minister of the marine. In his letter Fulton offered to sweep the British fleet from the Channel for the sum of two million francs. To justify his defection to England, Fulton lamely explained that had his torpedoes been successful, France could easily have duplicated them for use against England.[6] Fulton's obsession with submarine warfare was still so blinding that he could not come to terms with the fact that he was also jeopardizing the United States. Under the pretext of preventing American commodities from reaching Great Britain, the French had never stopped seizing American ships and cargoes. France was as much an enemy of America as was England.

———————

Anxious to be settled in New York by the start of the new steamboat season, Fulton did not remain in Washington for Madison's inauguration, but left with Harriet and the three-month-old Barlow on February 20. They traveled in their own carriage and stopped first at Philadelphia where Harriet went on a shopping spree. Among her purchases were gloves, stockings, a silk gown, a lace veil and handkerchief, ribbons, a shawl, and $3.00 worth of sheet music.

Fulton visited the Academy of Fine Arts and learned from Peale that the first year's exhibition receipts had been an encouraging $1,000. This "experiment on public curiosity" had been given so flattering a response, Fulton reported to West, that he was certain subscribers could be induced to set up a sinking fund to purchase more of his paintings. Fulton hoped they would buy "a few of the first merit," although, he tartly observed, "the public like quantity added to Quality even if it were blister plasters for their own backs."[7]

As always, writing West, and being of assistance to him, put Fulton in a cheerful mood. "I have a great big son Barlow Fulton," he boasted. "Everybody says he is a Beauty so it must be true. His mother has a great desire to see Europe and all the works of fine art. She has much taste for painting and draws very well in watercolours. She . . . Says my portrait is the handsomest She ever saw but that it is all owing to your art." His steamboat, he added, was doing wonders, having earned $16,000 in 1808. He expected the two boats he was building would clear $25,000, of which he would get half.

New York City in the spring of 1809 was bursting with promise. Domestic commerce and manufactures had been stimulated by the restrictions on foreign imports. When the Embargo Act was repealed in March, an immense surge of new energy was let loose. With a burgeoning hinterland, improved communication with the West, and confidence in its entrepreneurs, New York was determined to dominate the nation's trade. The designated port for the British packets, New York was the first to receive news from Europe. Express mail from Boston and Washington was fast. New York could not vie with Philadelphia in the cultural realms, but there were five daily newspapers; five more were published twice a week.

All the Weight on One Fulcrum

The Fultons took rooms at Mrs. Loring's. Harriet did more shopping and attended a theatrical performance, which, if it was the usual fare, lasted over five hours and included singing as well as two plays. They attend Verbecq's gala ball at which gentlemen were required to wear evening clothes and were requested not to dance in their boots. A demonstration of the minuet, the gavotte, the hornpipe, and a dance with a tambourine and a shawl were part of the entertainment.

On March 16, 1809, Fulton signed a three-year lease on a newly built house at 75 Chambers Street. Just north of City Hall, it was in a developing neighborhood, with pigs and cows roaming the streets, a good view of the city prison, and on the corner of Broadway, the wooden Board of Health building. It was, however, a substantial house with a stable. It had been built by Silas Talbot who was in the process of divorcing his wife. The rent was $750 a year plus taxes. Fulton also procured servants, at least one of whom was a young slave woman for whom he paid $200. At the time of purchase he promised to grant her freedom in six years, which under New York State's gradual manumission law he was not obliged to do.

Having at last established a household of his own, Fulton shot off to the city of Hudson. The *Steamboat*—now called the *North River*, because she was no longer unique—began service the first week in March. Too long and narrow to move quickly out of the way of other vessels, she had already been damaged in an accident with a sloop. Fulton's reaction was that sloops must be taught to avoid her, and he advocated strengthening the navigation laws to include steamboats.

Fulton made no attempt to pay Livingston a real visit on this fleeting trip, although he had not seen him in over nine months. Uninterested in day-to-day operations, Livingston was, in any case, fully occupied with breeding and selling his merino sheep. The two men had been associates long enough to sense that despite—or perhaps because of—their propensity for keeping each other at arm's length, their partnership flourished. In fact, Livingston was so pleased with the Hudson River enterprise that he at last agreed to expand their operation to the Mississippi. Initially they would establish a company to run passenger and cargo ships from New Orleans to Natchez, a 300-mile journey with comparatively deep and safe water. Fulton estimated investors would earn 27 percent return on their money and suggested that Livingston's brother Edward, who was living in New Orleans, might try selling a few shares to test the local market.

Robert Fulton

Since this was an ideal opportunity to weave Roosevelt into the web, Fulton proposed to engage him to survey the Ohio and the Mississippi rivers. He would be given $600 to cover expenses and an eventual share in the operation. Anxious to get a foothold in Fulton's and Livingston's enterprises in any way he could, Roosevelt accepted immediately. He and his adventurous wife Lydia set out for Pittsburgh in June.

Satisfied that he would get control of the western rivers before competitors had a chance to intrude, Fulton was inspired to conquer Europe as well. Undeterred by the raging Napoleonic wars, he wrote the Bavarian minister with plans for organizing a steamboat line on the Danube.

These ambitious plans for worldwide expansion helped Fulton mask from himself as well as from others that the eastern establishment was giving him "much trouble." Work on the *Car of Neptune* and John R. Livingston's *Rariton* had been delayed because the ship bearing copper from Paul Revere's foundry in Massachusetts was caught in a late freeze in Long Island Sound. John R., not understanding why his smaller and lighter boat could not go faster, displayed his utter lack of understanding of Fulton's theory of resistances and velocities by ordering McQueen to design a double set of wheels. Passengers on the *North River* complained that the fines were excessive and that the schedules were so poorly arranged they were required to spend two nights on a through trip between Albany and New York.

Compared to the tension caused by the recalcitrant Stevens, however, these troubles were trivial. As Fulton predicted, Stevens's high steam engine was a failure. Nevertheless, he had no intention of giving up the *Phoenix*. To help wear Stevens down, Fulton resorted to John R. as an ally, encouraging him to sue Stevens in state and federal court should he infringe on the New York–New Brunswick run. Stevens calmly accused Fulton of pomposity and informed John R. that his outburst had succeeded only in displaying the weakness of his claim.

Livingston joined the fray indirectly. Attacking Stevens for having taken down the fence that separated their properties on Broadway, he fumed. "I did not like just as I was leaving town [to] observe that you had removed the fence which your *father himself set* as the division between us after great deliberation and many consultations."[8] The intractable Stevens acidly replied that the carpenters had done it when he was out of town, and since Livingston himself was so seldom in the city, the same thing might well have happened to him.

Stevens certainly was feisty enough to savor certain aspects of his duel with Fulton and the Livingstons, but the sober truth was that he ardently wished to avoid going to court. Litigation did not suit his temperament, nor did he wish to spend the time and money. As a result he partially capitulated. Still refusing to acknowledge the validity of Fulton's patent and Livingston's monopoly, he prudently elected to take the *Phoenix* to Philadelphia and run her on the Delaware River to Bordentown.

This was a courageous decision. To reach Philadelphia, the *Phoenix* first must brave the open sea, a feat that Fulton had not yet envisioned as practicable. With Stevens's brilliant son Robert Livingston Stevens in charge, the *Phoenix* departed from Hoboken on Saturday, June 10, 1809, in a fog and light breeze. The first two days out were uneventful, but for the next eleven she was beset with "dirty squally weather," "great swells," and "very severe lightning, thunder and rain." The *Phoenix* did not reach the sheltering confines of the Delaware River until the evening of the thirteenth day. By then her boilers were "very foul." Unable to risk raising the steam, and with no wind to fill his sails, Robert was forced to drift upriver on the tide. He floated into Philadelphia on June 24 at nine o'clock, just as the midsummer twilight was giving way to night, and anchored opposite the Market Street wharf. Ignominious as the *Phoenix*'s arrival was, it in no way detracted from her glorious achievement. The vessel's survival through 240 miles of heavy seas more than justified Stevens's great faith.[9]

Impressed, Fulton laid aside his infringement claim for the moment and wished Stevens well on the Delaware. At the same time he began organizing a new company to operate ferries from New York to Powles Hook, the highly lucrative run he had recently offered to Stevens.

———

When Fulton was invited to join the elite and influential American Philosophical Society in the spring of 1809, putting him in the same illustrious stratum as Livingston, Thornton, Stevens, Latrobe, and the Earl of Stanhope, he proudly explained to the secretary his plans for extending his steamboat empire: "Thus, you see my whole mind and exertions are directed to the steam boats, until I train my engineers and get the boats in useful Operation. This I have conceived a prudent and useful mode of working, one thing at a time and do it well, and thus mechanically speaking all the weight on one fulcrum."[10]

Fulton might better have described himself as a juggler who had not entirely mastered the art of keeping his plates in the air, but whose evident skills inspired other novices to jostle him and ruin his act. Content no longer with insinuations, Thornton launched an overt assault on Fulton's patents. Drawing on his expertise as clerk of the Patent Office, he "delicately" suggested "the propriety of putting less dependence on an exclusive claim to wheels on the Sides of a Boat." The idea had been published in the *Lexicon Technicum* in Isaac Newton's day, he said, and, as Fulton well knew, the U.S. law expressly forbade patenting ideas that had been previously published, no matter when or where.

Thornton then offered to be Fulton's discrete support and eventual partner. "These Impressions suggested to me the Idea of keeping secret your Calculations on which you think so much depends. . . . The *Lexicon Technicum* I refer to is in my possession & I have kept its contents secret from those with whom you are contending."

If Fulton still believed his patent good, Thornton suggested he test it in an amicable suit with Stevens, although such a course would stimulate competition by publicizing both the processes and the profits. In his circuitous way Thornton was still attempting to obtain a percentage of Livingston's and Fulton's partnership in return for the use of his patents which, though unproven, he insisted were far stronger than Fulton's patent and, including the latest, prior to it. "I consider a connection with you desirable, not only to avoid but to repel opposition, & because I know you are scientific, & more to be depended on than any other of my Acquaintaince," he unctuously wrote. "I have been solicited to enter into partnership with others, but shall decline all engagements until I know your final determination."[11]

Fulton was not to be thrown off balance. He scornfully retorted he was perfectly aware that side wheels had been used on horse and man-powered boats in Europe for over a hundred years and that experimenters had tried to propel steamboats "with paddles, swans feet, smoke jack flyers, endless screws, endless chains, Long boats, Short boats, high Steam engines, and Boulton and Watts engines." None, however, had succeeded. If the steamboat was an old invention, he asked where it was. Clearly, it was nowhere until his discovery of the correct proportions and velocities. These principles were to be found only in his patent, and those who did not understand them were "groping in the dark without rule or guide." Such was Stevens's case and Thornton's as well.

Still Fulton did not care to cut off all communication with Thornton. Characteristically, he could not resist offering still another idea for improving wheelboards and inviting Thornton to comment on it. Nurturing their social relationship, he promised to deliver Thornton's remembrances to Mrs. Fulton and sent his own genial regards to Mrs. Thornton and "her mama." Asserting that little more could be done to increase speeds with a Boulton and Watt engine, Fulton explained in a final burst of candor, "I am so situated that I must stand or fall by what I have done. I cannot make any new association of partnership or adopt any new plan until it is proved not to encroach on me and to be better than my own."[12]

Incapable of going ahead on his own, Thornton turned again to Stevens. Stevens proudly informed him he was established in Philadelphia where Fulton probably would not disturb him and brushed his advances aside. "I have hitherto proceeded on my own bottom entirely," he wrote, "and feel the fullest confidence of being eventually successful."[13]

This pernicious jockeying for position did not prevent Fulton and Harriet from spending much of the early summer in the country. Harriet was always happiest when surrounded by her family, and Teviotdale, with its lawns and gardens and nearby creeks, was a healthy, amusing haven for little Barlow who was just beginning to walk with some authority. Fulton, however, was restless away from New York and his work. He needed the activity, conveniences, and excitement of city life. Although he enjoyed the countryside aesthetically, he did not romanticize it, but approached it as territory to be settled with neat towns and industrious people. He could only have had ambivalent feelings toward the Livingston domain where hardworking farmers were denied land ownership by the Livingstons' feudalistic land policies.

Moreover, away from the daily demands of the steamboat operation, Fulton was depressed by the "most unpleasant Vacuum"[14] created by his break with the Barlows. He told Barlow he had agreed to live at Kalorama only because when he returned to America he had had no thoughts of marrying and gave him stern advice about how to manage his finances so that maintaining Kalorama on his own would not be a burden. Fulton missed Ruth and Barlow's companionship. He invited them to visit Teviotdale. They refused on the grounds that the great distinction of delivering the Fourth of July Oration before Congress had been conferred on Barlow and he was busy preparing his address. Eager to demonstrate his unabated devotion, Fulton dashed off a spirited first draft of a speech full of good sense and idealism and complete with pauses and rhetorical flourishes, an exercise, he joked, "something like setting Hercules to play at nine pins." Reminiscent of Fulton's earlier tracts, the draft's message was that the Union must be kept from dismemberment by strong bonds of communication, education, and art. It also contained a glowing passage on submarine warfare, which Fulton exhorted Barlow to leave out if he thought proper. Finally, worried about Barlow's reputation as an atheist, he urged him not to forget his "belief in the wisdom of Providence and His goodness to us."[15] Barlow retained Fulton's ideas, which mirrored his own, and improved upon them. His final version was forceful, courageous, and well received. He was happy to espouse submarine warfare. But he did not visit Fulton at Teviotdale, or even in New York.

Fulton's and Livingston's second boat, the *Car of Neptune*, was launched on June 14, 1809. In the process the timbers in her keel were strained. The damage would have been far worse, John R. sourly reported to his brother, if she had been ballasted with water as Fulton had ordered. Planning to put her into service in the middle of August, Fulton was confident she would be the most elegant American passenger ship afloat. He looked forward to doubling the schedule to Albany and to reaping the profits as soon as she made her first run.

Meanwhile, the *Phoenix* was making a mark in Philadelphia. Stevens added entertainment to attract passengers. According to Peale, the boat was especially popular with boisterous young men, who treated her as a floating tavern. Mechanically, however, the *Phoenix* was far from perfect. Her paddleboards were too small and tended to wallow in the water. Built to weather the ocean, she was proving too clumsy for river work.

When Fulton saw Stevens's model of a modified engine at McQueen's, he concluded that his rival's back was at last against the wall, for the design was remarkably like his own. Livingston agreed that it was time to present Stevens with an ultimatum. Their much worked over joint letter has many disarming passages, but there is no question as to its message. "When relatives and friends grow cold towards each other, it is always to be lamented, yet when such an unfortunate event occurs there is more nobleness of soul in nourishing a spirit of concilia-tion than in persevering an error. If we have erred in judgment we are willing to make every reasonable acknowledgement and we sincerely hope you will meet us on like conditions,"[16] it gracefully began. Then it came to the point. If Stevens did not concede, at least privately, that his high steam engine had failed and that he was working under their patent, they would give the franchise for the run from Trenton to Philadelphia and from Philadelphia to New Castle to strangers.

Stevens still refused to capitulate. He replied that he had made unique improvements which he would patent. "Unless I am ready, *in forma pauperis* to subscribe to terms the most humiliating," he com-plained, "I am probably doomed to be pursued and persecuted on the Delaware in a manner similar to that employed on the New Brunswick run."[17] To save himself, he threatened to test the constitutionality of the New York State monopoly in court.

Both sides having finally exhausted their brave talk, Stevens, Liv-ingston, and Fulton compromised. On December 1, they agreed to share all present and future patent rights respecting steamboats. Fulton and Livingston would retain monopoly rights on all New York waters, in-cluding Lake Champlain and the run to New Brunswick. They also re-served for themselves the right to establish steamboat companies on the Mississippi and Ohio rivers. In return, Stevens could have Chesapeake Bay and the Connecticut, Delaware, Santee, and Savannah rivers and also the run from Long Island Sound to Providence, Rhode Island. If within seven years he had no boat on any particular water, that territory would revert to Fulton and Livingston. At the last moment Livingston sought to strengthen the agreement with an addendum stating that Ste-vens must "fully and absolutely recognize" his and Fulton's rights to all inventions and improvements specified in their patent as well as their exclusive right to navigate New York waters by steam for twenty years.[18]

Stevens signed the papers—without the addendum. No better than the faith and the intentions of the signers, the agreement signaled only a brief truce.

The Happiness
of the Earth

❖

Believing he had at last tethered Stevens, Fulton felt free to go to Washington after Christmas to stimulate government interest in submarine warfare. As Harriet was nearing the end of her second full-term pregnancy, he went alone and stayed with the Barlows at Kalorama. Joel had just bought twenty more acres to embellish the park and was busy making plans to beautify it. Ruth, whose health had been poor, typically began to feel better as soon as Fulton arrived. She did not mind that he ran about to "drawing rooms" in the evenings or that he admired the provocative Mme. Elizabeth Patterson Bonaparte. For the three of them, it was almost like old times.

Throughout the early winter, Fulton had been working on an illustrated pamphlet entitled *Torpedo War and Submarine Explosions* with which he intended to make his system known throughout the world as he had threatened the British he would do in 1806. Emblazoned on the title page were the words: "The Liberty of the Seas will be the Happiness of the Earth." He blanketed official Washington with copies, hoping to entice the legislators into funding further experiments and a full-scale demonstration. His chances were good, for Congress was still loath to spend the money to build up a naval force capable of offensive action. However, more than gunboats and land batteries were needed to protect the country's principal harbors, for the British bombardment of Copenhagen in October 1807, which killed over two thousand civilians and leveled half of the city, made the ruthlessness of the British clear. While the British and the French continued to prey on American ships, a convoluted piece of legislation called Macon's Bill No. 2 had occupied Congress all session. It excluded British and French naval vessels from U.S. territorial waters while it promised to open the door to trade with either country should it cease violating American merchantmen. If nothing else, another experiment with torpedoes would provide diversion from the tedium and the acrimony of the deliberations.

Though *Torpedo War and Submarine Explosions* was not so grand in scale as his *Treatise on Canals*, Fulton crammed into its sixty pages his whole social philosophy as well as detailed plans for submarine attack. Like "To the Friends of Mankind" and "Thoughts on Free Trade," composed twelve years earlier, it is shot through with high moral purpose. His goal in developing submarine warfare, Fulton declared, was to free America's genius and resources to pursue science, art, and education and thus create in Americans "a real grandeur of character, which would secure to them the respect and admiration of the civilized world."[1]

Offering his torpedoes as the most practical means to this Utopian end, he prophesied: "[W]ere America to try her finances to the utmost, and establish a marine equal to fifty ships of 80 guns it would be to us the greatest of misfortunes, for so many persons would become interested in obtaining a support from it, that, like England, we should continue adding, until our successors would find it a power superior to their liberty—one that would load them with taxes, press their children into senseless wars, nor leave them permission to complain."[2] With the money and energy it would cost to maintain a useless, nonproductive navy, Fulton stated that the nation could build an interstate communication system and a public school system as well: "Twelve canals, running from the eastern and northern parts of the United States to the south, each fifteen hundred miles long, and fifty miles distant from each other, equal to eighteen thousand miles; thirty canals, running from the sea coast to the interior, each six hundred miles long and fifty miles apart, or eighteen thousand miles—total, thirty-six thousand miles; . . . two thousand bridges, and two thousand fifty public establishments for education."[3]

Anticipating abuse for inventing a barbaric weapon, Fulton included a long essay, "On the Imaginary Inhumanity of Torpedo War." Playing on America's deep-seated fears he argued:

It is barbarous for a ship of war to fire into a peaceable merchant vessel, kill part of her people, take her and the property, and reduce the proprietor with his family from affluence to penury. It was barbarous to bombard Copenhagen, set fire to the city, and destroy innocent women and children. It would be barbarous for ships of war to enter the harbour of New-York, fire on the city, destroy property, and murder many of the peaceable inhabitants. . . . if Torpedoes should prevent such acts of violence, the invention must be humane.[4]

To defuse the accusation that he was nothing but a mercenary who had not hesitated to initiate both England and France into the mysteries of his system, Fulton justified his whole European adventure as an opportunity "to make many interesting experiments on a large scale." In fact, he declared, it was "a fortunate circumstance" that the explosion of the *Dorothea* was witnessed "by more than a hundred respectable and brave officers of the Royal navy," for if Congress should adopt them as a means of defense, they would be driven to respect America's rights.[5]

Since his return to the United States, Fulton wrote, he had improved both his anchored and his clockwork bombs by making them safer for the assailant and more lethal for the enemy. To the anchored torpedo he had added a simple deactivating device that could be set for a specific day when it would cause the torpedo to rise to the surface and, at the same instant, lock the detonating lever so that it could not strike fire. This would permit the mines to be checked for potency and to be relaid in varying patterns in order to confuse the enemy. He did not describe how it worked, but he offered to exhibit a working model in the future.

Fulton also unveiled a 27-foot, six-oared unsinkable boat to carry his harpoon gun. The gun was mounted on a swivel in the stern with the torpedo fixed on a platform behind it so it would clear the rudder when it splashed into the water. As this boat could be rowed at a rate of 140 yards a minute, Fulton calculated that the harpooner would be exposed to enemy fire for only four minutes. During this time he would be protected by four swiveling blunderbusses worked by marines who would carry pistols and cutlasses. Except "in case of emergency," Fulton explained, "our business is to run, to harpoon, and not to fight."[6]

Once trained, this special torpedo corps need practice only once a month. Otherwise it would cause the government no further expense.

In time of peace both the torpedoes and the boats could be easily stored. Thus, 650 torpedo boats, capable of protecting the six major East Coast ports, could be put into action for the same price as two highly vulnerable ships of thirty guns. Fulton urged Congress to authorize a full-scale demonstration with charged torpedoes. All he needed was $2,160 to train the twenty-four marines to man two boats. Declaring his personal commitment to the project, Fulton promised that if such a squadron were put under his command, he would be "responsible to his fellow-citizens for the courage which should secure its success." However, he emphasized that he had no desire for any official command. Referring to his steamboats, he claimed his private pursuits guaranteed his independence and freedom of action. "[T]hey are useful and honourable amusements," he said, "and the most rational source of my happiness."[7]

On February 17, Fulton exhibited his wares at Long's Hotel to an audience of over two hundred. Soaring to new heights of self-dramatization, he compared himself as a ridiculed and spurned inventor to Roger Bacon and Galileo. Even if Congress abandoned his invention to the chances of time, he declared, he would never forsake it but with his last breath: "Should I sink under the casualties of life it will be an orphan of the arts which I recommend to the guardianship of my fellow citizens; let them nourish it with the care I have watched over it for nine years past."[8]

Fulton's fanatic urgency was not as winning as he hoped. His friend, Samuel Latham Mitchill, deeply involved in the defense of New York Harbor, observed: "This trip to Congress has afforded him a considerable opportunity for displaying the talent he possesses, tho, I think he has had a considerable share of mortification. Captain Chauncey of the Navy, has, after all my favourable sentiments, almost convinced me, that it is very easy for a Ship or a Navy to prevent the ruin with which these exploding machines threaten them."[9] Chief clerk of the Navy Department C. W. Goldsborough told Commodore John Rodgers, "to me it appears visionary in the extreme. Altho' not a nautical man I can readily conceive that numerous expedients might be devised to secure a vessel from the effects of his Torpedoes. He has made some experiments—which have partly succeeded in demonstrating the principles that govern the application of his system. To my mind they are altogether unsatisfactory."[10] Rodgers was more blunt: "It was," he said, the most "Visionary scheme . . . to have originated in the brain of a man not actually out of his senses."[11] By means of booms, spars, ropes, chains, or nets, it was obvious to him that a vessel could be completely protected from torpedo attack.

In a display of defiance reminiscent of his frenetic behavior in England, Fulton went about Washington announcing that he was "prepared to encounter the ignorance of the multitude" and that, though "little wits and babbling orators" opposed him, the name of Fulton would be remembered with reverence when theirs had sunk into oblivion.[12]

Jefferson, to Fulton's gratification, tended to agree. Attributing opposition to pro-British federalists, he wrote from his retirement at Monticello, "I am not afraid of new inventions or improvements. . . . Your Torpedoes will be to cities what vaccination has been to mankind. It extinguishes their greatest danger . . . that the tories should be against you is in character, because it will curtail the power of their idol, England. . . . I sincerely wish the torpedo may go the whole length you expect of putting down navies. I wish it too much not to become an easy convert."[13]

The new secretary of the navy, Paul Hamilton, a tobacco planter from South Carolina who was inexperienced in naval affairs and burdened with a drinking problem, was also friendly toward Fulton's project. On February 26, despite the naval establishment's opposition, the congressional committee unanimously recommended that funds be allocated for experiments. Fulton returned to New York well satisfied.

No appropriation was forthcoming, however. Impatient for immediate action, Fulton wrote Senator Stephen Bradley, a republican from Vermont, protesting the delay and excoriating one of the members as "a very little man, who . . . turns Buffoon to amuse the company."[14] Finally, on March 30, Congress authorized the expenditure of $5,000 for torpedo experiments—double the cost Fulton had estimated in his pamphlet. Fulton was to demonstrate the results before the end of the session.

Fulton had, at last, achieved the objective he had so long proclaimed: the official involvement of his own country in submarine warfare. He panicked. His past failures, always glossed over or denied, could no longer be suppressed. Too clever not to credit his opponents' objections, he realized that, if he did not succeed this time, he might never be given another chance. To protect himself, he protested that he could not be prepared for a truly systematic investigation until early fall. Then he demanded that the principal officers of the navy give him their plans of defense so that he could contrive means of destroying or avoiding them. He insisted that the demonstration take place in New York Harbor where he would be able to employ his own workmen, rather than in Washington as he had initially suggested. Resorting to bravado, he declared: "My whole time and attention is now directed to ways and means for securing success. . . . [E]very plan of Booms, ropes, chains, nets etc. backing and filling which I have as yet heard of instead of being obstructions, will by a new combination on my part really facilitate my operations and enable me to destroy a vessel with much less risque to my men than if she had no such tackle."[15]

Neither the backing of the American government nor his anxiety about the results of the promised demonstrations dulled Fulton's appetite for world recognition of submarine warfare. Characteristically avoiding the proliferation of arms problems, he continued to do everything in his power to implement his system abroad. Not having received a reply from Barbé-Marbois, he sent copies of *Torpedo Warfare* to Volney, Monge, and Laplace. Explaining that he had abandoned the submarine boat because it was difficult to maneuver, he told them he had found a simpler method which "organized and combined with the courage of Frenchmen, will I am certain enable the Emperor to drive the English ships of war from the British Channel within twelve months." It would be a pleasure, he said, to send them one complete machine of each kind to serve as patterns.[16]

Still smarting from the British government's dismissal, he also sent ten copies of the pamphlet to Lord Stanhope with an absurdly abrasive cover letter. Explaining the improvements he had made and those he intended to make, he warned: "The depredation by your fleets of our commerce, the Impressing of our citizens, the Insolence of your commanders and the Injustice of your government towards these States Cries aloud for such coercion as shall produce a reform. And I am either wrong in my deductions from the most Interesting and so far satisfactory experiments, or this Invention will produce the happy consequence to my country which I contemplate."[17] Once again misjudging Stanhope's patriotism and pride, Fulton told Stanhope to distribute the books to such persons as he believed might comprehend the ultimate consequences of the invention.

In addition, Fulton sent six pamphlets to the Russian ambassador, asking him to bring the system to the attention of the czar and promising to send instructions and models. Soon afterward he dispatched a pamphlet to the Dutch ambassador as well.

Even in time of peace, such actions would appear treasonous. Yet, astounding as it may seem, there is no record that Fulton was accused of endangering the United States by making his inventions available to any country that would buy them. No attempt whatever was made to maintain even a modicum of secrecy about his system. *Torpedo Warfare*, which described his bombs in detail, was on sale for one dollar. Its availability was advertised in the newspapers along side *Tales of Fashionable Life* by Maria Edgeworth.

It was not quite true that Fulton was at liberty to direct his whole time and attention to his torpedo experiments, nor did he wish to. His drive to establish a steamboat empire before rivals usurped what he considered his legitimate territory—virtually all the inland waters of the nation—required myriad decisions that could not be postponed.

The Albany Company—inspired by the expectation of profits, by Albany's jealousy of New York City's commercial supremacy, and also by personal and political antagonism toward the Livingston family's proud exercise of power—had designs for a steamboat that blatantly ignored Fulton's patent and Livingston's monopoly. The Lake Champlain Company was brazenly running an exact copy of the *North River*. Aaron Ogden had joined forces with an inventor named Daniel Dod to convert his Elizabeth Town Point ferry to steam. Daniel French, who had patented an engine with side cranks and for whom Fulton had once inexplicably provided bail (which French had jumped), planned to contest Stevens on the Delaware.

The habitually contentious John R. Livingston was acting more as an adversary than as an associate. With every reason to be grateful for the liberal terms Livingston and Fulton had accorded him, he bleated that his profits were so low it would be impossible for him to operate the *Rariton* at all unless they waived their percentage of the receipts. Should they force him to run the boat at a loss to himself and a gain to them, he would sell her at auction. "Never shall he edge himself into any other enterprise which I can control,"[18] Fulton exploded, frightened that Ogden would take over the run to southern New Jersey.

Only in the West where their operation was still in the planning stages, did progress seem smooth. Nicholas Roosevelt brought back from his reconnoitering mission news of the immense emoluments to be earned on the Mississippi. There was enough trade in sugar and cotton alone, he reported, to occupy two steamboats from New Orleans to Natchez. Despite his previous disappointment with Roosevelt's services, Livingston agreed to send him to set up shops to build their first boat at Pittsburgh. In Pittsburgh, already called "the Birmingham of America," it was possible to build seagoing vessels of 450 tons, and float them down the Ohio and the Mississippi to New Orleans.

With so much steamboat business to distract him, Fulton found preparing for the impending torpedo demonstration "a long and tedious job." The harpoon gun he had advanced with such confidence proved neither accurate nor powerful. As an alternative, he designed a six-oared "torpedo boat." Suspended from the bowsprit was a 40-foot pole tipped with a torpedo and so balanced that the operator could elevate or depress it with his right hand while launching the torpedo with his left. Protected by movable spars, the boat looked in plan more like an ungainly water bug than a deadly attack vessel. In addition, Fulton contrived a gun-powered hook and chisel to cut ships' cables under water by remote control. However, even if this device succeeded in casting enemy ships adrift and depriving them of anchors worth $5,000, it did nothing to solve the essential problem of delivering torpedoes quickly, safely, and effectively.

Fulton was flailing about, and he knew it. Although at the end of June he announced he had everything in order for his New York demonstration, he was pleased when Rodgers, who had been appointed to represent the navy on the review committee, left town for the duration of the torrid weather, for Rodgers's absence gave him until September or October to perfect his performance.

Toward the middle of July, Fulton departed with his family for Teviotdale. Throughout the spring their lives had been in a state of upheaval. In April Harriet presented him with a daughter, Julia. At the same time they moved a few doors west to 133 Chambers Street. The house was much finer, but the neighborhood had not improved. According to a cranky letter Fulton wrote to the Common Council, the city's "scavengers" failed to remove the trash and manure the residents had been ordered to sweep into the middle of the street, with the result that the free-roaming hogs rooted in the rubbish, leaving the neighborhood as filthy as ever.

The country at least presented a change. Fulton particularly enjoyed the time spent with his children. Julia was a healthy three-month-old baby and the two-and-a-half-year-old Barlow, having recovered from a worrisome bout of "ague," was especially precious and engaging. "Now is the time he would please you," Fulton wrote the Barlows, "he begins to compound sentences and being fond of talking he makes droll and amusing English. Anty Babe, Unke Babe, Granemame, Ante Wive gone to Washington, is run over 100 times or more each day, then such a funny coaxing and handsome fellow you never saw."[19] Despite the fact Teviotdale was his mother-in-law's house, Fulton, with proprietary expansiveness, invited Joel and Ruthlinda to come and see for themselves. Fortunately, at least for Harriet, they were not disposed to accept.

When cool weather made New York City more comfortable, the evaluating committee assembled for the "ocular proof" Fulton had so sanguinely promised seven months previously. Neither Commodore John Rodgers nor Captain Isaac Chauncey, the navy's second representative, had changed his low opinion of submarine warfare. The members of the civilian committee, however, were Fulton's personal friends: Livingston was the chairman; other members included Morgan Lewis, Livingston's brother-in-law; Cadwallader D. Colden, a lawyer and steamboat investor; and Colonel Jonathan Williams, the country's foremost expert on port fortifications.

The demonstration Fulton arranged was elaborate, but for so important an event its agenda was surprisingly *ad hoc*. The first session, held at the City Hotel on Broadway, began at eleven o'clock on the morning of September 21. As he was wont to do, Fulton delivered a lecture on the principles involved. At the risk of boring his audience who had heard it all before, he attempted to put his entire work on submarine warfare into historical context with a soaring discourse on progress in the arts and sciences. Then with a torpedo placed on the table before him, he displayed a model of his torpedo boat with the 40-foot swivel pole.

For the mock attack, set for September 24, Fulton arrogantly requested Rodgers's *President*—one of the three largest ships in the United States Navy—to serve as a target. Rodgers offered the fine brig *Argus* instead.

Several thousand spectators collected at Corlear's Hook for the event. They were, however, quickly disappointed. At the last moment, the committee sent word that unfavorable weather prevented their meeting.

The next morning, the demonstration was again postponed because Livingston was indisposed and the weather had not improved.

While waiting, Fulton was allowed to examine the *Argus*. He was appalled to see that the brig's defenses were drawn from every warship's common equipment. She carried nine grapnels and twenty-five battering rams. The splinter net, suspended from the bow and wrapped around the hull over a framework fabricated from the spare studding-sail booms, formed a protective curtain. Fulton frankly admitted this shield would prevent him from applying torpedoes to her hull and begged time to reflect on how he might penetrate it.

To save face, he gave an informal demonstration of his machine for cutting submerged cables. Although it worked out of water as he had announced, he did not risk an underwater experiment. Instead, he tested his harpoon gun against a target about 5 feet square. It penetrated an oak plank to a depth of 5 inches, but only within a range of 15 feet.

The next day Fulton made several more essays with the harpoon gun, this time at the navy yard before the whole committee. He was not able to increase its range. Desperate, he persuaded the committee to return to Chauncey's house so that he could explain, with the help of models, the effects he had not been able to prove by actual experiment. As a special attraction he told them of a knife, activated by a series of explosive charges, on which he had been working since their last meeting and which he claimed could make so big a hole in the security nets that torpedoes could be spilled through it "in the same way that potatoes are commonly emptied from the body of a Cart."[20] The committee was not impressed. However, they agreed to review the working of the underwater cable-cutting device on September 28.

This demonstration was the most disastrous of all. The navy yard supplied a barge, anchored with an old 22-inch cable. Fulton could not even hook his cutting device to it. The gun fired properly, but the tide pushed his assault boat into such an awkward position that help had to be summoned to extricate it.

Delighted by Fulton's discomfiture, Captain Chauncey undertook to worsen it by utterly destroying the theory that a warship's guns would be useless against his torpedo boat at 20 yards. At a distance of 90 yards from the wharf, he anchored an 18-foot boat in which were placed boards representing three seated men. Discharging grape and canister shot from a 24-pound gun, he drove 73 bits of shot through the boat, 18 through the first board, 9 through the second, and 5 through the third.

Searching for relief from his humiliation, Fulton contended that the cumbersome defenses used by the *Argus* were too complicated to be mounted quickly enough to ward off a hit-and-run attack. To his astonishment, they were installed in fifteen minutes. There was nothing he could do but admit that his "want of nautical information" had led him into many errors. Glad to give him more rope with which to hang himself, Chauncey and Rodgers agreed to meet with the committee in four weeks to examine whatever improvements Fulton might be able to devise.

The weather was poor on October 29. On October 30, with only Chauncey, Rodgers, Colonel Williams, and a late-arriving Colden in attendance, Fulton exhibited a miniature model of a 300-ton vessel that he called a torpedo block ship. Its 6-inch-thick decks were musketproof, he said, and its 6-foot-thick sides were cannonproof. For attack, it was fitted with four 96-foot-torpedo booms supported at the inner end by double swivels and at the outer end by guys attached to a mast. Theoretically, the block ship would be moved against the tide by a hand-cranked propeller. Deploring his own "confined imagination," Rodgers called the vessel the *Nondescript*, then vividly characterized it as "a torpid, unwieldly, fifteen-sixteenths-sunk-in-water-dungeon," not calculated to supersede the necessity of a navy, particularly because the crew would be crammed in the hold "in as perfect darkness as if shut up in the black hole of Calcutta."[21]

On October 31, the weather was poor and there was no demonstration. On November 1, patience and curiosity expended, only a handful of observers showed up. Fulton's cable-cutting device finally succeeded in severing a 14-inch cable under water. Nevertheless, Rodgers, who was not present, remained unconvinced of its usefulness. Any ordinary seaman, he commented, would think up a defense in twenty minutes.

Grasping at straws, Fulton exhibited a torpedo that had been anchored in the East River near the navy yard for a month and explained the effect of the tide upon it. But he did nothing to prove its effect as an engine of war. After this fiasco, the committee adjourned for the final time, having exacted a pledge from Fulton that he publicly acknowledge the incorrectness of all such parts of his system not proven effective by his experiments.

It is incredible that, with his most cherished project at stake, Fulton was so ill-prepared for these demonstrations. He was certainly resourceful and experienced enough to figure out in advance the kind of defenses that might be used. Although Fulton was caught up in the excitement of the experiment and the magnitude of the project, his lack of organization and clear direction was evident throughout. He spent only $1,500 of the $5,000 Congress had appropriated. It was almost as if he did not wish to succeed, that he was driven by some inner compulsion to destroy the reputation he had striven so fiercely to create.

This chronic impulse to self-destruction was the dark side of Fulton's genius. It found expression in the gratuitously surly passages of his canal book. It tainted his early relationships with Stanhope and Livingston and his negotiations with the British government. It was as if the tension produced by feeling beleaguered was a necessary stimulus to his creativity. Like other human beings, Fulton did not comprehend the full range of his inner compulsions.

Nevertheless, though peevish and obstinate, Fulton's behavior was less maniacal than during his final months in England. He fumed, but he did not lose his temper and harass his examiners—at least on paper. He was, perhaps, more secure in 1810 than he had been in 1806. His steamboats had brought him fame and seemed certain to make him a fortune. He was married and had children. He had become a man of substance. William Lee, an American entrepreneur and minor diplomat whom he had known in Paris, summed up Fulton's situation: "My friend Fulton lives in a handsome house, keeps an elegant carriage, has four servants, two children, and sees his friends once a fortnight for $4000 per annum."[22]

Typically, it was not long before Fulton was again awash with optimism. Comparing himself to a man who, having shown an ounce of powder to Julius Caesar, was put down by the Roman legion as a madman, he implored Livingston to write a private letter to the secretary of the navy urging new experiments. The text that Fulton provided was over sixteen pages long. Its salient point was that a ship loaded with grapnels, nets, and spars would be an easy target. Still faithful to the concept of submarine warfare, Livingston was glad to comply. Though more reluctant than Livingston to copy Fulton verbatim, Morgan Lewis and Cadwallader D. Colden also delivered favorable opinions.

Having done all he could do from New York to reinstate torpedo warfare, Fulton was feverish to get to Washington. Ruth had been injured in a carriage accident and, although she at first made light of it, Barlow wrote there was little hope of her recovery. However, it was not until after the first of January that Fulton was settled at Kalorama—

probably without Harriet and the children. By that time Ruth was on the mend.

The majority report of the Committee on the Torpedo Experiments was issued in early February 1811. The report made abundantly clear Fulton had not demonstrated that the government should rely on his submarine system as a means of national defense. Instead of the promised confession of failure, Fulton's reply was a mixture of genial regret, brash truculence, and cheerful hope. He admitted the experiments were badly executed, but, drawing parallels with the abused seventeenth-century fortifications genius Sébastien Vauban, he derided all who questioned his ultimate ability to place a torpedo under a ship in defiance of its resistance.

The mood of the country had changed; war instead of commercial restrictions was favored as a means of securing U.S. maritime rights. Since Fulton's system would not impinge on the recently initiated program of building a strong conventional force, Secretary Hamilton saw no harm in Fulton's using for further experiments the $3,500 of the $5,000 initial appropriation that remained unspent.

Fulton thus survived his ordeal. The strain, however, took a decided physical toll. A boil erupted on the side of his nose and became so inflamed he was confined to Kalorama. The atmosphere there was far from restorative, for the household was in turmoil. Barlow had been appointed minister plenipotentiary to France. His difficult mission was to find out if Napoleon had revoked the edicts under which France had been seizing American ships. He was also expected to procure the release of sequestered ships and indemnities for those that had been confiscated. Although Barlow claimed the sacrifice of ease and comfort on his part would be too great and the prospect of doing the public good too little for him to take any satisfaction in the mission, it was obvious he would accept the honor. Fulton dreaded his departure.

The Cupidity of Many

❖

It would have been helpful to Fulton if, while he was absent from the New York arena, a few of the difficulties besetting his steamboat empire had solved themselves. They had not.

The fault did not lie entirely in Fulton's proud, compulsive personality. The structures necessary to support his dream of a united and prospering nation simply did not exist. Except between the largest cities where there was express mail, communication was painfully slow. The movement of passengers and goods whether by horse, stagecoach, wagon, or boat was constrained by the vagaries of the weather. Banking was chaotic, there was no specialized labor pool, and the management techniques necessary to operate a large, capital-demanding operation had not even been imagined. In fact, few of Fulton's contemporaries were capable of understanding the commitment of time and money required for a long-term enterprise. Speculation was the passion of the day. The few great fortunes that had been made rather than inherited were amassed by dealing in ship cargoes, military contracts, or quick-turnover real-estate schemes. Fulton was almost unique in grasping the challenge of investing in the country's basic development.

Virtually unaided, Fulton undertook every aspect of the work himself—designing, manufacturing, marketing, financing, researching, supervising day-to-day operations, planning for future growth, and lobbying government officials. Those men equipped to help him because of their vision, inventive genius, or mechanical skill were necessarily real or potential rivals whom he could never fully trust. Even Stevens, who of all Fulton's associates was by temperament and talent the most capable of giving him support, was unreliable. Stevens had procured a patent for an improved engine that Fulton would use, but he had no intention of cooperating further with Fulton unless it served his own ambitions.

With two able sons to work for him, Stevens was taking advantage of his agreement with Fulton and Livingston to start a line of boats that would run on the Delaware between Philadelphia and Wilmington and on the Chesapeake between the Elk River and Baltimore, competing with the turnpike to Washington. He expected Fulton to secure subscriptions from President Madison and other high-level government officials "to give weight & respectability no matter how few shares,"[1] but he still refused to provide a written statement that he was working under a franchise from Livingston and Fulton. Moreover, Stevens was soliciting the legislature of Virginia—a territory not included in his agreement—for a monopoly in his own name. He had also applied to the Corporation of the City of New York for a lease to run a steam ferry from his property in Hoboken to the Bear Market in Manhattan. This, of course, would divert traffic from the Powles Hook ferry for which Fulton was already building two boats.

When on January 24, 1811, the Legislature of New Jersey retaliated against the enforcement provision of the New York State monopoly by authorizing its citizens to take the boat of any New Yorker who seized a New Jersey boat and hold it until the Jersey boat was safely returned, Fulton remembered Stevens's warning that the New Jersey courts would never tolerate the New York State monopoly. He could only suspect that, if Stevens had not instigated this alarming piece of legislation, he at least supported it. Fortunately Livingston was able to run still another monopoly refinement through the New York State Legislature. It put sharp teeth into the 1808 Act. The penalty for infringement was confiscation of the boats. Since an injunction could be issued as soon as a rival's boat started running, this Act threatened perpetual injunction against competition in New York State waters.

Not wishing to rely so heavily on the monopoly, both because it placed him in an inferior position to Livingston and because its jurisdiction was limited to New York State, Fulton attempted to fortify his 1809 patent. The improvements he offered were: four methods for throwing the water wheels in and out of gear; the wheel guards with their storage bins and "commodities for men"; the placement of the steering wheel near the center of the boat and the air pump and wheels rods behind the cylinder; the use of oak braces to support the engine for boats over 60 or 80 feet; the concept of combining sails with steam, and the finding that 50-ton boats used power more efficiently than boats under 50 tons. The last he cited as his most valuable discovery and brashly claimed patent coverage for all steamboats exceeding 50 tons.

This new patent application, over which Fulton labored at length, was at best an exercise in self-deception, a display of exhausted imagination. It did nothing to shore up his original patent. Rather it gave William Thornton a perfect opportunity to unleash his scorn publicly. Castigating Fulton for his "unworthy" attempt to restrain anyone from building a large boat, Thornton told him that as chief of the Patent Office he was obliged to enter an official protest against the patent because it offered nothing sufficiently new. He reminded Fulton of his own patent for stern wheels or paddles, which he had obtained on January 16, 1809, three weeks prior to Fulton's first patent. In addition, Thornton claimed priority for the use of sails with steam. He even took credit for the invention of side wheels—or so he wrote Fulton in an unmailed letter Fulton "accidentally" saw on a visit to Thornton's office when Thornton was not in. Thornton next published for general distribution a pamphlet on how to file a patent application. It made clear his control over the formal aspects of patent applications. Finally, he granted himself another patent for an improved steam boiler. It was, he boasted, light—"not a brick in it"—and safe; it would not melt when raised to high pressures.

In a fit of sarcasm, Fulton said that if Thornton succeeded in building a boat that would go 6 miles an hour with 110 tons of freight, he would reimburse him for his expenses and give him $150,000 for his patent. If Thornton could produce a convincing drawing, he would join him in expenses and profits. Such mockery was, of course, foolhardy. Thornton's desire for "fame and emolument" was as relentless as his own. Desperate for money to maintain his handsome style of living, he was determined to capitalize on his steamboat inventions in any way he could.

Thornton was, in fact, in the process of establishing a rival Wilmington steamboat, and taking advantage of his official position, he was attempting to lure the Albany Company into using his patented engine. The twenty wily entrepreneurs who composed the Albany Company were better informed than Thornton realized. They had already weathered one failure when they tried to implement a locally invented method of propulsion based on the motion of a pendulum, and they were not about to throw in their lot with Thornton who had never built an engine or a boat on his own. Believing there was less risk in copying Fulton's proven designs, they had already started building two boats on the model of the *North River*, significantly called the *Hope* and the *Perseverance*.

The Albany Company's cold response did not stop Thornton from importuning them. As a gesture of his good faith, he supplied them with a draft request to the New York State Legislature for the abrogation of Livingston's monopoly. In this document, Thornton reasoned that Fitch's federal patent had rendered the monopoly invalid and that when Fitch's patent expired every American citizen became possessed of the power of navigating with steam on all the rivers, lakes, and bays of the United States.

On April 2 the Albany Company's first steamboat, the *Hope*, sailed down to New York City in 22 hours for final work on her engines. She was a handsome craft—faster, the Albany Company boasted, than any vessel yet built. The rivalry was immediately perceived as an upstate-downstate battle. Envious of New York City's commercial and financial preeminence, the Albanians, as the residents of Albany were then called, saw the *Hope* as a symbol of their resurgent importance. When the *Hope* returned to Albany in late June with fifty passengers aboard, she was greeted by throngs of proud citizens accompanied by a band playing "Washington's March" and other patriotic airs. Her running time was 38 hours against the wind.

Almost an exact copy of the *North River Steam Boat*, the *Hope* challenged both the monopoly and the patent. She was, Fulton raged, "an example of the unblinking roguery of mankind, an outrageous assault on my rights & the useful arts of our country in their very infancy."[2] He was jubilant when a breakdown forced the *Hope* to be temporarily laid up. However, he did not deceive himself that the Albany Company would be disposed of without a lawsuit. He immediately began collecting evidence in defense of his patent.

Setting aside his claim to "unique combinations" as too risky, he elected to prove he was the first person to have conceived of using side wheels with steam. To establish a date prior to 1798 when Roosevelt fruitlessly suggested the idea to Livingston, he wrote Lord Stanhope for corroboration that they had discussed side wheels as far back as 1793, enclosing a copy of a letter advancing his ideas for propelling boats by steam that he claimed to have sent to Stanhope at the outset of their acquaintance. With it he sent a page of drawings that he said represented models he had made to demonstrate them.

Stanhope neither certified nor returned the letter and drawing. Although it is not likely, he may simply have overlooked them. In 1811 Stanhope was embroiled in a disagreeable lawsuit with his eldest son over the management of their patrimony and was prostrated with grief over the death of his mother. He had become more and more of a recluse, yielding much of the control of his life to his Bohemian mistress, Mrs. Lackner. Nevertheless, he saved Fulton's copies of the letter and drawing. The question therefore arises as to what happened to the 1793 originals. Since Stanhope had a predilection for filing every scrap of paper with writing on it, it is possible that he deliberately destroyed the original because he did not want his work on steam navigation to appear dependent on Fulton's ideas.

At the same time, it is more probable that Fulton's alleged 1793 letter was a fabrication of 1811, for in 1802, when he seriously began designing a steamboat, he was at first convinced of the superiority of an endless chain of paddles. It was only after a year's intensive experimentation that he changed to single side wheels with fixed paddles. Moreover, the style of the November 4, 1793, copy is infinitely more restrained than the excited slapdash letters about the lock carriage that Fulton wrote to Stanhope at the end of November 1793. It also contains such odd phrases as "In June '93 I began the experiments," where "Last June I began the experiments" would have been more natural, and it is surprising that he referred to himself as "a young man." Even the date, November 4, is suspect; it was on that day that Fulton wrote Boulton and Watt in 1794.

The copy of the purported November 4, 1793, letter, the certification of which was of such great importance to Fulton, is:

> My Lord, I extremely regret not having received your Lordship's letter in time to have the pleasure of an interview at Exeter as a Mechanical conversation with your Lordship would have been infinitely interesting to a young man. To atone for such loss and conform with your Lordship's wish I have made some slight drawings descriptive of my ideas on the Subject of the steamship which

I submit with diffidence to your Lordship. In June '93 I began the experiments on the steamship; my first design was to imitate the spring in the tail of a Salmon: for this purpose I supposed a large bow to be wound up by the steam engine and the collected force attached to the end of a paddle as in No. 1 to be let off to urge the vessel forward. This model I have had made of which No 1 is the exact representation and I found it to spring forward in proportion to the strength of the bow, about 20 yards, but by the return of the paddle the continuity of the motion would be stoped. I then endeavoured to give it a circular motion which I effected by applying two paddles on an axis, then the boat moved by jerks. There was too great a space between the strokes; I then applied three paddles forming an equilateral triangle to which I gave a circular motion by winding up the bow. I then found it to move in a gradual and even motion 100 yards with the same bow which before drove it but 20 yards.

No. 2 is the figure of my present model in which there are two equilateral triangles, one on each side of the boat acting on the same shaft which crosses the Boat or Ship and turns with the triangles; this, my Lord, is the line of experiment which led me to the triangular paddles which at first sight will convey the Idea of a wheel of perpendicular oars which are no longer in the water than they are doing execution. I have found by repeated experiment that three or six answer better than any other number as they do not counteract each other. By being hung a little above the water it allows a short space from the delivery of one to the entrance of the other; it likewise enters the water more on a perpendicular as the doted lies will shew its situation when it enters and when it is covered the circular dots exhibit its passage through the water. Your Lordship will please to observe in the small wheel with a number of paddles A.B.C. and D. strike almost flat in the water and rise in the situation whilst E. is the only one that pulls, the others act against it which renders the purchase fruitless; while E. is urging the Ship forwards B.A. is pressing her into the water, and C.D. is pulling her out: but remove all the paddles except E. and she moves in a direct line. The perpendicular triangular Paddles are supposed to be placed in a cast Iron wheel which should over hang above the water—it will answer as a fly and brace to the perpendicular oars. This Boat I have repeatedly let go and ever found her to move in a steady direction in proportion to the original purchase. With regard to the formation of ships moved by steam I have been of opinion that they should be long, narrow and flat at bottom, with a broad keel, as a flat Vessel will not occupy so much space in the water; it consequently has not so much resistance. A

letter containing your Lordship's opinion of this mode of gaining
a purchase on the water and directed for me at the post office, Exeter, will much oblige your Lordship's most obedient and
Very humble servant,
Robert Fulton
Torquay, November 4th,
1793.[3]

Not content with soliciting so great a favor as the validation of this
document, Fulton pressed Stanhope to let him know in a private letter
whether any steamboats were operating in England or Ireland. His contention was that he was presently the only person in the world capable
of building a commercially viable steamboat. Then, arrogantly concluding with the false and insulting statement that he had so far improved
his torpedoes that they were practically invulnerable even to the ingenious methods Stanhope himself had contrived, Fulton willfully destroyed any precarious chance of enlisting Stanhope's assistance.

As his next step in assembling material for the impending legal battle, Fulton ordered copies of the twelve patents issued since 1791 relating to propulsion of steam vessels. This expensive undertaking occupied
a draftsman from May to July. At the same time he wrote to Elihu
Whitney, who had suffered repeated incursions on his cotton gin patent, asking what action he had taken. Whitney's discouraging response
was that local juries favored infringers who were, of course, their friends
and neighbors. "A patent," he commiserated, "is but a species of right
which but *few* can acquire & will always be liable to be trampled under
foot by the many."[4]

In addition, Fulton wrote an essay entitled "Invention in Mechanics" as a basis for the depositions he intended to extract from favorable
witnesses. With little variation, he once again laid out his belief that
novelty consists of making a judicious choice among many existing elements to form a new combination and that to be patentable the idea must
be both workable and useful.

Then to establish that he was the first to prove the superiority of
side wheels over paddles, skulls, and endless chains—as opposed to having merely thought of them or tried them—he asked Barlow to testify
to his large-scale demonstration in Paris in 1803. In an extraordinary exhibition of hubris, he commissioned Barlow to make Thornton swear
that to the best of his knowledge Robert Fulton was the first to apply a
waterwheel to the side of a boat propelled by steam, that his patents

were valid discoveries, and that there was no steamboat in service in Europe and never had been. "Get him to call on you, get him in a private room, no evidence," Fulton directed. "Point out to him in firm language the mischief which the Albanians avow and for which we will pursue him if he does not immediately do us all the justice in his power."[5]

Barlow should have warned Fulton that he would only solidify Thornton's animosity. Instead, although he was busy with preparations for his trip to France, Barlow applied himself to the task with relish. He called for Thornton in his carriage before breakfast and kept him out until eleven o'clock, by which time he had succeeded in persuading Thornton to admit Fulton's claims with respect to Europe. Nevertheless, Thornton continued to insist he had suggested wheels over the sides to Fitch and had planned to use sails with steam on his projected Mississippi boat. If he liked wheels over the sides so much, Fulton snapped to Barlow, why had he left the idea dormant for twenty years, depriving the public of their use?

This thrust was wasted. Thornton was seriously ill. At the time of Barlow's carriage ride he had a high fever, which Barlow attributed to his drunkenness the previous night, but which lingered on. As Barlow gleefully wrote Fulton, "The poor fellow can depose nothing now unless it be his bones. He has not recovered from his fever & it is thought by some that he never will."[6]

On August 1, Barlow sailed from Annapolis for France with Ruth, her niece Clara, and one of his nephews. Fulton was not able to leave New York to see them off. In a romantic farewell Barlow wrote: "I go with an ardent wish, but without much hope of doing good & with full intention, though with a feeble hope, of living to return. . . . God bless our dear friends, Harriet & Fulton."[7]

Before his departure, Barlow entrusted the Thornton documents to Fulton's aggrieved rope-making partner Nathanial Cutting—a most imprudent gesture. At the time, however, there was nothing Cutting could do. Thornton's health did not improve. Throughout the fall he lay in bed, so fatigued, he complained, that he could read only a few lines of the dictionary at a time.

Fulton's and Livingston's plea for an injunction and treble damages against the Albany Company for infringement of their patent right was heard during the summer session of the Circuit Court by federal Judge Henry

The Cupidity of Many

Brockholst Livingston—a second cousin and close neighbor of Fulton's partner. Their battery of lawyers was led by the Irish emigre Thomas Addis Emmet whom Fulton had met in Paris. Emmet's brilliant intellect and luxuriant fancy was balanced by the meticulous, reflective style of Cadwallader D. Colden, a member of the torpedo committee who had become Fulton's friend and personal lawyer. Fulton's record of the proceedings survives. The arguments advanced were those he and Livingston had formulated in their disputes with Stevens. The notebook is interesting principally for Fulton's sketches of the participants.

On August 3, Judge Livingston dismissed their plea on the grounds that an injunction before full trial would be excessively punitive to the Albany company. The action then shifted to the state court. On August 6, with the concurrence of their lawyers, Livingston and Fulton agreed to file a bill in Chancery Court, where matters of equity were decided, asking for possession of the Albany boats and treble damages.

This information did not deter the Albany Company. In early September, its *Perseverance* joined the *Hope* in competing with the *North River* and the *Car of Neptune*. At every opportunity the opposing captains challenged one another to race. Each side charged that the other held down the safety valves in order to raise steam pressure. Betting on the boats became a favorite New York pastime.

At the Albany end, the captains spent their time vying for passengers. "All the Taverns are filled with people inimical to our establishment," Captain Andrew Bartholomew of the *North River* wrote Livingston. "I have seen this time up people to come on board & view my boat and acknowledge my accommodations were far superior, and after all be persuaded to take passage in the *Hope*, crowded into a berth better fit for a Coffin than to Sleep in." At the same time Bartholomew was forced to report that his boat was infested with bugs. "There has not been a trip since warm weather has come on when the weather would permit but we have taken all the Beding out and Scalded the bottom. This we have found to keep them down the best but the Boat is full and I do not believe they can be got rid of without burning the boat to ashes."[8] All these problems added up to the fact that the *Hope* sailed with all berths taken and Fulton's boat with only twenty.

Although Livingston was plunged into grief because two of his young grandsons had died, he pulled himself together sufficiently to attend to the state case. In addition to his covey of New York–based lawyers he tried to engage Abraham Van Vechten, an Albany attorney who had worked for him previously, but Van Vechten changed sides and returned Livingston's retainer with the excuse that several of his relations were among the twenty Albany defendants.

Fulton continued to collect depositions. Robert McQueen stated that the *Hope*'s success depended entirely on copying the *North River*. Roosevelt, who desperately needed his job in Fulton's Pittsburgh operation to save him from financial ruin, was prevailed upon to confess that his early experiments with Livingston had failed because he did not comprehend the principles Fulton had since demonstrated. Fulton's steamboats, Roosevelt declared, were a new science not practiced or written in any work he had seen. In fact, he felt so forcibly the utility of Fulton's design that he was now building a boat under Fulton's patent to be navigated on the Ohio and Mississippi rivers.

The bill against the Albany Company was filed on September 14. After relating the history of the several acts that constituted their solemn contract with the state, Fulton and Livingston argued that they had faithfully fulfilled the contract's requirements and, therefore, were entitled to the uninterrupted enjoyment of the exclusive rights it conveyed. The *Hope*, having violated their rights, must be forfeited. According to law it belonged to them. Chancellor John Lansing, recognizing the case as highly complex and of signal importance, was unwilling to take precipitate action. He postponed a decision by directing the Albany Company to show cause by the first day of the next court term why an injunction should not be issued.

"We are head over heels in the law, what the issue will be I know not," Livingston wearily wrote his brother Edward. "We cannot expect justice from our enemies and our friends are fearful of granting it, lest it appear they love us."[9]

Early in November the parties were back in court. The Albany Company argued that Fulton's patent was nonsense and that the monopoly was contrary to the commerce clause of the U.S. Constitution. The states could not dispose of navigation rights in the same way as other common property. Chancellor Lansing examined pertinent law from Justinian through the Magna Charta, Elizabeth I, and Blackstone and found that the case from "its novelty, its importance and perplexity" was "incapable of being considered so clear and plain as not to admit of doubt."[10] He again refused the injunction. Fulton and Livingston's only recourse was an expensive and time-consuming appeal to the Court of Errors. As this was composed of the governor, two senators, the chief

The Cupidity of Many

judge, and two other judges and was politically oriented, they hoped for a more sympathetic hearing. The appeal would not come up until March 1812, giving them three months over the winter to refine their strategy and, if all went well, settling the case favorably before the commencement of the next steamboat season.

Despite the incursions of the *Hope*, the Hudson River boats were lucrative. The records are disorganized, but Fulton's share of the *Car of Neptune* alone seems to have brought him almost $10,000. Plowing the money back into the business, he proceeded with their third boat, sorely needed to replace the *North River* which, as well as being infested with vermin, was showing her age by slowing down. Convinced that the best way to prevail against infringers was to provide ever more luxurious and convenient service, Fulton decided that the *Paragon* was to be a floating palace, 170 feet long and 28 feet wide. Fulton himself probably submitted the illustrated account that appeared in the magazine *Port Folio* shortly after she was put in service:

In the rear of the works you descend a mahogany stair-case to a large platform; on the one hand is the captain's state room, on the other a water closet, opening into the ladies' cabin, which contains sixteen births [*sic*] and eight sofas, furnished with beds, when required; opposite to this is the ladies' dining room, which is about thirty feet long and twenty-six wide; it contains twenty births and ten sofas; adjoining to this on the right hand, is a pantry through which you pass into a kitchen, provided with two ovens, a grate for roasting, several boilers and steam boilers, in which dinner can conveniently be dressed for one hundred and fifty persons; connected with this is a dining room for the sailors and servants; these are all on one side of the works: on the opposite is a steward's room and pantry, with four births and binns for seaman and servants' clothing, none being allowed trunks; here also is a handsome apartment for the engineer, with two births for himself and the pilot. In front of the works you descend by another mahogany stair-case into the great cabin; this is forty feet long and about twenty-five wide, and has twenty-eight births and twelve sofas, accommodated with beds: on the right hand as you enter is a large pantry which communicates with the kitchen by the servants' room and with the cabin: on the left hand is a large bar room. In front of this cabin is a forecastle with births for the use of the seamen. The whole number of beds for passengers is one hundred and four, besides those for the accommodation of the captain, officers, seamen, and servants. The births are so wide as conveniently to admit of two persons, when the boat is crowded, and it is agreeable to the parties. The cabins, besides side windows, are lighted by large sky lights so as to be perfectly airy, and are elegantly furnished with carpets, looking glasses, etc. The meals are served on china. Every upper birth, except a few near the wheels, has a large window, and each has a shelf for the reception of the hat and clothes of the person that takes it. The curtains, which are of fringed muslin with silk drapery, are so contrived that the cornice to which they are fixed draws out, and thus forms a little closet in which a person may dress without being seen from the cabin. On the out work that defends the wheels, and which projects both before and behind them, are staircases to descend into a boat; wells for fish, and necessaries; bins for fuel, which is never suffered to encumber the decks that are left free for passengers to walk, under awnings that cover almost the whole vessel. . . . A singular advantage of this vessel is, that being built principally of red cedar and pine, and very strongly timbered, and carrying no ballast, were she to fill with water, the passengers would incur no danger, the timber being more than sufficient to float all her weight.[11]

With so much work under way and still more planned, Fulton and Livingston agreed they would be well advised to set up their own facilities in Manhattan for equipping and maintaining their boats. Early in November they signed a two-year lease for a lot on the corner of Beach and Washington Streets on which stood an old steam sawmill. They put Charles Staudinger in charge of converting it to workshops.

The *New Orleans*, the boat Roosevelt was building at Pittsburgh, was launched at the end of September. There are no drawings or detailed descriptions of this vessel, but she was patterned after the Hudson River boats and apparently had two cabins, portholes, and a bowsprit and was painted sky blue. During the last weeks of construction Fulton realized she drew too much water to ply the Ohio on a regular basis, and he ordered Roosevelt to take her to New Orleans. He was to establish service from there to Natchez, a run of only 300 miles in relatively deep, unobstructed waters not unlike the Hudson. The profits would be great, since they had already obtained an exclusive privilege in the Territory of Orleans and would be protected from rivals in that segment of the river. The boat was named New Orleans.

With a captain, engineer, six hands, Roosevelt's wife Lydia—in the eighth month of her second pregnancy—their infant son, two servants, and a Newfoundland dog named Tiger aboard, the *New Orleans* began her historic 2000-mile journey southward on September 27. Fulton sanguinely expected the boat to reach New Orleans within a month. The outfit arrived at Cincinnati in one day and at Louisville in four. There they were delayed because low water made the Falls impassable. Roosevelt put on a great fête for the inhabitants and made excursions to Cincinnati. Lydia gave birth to her child. It was not until the end of November that they were able to navigate the Falls.

When Fulton heard the *New Orleans* was safely past Louisville, he was in Washington lobbying for a special bill extending the time limit of his patent. Congress was against such legislation in principle because it benefited an individual rather than the general public and, in his case, because it was evident he would be amply reimbursed for his efforts long before his original fourteen years elapsed. Fulton was convinced, however, that with steady perseverance, great patience, and politicking, he would be able to push it through. He was mistaken. The Albanians, taking the opportunity to strike yet one more blow, filed a memorial against the bill, which they characterized as the "introduction of an odious oppressive favoritism in subversion of Justice and of right."[12] Moreover, since Fulton was not a true inventor, the Albany entrepreneurs demanded his patent be repealed. Thornton must have led the attack, for Fulton threatened to take him before the district court for stealing his patent for wheels at the stern, then attempting to extort $5,000 a year for the use of it.

Stevens was also behaving badly. He raced his *Juliana* against the Hudson River boats and declared in the press that she reigned victorious over New York State waters. Of all their enemies, Fulton growled to Livingston, Stevens had inflicted the most injury.

EIGHTEEN

Fickle Fortune

❖

The year 1812 started badly. January and February were filled with petty irritations and fundamental problems. The sloop owners claimed that Fulton's steamboats wintering at the city's wharf prevented vessels with firewood from unloading. Fulton was more in debt than ever before because of unavoidable advances from his personal funds for the construction of new boats. The litigation against the Albany Company had already cost the partners over $2,000, and Livingston, who was in Albany doing what he could to further their cause, was accused of bribing the judges. Although Fulton had written Stanhope a second urgent letter, he received no answer. A wide segment of the Mississippi region was devastated by earthquakes, yet Roosevelt sent no reassuring word of the safety of the *New Orleans*. On January 24, an arsonist set fire to the Beach Street workshops, destroying the building and most of its contents.

Tired of contention and feeling his sixty-five years, Livingston was disposed to be philosophical. "[W]e must make the best of it and brest our evils boldly. Fortune is too fickle to hold the same course long and I trust in god that she is now about changing," he stoically reflected, as he advocated buying a fierce dog to guard the boats in Manhattan.[1]

Fulton had no such reservoirs of patience. He was frightened. Even if the appeal in the Albany suit was successful, there would be other rivals. Having failed to win congressional approval for a special extension of the life of his patent because of opposition generated by Thornton and the Albany Company, he stayed in Washington until February 25, lobbying for revisions of the general patent law. All patents should be granted for at least twenty-one years, he believed, to make up for time lost in litigation. In addition, some way must be found to protect inventors from theft of their ideas by workmen or associates while in the development stage. "[I]f the nation could respect the labours of mind and do justice to them as is done to the labours of every vulgar pair of hands we might perhaps become as rich as some cotton planter or merchant," Fulton wrote Thomas Law, a Washington lawyer and speculator. "Preach this good doctrine in the highways & public places. Call on sinners to repentance. Hell is full of nonbelievers and Oh how I should grieve to see my good friends damned."[2]

In a direct attack on Thornton, he also urged the inclusion of a clause that prohibited the superintendent of the Patent Office from taking out patents in his own name. The secretary of the treasury was not allowed to deal in stock, he reasoned, and the secretaries of war and navy were not permitted to trade in military stores. Belaboring Thornton for using his office for his own benefit, he complained to Secretary of State James Monroe: "[H]ere lies the evil: the Doctor takes patents, exchanges Barters and then disputes the rights of all who interfere with his pretensions."[3] His own case was but one example.

Thornton vowed he would make Fulton "sweat" for his "malevolent Heart."[4] He attacked Fulton in the press and extracted a statement from Henry Voight, Fitch's erstwhile partner who had become the superintendent of the U.S. Mint, that Fulton had taken the idea for a steamboat from Rumsey when he was in England, that he had brought all his machinery from Europe, and that he had accepted 30,000 pounds from the British for suppressing his torpedo scheme. Thornton continued to encourage the Albany Company and tried to attract backers for a rival Mississippi boat, which he claimed would go 5 miles an hour against the current and cost $10,000 less than the *New Orleans.*

To an alarming extent, Fulton was excited by this exchange of acrimony and seemed to draw creative energy from it. It was a dangerous way of life, but, like the other inventors with whom he was dealing, he acted compulsively. As if he did not already have enough enemies, he deliberately antagonized Oliver Evans, whom he actually respected as one of America's three true inventors—the other two being Elihu Whitney and himself.

Evans had begun working on steam engines in the 1780s. In 1803 he installed a high-pressure engine in a boat at Louisville, Kentucky. It performed satisfactorily, but the boat ran aground. Needing money, Evans sold the engine for use in a sawmill—which was soon burned down by hand-sawyers who perceived their livelihood threatened. In 1804 Evans obtained a patent for a small steam engine that he claimed produced pressures up to 150 pounds per square inch and, in a virtuoso display of inventiveness, he attached one to the dredge he built to remove noxious sludge from the Philadelphia waterfront. To transport this amphibious digger—or *Orukter Amphibolos*, as he called it—the 1½ miles from his foundry to the water he mounted it on huge wheels, making it into a steam locomotive. An inveterate promoter, he ran this monstrous 15½-ton rig around the Central Square waterworks building for several days. Then he drove it into the Delaware, floated the undercarriage off, added a paddle wheel—or so he later said—and propelled it up the Schuylkill. Evans never lost interest in adapting his high-pressure engine for steamboats. In 1808, he had tried to persuade Livingston and Fulton to use one in a Mississippi boat but, satisfied with the performance of their Boulton and Watt engine, they had refused.

Fulton and Evans might at least have been comrades in adversity, for Evans suffered continual abuse and financial loss because of the weakness of the U.S. patent law. In fact, he had burned all his drawings and descriptions of new inventions in 1809, because a federal court had declared one of his patents invalid on a filing technicality and had ordered him to repay all the licensing fees he had collected. Instead Fulton allowed him to become a competitor. At the moment Evans was building an engine for a Massachusetts canal boat and in Pittsburgh his son George had begun a 120-foot steamboat to carry passengers from New Orleans to Natchez rivaling the *New Orleans*.

Fulton was perfectly aware of the advantages of weight and fuel savings of high-pressure engines, but he distrusted them. He did not think the art of machine making sufficiently advanced to produce an engine strong and reliable enough to be used in steamboats of the size he operated. Yet, with competition pressing on all sides, Fulton realized he must investigate high steam further, and he wrote Evans asking for information.

At the outset Fulton and Evans corresponded pleasantly, even though Fulton thought Evans wanted too much money for the use of his patent. As Evans put it to Stevens—with whom he was simultaneously advancing a cooperative arrangement—"Mr. Fulton and myself are cultivating friendship, for our mutual interest."[5]

Fulton stopped in at Evans's foundry, the Mars Works, on his way through Philadelphia in late February. There is no record of what they discussed, but after that visit Fulton's behavior toward Evans was not even studiously polite. In a needlessly scornful letter he bet Evans a beaver hat he could not make a boat run 10½ miles an hour in still water and another hat or suit of clothes it would not run 9 miles an hour. Evans, who had a reputation for being proud and grasping, ridiculed Fulton's patents as useless and stepped up the schedule for his Mississippi boat.

As Livingston predicted, fickle Fortune at last changed her course. The first good news was that the *New Orleans* had descended the Mississippi safely in 259 hours, or just over 8 miles an hour. It was a truly heroic voyage. Between Pittsburgh and Louisville an immense comet illuminated the northern sky. Then it disappeared. Two weeks of severe earthquakes followed. From the sea coast to the Mississippi the central portion of the country was shaken. In Tennessee stone houses tumbled down. Fissures opened in the land that remained marvels for decades to come. Hurricane winds whipped the already turbulent river to terrifying heights. Eighty miles below the mouth of the Ohio the current was three times its normal speed. The channel, when it could be found, boiled with plunging tree trunks and mud. When the wind at last subsided, the unnatural calm was so oppressive the boat hands spoke in whispers. The long days were tense with fear of Indian attack. The silence of the sleepless nights, when the steamboat was tied up, was broken only by the rushing water, the restless prowling of the Newfoundland dog, and the sporadic cries of Lydia's baby. A fire, started by the cooking stove, almost destroyed them all.

Roosevelt was greeted by an ecstatic populace when he arrived at New Orleans on January 12, 1812. His steamboat had conquered the Mississippi. Western trade was suddenly released from its bondage to the wagoners of the East. Now able to serve both the incoming and outgoing commerce of the vast interior of the country, New Orleans expected to become the premier port of the nation.

Roosevelt responded to the acclaim by taking the cheering citizens on festive excursions. Then, on January 21, he departed for Natchez with a full cargo and three hundred passengers.

For Fulton, the only sobering aspect of these triumphs was that he heard of them third hand, "from a Gentleman who had a letter from hi[s] brother."[6] From the time the boat passed the Falls at Louisville, neither he nor Livingston received one word from Roosevelt directly. Weeks passed and still their only reports of the *New Orleans* were from travelers and the newspapers. Roosevelt sent no accounts of the trips or the profits. Basking in his celebrity and determined to act independently, he obviously had not been "woven into the web."

Fulton and Livingston, however, were distracted for the moment by their preoccupation with the lawsuit against the "Albany picaroons." In early March, they at last savored victory. The Court of Errors, having examined the case exhaustively, upheld their monopoly. It accepted Emmet's two-pronged argument that the federal patent law only made a machine tangible property, "by clothing the productions of the mind with the attributes of personal property."[7] New York State might fill up the mouth of the Hudson, so as to prevent the navigation altogether and, although the citizens might deplore the folly of the measure, it would be an act of sovereignty to which all must submit. The only control of such an exercise of power was the good sense of the legislature responding to the interests of the people.

In his meticulous opinion, Chief Justice James Kent, regarded today as one of New York State's keenest jurists, wrote that to prohibit the states from conferring monopolies would be a "monstrous heresy," for it would annihilate the legislative power of the states. With an eye to practicality, the court further stated that the injunction was one of the most salutary powers of a court of equity; it prevented a multiplicity of suits that could only end in ruining the holders of monopolies.

Fulton's relief was immense. "My Great law contest in which I had every thing at Stake [and which] so occupied me and worried my mind" has succeeded, he wrote Barlow. "I have beat my enemies in law, the court of Errors has laid their boats under an Injunction, they will be condemned to us and our state grant will be confirmed for 26 years to come. I am now tranquil on this important point. . . . I am in better health than I have been for many years."[8]

Livingston perceived the victory as his own work and, proud of his achievement, took the occasion to impress on Fulton that his exertions for the monopoly were fully equal to Fulton's superintendence of the works. "Do you believe that without my aid you would ever have got thru' this controversy?" he wrote. "Were not our very counsel of opinion against us & Had I not to commence by convincing them?. . . The boats might be built under the superintendence of Staudinger, but your law suit could have been carried on by no one but myself as has been so [since] its commencement. Nor could the necessary funds have been raised as we wanted them without my credit."[9] To emphasize his superiority, Livingston insisted Fulton curb the waste and extravagance of the previous year by introducing a more regular system of bookkeeping.

Fulton was too pleased with the results in Albany and too busy with the operation of the enterprise to be irritated by Livingston's deprecating treatment. In addition to repairing the Hudson River boats, including inserting a sheet of lead and a sheet of copper separated by a 2-inch space for circulating water beneath the *Paragon*'s boiler, he was working on two new boats, a ferry for the Powles Hook Ferry Company, called the *Jersey*, and a small version of the *North River* called the *Firefly*, in which Livingston and Captain Arthur Roorbach were principal investors.

Fulton was far more interested in the *Jersey*, for the prospective profits were immense and the design was new. She was a catamaran, 32 feet wide and 78 feet long with the wheel between the hulls to protect it from the river's strong north-south wave motion. One side was for passengers. The deck was fitted out with neat benches covered with an awning. Below was a small cabin, only 5 feet high, but with a stove for warmth in winter. The other side was left free for horses, carriages, and cattle. The ferry's bottom was rounded, and there were rudders at both ends so that she could move with either end foremost. To turn around she simply reversed her paddle wheels. Fulton designed floating stages and complicated but effective shock repellers to facilitate docking. So that service need never be interrupted, he even contemplated adding steam-driven ice breakers.

Fulton was in haste to put his *Jersey* in operation, for the previous September Stevens began running the steam ferry *Juliana* between Vesey Street and Hoboken. She made as many as sixteen trips back and forth in one day, carrying an average of one hundred passengers. Stevens was not yet trespassing on the Powles Hook Ferry Company's territory, but Fulton knew him well enough by now to expect him to. In the meantime Stevens lost no opportunity to announce that his machinery was superior to Fulton's and that the *Juliana* was the fastest boat on the Hudson River.

Fulton also looked to the *Jersey* as a way to smooth his relationship with Harriet. Because ferries were not specifically mentioned in the 1802 agreement, he risked treating them as a separate entity to which Livingston had no right, and he promised her she could have the full patentee's fees as pin money. The ploy did not work. Livingston did not intend to relinquish a penny of profit. "[I]s it reasonable that you should shut me out of the ferry" he scolded, "& thereby introduce a complexity in our accounts which will be found very troublesome."[10] Fulton capitulated without an argument. Then, since he had already spent $1,000 of his own on the *Firefly* to pay for coal, iron, and blacksmiths' wages, he dunned Livingston for payment. In a pseudo-jocular vein he wrote: "I am so poor as to be pressed by my Bills in the Banks and children looking for bread so that you so rich must try to let me have at least $3000 and $1000 to meet the expenses of the Firefly, total 4000 with which I hope I can carry you through until the Firefly runs."[11]

His "poverty" did not prevent Fulton from projecting a boat to run between New York and Norwich, Connecticut, through Long Island Sound. He designed her with a rounded hull to withstand the dangerous currents of the Hell Gate. Fulton also laid plans to build a drydock; they now pulled the boats up on the beach near the city of Hudson to work on their hulls, an arrangement obviously inefficient for a larger fleet. Because either buying or renting land on the Manhattan waterfront had become too expensive for such an establishment, Fulton started looking for a suitable property in Jersey City where he could build machine shops as well.

On March 26, Fulton advertised the opening of the season in the newspapers. The *Car of Neptune* would commence on March 31, going as far north as the navigation permitted. All three of his boats were soon running full of passengers. With the *Hope* and the *Perseverance* under injunction, there was no competition. By autumn, Fulton exultantly informed Barlow, he would at last be out of debt.

Fulton's elation, unhappily, did not brush off on Harriet. She was seven months pregnant—"getting fat," as Fulton put it to Barlow. In May they had moved to a handsome house on the corner of State and Marketfield Streets, opposite Bowling Green, and throughout the spring she felt so well that on May 29 she gave a "splendid entertainment" aboard the *Paragon*. Regaled by a band and an eighteen-gun salute from the English cruiser H.M.S. *Bramble*, whose commander was the guest of honor, the party steamed up the East River past Corlear's Hook, then down through Buttermilk Channel to Staten Island and back to Manhattan. Despite the fact that any day Congress was expected to declare war against Great Britain, it was a brilliant social event.

Harriet's temper wore thin, however, as spring turned into summer and Fulton delayed their trip to Teviotdale where the baby was to be born. She was especially irritated because the *Jersey* was already reaping large profits that Fulton neglected to pass on to her. Still in hot and humid New York on July 29, she composed a scathing letter to Livingston complaining of Fulton's callous behavior toward her. It is remarkable that Livingston did not destroy it as soon as he read it—out of discretion if not out of sympathy:

> As my husband in his good nature and thoughtless way has been disposing of my property without consulting me and you are involved in the horrible sin against a defenseless woman, I must appeal to you for justice. Know then that when the Steam Ferry boat was commenced he gave to me for present pin money and future support of my Children in case of accidents the whole of the Patent rights to the ferry which he said he possessed by contract with you. Yesterday on claiming this right I was surprised to hear him say he had given you half of it and he was so delicate on this point that I am forced to negotiate with you. Say my dear Sir, have I not a prior right? in honor is it not mine? To you it is no object, and if it is, you must make Fulton abandon to you the patentee's right in the Firefly, or on Lake Champlain, or Mr. J. R. Livingston's boat—for I cannot give up my claim, it is under my eye, where four times a year I can get pocket money, indeed my heart is so set on it that, your generosity must meet my wishes— and I will make Fulton do the same for you.[12]

Harriet had every reason to be angry with Fulton for breaking his promise. Some of the bitterness she poured into her plea may also have been caused by the emotional turbulence that often signals the approach of childbirth. But such seething dissatisfaction could not have been caused by an isolated incident. Far deeper frictions must have marred their relationship. Money was certainly a primary factor, for Harriet was accustomed to income derived from the passive collection of land rents and did not—or refused to—understand that to establish his steamboat empire, Fulton must reinvest his profits.

Perhaps more serious, the steamboat enterprise required Fulton's constant attention. His first passions were absorbed by managing, contriving, and dreaming his great works. Unlike other men she knew, the center of his life was not his home and friends' drawing rooms. No dilettante, Fulton was committed to an ambitious career. At the beginning, this may have excited Harriet. But, after four and a half years of marriage, such outward manifestations of his success as their new mansion and the occasional use of his steamboats for parties did not compensate for his neglect.

Fulton's profound attachment to the Barlows, which had not been weakened by their move to Paris, could only have increased Harriet's antagonism toward Fulton. While she remained on the periphery, the three continued to find both large and petty ways to keep their lives entwined. Ruth begged Fulton to send sugar because it was so expensive in France. She expected Harriet to buy English cambric for her, since none was available there. Ruth was commissioned to procure a box of harp strings for Harriet, but she bought the wrong kind. Fulton asked Barlow to give Harriet's brother Walter a berth as secretary to the mission, but he did not comply. Still, Fulton commissioned the Barlows to buy French carpets, chandeliers, dinner plates, and other embellishments for the mansion he intended to build as soon as his profits were sure and the war was over.

As Latrobe had so caustically observed, Harriet was a commanding woman. But her attempts to dominate Fulton were bound to be frustrated. That the law vested control of her property in her husband was a fact she could accept, but it angered her that her influence was marginal in areas where other women held sway. She felt, and indeed perhaps was, emotionally abused. It is noteworthy that she spoke of "my" not "our" children and that she vividly entertained the possibility that her husband could meet with an incapacitating, if not mortal, accident.

Fulton must have been worse company than usual during this period, for the strain of managing his empire multiplied as it expanded. Safe in faraway Louisiana, Roosevelt informed neither him nor Livingston about the *New Orleans*'s performance or profits. In addition, all Fulton's applications for twenty-year monopolies on the Ohio and Mississippi, except in the Territory of Orleans, had been refused, although he promised to move merchandise at two-thirds the cost and in half the time required by conventional boats. Ohio epitomized the opposition. "The importance of this species of commerce to western people is too great and too obvious to require comment," the legislature declared. "It would therefore be dangerous and impolitic to invest a man or set of men with the sole power of cramping, controlling or directing the most consider-able part of the commerce of the country for so great a period."[13]

Fulton should have had the wisdom to go west himself. Consider-ing the importance he had always attached to the Mississippi, it is sur-prising he did not. However, he was reluctant to spare the time even a quick inspection would require. Instead he sent Harriet's brother, John Livingston. Still in his early twenties and with little more experience than that afforded by manor life, he was at least eager, and since Fulton treated him indulgently, he could be expected to be loyal. John's orders were to take over the supervision of the New Orleans and Natchez line from Roosevelt and to set up companies to run one boat from New Or-leans to St. Louis and one from New Orleans to Louisville. His salary was excellent—$1,000 a year plus traveling expenses and his keep when he was on board ship.

When John arrived in New Orleans, Roosevelt was at Natchez. John soon caught up with him, but Roosevelt refused to surrender the boat. His honor was at stake, he declared, because he had extended his per-sonal credit to raise $6,000 of the $34,000 cost. As a compromise he pro-posed to take the receipts from the freight to New Orleans. John stood his ground. Roosevelt laid claim to the use of the boat for a year. Hav-ing learned she had already made a great deal of money, for which Roo-sevelt had not accounted, John finally threatened a lawsuit. At last frightened, Roosevelt handed over the *New Orleans*. However, he still refused to show John his records. John later discovered that Roosevelt was heavily in debt. A compulsive speculator, he had bought a snuff mill and a distillery in Pittsburgh, both of which turned out to be poor investments. To capitalize on the first trip down the river, he took mer-chandise on credit for sale in Louisville and lost money on that trans-action as well.

Although the boat's reputation had been damaged by Roosevelt's erratic management, John was confident he would soon have the oper-ation running smoothly. He expected to make a round trip from New Orleans to Natchez every three weeks and clear between $1,500 and $2,000 a month. John was not so sanguine about his ability to sell shares in the new Mississippi Navigation Company, however. The terms Ful-ton specified were, he thought, far too stringent. They stipulated that 5 percent of the profits, after Livingston and Fulton received their half as patentees, would be placed in an accumulating fund to be used for re-pairs and new boats. The reasonable intent of this provision was to guarantee the stability of the company and its smooth transition into a great enterprise and also to prevent speculation, but since New Orleans investors were able to get over 25 percent in short-term ventures, John found few subscribers. When, with Fulton's permission, he modified the terms—he did not say how—he sold $20,000 worth of shares in less than a week.

Edward Livingston was a heavy investor. He also provided invaluable legal and financial assistance. Fulton had corresponded with him since 1807 and had met him on one of Edward's occasional visits to the East. He enjoyed him for his extraordinary intelligence, and his sharp eye for business and probably also for his charming Creole wife. Fulton was satisfied Edward could weather adversity honorably, for in 1803 when he was simultaneously mayor of New York City and federal district attorney, he pledged his entire fortune to cover the theft of customs house bonds by a subordinate. He was, in fact, in New Orleans hoping to recoup his reputation and his fortune.

In return for his advice, Fulton offered Edward, free of patentees' fees, the franchise for the Red River, a western tributary that flows into the Mississippi midway between Baton Rouge and Natchez. So that Edward would not encroach on the Mississippi Navigation Company's territory in his enthusiasm to develop the vast tracts of land he owned in the area, Fulton stipulated that all cargo must originate at least 20 miles inland of the Red River's mouth. Cargo might be deposited, however, on the Mississippi and also on the Black River, which branched off from the Red River. To prevent any misunderstanding, Fulton drew a detailed map for Edward's records.

Roosevelt returned from the West in late June with sparse and inaccurate records of his expenditures for the *New Orleans*. He had, or so he said, paid out $3,000, most of which was signed for by his clerk. However, he had no vouchers. He insisted that he had spent $2,000 more on furniture for the boat, but he had no inventory. There was, Fulton warned Livingston, ample reason to suspect dishonesty. They must bring Roosevelt to rigid account, then have nothing more to do with him.

It was not that easy to dispose of Roosevelt. His claim of having proposed wheels over the sides in 1798, backed up by his 1800 contract with Livingston, remained a real threat to their patent. Prudence—or as Fulton euphemistically put it, his "friendship for the family"—dictated that they make still another attempt to buy Roosevelt off. Taking advantage of his indebtedness, Fulton put together a proposal by which, under a trusteeship, he gave Roosevelt's wife, Lydia, one-third of the patentees' fees for the *New Orleans* or its replacement and one-third of the fees for whatever steamboats they might run between Pittsburgh and the Falls of the Ohio, to be paid quarterly and to devolve on her children should she die or remarry. Roosevelt accepted because it was a handsome settlement and because it would put the money beyond the reach of his creditors. He was certain Lydia's love for him was so strong that she would make the money available to him to do with as he saw fit. Since the agreement could be interpreted as Fulton's recognition that Roosevelt suggested side wheels in 1798, it was for Fulton a painful compromise and, as it turned out, merely a stopgap solution.

Fulton and Livingston were faring only slightly better in their dealings with the Albany Company. Rather than resorting to the courts once more, Livingston and Fulton elected to negotiate the disposition of the *Hope* and the *Perseverance*. Although Fulton complained the boats were so cheaply built they were good only for firewood, he expected John R. to pay $12,000 for the *Hope*, enough to cover their legal fees. If he did not, Fulton and Livingston could run her to Tappan, New York, for a year, perhaps netting between $8,000 and $10,000, and then remove the fittings and engines to use in another boat and sell the hull for use as a calf-hauling scow.

Fulton and Livingston advanced several proposals on this order, but the "scandalous and obstinate villains" liked none of them. There seemed no end to the Albany Company's animosity. Probably inspired by Thornton, they accused Fulton of having persuaded one Fletcher to forge his signature on the 1809 patent application, which Fulton had, in fact, done.

Such were the tensions surrounding the birth of Harriet and Fulton's third child. Having arrived at Teviotdale barely in time for the event, Harriet was delivered of a daughter on August 6. She was named Cornelia after Harriet's mother. Fulton described his family as "happy as doves in a basket,"[14] but he was again afflicted with so festering a boil on the side of his face that he could not see out of one eye and was in great pain for over two weeks.

Livingston was also seriously ill, unable, in fact, to write his own letters. The doctors described his malady as "apoplectic and paralytic seizures," caused, they thought, by "a fulness of the blood vessels of the brain."[15] They cautioned him to avoid the tensions of business and pre-scribed bleeding, infusions of bark of nitrate and "due attention to diet and to the state of the bowels." The treatment had little positive effect. Fulton must have realized that Livingston's affliction might prove per-manently incapacitating, but he was too dependent on Livingston both personally and professionally to admit it. Fulton continued to make de-mands on him as if he were perfectly well.

On September 15, a complicated compromise was reached with the Albany Company. It was a reprieve, if not the victory Fulton claimed. The Albanians were permitted to sell the boats to anyone who had ob-tained a license from Livingston and Fulton. The net profits would be divided equally between the two parties. However, if the Albany Com-pany took on the Lake Champlain franchise, they could keep the boats. For this they would pay an annual rent of $10 and defend the territory from invaders at their own expense. The Albany Company evidently did not think it wise to become stand-ins for Livingston and Fulton in Lake Champlain litigation, for they did not take the option. In Decem-ber Fulton bought the *Hope* for $11,000. Somehow Aaron Ogden se-cured an interest in the *Perseverance*.

The removal of the Albany Company's boats from the Hudson River did little to solve Fulton's fundamental problem—the lack of an active associate with mechanical expertise as well as the vision to make long-term investments. Livingston, his relatives, and his friends, though use-ful for their financial and social connections, were not able to fill this function. Stevens was not even marginally obliging. On the contrary, he enticed artisans from Fulton's shops to work on his latest boat, a fast and elegant ferry for the Delaware, which would become renowned as the *Old Sal*. Flouting the monopoly and Fulton's patents, Stevens was using the *Juliana* to carry horses, gigs, cattle, carriages, and freight as well as foot passengers across the Hudson. Then in early autumn he went on a junket to Virginia and North Carolina to procure monopolies for himself. His plan was to run one boat from Baltimore to Norfolk, Virginia, another on Albemarle and Pamtico sounds, and a third from Kingston to Charleston, South Carolina. No part of this 690-mile route, of which only 100 miles required land carriage, was within the territory conceded to him by Livingston and Fulton, yet Stevens used his asso-ciation with them as a basis for his petitions.

Realizing he had to act fast to dominate the southern waters, Fulton cast about for an agent who could lay the groundwork for him. The best he could find was Latrobe who, because the government had abolished his position as surveyor of buildings, had been pestering him all summer for work. Despite Latrobe's personal involvement with Roosevelt, he seemed a good choice. His major contribution to the Gallatin report on public roads and canals spoke for his expertise in the field of transportation. He was also experienced with steam. The previous year he had installed an engine capable of simultaneously operating a forge, bellows, and block mill in the Washington Navy Yard. One of the pumps on his Philadelphia waterworks project also drove a copper rolling mill. At the moment he had a contract to build water pumps and a sugar mill engine for New Orleans. Latrobe was unquestionably the most imaginative and technically proficient architect in America. He was also an artist and an ardent supporter of the arts as well as an intimate of the Barlows—all of which made him a potentially congenial and useful associate.

However, Latrobe had a volatile temperament. A compulsive worker, he was vain and irascible even when work progressed smoothly. Under stress he was prone to nervous collapse. His moods followed a typical pattern. Blithe optimism and solid creativity suddenly gave way to petulant, groveling demands for affection and attention, which, if not gratified, disintegrated into devious attacks, especially on his patrons. A period of abject remorse often followed, after which the cycle began again. In addition, although professionally competent, Latrobe was incorrigibly extravagant and a bad bookkeeper. Perhaps because Fulton recognized in Latrobe many of his own characteristics, he chose not to question how these multiple defects might affect a long-term business relationship. Latrobe was to solicit subscriptions for a Potomac boat. His pay would be a percentage of the receipts.

About the same time, Fulton also hired one John Devereux Delacy, a speculator and attorney of flamboyant charm who had helped peripherally with the Albany negotiations. Like Latrobe, Delacy had pressed Fulton for work. Delacy's job was to set up the Norfolk–Richmond line at a salary of $2,000 a year, paid by the investors as part of their subscription.

Latrobe was, from the start, an ardent agent. He corresponded copiously, scolding Fulton when he did not reply immediately and precisely. He kept close watch on their rivals, worrying about them even more than Fulton did, and on Delacy who was said to be "a bad actor."

Then, without checking with Fulton, Latrobe extended his territory by accepting Secretary of the Navy Paul Hamilton's bid for the Savannah, Georgia, franchise.

Despite this energy, Latrobe could not fill the Potomac boat subscription. It was not his fault, he said. Although he persuaded President Madison to give it his imprimatur by taking five shares, he was unable to counteract opposition from the ferry owners and from bridge and turnpike interests. The problem, as he saw it, was twofold: Fulton had not procured a Virginia monopoly, and the rumor that his patent was not valid discouraged subscribers. Latrobe raised only $20,000 of the $25,000 he promised.

Fulton did not mind. "[T]he spirit and address with which you do business gives me more pleasure than any perspective of emolument," he wrote on November 23.[16] He assured Latrobe that the patent was secure and that his 1793 letter to Stanhope proved conclusively he had thought of wheels over the sides before Roosevelt. But he was not happy with Latrobe's meddling with the Savannah boat; that, he informed him, was in Delacy's territory.

Fulton was even more satisfied with Delacy's performance. He was so prompt in filling his subscription with "a respectable body of gentlemen" that Fulton asked him to help Latrobe to promote the Potomac boat in order to speed the completion of the line from Washington to Norfolk. In addition, he sent Delacy a petition and draft of a monopoly law to present to Virginia legislators. "Take care," Fulton advised, "ask advice of friends on the spot and do not by asking too much risque to get nothing."[17]

Latrobe and Delacy were useful adjuncts, but Fulton still required help from Livingston. Expecting at least sympathy for the heavy work load he shouldered, Fulton catalogued his extensive efforts: new machinery for the *Car of Neptune*, two Mississippi boats, one for the James River, one for the Potomac, one for Long Island Sound, two East River ferryboats, and two Ohio boats—all undertaken on the express condition that he would superintend each one of them. In addition, he had begun the drydock and shops in Jersey City and, because Paul Revere's copper was too often brittle, he was considering setting up his own smelting mill. To extend their enterprise abroad he enlisted the help of Paul Svinin, the Russian ambassador to the United States, and John Quincy Adams, the American ambassador to Russia, to procure an exclusive right to run steamboats from St. Petersburg. He urged Thomas

Law who had connections in India to set up a company for the Ganges
River.

Despite his global outreach, Fulton continued to supervise every
detail of the Hudson River operation himself. As always he was concerned with the well-being of the men who worked for him. He insisted
on raising the captains' annual salaries from $600 to $800 in the current
year and to $1,000 in the future. "Our establishment being a very lu-
crative one," he wrote, "our captains should have the means of appearing like Gentlemen."[18]

With every aspect of his steamboat empire clamoring for attention and
his principal partner gravely ill, it is extraordinary that Fulton should
have agreed in early October to become one of the commissioners for
the Canal Street project, a real estate venture designed to convert the
canal that drained the Collect and Lispinard Meadows into high-priced
residential property. However, it gave Fulton an opportunity to indulge
an interest in urban design that must have dated back to his time in England, for when there he made a rendering of elegant row housing with
the philosophic caption: "Some thoughts on colonnad architecture, a mode
of building which should be universal in the cities of America. They are
in every respect comfortable and produce a great economy. But in such
work we move slow to improvement, and, like all mankind, follow old
habits rather than contemplate new."

Elihu Whitney and T. H. Poppleton, an engineer from Baltimore,
were fellow commissioners. Although Poppleton was engaged to do the
surveying, the meetings, many of which took place at Fulton's house,
often occupied whole days. The three men examined the subject in all
its shapes and variations, including constructing a navigable canal instead of a street between the house lots. Although Poppleton was engaged to do most of the work, when they fell behind schedule, Fulton
took on the task of preparing drawings. Unfortunately, the "books of
plans and other drawings" have been lost. However, the imprint of his
ideas on the written material is strong, especially the cost benefit statement, which demonstrated the great revenues that would accrue to the
city if their plan was adopted.

At the same time Fulton amused himself by exposing the season's
most popular entertainment, the impresario Redheffer's perpetual motion machine. Listening to its uneven sound, Fulton realized it was moved

by a crank. To the delight of a crowd of onlookers, he traced a thin piece of catgut through a wall to a hidden room and surprised the operator patiently turning a wheel. He then drew a cartoon caricaturing the rapt expressions of the dupes of the fraudulent contrivance.

In December Fulton was given the "Freedom of the City," a ceremonial gesture honoring him for the "important and beneficial services rendered to the United States in general and more particularly to the interests and accommodation of the City" by his invention and improvement of the steamboat.

These activities were welcome distractions from the corrosive fear and the anger with which Fulton responded to Livingston's persistent illness. A trip to Lebanon Springs and a prodigious array of medicines had not arrested the deterioration of his health. Latrobe acidly characterized his state of being as "imbecilic." Still refusing to admit that his partner was dying, Fulton informed Robert L., who was handling his father-in-law's affairs, that he expected Livingston to take over the finishing of the Long Island Sound boat and the establishing of the East River ferries.

NINETEEN

Two Such Friends

❖

Robert R. Livingston suffered a fatal stroke on February 25, 1813, while at the supper table with his family. Fulton should have been prepared by his long illness, but the news, when it reached him in New York, was devastating. Although a difficult partner and never as intimate a friend as Fulton liked to presume, he had been a strong support. Now that he was dead, Fulton realized that Livingston had become indispensable to him. He no longer relied on Livingston's credit and social connection, but he desperately needed the feeling of continuity provided by their long labor for a shared vision. Vain, feisty, self-deceptive, and arrogant as they both were, they recognized their mutual dependency and never tried to crush or displace each other. In subtle ways they always came to each other's assistance. There was in their association an overriding pride that kept the partnership from falling apart. They both drew pleasure, as well as "fame and emolument," from it.

To have suffered so profound a loss should have been sufficient evil for that melancholy day, but within a few hours, Fulton learned that Joel Barlow had been dead for two months. Frustrated by week upon week of fruitless attempts to discuss with Napoleon's underlings France's payment of indemnities for illegally seized American ships, Barlow had left the comfort of 50 rue de Vaugerard and set off for Wilna, Poland, where Napoleon had established an interim court during his Russian campaign. Having worked his way through the war-devastated wastes of Poland, Barlow arrived at Wilna only to learn of Napoleon's defeat in Moscow. Nevertheless, he valiantly, and perhaps rashly, decided to remain at the court on the chance he might be able to bring America's cause directly to the emperor. On December 5, Napoleon abandoned his army and by December 18 it was known he was in Paris. Barlow then joined the awful retreat. Traveling day and night in his own coach, he passed safely through Warsaw and had almost reached Cracow when he became so weak from fatigue, exposure, and fever that he was forced to halt in the bleak village of Zarnowiec. Two days later, December 26, 1812, he died. The news did not reach the United States until the end of February 1813.

Although Fulton's partnership with Livingston and his growing family had come between him and Barlow, Fulton never stopped loving and needing him. For close to sixteen years Barlow had given his life a sense of rootedness. He had been a father as well as a companion to him. Without Barlow Fulton felt abandoned and exposed. "None knew him as well as I did," he mourned to Jefferson."[1] He was, he might have added, a part of myself. He could not even draw solace from comforting Ruth; she would not return from Paris until autumn.

Fulton never recovered from this double bereavement. His grief was abiding and corrosive. "I feel it most sensibly," he lamented to Edward Livingston. "Two such friends of such rare talents are not to be replaced in a whole life."[2] The irrevocable loss affected his health and his judgment. Depressed at having outlived his friends, he talked to Latrobe about giving up his steamboat enterprises.

Livingston's death had grave practical consequences as well, for it immediately altered Fulton's relationship with his many Livingston associates. Even during his protracted illness, Livingston, as acknowledged head of the clan, had been able to temper, if not control, the personal ambitions and animosities of the brothers, cousins, and in-laws he and Fulton had deliberately drawn into the steamboat venture. Without his commanding presence, they ran rampant.

To make things worse, Livingston had left his estate in frightful disorder. The validity of his will, made on the occasion of his departure to Europe in 1801, was questioned. Moreover, it made no disposition of his steamboat interests, which were listed in the appraisal as of no value. Livingston had left no proper record of his financial transactions with Fulton or of the agreements and promises he and Fulton had extended to John R. Livingston, young John Livingston, John Stevens, or any of the other participants in the steamboat enterprise. There was not even a clear accounting of receivables and debts. This made Fulton especially vulnerable to attack by the heirs—Livingston's widow Mary Stevens Livingston, and his sons-in-law Edward P. Livingston and Robert L. Livingston—for whom the magnitude and complexity of the enterprise was utterly bewildering. Since all three were exceedingly eager for profits, but none was desirous or capable of making a serious contribution to the business, they were frightened of, rather than grateful for, Fulton's labors. Their dependence on him merely fanned their innate distrust of him as an outsider. When they discovered Livingston had died owing Fulton more than $27,000, they were appalled.

It was perhaps fortunate for Fulton that Edward P. and Robert L. were so jealous of each other that they found it almost impossible to act in concert. Edward P. was the more intelligent of the two—he was a lawyer and had been a state senator—but he was diffident and sensitive to imagined injuries. Robert L. had been Livingston's amanuensis during his illness and enjoyed a more intimate relationship with his mother-in-law, the sole executor. At Clermont he continued to share the mansion Livingston had built. Standing above and more luxurious than the older Clermont Edward P. had inherited through his wife, it was a tangible symbol of the chancellor's personality and the psychological seat of family power.

By law, Mrs. Livingston was assigned one-half of her husband's steamboat interest and one-third of the net proceeds. While she evidently preferred Robert L. of her two sons-in-law, she was loath to cede authority to either of them. To advise her she retained William Wilson, who in addition to being her husband's estate agent and physician, was a lawyer and, as the first judge of Columbia County, had jurisdiction over probate matters.

Robert L. was able to tolerate Wilson with some complacency, but Edward P. distrusted him. He accused Wilson of conducting the probate illegally and as far as he and his family were concerned "in a most unfriendly manner." Reluctant to play an active role in the settling of the estate or in the management of the steamboats, Edward P. sequestered himself at Clermont. Fearful that Robert L. or Mrs. Livingston might accuse him of interference, he put the few steamboat papers he possessed in a trunk without examining them—or so he said. All he could bring himself to do was collect receipts occasionally from the steamboat captains.

Edward P. and Robert L., however, strongly agreed on two points: their unwillingness to advance more money and their method of dealing with Fulton. Land rich and cash poor—as befit Livingstons—they both claimed to be in debt. Therefore, they would proceed with caution, avoiding further speculation and, where possible, disposing of future rights. For his efforts in supervising current operations, they would pay Fulton a salary.

To be offered wages like any employee profoundly affronted Fulton. Perceiving himself as equal to—if not better than—the unenergetic Livingstons, he told them he was entitled to live as respectably from his mental exertions as they did from their inherited land and that it was help, not money, he needed. His heavy work load had so impaired his health, he wrote Edward P., that he had not been able to eat solid food for four months. Edward P. and Robert L. were not sympathetic.

Depressed and exhausted as he was, Fulton continued to produce remarkable results. The *Firefly* opened the Hudson River season on March 17 with a run to Peekskill and scheduled stops at Tarrytown and Mt. Pleasant (Ossining). "As she is a remarkably swift Boat, her passage will be short; Passengers will breakfast before they come aboard. At twelve they will be furnished with crackers and cheese there being no conveniences on board for cooking, although her accommodations are otherwise elegant," Fulton's advertisement stated.[3] At the end of the month the *North River* and the *Paragon* were able to get through the ice flows to Albany. The *Car of Neptune* was having her engine rebuilt to bring her up to the speed of the *Paragon*, but she was afloat by May 21. That same week, the Long Island Sound boat was launched. She was, Fulton boasted, "such a masterpiece of workmanship" he would not be afraid to cross the ocean in her. Proudly he called her the *Fulton*. The Potomac and James river boats, the *Washington* and the *Richmond*, were launched soon afterward.

On June 8 Fulton signed a covenant with Harriet's brother-in-law, William Cutting, that enabled Cutting to take over the lease for two steam ferries on the East River they had extracted from the city after a year's negotiations. Cutting was to pay the city $4000 a year for rent. He could charge twice the fare of man- or horse-propelled vessels, but was required to offer a special rate of $10.00 a year for commuters. One ferry was to ply between the Battery and Pierpont's distillery on Long Island and from there to Williamsburg about a mile above the navy yard, then, crossing the river again, to a point a mile above Grand Street and back to the Whitehall Slip. The other would run between Beekman Slip and the old ferry at Brooklyn. For the patent right, Cutting was to pay Harriet $1,000 a year in semiannual installments. Livingston's death made it easier for Fulton to give her the pin money she had demanded the previous year. Fulton was to advise Cutting on building, repairs, and improvements when requested.

In addition, the dry dock and workshops at Jersey City were almost complete. So far they cost $21,913—a valid reason for Edward P.'s and Robert L.'s anxiety about expenses. However, they were unique in the New York area. The building where the engines were to be built was two stories high and contained boring, turning, and drilling mills and a model shop. A second building housed the smiths' shop with mine forges and the third, a boiler shop, had an oven, molds, punchers, and cutters. The dry dock was the first of its kind in the country and necessary for ongoing operations.

Work on the eastern waters would have been in splendid order had it not been for the orneriness of both John R. Livingston and John Stevens. John R. refused to pay his licensing fee on the grounds that he had as yet made no profit on the *Rariton*. Urging John R. to develop his ferry rights to Staten Island, Elizabethtown Point, and South Amboy before Aaron Ogden usurped them, Fulton insisted that his earnings were three times as great as he had expected and reminded him that he had not contributed a cent toward the lawsuit that had so effectively protected his interests.

Stevens was, as usual, an even greater plague. Delacy had not been quick enough to prevent the North Carolina legislature from granting Stevens a monopoly for navigating with steam on the state's waters. Insulted by this scandalous imposition, Fulton ordered Delacy to seek a repeal of the grant on the basis that Stevens's application was fraudulent; he could not put steamboats on North Carolina waters without violating Fulton's U.S. patents. To aid Delacy, Fulton sent him a copy of the "humane" grant he and Livingston had made to Stevens in 1809. It included the acknowledgment of Fulton's invention of steamboats that

Stevens had never signed. To stir Delacy's ardor, he offered him 5 percent of whatever subscriptions he raised for waters south of Baltimore
and $6.00 a day for expenses.

In addition, Stevens continued to run the *Juliana* from the Bear
Market at Duane and Day streets in Manhattan to his own property in
Hoboken. Although he promised to substitute his own patented system
of paddles for side wheels, Fulton refused to tolerate Stevens's infringement any longer and told Colden to prepare an injunction.

As in the past, the threat of litigation caused Stevens to retreat. The
main purpose of his venture into North Carolina may have been to gain
a bargaining point, for he soon informed Colden that for the sake of peace
he would cede Fulton and the Livingston heirs half of the North Carolina monopoly for the right to run steam ferries to Hoboken. Fulton was
glad to agree, but only if Stevens acknowledged his dependency on his
patents and raised the percentage to two-thirds the North Carolina grant.
Should Stevens comply, he could run his steam ferry free of licensing
charges for foot passengers. For the privilege of transporting cattle, horses,
and carriages, Stevens must negotiate a separate contract with the Powles
Hook Company which, Fulton well knew, counted on that trade to make
its line viable. In addition, Stevens must allow them to use all his inventions—which, shortly before, Fulton had brazenly denied existed.
Moreover, Stevens must promise not to build boats for any waters not
already assigned to him.

Stevens rejected this proposal out of hand. Fulton ordered Colden
to commence court action and sardonically wrote Edward P.: "I propose
that all boats working under our patent have that acknowledgment painted
in large letters on the top of the engine frame, thus: LIVINGSTON
and FULTON'S PATENT. This will show pirates and the public that
there is unanimity among us."[4]

While Fulton exerted these protean efforts to build a steamboat network
that he believed would bind and strengthen the nation, the conflict with
England threatened to destroy what precarious unity the United States
had managed to forge in thirty-five years of independence. Although war
was long anticipated and important segments of the population were jubilant when it was finally declared, the country was ill prepared. As a
result of the Jefferson administration's reluctance to plunge into debt for
defense and the Madison administration's vacillating policies, the army

was a pitiful shambles of survivors of the Revolution and a handful of ill-trained recruits. The navy boasted no more than 20 seaworthy ships. The frigates—*Constitution, President*, and *United States*, each rated at forty-four guns, were the largest. Against this tiny fleet was arrayed the great British force of over 1,000 ships. Admittedly, most were engaged in the struggle with France, but, on the American station—between Newfoundland and the Leeward Islands—were five ships of the line, each carrying over seventy-four guns.

To make up for the nation's lack of naval power, the U.S. Congress passed an Act on June 26 authorizing letters of marque and reprisal— that is, commissions for commercial vessels to seize or destroy British ships and cargoes. These privateers, armed at the expense of the owners, were internationally recognized as extensions of regular navies and were governed by explicit rules; if captured, for instance, the crews were treated as prisoners of war. The rewards were handsome. Half the purchase value of a captured ship, determined and paid by the government, went to the owners, half to the officers and crew. The bounty for a burned or destroyed ship was $20.00 for each person aboard at the commencement of the engagement. In November, to make this service even more enticing, the usual customs duty of 40 percent on prizes was lifted.

Not only was privateering a quick way to a fortune; it also appealed to Americans' sense of independence and their desire for revenge against the British for attempting to crush their fast-growing maritime trade. Almost overnight American merchant ships were converted into privateers, and new ones were built, mainly schooners of a design perfected in Baltimore, then the world's fastest and best handling ships. Seamen, out of work because of the decline in shipping during the long prelude to the war, flocked to them. Having been preyed upon by the French, the British, and the Barbary pirates for over fifteen years, the men were seasoned. Their sorties were so successful that the anti-war faction complained that bounty payments were draining the Treasury dry.

The nation's heavy reliance on civilian efforts gave Fulton an ideal framework in which to further develop and implement his system of submarine warfare. In fact, the setting could not have been more propitious if he had invented it himself, for at stake was freedom of the seas. It is surprising, therefore, that although the government and the public were more sympathetic toward torpedoes than ever before, Fulton presented no grandiose schemes. Chastened, perhaps, by the dismal outcome of his last demonstrations and caught up in the expansion of his steamboat enterprise, which he had no intention of slighting, his approach was cautious. He wrote Secretary of War William Eustis and Secretary of the Navy Paul Hamilton that he had twelve torpedoes with which he could conduct experiments, and he tried to engage Elihu Whitney to make locks for them at his weapons factory in New Haven. When Whitney refused because he was tied up filling government firearms contracts, Fulton arranged to have nine fabricated at Harpers Ferry, where, because it was the site of a government arsenal, there were reliable workmen. A French watch maker in New York agreed to work on the remainder. If none of the twelve torpedoes produced the desired effect, he wrote Eustis, he would give up the project entirely.

During the first six months of the war, the Americans scored a series of extraordinary triumphs over the British on the high seas, and Fulton did little more than put his preparations in motion. It was only when the enemy gained the upper hand and, at the beginning of 1813, began a campaign of blockading and pillaging towns on the Delaware River and Chesapeake Bay, that he applied himself seriously to introducing his torpedoes into actual warfare. His objective was to form a private company that would maintain a corps of men trained in their use. Their successes would, he hoped, persuade the government to integrate his submarine system into its defense strategies.

There were still strong pockets of opposition to his unorthodox and unproven devices. For example, General John Armstrong, who replaced Eustis as secretary of war in January 1813, firmly announced that the United States would never adopt a mode of warfare that could so easily be turned against its own ill-guarded cities. To counter this opposition Fulton used all the influence he could muster to get a bill passed that would give torpedo boats a status equivalent to that of privateers. Latrobe and Delacy acted as his on-the-spot lobbyists, and on March 3, 1813, Congress passed an act that made it lawful to use submarine weapons of any kind to burn, sink, or destroy British war vessels. The bounties would be the same as those accorded to privateers.

On March 26, Fulton signed an agreement with Samuel Swarthwout—an exonerated accomplice of Aaron Burr in his attempt to seize the territory bordering the Mississippi—whereby Fulton would supply at least six torpedoes with instructions for their use and two rowboats commissioned as privateers to deliver them. Swarthwout would mount the operation for $100 a month, one-fifth of the bounties for ships destroyed, and one-sixth of those taken as prizes. The remainder would belong to Fulton.

Fulton's instructions for deploying the torpedoes were characteristically explicit. It was best to use whale boats of six or eight oars, he wrote. The oars should be well muffled and painted, like the boats, a faint gray. The men should wear white flannel overwaist coats and white flannel caps, for white would absorb a gray tint from the water and the sky. Black, rainy nights when the wind ruffled the water were most favorable for attack, since all hands except the watch would be sheltering between decks.

Fulton's directions, complete with sketches, for launching the torpedoes made an assault seem more like a gigantic fishing expedition than deadly warfare, but it had the great advantage of using materials at hand. To place contact torpedoes the operator was to take the top of a pine or any small tree with many long and tough branches, from which he was to fashion a great barbed float. The torpedo was to be tied to it with a line up to 90 feet long and the whole device dropped within the target ship's mooring by an auxiliary boat. Meanwhile the main launching boat, which could be as far away from the target as 1,000 feet, would row in a great circuit drawing the line tight so that the tree-hook would catch the cable. Calculating the tide and the friction of the water, the distant line manipulators would guide the torpedo beneath the keel of the ship. All that was then necessary was to pull a second line attached to the trigger. While enjoying the mighty explosion, the crew would retreat. Should the action be discovered by the enemy, the auxiliary boat was to act as a decoy, rowing 100 or 150 feet ahead and firing blunderbusses and muskets. If it was necessary to retreat by land, the boats and torpedoes could be loaded onto wagons packed with straw and the whole rig disguised as a provision cart.

Unfazed by the complexity of the task, Swarthwout put two boats carrying twenty men and four torpedoes in the Delaware estuary on April 1. It was not until May, however, that he found his quarry, the *Poictiers*, one of the British seventy-four-gun vessels, which had been pillaging and burning defenseless settlements along the shore since February. Swarthwout prepared his bombs, but the governor prevented him from launching an attack because the *Poictiers* carried were American prisoners aboard. Fulton was furious when he learned of the governor's intervention. The decision was laudable, he sarcastically complained to the secretary of the navy, only if the British having butchered old women and children could be considered humane. The obvious lesson to the enemy was that they could always protect themselves by carrying a few prisoners.

Fulton contracted for a second expedition with Elijah Mix, described by Latrobe, who recruited him, as "young, unmarried, and a sailor from his cradle."[5] For some unknown reason his contract was much better than Swarthwout's. He was to receive two-thirds of the bounties to Fulton's one-third. The torpedoes with which he was supplied had been found by Latrobe heaped haphazardly on the upper floor of a warehouse in the navy yard, probably the remnants of the Washington demonstrations.

In early June, Mix set forth from Baltimore, having sited fourteen armed enemy vessels within three miles of the harbor. He hooked a torpedo to one ship's hauser, but because he had meant to attach it to the rudder, he fled, abandoning the bomb. He was lucky to recover it the following night. Although no damage had been done, the British growled that Mix's attack was villainous, invidious, improper, and cowardly, never reflecting, a Virginia newspaper commented, that their own government had once paid Fulton a handsome stipend for this very invention and that they themselves were using Congreve rockets and land mines. Undeterred by the threat of torpedoes, they continued to molest helpless civilians. Frenchtown, the entrepôt village at the head of the Elk River, was destroyed, and Hampton was unspeakably ravaged; neither its women nor its children were spared.

In a boat called the *Chesapeake's Revenge*, Mix moved his equipment to Lynn Haven Bay near Norfolk, Virginia. His prey was the *Plantagenet*, a ship of the line. His first six attempts on consecutive nights were unsuccessful. But on the seventh he approached close enough to launch a torpedo. Just before it floated beneath the ship, the device exploded. The "scene was awfully sublime! . . . It was like the concussion of an earthquake, attended with a sound louder and more terrific than the heaviest peal of thunder," *Niles Weekly Register* reported. A pyramid 50 feet in circumference was thrown up 40 feet; "its appearance was a vivid red, tinged at the sides with a beautiful purple. On ascending to its great height it burst at the top with a tremendous explosion and fell in torrents on the deck of the ship which rolled into the yawning chasm below and nearly upset."[6] The *Plantagenet* survived the turbulence, but thereafter she was guarded by one seventy-four-gun ship, two frigates, and three tenders. The British fleet would never again feel quite safe in American waters.

If Fulton was alarmed by the failure of Swarthwout and Mix to destroy a single enemy vessel, he did not write about it. He was engrossed in experiments with underwater cannon, not as a substitute for torpedoes but as a surer and more acceptable way of delivering explosives beneath the surface of the water. Despite universal doubt, Fulton was certain that ordinary cannon, shot under water, would retain enough force to penetrate the hull of a frigate.

Even though he said he had developed submarine weapons for the benefit of the country, Fulton was quick to patent this invention. He then signed a contract with Commodore Stephen Decatur, the commander of the *United States,* to develop and exploit it. Renowned for his fearless boarding actions during the Tripolitan War and for his recent prize-taking sweeps across the ocean, the handsome, gallant Decatur was the idol of the public and of the navy itself. Of him it was said: "in contest an eagle, in chasing a lark." Like Fulton he was avid for fame and fortune. According to their agreement, neither he nor Fulton was bound to execute an attack against the enemy. Rather each was to use his influence and intelligence to make the cannon practicable. If the United States was at war, they would employ the weapon against its enemies. If the nation was at peace, they would introduce it among the maritime nations of Europe. They would divide expenses equally.

Fulton began formal experiments on May 19. First he submerged a 2-foot gun, loaded with a 6-pound lead ball and an ounce of powder, in 3 feet of water. Igniting it through a long tin tube, he was pleased that the ball passed through 18 inches of water and a yellow pine plank 18 inches thick and that the gun did not burst. To find out what would happen if part of the gun was in water and part in air, thus subject to different pressures, he ran the muzzle through the bottom of a 3-foot wine cask filled with water and laid against a pine post. The ball passed through the water, demolished the cask and entered 7 inches into the post. Fulton then built a box to test the gun with its muzzle in the water and its breech in the air, as would be the case if it was mounted in a ship below the waterline. At a depth of 4 feet it fired through 12 feet of water and 15 inches of yellow pine without any injury whatever to the gun. The series continued with larger cannon, heavier charges and balls, and denser targets until Fulton was convinced he had proved the "undeniable principle" that a broadside of only two 9-inch balls discharged from a cannon 8 feet below the waterline could sink a first-rate warship in a matter of minutes.

In his subsequent experiments Fulton explored ways of keeping water from entering the vessel during firing. His ultimate solution was to fit the muzzles of the guns into watertight cylinders that supplanted the usual portholes and operated on the same principle as a piston of a steam engine or a forcing pump. The water side was outfitted with a strong sliding valve that could be opened from inside the vessel just as the gun was run into the cylinder, and closed when it recoiled.

To carry the Columbiads, as he called his cannon, Fulton designed a ship that he said was virtually invulnerable. Her sides were made of pine logs 8 feet thick. Raising above the deck, they would protect the men working the sails and, at the same time, render the ship so buoyant as to be unsinkable. For harbor defense and eventually for sea service, Fulton proposed to equip the vessel with a steam engine. The masts were easily dismounted, and since the deck would not be used during combat, it could be slanted to at least 25 degrees to impede boarding. Such a steam vessel could "play round the enemy in a light wind or none at all, take her choice of position on bow or quarter, and sink her with little danger to herself," Fulton boasted.[7] For the $600,000 it cost to build and outfit one seventy-four-gun ship, he could build seven such vessels, making the United States navy the most powerful fleet in the world.

Excited by these accomplishments, Fulton sent Jefferson, his reliable supporter, an illustrated recapitulation of the experiments. Hoping his new invention would, like the steamboat, prevail over "doubting friends and presumptuous enemies," he urged Jefferson to use his still considerable influence to stimulate support in Washington.[8]

Jefferson, who had great respect for Fulton's inventiveness—Fulton had just provided him with an analysis of the heating properties of an elegant soapstone fireplace insert—wrote back enthusiastically: "[A]s we cannot meet the British with an equality of Physical force we must [do] it by other devices in which I know of nobody equal to yourself and so likely to point out to us a mode of salvation." But once again he was disappointed that Fulton had not returned to his *Nautilus*. "I confess I have more hopes of the mode of destruction by the submarine boat than any other," he admonished. "No law of nature opposes it, and in that case nothing is to be despaired of by human invention, nor particularly by yours. Accept the just tribute of an American citizen & of a friend."[9]

Fulton's relationship with Decatur, in contrast, was, for the moment, a good deal less supportive. Decatur simply did not answer his letters. Fulton fumed:

> I cannot conceive that after I have laboured 13 years at great expence on experiments which produced the one in question and even had it all arranged before we Spoke together on the subject that you can hope for me to have all the labour anxiety and negotiations with government or Individuals to bring it into actual practice and Share its emoluments, if you will not even draw a pen in its favour or give all your Influence to promote its success. . . . [U]nless an answer To my former letters arrives by return post I shall conclude you have declined any interest in my experiments & this new mode of warfare, nevertheless I shall have the highest respect for your many Virtues."[10]

Decatur, at that time, was penned up in the Thames River at New London where, having run the blockade of New York, he had taken the *United States*, the *Hornet*, and his most recent prize, the *Macedonian*. Sir Thomas Masterman Hardy, the late Lord Nelson's affectionate friend, immediately sealed the port with his *Ramilies*; Decatur's ships would remain locked in for the duration of the war.

Decatur was deeply hurt by Fulton's diatribe and wrote at once to reproach and placate him. Fulton, who was fascinated by Decatur, gracefully justified his outburst as excess ardor. "If we succeed to render it of importance to our country there is Sufficient of fame In it to gratify the whole nation, of course more than Sufficient for each of us," he wrote. "Of fortune it may produce you as much as Stephen Girard possesses. You would then be envied, perhaps abused, for getting wealth through the medium of doing good. There is another discovery which you have made which pleases me as much as firing guns through the side of a Ship. You have discovered that we are in disposition alike. I would be as much like you as possible."[11]

Decatur wanted only to get rid of the *Ramilies*, which kept him so ignominiously confined. Fulton sent James Weldon, who worked with Swarthwout, to destroy the *Ramilies* with torpedoes. Decatur reported that Weldon appeared to be prudent and persevering, but that he could do little because of the brightness of the moon. There is no record that Weldon attacked the *Ramilies*. Others tried, however. A man from Norwich built a crude diving boat and torpedo patterned on Bushnell's *Tur-*

tle and on his third attempt succeeded in screwing his torpedo into the copper hull. The screw broke and when he came up for air the *Ramilies* sighted him, cut her cable, and fled.

The most dramatic assault was contrived by a New York City man named Scudder, whose family had been killed on the western frontier by British-recruited Indians. He loaded a common schooner with flour and naval stores, among which he hid ten casks of powder and turpentine triggered by a device similar to those used on Fulton's contact torpedoes. As some New Londoners were provisioning the British, the *Ramilies* sent small boats to unload her. As soon as the first barrel was moved, the schooner exploded, thrusting a column of blue that burst like a rocket 900 feet in the air. At least twelve of the *Ramilies* crew were killed. Hardy was so unnerved that he kept the *Ramilies* in constant motion and swept her bottom every two hours night and day. He was so incensed at being attacked by mercenaries using vile and pusillanimous weapons that he abruptly changed his relative beneficence toward the inhabitants along the coast and proclaimed that if he heard again of such devices in his waters he would order every house near the shore destroyed.

Bostonians, many of whom had made fortunes supplying the British, sided with Hardy. A local newspaper declared:

> [I]t is high time to calculate the cost which the innocent merchant as well as coasters will have to pay for such ingenuity. Should a single ship be destroyed in this way there will not be an American vessel of any description that should come within the power of the enemy that will escape destruction: nor will *our towns which are at present respected* escape the general wreck . . . and *"the dogs of war"* will then in reality be let loose upon us, crying "Havoc and confusion."[12]

Fulton was not deterred. He drew up plans for yet another torpedo-carrying boat and for a mighty steam-propelled frigate, which he called the *Demologos*, Voice of the People.

Useful and Honorable Amusements

❖

Fulton's preoccupation with submarine warfare served only as an irritant to his relationship with the "representatives," as they termed themselves, of his late partner. Unlike Livingston, they were fascinated neither by its scientific complexities nor by its potential usefulness for national defense. It was simply one more thing that diverted energy from their mutual steamboat concerns.

Since it was not fame but emoluments in which they were most interested, they continually harassed him about expenses. Fulton resented their attitude. "I enclose you a letter from france, 19 cents postage which someone must pay because I have turned economist," he snapped at Robert L. "But what is more I have $5600 of bills to pay . . . plus $1500 to keep the works going and provision for the $11,000 due on the purchase of the *Hope*."[1] In reply, his brother-in-law sent the nineteen cents together with the information that, because the accounts were incorrect, Mrs. Livingston had been obliged to ask Judge Wilson to straighten them out. Fulton sarcastically suggested that for their contribution Robert L. and Edward P. might endeavor to establish an ice house at Albany and a fruit and vegetable garden at Red Hook. "An exclusive right for 25 years yet to come," he told them, "merits such a garden for *economy*, Luxury, and *Popularity*."[2]

On October 28, 1813, the Livingston heirs, with the help of a battery of lawyers, finally mediated an agreement on the disposal of the steamboat segment of his estate. The sons-in-law renounced all legal right to the one-tenth profits Livingston had allowed them during his lifetime but had never actually transferred to them; in return Mrs. Livingston conveyed to each a one-third interest in her husband's half, reserving one-third for herself. Thus, none of them possessed the twenty shares which, according to the October 10, 1802, agreement, were necessary to be a voting partner, yet each was still liable for all debts. The signing did little to mitigate their animosity toward each other or toward Fulton, to whom the estate still owed over $17,000.

Wearied and perhaps frightened by the prospect of more inconclusive squabbling, Edward P. advised Robert L.—who in search of a milder and more healthful climate had taken his family and Mrs. Livingston to Washington for the winter—that it would be in their best interest to give Fulton absolute control for the four years it would take him to finish the work already contracted for. Fulton would receive $3,000 a year, $1,000 for a bookkeeper, and their interest in the Ohio and its tributary streams, the Missouri and the Arkansas.

Robert L. agreed with Edward P. that compensation ought to be allowed the "active partner," but, having made inquiries about the trade expected on the Mississippi, was loath to relinquish such great potential profits. He and their mother-in-law preferred to set up an office in New York with an agent and one or more clerks to handle all operations. Fulton would only supervise, for which he would receive "the Sum of $2000 or thereabouts . . . added to the first cost of Every boat that may be built."[3]

Fulton was enraged at this offer. In lieu of a salary, he retorted, he wanted their whole interest in the Mississippi Navigation Company. This he needed to improve the hitherto neglected fortunes of his own relatives. As to the other Mississippi work, he would carry it on only if Robert L. and Edward P. supervised the assorted lines, which were to run from Washington to Florida. Robert L. testily accused Fulton of wounding his feelings and those of Mrs. Chancellor Livingston. As a coup de grace, he informed Fulton that his father-in-law firmly believed that the United States patent was defective and that the success of the enterprise resided solely in the New York State monopoly. Thereafter, Robert L. returned all correspondence from Fulton unopened.

Fulton then struck out at Edward P. Listing the assistance he had selflessly accorded members of the Livingston family, Fulton complained bitterly that they had refused to give him the means of aiding his own family by one river grant. To emphasize his displeasure, Fulton threatened to sell off his shares and leave the Livingstons to their own devices.

Both Fulton and the heirs would pay for wasting their energy in this fruitless manner. While they squabbled, Aaron Ogden, who had built a steamboat named the *Seahorse*, was acquiring a monopoly covering all the waters of New Jersey. His exclusive privilege would interfere with John R.'s run up the Raritan River to New Brunswick and with the Powles Hook ferries, generating a series of debilitating and ultimately disastrous lawsuits. Ogden was a powerful foe, for he had become governor of New Jersey that October. Flouting Fulton's monopoly and New York State's claim to the Hudson River up to the high-water mark on the Jersey shore, the *Seahorse* plied between Elizabeth Town Point and Powles Hook. Passengers bound for Manhattan were transferred to a barge that docked at the Whitehall slip, virtually beneath the windows of Fulton's house. At Elizabeth Town Point passengers bound for Philadelphia took the same stagecoaches as those from John R.'s *Raritan*. Their competing notices, advertising a 9:00 A.M. departure with arrival in Philadelphia by noon the following day ran side by side in the newspapers.

To add to his troubles Fulton was embroiled in a nasty suit with John L. Sullivan of Boston, who had contested his patent application, filed earlier that year, for towing boats by steam and warping them over rapids by means of their engines. The case was arbitrated in Hartford, Connecticut, in late November. Fulton was able to prevail on Elihu Whitney to journey forth from New Haven to appear in his behalf. Initially Fulton intended to accompany him, but as the date drew near he excused himself, lamely explaining that friends who required his attention had unexpectedly come to town and that he did not think his presence would be useful anyway. Instead, he sent Delacy, who had achieved the status of his trusted assistant.

As evidence of priority of invention, Latrobe—who had submitted the contended patent in Fulton's behalf—deposed that he and Fulton had discussed the subject in 1809 or 1810. For additional proof of his original contribution to towing boats, Fulton sent his *Treatise on Canals* although, he conceded, it did not link the principle of concatenating boats with the use of steam. "The honest truth is that I had In contemplation to make Steam boats draw after them loaded boats as early as 1802–1803," he confided to Delacy, but "As my boats have been constructed for passengers on deep waters, I did not think of practising this mode of Navigation until I commenced building merchant boats for the Ohio."[4]

The suit was just the opening that Thornton, hovering spiderlike over all Fulton's affairs, had been waiting for. With no attempt to disguise his partisanship, he gave every assistance to Sullivan. The correct approach, he advised, was to contest the form of the patent application rather than its novelty.

On December 18, Whitney sent Fulton the arbitrators' mortifying decision: the idea of towing lines of boats belonged to mankind; concatenating the boats in such a way as to eliminate resistance belonged to Fulton, and that of warping a boat forward by means of a steam-driven windlass was Sullivan's. The decision was reached, as Thornton predicted, solely on the legal form of the competing applications. "Yours (if it may be called an application at all) being so imperfect and incomplete," Whitney scolded, "that a Patent could not be issued upon it if there was no interference."[5] As Sullivan had complied with all the requirements, he was awarded the right to a patent for a steam tow boat.

Fulton brushed the decision aside. At the moment he had much else to cheer him. Stevens had given up his intrusion on the Powles Hook ferry franchise and sent his intrepid *Juliana* through the blockade to Killingworth, Connecticut. The elegant Long Island Sound boat, *Fulton*, was at last finished. She won a race against the *Paragon* and the *Car of Neptune* hands down. The dry dock in New Jersey was more perfect than Fulton had anticipated. "At any time in 24 hours," he boasted, "we can get one of our boats high and dry to repair and clean."[6] When the *North River*'s hull was examined, it was found to be "as straight as an arrow" despite six years' hard running. Delacy had deposited the applications for his catamaran steam ferryboat at the U.S. Patent Office and had then gone on to Virginia to form a company on the Appomattox River and to petition the legislature for a state monopoly. Based on information Delacy sent him, Fulton was writing a promotional pamphlet called *Report on the Practicability of Navigating with Steamboats on the Southern Waters of the United States* in which, describing himself as a political economist, he envisaged a steamboat network running from northern Vermont to east Florida. To cap it all, the 1813 receipts from the North River Company were over $119,000, which was $25,000 more than in 1812.

The news from Pittsburgh was encouraging as well. John's first boat was nearly complete. The second was already framed out. Fulton indulged in the wry pleasure of naming them the *Vesuvius* and the *Aetna* after the bomb ketches Rodgers had once commanded in New Orleans, and because of the great clouds of smoke they belched forth. A friend returning from Pittsburgh praised Fulton's young brother-in-law as "an industrious fine fellow much respected," which made Fulton so light-hearted that he passed the compliment on to John, adding, "all this is good and true, now as he has a fine daughter *all goodness and innocence*, could you not aid her with some of your experience to journey through this wicked world?"[7]

To carry on the Ohio Navigation Company for which Roosevelt was the original agent, Fulton had sent Latrobe, who begged for the job, to build a boat at Pittsburgh to run between there and Louisville. In May Latrobe settled his libel suit against Thornton by accepting $1.00 for damages and, during the summer, he hired workmen in Lancaster and sent them ahead to Pittsburgh together with his servant and wagonloads of furniture. With a $1,500 advance from Fulton, Latrobe finally set out himself in early September. Traveling with his wife and three children in a handsome olive green carriage of his own ingenious design, he arrived on the first of November. On the ninth he sent back the enthu-siastic news that, despite the bad weather, he had "got on with more business than I perhaps ever did in the same time."[8] Since he found the Allegheny an astonishingly rapid river with a shoally, gradually sloping bed unfit for launching boats, he chose a site for his shipyard on the Monongahela where the current was moderate and he heard there was always sufficient water to launch a boat. Near the ramparts of old Fort Pitt, the site was adjacent to the Mississippi Navigation Company's yard. Because of their proximity he would be able to reduce expenses by leas-ing major machinery from John. Despite rapidly rising property values, Latrobe persuaded the Irish owner, the proprietor of a glassworks and a brewery, to lease it for one year with an option to renew for up to five years at "a moderate rent"; he did not yet know how much it would be. From the same landowner he also rented a large brick residence, suitable for a gentleman of his importance.

Latrobe was full of praise for John's work and optimistic about his own steamboat, which he expected to be in the water in March and at Louisville in time to transport to Pittsburgh the first cargo the *Vesuvius* brought up from New Orleans. He claimed he could build his ship to run twice as fast as the North River boats. Overcome with gratitude by the thought of this bright future, he wrote Fulton: "In a few words let me thank you most truly & sincerely for having placed me here. After

25 years toil for the public, I shall at last owe ease & competence to the friendship of an individual."[9]

Edward Livingston, who passed through Pittsburgh on his return from a short trip east, was not so enthusiastic as Latrobe about Pittsburgh as the seat of their construction operation. The paramount flaw was the delay and risk of bringing the boats over the Falls of the Ohio at Louisville, for which no insurance could be obtained. In addition, lumber was hard to find and of poor quality. Common labor commanded twenty-six dollars a month, and food was so expensive that the carpenters sent from the East were forced to bring supplies with them or spend their entire wages on room and board. Moreover, any improvements made to the workshops only enhanced the value of the property and, consequently, raised the rent. Even if they continued to fabricate their engines at Pittsburgh, because neither good iron nor experienced workers were available at Louisville, Edward urged that they buy land for new shipyards below the Falls.

Such a move had already occurred to Fulton. He suggested a piece of ground two miles below Shippingport. It was, in all probability, land he had just contracted to buy from Roosevelt. Consisting of 1,000 acres 100 miles above the junction of the Ohio and the Mississippi, the site was purported to have an inexhaustible supply of coal from which he hoped to fuel the Mississippi boats. Since, sight unseen, he paid $4,000 plus a $1,000 annuity for it, it is probable the purchase was one more means of placating Roosevelt.

Edward also criticized Fulton's "accumulating fund." It would be better, he insisted, to take a 6 percent loan backed by a total or partial pledge of stock. "[W]e shall by paying six receive thirty or forty per Cent and, when the first loan is expended in the Construction of two other boats, we shall have a sufficient pledge for another to Double the amount," he pointed out.[10] Should the subscribers refuse to go along with his plan, he promised to take $20,000 of the loan himself.

Fulton valued Edward's energetic advice and his financial commitment to the enterprise. Taking advantage of his legal abilities, he also counted on him to pursue the infamous Daniel French who had built a small steamboat not far upriver from Pittsburgh. This vessel was already proceeding down the Ohio, her wheel in the stern, thus infringing on Fulton's patent and, as she crossed into Louisiana, his monopoly. Rather than become involved in a test of his patent, Fulton told Edward to attack French on the basis of the monopoly, which he asked Edward to have strengthened by the addition of amendments along the lines of the New York State penalty clauses. Finally, to put the Mississippi Navigation Company on better footing, Fulton requested Edward to attend to its incorporation.

As a major stockholder in the Company, it was in Edward's interest to perform these tasks. As a first-rate lawyer he enjoyed them and did them well. Nevertheless, he was convinced that it was of the utmost importance that Fulton go to Pittsburgh to inspect the workshops and travel the steamboat routes. Advocating the trip in glowing terms, he wrote: "You can have no idea of the riches & future consequence of the Country without seeing it. Under all the disadvantages of extreme cold, & villainous Weather its beautiful features delight me. . . . Tell Mrs. Fulton that she must not be frightened by the journey over the mountains. Even the fatigue may have its charms for the law of the sublime in nature and that of the beautiful will be found in all its perfection when the banks of the Ohio are clad in their robes of Spring."[11]

It would have been well for Fulton if he could have entrusted the work of the eastern enterprises to a reliable associate or manager for a short period of time and followed Edward's sound advice.

––––––––––

In January 1814 Fulton suffered his chronic seasonal cold, which this time developed into a serious inflammation of the lungs accompanied by a severe cough and pain in the chest. However, these symptoms, together with the bleeding, purging, and chemicals administered to combat them, did not blunt his nervous energy. From his bed, where he should have been resting, he laid plans for the oncoming steamboat season, and he continued to devise new ways to deliver torpedoes. His latest idea was an iron-plated vessel that could be submerged by pumping water into an enclosed chamber so that the deck was barely above the surface of the water. Large enough to contain one hundred men, she was to be propelled by a wheel moved by a shaft pushed backward and forward by the crew. Fulton called his virtually cannonproof and silent vessel the *Mute.*

All this was not enough to satisfy Fulton's need to be "always big with some new project," however. Simultaneously, he embarked on a series of complicated new ventures, the most novel of which was a scheme to supply coal from the Ohio River valley to New York City. Coal was not used for heating in New York until 1810, and it was still considered a great curiosity. But the price of wood was rising as supplies dwindled to the point that the state legislature offered a reward of $1,500 to anyone who could find coal within transportable distance of the Hudson. Fulton had a special interest, of course. His steamboats alone burned 17,000 loads of wood annually.

To carry out this project, he had three partners: his physician Dr. Archibald Bruce, Dr. Richard DeWitt, and Peter Jay Munro—no Livingstons for once. Each possessed a one-quarter interest. Fulton wrote the company's prospectus. The operation he described used steam power throughout except, to reduce costs, on the barges in which the coal would be floated down the Mississippi. Coal-fired steam engines would be used in the mines and to cut the lumber used in the barges. When the coal arrived at Fort Plaquemine below New Orleans it would be hoisted into company-owned colliers by means of steam-operated machinery. At New York it would be unloaded into their coal yards again by steam. Because of the savings in manual labor, the total cost at New York would not exceed nine dollars a ton—far cheaper than Liverpool coal, as cheap but of better quality than Virginia coal and infinitely cheaper than coal from the headwaters of the Delaware and Susquehanna Rivers which, because of the cost of land carriage, could not compete at all. Even with the use of so many steam engines, a host of jobs would be created in the mines and in the coastal transport and in the shipbuilding trades. The operation itself would give full employment for at least 246 men. "From every point of view," Fulton asserted, "the plan here contemplated is interesting to the public, to this city and its manufactures."[12]

The "certain resource for obtaining a supply of fuel of the best quality and in sufficient abundance for every purpose," which Fulton so enthusiastically offered was the land he had purchased from Roosevelt. A 6-foot stratum had been dug without arriving at the bottom, he unequivocally stated. The coals were of the same kind as found at Pittsburgh. Their excellent quality was proved by their use to fire the boilers of the *New Orleans* on its maiden voyage.

All this Fulton fervently hoped was true, for, though he knew coal was essential to the growth of industry in America and he wished to be in the forefront of its development, his immediate objective was to reinforce his grip on Mississippi River navigation. In return for his organizing work, the company promised him the exclusive right to furnish coal for consumption by steamboats at a guaranteed price of 50 cents a chaldron, that is, between 32 and 36 bushels. "This power has always been contemplated by me," Fulton confided to Peter Jay Munro, "to strengthen my command over the steamboats and secure my rights on them."[13]

Fulton's new partners were happy to comply. Their interest was to use the coal supply company as a vehicle for establishing a bank, a purpose they endeavored to play down because banks were then notorious havens for speculators. A satirical notice in the newspaper, for instance, advertised a Clam Bank promoted by Thomas Codfish, Peter Crab, Abram Sturgeon, and Simon Terrapin. It was to be funded by initial capital of a million and a quarter dollars with the purpose of providing the citizens of New York for one year with sound and good young clams at a price not to exceed 18¾ cents a hundred and for the purpose of banking if any surplus remained.

Knowing that the legislature would regard their incorporation with a cold eye, Fulton and his partners agreed to dissolve their association if they were denied corporate status. The incorporation was granted in April. However, when the "inexhaustible" mines were eventually explored they were found to contain no coal. Most of the land was, indeed, below the waterline. No investigative survey had ever been made. Fulton was forced to pay for the land himself. The only positive outcome of this venture was that it caused Fulton to enter into correspondence with his brother Abraham, then a teacher living in Louisville. Apparently Fulton asked him to investigate additional coal lands and also property suitable for wharves and shops at Shippingport. Only two of Abraham's letters have survived. Both express strong affection for his older brother and, despite years of separation, the same sense of family solidarity that characterized Fulton's early letters to his sisters.

Fulton's second project was the promotion of the great New York State canal that was to join the Hudson River to Lake Erie. In this Fulton was on much surer ground. Plans for the canal had been in the making for the past twenty years. In 1811, he was appointed a member of the commission to study the project. Although it would be a large canal and would undoubtedly siphon off much of the Ohio and Mississippi trade ultimately bound for the east, it was the kind of project in which he had so long believed. He supported it with zeal.

Fulton chose to promote the canal in a pamphlet comprising letters exchanged with Gouverneur Morris, the distinguished president of the Board of Commissioners. Both contemplated with horror the possibility that the products of the vast western lands would come east by way of the St. Lawrence and Canada. Fulton went so far as to state that the canal route would be cheaper in most cases than the Mississippi, even with steamboats. Using arguments similar to those expressed in his *Treatise on Canals* twenty years previously—not because he had lost touch with the subject, but because he had so well grasped the essentials at the out-set—Fulton described the canal as "a great labour-saving machine in the possession of a prudent and skillful manufacturer."[14] Moreover, because of its vast catchment area, investors could comfortably look forward to a truly stupendous return on their money.

Morris's reasoning so exactly mirrored Fulton's that he seemed to be acting as a personal booster. His only important divergence of opin-ion was that, to further reduce the cost to the shipper, he opposed charging tolls. His fond hope was that the federal government could be prevailed upon to provide loans that would cover the entire expense or, if not, that the state of New York would back private loans.

Critics of the canal to Lake Erie pointed out that the natural com-munication between the Atlantic Ocean and the West was through Lake Ontario, and that state money should not be used in a risky venture that would benefit only the men through whose now unsalable land it would pass. John Stevens warmly argued that railways and steam carriages would provide far better communication than canals, because rails offered far less resistance than water and because service would not be interrupted because of ice. Such railroads, he pointed out, would be cheaper, faster, and more reliable. With engines similar to the one he had designed for the *Juliana*, he was certain he could make a steam carriage average 4 miles an hour. For a brief time in 1812 Fulton had shown an interest in rail transportation, but Livingston had been successful in discouraging him from pursuing it. Like the general public, he deemed these railways ex-pensive to build and prone to accident, simply another of Stevens's far-fetched ideas. At any rate, it was the war with England rather than op-ponents that delayed the construction of the Erie Canal. In 1814 the British were firmly entrenched along the Canadian frontier. The end of the conflict was nowhere in sight.

With so many mechanical schemes teeming in his brain, it is remarkable that Fulton was able to paint. It was, however, an activity he obviously could not live without. During these busy years he painted at least twenty excellent miniatures. The subjects are prominent New York, Philadelphia, and Washington men and women. Most fascinating are his portraits of Mrs. Oliver Hazard Perry, Mrs. Manigault Heyward, Mrs. Stephen Van Rensselaer III, and his wife Harriet. All are seated in similar positions, and all wear the low-necked gauzy gowns held close by jeweled belts high under the bosom that were so fashionable, yet each is artistically and psychologically unique. Mrs. Perry appears a graceful young matron, Mrs. Heyward a voluptuous though highly romanticized beauty. In contrast, the miniature of Mrs. Stuyvesant is reminiscent of his early Philadelphia style. She is not pretty, but both her expression and the painting itself are enormously seductive. The portrait of Harriet is by far the most forthright. Unlike the other women, she looks firmly away from the viewer.

Fulton also painted a miniature of his mother-in-law, on the reverse of which is an unfinished portrait of his son, Barlow. Undoubtedly he painted his little girls as well, but only one survives, a double portrait of Barlow and Julia. In a beguiling conceit, the children are costumed in Elizabethan dress. Apparently John was the only one of his Livingston partners whose likeness Fulton cared to capture; thus far, none other has been found. Of John there is both a miniature and a large oil painted on wood. His handsome, aristocratic face has a petulant air. That Fulton did not ask Edward P., Robert L., or John R. to sit for him is not surprising, but it seems extraordinary, given his prolific output, that he did not paint Robert R. Livingston either from life or from memory.

Fulton himself sat for Rembrandt Peale at this time. Sleek and plump cheeked, the portrait has none of the raw-boned intensity of the earlier likeness by his father, Charles Willson Peale. And, as in the past, Fulton painted several self-portraits. Each is utterly different in tone and in style. One is a miniature, a translation of the portrait of him by West, in which Fulton depicts himself as very young and lean, his hair carefully combed in a voguish ruche. At the time, he was giving art lessons to Emmet's young daughter, Elizabeth, and since it is so similar to her portrait, Fulton very well may have painted it for her instruction and encouragement. Another self-portrait is a pencil and chalk drawing that Fulton presented with a personal inscription to America's first naval architect, Henry Eckford, who supervised the building of the Great Lakes fleet. In it Fulton's eyes have a haunting, worldly-wise expression. His once thick curly hair is thinning, and his side whiskers are straggly. He looks his nearly fifty years. The most amusing of the self-portraits is a quick pencil sketch. A caricature of the West portrait, Fulton leans comfortably back in a light chair and puffs on a long thin cheroot. He seems to be pondering with enjoyment some knotty but solvable problem.

That Fulton produced so many portraits when he was fully occupied by his steamboats, marine weapons, and other affairs suggests that painting was for him a way of enriching his relationships with friends, a means of socializing that permitted him to remain emotionally detached.

Through his self-portraits Fulton seems to have probed his own psyche. The personality they reveal is so protean that it is difficult to believe they are by the same painter and of the same man. The composite image is multifaceted but fragmented, a man sometimes at war with himself, sometimes deluding himself, and always revealing himself. His mercurial nature is apparent in portraits of him by other artists, but it is even more forcible in his own.

Fulton undoubtedly obtained much therapeutic diversion from his extraneous business projects and from painting, but his abrasive dealings with the Livingston heirs remained a burden. The Livingstons found Fulton overbearing and Fulton thought them stupid. "My partners are not men of business," he confided in Delacy, "they cannot conduct any part of it themselves, nor will they compensate me for a state of slavery."[15] The acrimony between them was intensified by the deteriorating health of Mrs. Livingston, which cast an uncertain shadow on their future association.

Nor was Fulton's grand house on Marketfield Street a haven of peace. Harriet, still nursing their third daughter, Mary, who was prematurely born in July, was again pregnant and threatening miscarriage. Ruth Barlow, who chose this time to pay them a visit, lamented to Clara that Fulton was oppressed by a growing family and steamboat debts. She herself was beset with violent nervous headaches, inflamed teeth, and painful eyes.

Such surroundings could not have helped Fulton deal with a major assault on his New York State monopoly. This time the contest was more intense, for it played out in the state legislature which was necessarily far more responsive to public opinions than the courts. On January 25 Aaron Ogden petitioned the New York State Legislature to repeal or modify the "manifestly unjust" steamboat monopoly acts. Because of the complexity and importance of the matter, a special committee was set up to examine his plea. The hearings began on February 26. Neither Fulton nor Edward P. nor Robert L. attended the opening sessions. Of all the principal associates only John R., sorely afflicted with gout in both feet, was in Albany. Emmet and Colden again served as their principal counsel.

Ogden was armed with advice from Thornton and an assignment of Fitch's rights, purchased for one dollar from his administrators. "[W]ith great force and cunning," he delivered a series of speeches against the monopoly, some lasting over three hours. To demonstrate that his engines, built on Fitch's pattern with improvements by Daniel Dod, were substantially different and better than Fulton's, he brought models. His principal arguments, however, constituted an attack on both Livingston's and Fulton's probity. Livingston, he maintained, had falsely sworn he actually possessed a new mode of applying a steam engine to propel a boat when all he actually did was think of one that was impracticable. Fulton, he asserted, had fraudulently used, as a basis for his U.S. patent, tables of resistances and velocities that were previously published in Charnock's *History of Naval Architecture* in England in 1802.

Sensing that the committee, dominated by upstaters and Federalists, would vote against the monopoly, Colden requested a postponement until Fulton could appear. It was denied, and that evening Emmet delivered himself of a passionate six-hour oration, attempting to persuade the legislators that Fulton's reigning interest was solely to benefit the state and the nation.

With so much at stake, Fulton never should have remained in New York City. His official excuse was that he was perfecting ways to defend New York Harbor. However, the real cause of his avoiding the hearing was his hope that Ogden would accept a "reasonable accommodation"—as, indeed, he would do, but not until he had suffered more litigation and Fulton had died. Impressed by Ogden's influence, energy, and legal ability and fearing the long-term consequences if he was left to act independently, Fulton urged Edward P. to offer Ogden one-third of a joint concern in return for the use of his *Seahorse* and his wharves at Elizabeth Town Point. Since this solution impinged on the New Brunswick run, John R. refused to cooperate. Infuriated, Fulton snarled via Colden that John R. was not reasonable and that he would support Ogden's claims with all his means. Fulton pointed out that as the only voting partner he alone had the power to stop Ogden's boat, and, if necessary, he would withhold exercising that power until John R. agreed.

He gave Colden permission to show this letter to Ogden, whom, he asserted, he did not wish to place "in a state of desperation from ruined Fortune."[16] He added that Ogden need only acknowledge in writing that Fulton was the inventor of the steamboat and that his patent and monopoly were valid.

If Colden did as Fulton suggested, he must have received a sharp retort from Ogden, for, in an abrupt change of strategy, Fulton excoriated Ogden for attempting to destroy his character. Ogden's arguments, he said, were "a basket of scraps, conjectures, and abortive essays." His vile objective was to destroy confidence in state contracts and to place inventors' property "in a position so insecure, as to destroy every mental exertion."[17]

This diatribe did no good. In the first round, Ogden prevailed. On March 8 the committee found that steamboats built by Livingston and Fulton were in substance the invention of Fitch, patented in 1791. Stating that neither Fulton's patent nor Livingston's monopoly was legal because neither advanced new ideas, the committee drew up a bill granting Odgen relief.

Colden was able to postpone the hearing on the bill until Fulton could be present. Fulton delayed his departure until March 12 when the *Car of Neptune* opened the 1814 season, probably running as far north as Poughkeepsie. On the way to Albany he stopped off at Clermont to see Edward P. and borrowed a topcoat from him, but he could not persuade him to travel to Albany, for yet another of his little children was dying.

Fulton addressed the State Assembly in his own behalf. Characteristically, he played the role of persecuted genius. Pleading that his invention was obviously new because in the face of disbelief and ridicule he had established the first steamboat line in the world, he pointed out that, because of his labors, the state now possessed the most rapid, cheap, commodious, and elegant conveyance on earth. In contrast, Ogden's sole motivation was to cut in on John R. Livingston's profits. Any loss Ogden sustained, therefore, was caused by his own error in judgment and not by the Livingston-Fulton monopoly.

Informing the Assembly that his company was $77,700 in debt and that it would take five years with four boats in daily service between Albany and New York to break even, Fulton sought the legislators' high-minded sympathy by describing how chilling the violation of inventors' just claims was to the spirit of enterprise.

Fulton then produced depositions from Staudinger and Latrobe and, to reinforce his claim to original invention, he exhibited what he asserted was a true copy of his letter to Lord Stanhope, dated November 4, 1793, in which he discussed using side wheels as a means of propulsion. This evidence, it was reported, gained Fulton many supporters.

Emmet's final oration displayed all the Hibernian theatricality for which he was so famous. Addressing Fulton directly, he warned that, no matter how the present case was decided, "interest and avarice" would always rise against him:

> You rely too implicitly on the strength of your rights, and the sanctity of the obligations on which they are founded. You expect too much from your well-earned reputation, and the acknowledged utility to mankind of your life and labours. You permit your mind to be engrossed with vast and noble plans for the public good. You are inconsiderately sinking your present income in the extension of public accommodation by steam-boats. You are gratuitously giving your time and talents to the construction of that great national object, your stupendous invention for maritime defence. . . . Artful speculators will assuredly arise, with patriotism on their tongues, and selfishness in their hearts, who calumniating or concealing your merits, will talk loudly of your monopoly—who will present it as a grievous burden on the community . . . who will exaggerate your fortune. . . . Yes, my friend!—my heart bleeds while I utter it; but I have fearful forebodings, that you may hereafter find in public faith a broken staff for your support, and receive from public gratitude, a broken heart for your reward.[18]

On March 30, Ogden was denied his petition by a vote of 51 to 43. The monopoly rights bestowed on Fulton and Livingston in 1808 and 1811 were upheld intact. In triumph Fulton wrote to Delacy, "I came here to defeat Aaron Ogden's projects which I have done in the most satisfactory manner."[19] But to Colden who returned to New York before the vote was taken, he wrote: "You happy, happy man to be at home with your wife and family while I am very, very alone."[20]

The Nation's Benefactor

❖

If Fulton nourished any hope that the narrowness of their victory in Albany would stimulate Livingston's "representatives" to give him more support—in their own interest, if not in his own or the country's—he was soon disillusioned. On March 26, 1814, Mrs. Livingston died in Washington. She left no will, and even before her body was interred, Fulton and her heirs were forming their battle lines. Fulton asserted that Edward P. and Robert L. were assigns of Mrs. Livingston and not of her husband and, therefore, according to the 1802 agreement were simply shareholders with no vote. He had Emmet's corroboration for this interpretation and he insisted that they pay their half of the outstanding debts immediately.

Appalled to find the enterprises were well over $60,000 in arrears, Edward P. refused to take any action until he had a close financial accounting. To make clear he would advance no more money, he pleaded insolvency. "That you may not suppose I have money locked up I will briefly state that I have now notes of my own out, which I have agreed to reduce by installments. The personal Estate left by the chancellor including his Bank Stock and the shares of the New Orleans boat will not more than meet his debts and if not carefully managed may not be enough."[1] Fulton countered by complaining that he could not "superintend the various works, correspond, attend to contracts, create companies and contest piracies throughout the continent" without some help, and urged him and Robert L. to come to New York so they might settle their differences in person rather than through expensive counsel and time-consuming correspondence.[2] Edward P. icily replied, "It is true that you have sometimes requested me to prescribe what I am to do, I shall not notice any such directions, nor can I consent that you shall undertake what you may think proper and assign any particular business to me."[3] Fulton then ordered the captains to pay all receipts only to him and contemplated firing them if they failed to comply.

The quarreling between the three men extended even to the scheduling for the 1814 season. Fulton did as he pleased. To replace the *North River*—which, despite the trueness of her hull, was slowing down—he rented the *Richmond*. Intended for the James River, she had not been sent to Virginia because the British blockade effectively closed the port and, in fact, prevented all coastal shipping. Since the *Fulton* could not be put on Long Island Sound for the same reason, Fulton ran her to Albany as a weekender with a guaranteed limit of fifty-five passengers and a fare of ten dollars. This annoyed Edward P. who protested that such distinction was undemocratic and, far more serious, that it might induce the state to enact legislation regulating the number of persons to be carried in public passage boats. Fulton ignored his advice. The *Fulton* retained her luxury status throughout the summer.

Fulton's paramount worry in the spring of 1814, however, was that such control as he retained over the Mississippi enterprises was slipping from his hands. The cost overruns were frightening. When John asked for $10,000 to finish the *Vesuvius*, which was already far behind schedule, Fulton sent him $6,000, enough, he caustically commented, to start the next boat as well. It was even more painful for Fulton when he learned that John had sold to Edward his one-sixth interest in the patentee's rights. "It is obvious if the Rights are good for him, they must be so for you," Fulton snapped. "In fact when I gave you a Sixth it was under the impression that it would give you from 2 to 3 thousand a year. . . . it would have made you and your excellent Mother happy at Teviotdale, you have indeed thrown it away, defeated my best wishes."[4] Fulton was concerned that Edward would expect the one-sixth to apply to all future boats, whereas John was to get the percentage only on the boats he actually supervised.

Edward was, in fact, trying to buy an additional one-sixth interest from Edward P. or Robert L. It is a measure of their lack of true communication that he expected Fulton to negotiate the transaction for him.

Moreover, he urged Fulton to move the Pittsburgh establishment to a site he had located at the mouth of the Cumberland River, not far from the junction of the Ohio and the Mississippi where there was coal as well as an abundance of timber. His intention was to put John in charge "on liberal terms," then transfer the directorship of the Mississippi Navigation Company from New York to New Orleans.

All at once Fulton was struck with the disagreeable notion that Edward might be scheming to usurp control in the West. Compulsively, he sent off a strong letter accusing him of grabbing the Red River, of trying to take over the Mississippi freight business, and worse, of ingratitude.

Wounded by Fulton's lack of confidence in his judgment, Edward patiently explained the disadvantages of keeping the management in New York. "First, if any of your captains or other agents should misbehave, should embezzle your property . . . or render himself disagreeable to your employers who is to Displace him? The evil must continue for three months until representations can be made & your answer obtained & is there not some greater risque that you will be deceived by false representatives." Furthermore, the local residents would never grant corporate status to a New York–based concern. They might even contest the patent. "This I know from being on the Spot, you do not know of because you are at New York," where, he pointed out, Fulton's endless troubles should have taught him about the precarious nature of the steamboat business.[5]

There was, of course, much truth in what Edward wrote. Although Louisianans were glad to use the capital raised in New York, they viewed steamboats as a way of breaking their subservience to the East and would not invest in an operation controlled by New Yorkers. It was obvious to both Fulton and Edward that they must compromise. Fulton admitted that the profound financial dislocations caused by the blockade of New Orleans made it difficult for subscribers to find ready cash and, therefore, offered those in arrears three months to pay up. He agreed to place the governance under a president and eight directors, elected annually starting April 1, 1815. However, the patentees would retain one-third of the shares, hence control of one-third of the votes, exclusive of what they owned personally, and the boats would continue to be built under the supervision of Fulton or his appointee.

Latrobe's behavior was even more disquieting than Edward's. Two weeks after his arrival, he suffered so serious a nervous collapse that he was unable to work or even write letters. Yet his first order of business when he recovered was to set himself up in the house-construction trade. As he boasted to Delacy, "With luck—or prudence—I can make a competency here out of a number of things in which I am engaged And, in fact, if I do not make money here I shall be the only inhabitant of the place . . . who does not grow rich. . . . Mud and smoke are the only evils."[6]

It was not until December 23 that Latrobe laid the keel to his boat. Then he was full of cranky complaints. John's company, to whom he had given some of his best materials, had been "egregiously disappointing . . . of no use to me scarcely, beyond the example of what to follow and to avoid." The boiler Fulton had specified was "a great evil in its size." The *Vesuvius* was a ridiculous name; his boat would be called the *Buffalo* as befitted an American vessel.[7]

February brought three weeks of terrible rains, interspersed with frost. The river flooded to within a foot of the *Buffalo*, making it impossible to work. Nonetheless, during this "interregnum" Latrobe built two barges for his own account and begged Edward to give him the contract for his Red River boat. He built elaborate workshops in which he planned to make engines for his own clients. For his personal tools which had gotten mixed in with the company's, he simply charged the company $4,000, promising to buy them back later if the company insisted.

Since his arrival in Pittsburgh, Latrobe had drawn large sums on Fulton without rendering any accounts. Fulton's demands for records produced nothing but protests that he had, indeed, kept separate books for expenditures on shops, boat engine, tools, patterns, and contingencies, but had not sent them east because they were "too voluminous." Scenting a situation not unlike the one he had suffered through with Roosevelt, Fulton threatened to stop all funds unless Latrobe improved his practices.

Latrobe was, of course, incapable of changing. He merely responded with a frenetic rush of letters alternating obsequious flattery with assorted bits of useful information. "I shall be a true soldier to you & indulge in no new scheme to the risk of the reputation of your *boats*," he promised. "This *policy* as well as *gratitude* will dictate altho' I own the latter is the strongest for I have to thank you for peace of mind and cheerful prospects that I have not known in many years." To detract attention from his endless pleas for money he warned Fulton about competitors. "Half a dozen pirates are whisking about me & laughing at you and me & our company," the most serious of whom were Evans and French.[8]

When Fulton notified Latrobe he would not honor further drafts on his account, Latrobe replied that he could not finish his boat for the initially agreed upon cost of $23,000 because of inflation. John's *Vesuvius*, he pointed out, cost almost twice the original estimate, even though he had been able to buy most of his materials before prices rose. He therefore took it for granted his *Buffalo* was also to be completed even at increased cost.

Taking advantage of a sudden rise in the river, the *Vesuvius* set off for New Orleans on May 2. Patterned on the Hudson River boats, her keel measured 160 feet and her beam 28 feet, 6 inches—7 feet shorter but 2 feet wider than the *Paragon*. The entire hold, except for the machinery and the ladies' cabin, was devoted to cargo. She could carry eight hundred bales of cotton and one hundred passengers. On the deck was an elegantly appointed cabin with twenty-eight double berths on each side. Typically, Latrobe's appraisal was an ebullient mix of opinions and emotions. The *Vesuvius*, he said, was "the most magnificent vessel that ever floated—a little leaky, perhaps, and the engine a little lazy like all new engines, but this might be due to the poor quality of coal, which produced thick smoke. With wood, she might go faster."[9]

As the day on which to put the *Buffalo* afloat, Latrobe playfully chose Friday the thirteenth. It was, he gleefully reported, a "very Desparate launch." In the ten days since the *Vesuvius*'s departure, the water level had fallen dramatically. Although Latrobe engaged forty men to lengthen the wharf, the drop was still 10 feet. The *Buffalo* struck the wharf as she slid "safely and handsomely" into the river, an injury, Latrobe claimed, not worth five dollars.[10] But, to pay the workmen and all debts so that this thrilling event could take place, he confessed he had drawn another note for $2,500.

With "nothing but ruin" staring him in the face Latrobe still insisted on finishing the *Buffalo*. He would mortgage the first cargo if necessary. However, "ruin" did not stop him from starting to build a tugboat of his own design. Much smaller than the *New Orleans* or *Vesuvius* so as to accommodate the summer shallows of the Ohio, he had already named her the *Harriet*. Declaring that every farthing he earned as an architect went into his boats, he exhorted Fulton to make a "grand exertion" for him. "I will stand any ordeal you can subject me to. I shall not now be disgraced. . . . Yours very sincerely & much more faithfully & usefully than you believe."[11]

This last was a lie. Before the ink was dry, Latrobe filled a letter with bitter complaints to Delacy. "I am working for my employers like a horse," he whined. "It is the business of Roosevelt over again only that my accounts & vouchers are in better order."[12] Then he appointed Delacy his attorney to make Fulton believe he was not so much of a fool to put his neck into a halter and no rascal to do anything that deserves one.

Fulton, in the meantime, had written to Henry Baldwin, Ruth's brother and the federal judge in the western district, requesting him to attach Latrobe's shops for benefit of the Ohio Company subscribers. In the same mail pouch Fulton sent a letter to Latrobe, castigating him for incompetence and for lack of gratitude for the many benefits that had been conferred on him and his family. Separated by so great a distance, the headstrong, capricious Latrobe and the irritable, egocentric Fulton took equally self-destructive stances, deceiving themselves as to the righteousness of their intentions. Their subsequent letters are filled with spiteful recriminations when they are not suffused with emotional pontificating.

Fulton's health as well as his pride was affected. "[H]is stomach became so deranged," his doctor later wrote, "that he was in a great degree restricted to the exclusive use of animal food, and a glass of weak brandy and water as the principal drink at his meals."[13] His liver and bowels became "torpid." He was advised to decline all social engagements, to observe the strictest regularity in his meals, and retire at an early hour.

To compound his physical problems, Fulton's chief engineer Lewis Rhode, whom he had personally trained, was mangled while fixing the machinery of the new East River ferryboat and died. Fulton stood weeping by his side during the last hours as if Rhode were his own child. A close friend of this period recalled that often in company Fulton would become silent and abstracted and, for as long as a half an hour, stare at the tablecloth so intensely he seemed to be counting the threads. Nevertheless, in the midst of his turmoil, Fulton summoned the energy to write West with characteristic enthusiasm: "I am endeavoring to be in the mechanic arts what you are in the fine art of painting by steady attention to one of the most useful kind, I mean steamboats. I have great reason to be satisfied with my success both as to private emolument and public

Utility . . . in a few more years we shall have the most elegant, cheap, rapid and extensive inland communications in the world." [14]

Fulton's ill-considered reluctance to inspect the Pittsburgh works in person was caused, at least in part, by his preoccupation with his steam frigate. Vastly increased protection of the nation's harbors was urgent, for the overthrow of Napoleon Bonaparte in April 1814 had released the full might of the British army and navy against the United States. By early summer 14,000 seasoned troops had been dispatched for America to mount a triple offensive against Lake Champlain, the Chesapeake, and New Orleans. Steadily increasing numbers of warships reinforced the blockade. Every major port along the coast—even Boston, the center of British sympathizers—was terrified of invasion.

The previous Christmas Eve, Fulton had displayed plans for his steam frigate before a group of prominent New York citizens who had assembled for the purpose at his house. Among them were former Secretary of War Henry Dearborn; Morgan Lewis, recently appointed quartermaster general of the United States Army; Samuel Latham Mitchill, now a U.S. Representative; Thomas Morris, a member of the New York State canal committee; Fulton's lawyer Cadwallader D. Colden; and Stephen Decatur, who had taken a holiday from his still sequestered ships at New London.

Immediately afterward Decatur hurried back to New London with drawings and a model to present to high-ranking naval officers. Six of them signed an affidavit stating that the steam frigate promised to be "more formidable to an enemy than any kind of an engine hitherto invented" and that it was in the best interest of the United States to carry it into immediate execution. [15] Oliver Hazard Perry, whose victory at Lake Erie and terse dispatch—"We have met the enemy and they are ours"—had made him a national hero, was one of the steam frigate's most ardent supporters. Fulton used this fine testimonial to lobby in earnest. The new secretary of war, William Jones, and the Speaker of the House of Representatives, Henry Clay—another of Fulton's close acquaintances—were his special targets. The steam frigate "can *scarcely* be considered as an experiment," Jones told the House Naval Committee, "because all the principles which enter into its construction are *perfectly demonstrated* and reduced to practice, and only require combination to produce the *desired effect* with *certainty.*"[16] Perry testified in its favor as well. And by the end of January, Clay had the pleasure of reporting to Fulton that the sentiment in Washington was "not merely of passive acquiescence, but of positive conviction in its utility."[17]

In New York the men who had met at Fulton's house formed the small but powerful Coast Defense Committee to raise private money, a project that failed, although John Jacob Astor was now a member. On March 23, Fulton wrote President Madison suggesting New York State might lend the money, if the U.S. Treasury would guarantee it. "[O]ne word from You," he wrote, "will give Vigor to the operations."[18] Congress was persuaded. On May 9, 1814, a bill was passed authorizing $1,500,000 for the construction of one or more floating batteries. New York was to have the first of them, built according to Fulton's plan and under his supervision.

Despite his commitment to the Livingstons to build passenger boats, Fulton ordered all hands at the Jersey workshops to begin the engine, machinery, and boilers. Adam and Noah Brown agreed to stop work on the sloop-of-war *Peacock* to build the hulls. Nevertheless, two months went by before the government authorized the Coast Defense Committee as agents to enter into contracts and to draw on naval stores. Almost another month passed before the ship's keels were finally laid.

While under construction, the vessel was called the *Steam Frigate* or *Steam Battery*. Neither Fulton's uplifting *Demologos* (the Voice of the People) nor the Coast Defense Committee's theatrical *Pyremon* (Vomiting Fire) caught on. A double-ended catamaran, she measured 167 feet on deck and 120 feet on the keel. Between the twin 20-foot hulls was a 15-foot space to accommodate the great paddle wheel. The engine occupied one hull, the boilers the other. When loaded she would draw 8 or 9 feet and was expected to move at 4½ or 5 miles an hour.

Although Fulton applied for a patent—Delacy deposited the papers with Thornton in March—he regarded the *Steam Frigate* as a gift to the nation and did not extract a patentee's fee for the use of the invention. His reward was to be the fame he had so long sought and 10 percent of the cost of the work he supervised, the going rate for ordinary engineering.

Since the Browns' shipyards and Youle's foundry where the bronze and copper work was cast were located on the East River and the workshops were across the Hudson River in New Jersey, Fulton was constantly in motion. Youle's foreman later described him as "exhausting himself night and day, in travelling from one shop to another either to alter mistakes or prevent others."[19] Few of his workers had experience in reading drawings. Because of the stiff blockade, materials were scarce. Moreover, the government, deep in a financial crisis, could not meet its payments. Fulton advanced his own money. It was not until August 17— coincidently the jubilee of the *Steamboat's* historic first trip—that he received an initial payment of $3,000 in Treasury notes. Still the mighty work proceeded at astonishing speed.

The preemption of the New Jersey shops as well as Fulton's time placed him in an awkward position with Edward P. and Robert L., and he perfunctorily invited them to invest in the enterprise. However, he expected them to pay him a fee for the use of his patent. Livingston's heirs, he pointed out, enjoyed no claim to half of his brains.

Edward P. and Robert L. had no intention of becoming enmeshed in this new venture, however. Instead, they used it as a framework for a complete recasting of their partnership agreement. The Hudson River enterprise was to be divided into 1,640 shares of which Fulton, the surviving original partner, would get half. Edward P. and Robert L. would take the other half and become voting partners, each with one vote. Fulton would have two votes as long as he retained at least five shares. Any partner could dispose of his shares as he saw fit. But only after the death of a partner would his heirs and assigns have a voice in the management. Until they paid their half of Fulton's advances—now almost $80,000— all other outstanding debts and the cost of two new boats, Edward P. and Robert L. would receive $6,000 a year. Fulton would take as his own all profits of the shops arising from the *Steam Frigate* up to $12,000. In return, he would render his services without compensation for boats under construction: "one for the Mississippi River, one for the Ohio River and . . . two new Boats for the Hudson River."[20] Other profits and expenses would be shared. The contract would be coextensive with the state grant—that is, until April 11, 1838.

This agreement was signed July 25, 1814. It reflected Fulton's paramount concern with the *Steam Frigate* as well as his desire to place himself on an independent footing now that he no longer needed the Livingstons' credit and social connections. He even contemplated retiring as soon as the specified contracts were fulfilled.

The agreement did little to improve Fulton's relationship with his partners, however, for he continued to insist that the Hudson River captains deliver all receipts directly to him.

On August 25, British troops burned Washington, so savage a premeditated outrage that even large segments of the English press expressed shock. Baltimore was the next expected target. On September 1, Fulton rushed off to Washington, hoping that the torpedoes stored at Kalorama had not been taken by the French ambassador who was renting it, and that he would be able to transport them to Baltimore in time to contribute to the port's defense. The Federal City was a heartbreaking ruin when he arrived. The splendid Capitol and the President's House were smoldering black shells. The navy yard had been set on fire by the commander himself to prevent its falling into enemy hands. All the public buildings, with the exception of the Patent Office—saved by Thornton who pleaded that the contents were private property—were demolished. The printing presses of the *National Intelligencer* were hacked to pieces, the type scattered in the street. The great bridge across the Potomac was destroyed. Kalorama, however, was spared, as were virtually all private residences, and Fulton found his weapons. Then he returned to Washington to dine with the President, who must have ordered Commodore David Porter to take the torpedoes with him in the wagon train that left Wshington on September 6 and which, appropriately, flew Porter's standard: "Free Trade and Sailors Rights."

When Fulton arrived in Baltimore, the city was expecting the British attack. Militia from the interior of the state and from Pennsylvania were massing. Every able-bodied male had volunteered to dig breastworks and ditches. Women and small children had been evacuated to the countryside. Fulton was able to persuade his former adversary Commodore John Rodgers to accept two clockwork and two fulminating torpedoes for the defense of the harbor.

His mission completed, Fulton dashed back to New York. He arrived in the evening of September 11, saw that his "dear family" was well, and barely stopping to rest, sallied forth to inspect the work accomplished in his absence at the Browns' shipyards and in his Jersey City workshops.

On September 12, the British began their assault on Fort McHenry. Ironically, Congreve's rockets have become a part of the American heritage, for the national anthem was composed during that dramatic and decisive engagement. There is no record that Rodgers attempted to use Fulton's torpedoes.

At the moment Fulton was too harried by the demands of his warship to brood. Such great hopes were vested in the *Steam Frigate* as the savior of New York City that special guards were hired to protect her from the steady procession of sightseers as well as from enemy spies. Fulton was well pleased when Commodore Porter was given the frigate's command. In what could only have been a jibe at Rodgers, Fulton promised the *Nondescript* would be launched in a month and would then have a more musical name.

On October 29, 1814, a bright autumn day, crowds of spectators thronged the shores and hills surrounding the East River to celebrate the launching of the *Steam Frigate*. The river and bay were filled with anchored vessels of war, festooned with all their colors. Man-powered craft and sailboats threaded their way among them. To those lucky enough to have procured places in advance, the horse-propelled ferry lying off Delancey Street afforded a fine view. Bands played aboard Fulton's steamboats as they "skimmed along as if by enchantment."[21] The air vibrated with the excitement of the glorious event.

At high tide, amid the roar of cannon and the shouts of 20,000 people, the great hull plunged into the water. A behemoth, dwarfing every other boat, she "set nobly in the water." She was christened *Fulton I*.

"I do not dispair of being able to navigate her from one extreme of our coast to the other," Porter wrote to the secretary of the navy. "The ease with which she can be towed with one steamboat renders it certain that her velocity will be sufficiently great to answer every purpose, and the manner it is intended to secure her machinery from the gunner's shot leaves no apprehension for its safety. I shall use every exertion to prepare her for immediate service; her guns will soon be mounted and I am assured by Mr. Fulton that her machinery will be in operation in about six weeks."[22]

There is, surprisingly, no contemporary record or even remembered account of how Fulton himself reacted to this culminating triumph. He must have been emotionally spent. Moreover, much work still needed to be done. The engines were not yet finished, nor was all the armament procured.

On November 21, in another festive harbor parade, the *Fulton I* was towed by the *Car of Neptune* and the *Fulton* steamboat to the wharves of the workshops in Jersey City. At first, work was held up by a long period of rain and by an exhausted U.S. Treasury, but slowly the frigate began to take final shape. Two stout masts for lanteen sails and two bowsprits for jibs, requested by Porter, were mounted. Two long guns and a 32-pounder were lightered across the bay from the navy yard. Twenty-four cannon captured from British ships were laboriously transported overland from Philadelphia. Fulton's only disappointment was that the underwater cannon he had counted on were never built. At that time in the war, there was neither the metal nor the workers to make them.

Fulton described the steam frigate's finished dimensions as: length 167 feet, breadth 56 feet, depth of hold 12 feet, height of gun deck 8 feet, thickness of sides 5 feet. The engines had the power of 120 horses. The great copper boilers weighed 24 tons. Fired by wood, the furnace was adapted to provide hot shot as well as power. The frigate sailed either end foremost. Her paddle wheel was reversible, and there were two pairs of rudders. The cost came to approximately $240,000, including the guns, coppering, sails, anchors, cordage, joiner's work, and armament.

The citizens of Philadelphia and Baltimore were so impressed by the *Fulton I*'s apparent power they pleaded with Fulton to build steam frigates to protect their harbors. Fulton helped them with information, but told them that he could not trust the construction of the machinery or the fittings to be directed by any one but himself. He was far more interested in building a prototype *Mute* to be used as a tender for the frigate. To obtain the $15,000 in government funds he needed, he asked Richard Rush, the U.S. attorney general, to solicit the President's backing.

In addition, he wrote his former adversary Commodore Isaac Chauncey a glowing letter about using iceboats on Lake Ontario to destroy the British fleet, which was frozen in for the winter. The boat he proposed was similar to the one Livingston and Stevens had built for pleasure on the Hudson. Fulton sent Chauncey a rough sketch depicting a simple triangle with three iron runners, one of which would also serve as the rudder. Gaff rigged with provision for a jib, the iceboat would move at 60 miles an hour, Fulton promised. His strategy was to load the boats with combustibles and send them into the British stronghold at Kingston. The "courageous" and "enterprising" assailants would ignite the payload as they entered the harbor, then chain the iceboat to the enemy's immobile vessels, instantly retreating in accompanying iceboats. Spellbound by his own imagination, Fulton wrote Chauncey, "Here all nature's laws are in favor which gives little friction or resistance. . . . Please to give me your reflections as soon as possible and again permit me to repeat not one *hint* the most *obscure.*"[23] The success of his steam frigate seems to have made Fulton light-headed.

Stag at Bay

❖

When John Livingston's *Vesuvius* arrived in New Orleans, she was greeted by a cheering populace. The steamboat had made the long journey at just over 8 miles an hour. Edward and the other shareholders put on a gala entertainment to which they invited the governor and the committee named to certify her speed and fix her freight schedule. They were rewarded with "a very liberal allowance," Edward reported to Fulton, "an average of four and a half cents for heavy cargo and six cents for light cargo."[1] However, because even smugglers were unable to evade the British blockade, he doubted they would have a full load for the return trip.

Edward's discouraging prediction was only too true. The *Vesuvius* sailed from New Orleans in the middle of June with receipts from freight and passengers of at most $5,000, less than half what she would have made if the boat had arrived as promised in March, before the blockade was strengthened. Nevertheless, Edward ordered the captain to put the passengers bound for Pittsburgh into barges at Louisville so that the boat could return immediately to New Orleans, and anxious to have the *Aetna* completed, he called for another payment from the subscribers. Quite probably prompted by Edward's desire to have both steamboats physically in his territory, these decisions, nevertheless, had the effect of restoring Edward to Fulton's good graces. With two boats running between New Orleans and Natchez, Fulton felt that the Mississippi operation was at last moving toward a sound footing.

Fulton's and Edward's pleasure was short-lived. On July 7, several miles from Baton Rouge, the *New Orleans* struck a stump. Somehow the captain got the passengers and much of the cargo safely to shore in the middle of the dark, rainy night. But, although he threw the fuel overboard, by morning she had sprung a leak and sunk. Fulton took the news with exemplary calm. Almost as if he delighted in the opportunity to exercise his problem-solving abilities, he instructed the captain to extract the machinery, clean it well, boil it to prevent rust, and store it carefully. He was then to go to Pittsburgh, with the salary of both an agent and a captain, to supervise the building of a new hull. On her maiden voyage, the *Aetna* could tow it to wherever he had left the engines, install them in the new hull and be back in service. "Spirit and energy," Fulton sententiously moralized, "will repair evils and add to your resources. . . . If all we lose is her hull or woodworks we may consider ourselves fortunate."[2]

Not long afterward, the *Vesuvius* ran aground when the pilot left the channel to take a shortcut deep in unsettled country just south of the Kentucky-Tennessee border. Fulton called on John to apply to Tennessee for state militia both to protect the boat from Indian attack and to help dig a channel through the sand bar so she could back out more easily as the water rose. Then John was to go to New Orleans to pry more money from the subscribers. Taking advantage of the fact that the twin disasters had depressed the price of steamboat shares, Fulton advised him to buy up as many as he could.

The vicissitudes of this difficult season cost Fulton more than immediate profits. While his boats were out of service, competitors made steady gains. Having banded together with a savvy riverboatman named Shreve, Daniel French was already earning good money between Louisville and Cincinnati with the 75-ton *Dispatch*. Her sister ship, the *Enterprise*, had achieved astonishing speeds during trials. Built to run between Pittsburgh and Louisville, she threatened to usurp the territory that was to have been the sole province of Latrobe's *Buffalo*. George Evans's boat was also running out of Cincinnati. To circumvent Fulton's patent, she was built without rims on the paddle wheels.

Latrobe found the rivalry exciting. Although he would suffer financial injury, he was thrilled by the idea that Fulton might be bested. He unctuously wrote Fulton, "I preserve a profound silence to all our friends as to any difference between us. You will find me the most honest & friendly of all your connexions within six months from this day."[3] At the same time, he confided to Delacy "as to Fulton the violence of his passions gets the better of his natural justice. . . . I fear he cannot bear prosperity as well as he ought."[4]

This ambivalent behavior signaled another nervous collapse and, throughout the fall, Latrobe grew more stubborn. "I am not going down from here until I go in our boat," he warned Fulton.[5] Berating Latrobe for speculating in land to the neglect of his steamboat obligations, Fulton peevishly replied, "Had I never attempted to help you I should have saved myself much mortification and trouble and have had your good will."[6]

Fulton's relationship with Edward also deteriorated. Fulton threatened Edward's New Orleans associates with forfeiture for not paying their subscriptions. At the end of his patience, Edward confronted him. "It is time for our mutual *interest* to say nothing of our Credit that these bickerings should cease. You say that you and the New York subscribers are in advance. Let us know what it is & it shall be paid. But we have been kept in almost unjustifiable ignorance of what has been passing as to our interests. For instance I just learn that the *Aetna* was launched in July last & I learn it by *chance* in November." Accusing Fulton of carelessly citing inconsistent and therefore misleading figures, he concluded: "Should the patentees or the New York proprietors attack me I k[now] how to defend myself & of this I am sure, that they will not gain but will lose by a Contest."[7]

While Edward and Latrobe were complaining, Fulton, without informing them, offered the Mississippi boats to the government to transport troops and ordnance to New Orleans. No other way was as "rapid, commodius or cheap" as steamboats, Fulton asserted, promising Secretary of State Monroe that the *Vesuvius* would be afloat within a month, that the *Buffalo* would be finished in six weeks, that the *Aetna* would descend from Pittsburgh before ice formed, and that the *New Orleans*'s hull would be finished in December or early spring. These four ships could take troops from Tennessee and Kentucky to New Orleans in fifteen or twenty days and return in thirty-five or forty days. "Such rapid movements to meet the enemy will give power and confidence to the Nation," Fulton declared, "& I hope reflect honor on the Administration."[8] All Fulton needed was $40,000. If the government advanced that sum, he would place the boats at its disposal for only $15 a soldier from

Louisville to New Orleans, $30 for the return trip. Alternatively, the government might charter the boats to be at any given place to wait its time and convenience for $2,000 a month plus the crews' wages and all other expenses. Compared to potential earnings in commercial service, this was not an unfair rent.

At the same time Fulton asked President Madison, "with a frankness which I am certain you estimate more highly than any circuitous measures," to appoint him secretary of war for twelve months to replace William Jones, who was about to retire.[9] Fulton even went so far as to enjoin Ruth Barlow, who was in Washington, to use her influence with Mrs. Madison in his behalf. As might be expected, this awkward campaign failed. Benjamin Crowninshield, a successful Boston merchant and a far more politically acceptable figure, eventually got the job.

The many tensions of the fall did little but aggravate Fulton's poor health. In December he made a will, leaving Harriet $9,000 a year during her widowhood and $3,000 should she again marry. For the support of their children, she would receive $500 a year for each child until twelve years old when the amount would be increased to $1,000. Payments would stop as they reached twenty-one. Harriet was also to have the use of the household furniture, carriages, horses, and silver during her lifetime. To his brother and sisters, Fulton bequeathed legacies consonant with what he believed were their needs. Abraham was to have $3,000; Betsy would receive $1,000 plus the use of her mother's farm for her lifetime, after which it was to be sold and divided equally among her children; Belle was to receive $2,000; and to each of the children of Polly, who had recently died, he left $500. All loans he had made to his brother and sisters were canceled.

Fulton left the remainder of his estate to his children. Sons would get their capital when they reached the age of twenty-one or before that if they had already married. Daughters, however, were to receive only the interest on the capital for, he carefully explained, "a girl must be guarded against the misfortune or imprudence of a husband." Three-quarters of a daughter's inheritance must go to her children at her death; one-quarter she might leave as she saw fit. If all Fulton's children died before Harriet, half of his estate was to be used for the promotion of a national institution for historical and scientific paintings. The other half was to be at her absolute disposal. Lest Ruth feel neglected, Fulton left her all the copies of the *Columbiad* then in his possession and deferred payment of the $7,000 debt owed to him by Barlow. Tired and ill as he was, it undoubtedly gave Fulton satisfaction to knit the strands of his life so neatly together and to believe that, should he die, his beneficent influence would extend beyond the grave.

Sometime in the autumn of 1814, Fulton began to realize that John Devereux Delacy was not a dutiful aide-de-camp in whom he could confide, but a scheming manipulator. "This busy and bold intriguer," Fulton complained to his friend John Vaughn, was soliciting backers in his own name for a steamboat from Manhattan to Shrewsbury, New Jersey, which he had neither the mechanical aptitude, patent, nor state right to do. Moreover, during the past eighteen months, Delacy had piled up debts amounting to $4,600. Refusing to suffer such an "embarrassment," Fulton fired him.

Delacy had, in fact, shifted his allegiance to Roosevelt who he was convinced would be a more useful stepping stone to fortune than Fulton. Roosevelt had just received patents for the use of gunpowder and gases to power every kind of machinery and for using wheels with adjustable paddles to vary their purchase on the water which, added to his work with Livingston in the 1790s, placed him in a strong position to contend Fulton's domination of steam navigation.

When Latrobe heard that Roosevelt had banded together with Delacy to mount an attack on Fulton's patent and monopoly, he reminded Fulton that he had never liked Delacy. But, in the same breath, he pointed out that any success Fulton had enjoyed with Congress he owed to Delacy's "energy & to those qualities which (while they do not exactly constitute him a polished Man of the world) have a very great effect with the Public." Promising he would not help Roosevelt and Delacy—except "in open & honorable defense of his own work and character," he demanded that Fulton take prompt measures to put the *Buffalo* in operation and also retract his accusation that Latrobe speculated with the company's money[10]

Fulton replied by ordering Baldwin to attach Latrobe's boat and shops without delay. Latrobe, however, was too quick for him. He gleefully put the shops in the sheriff's hands as security for his debts, and mixing self-pity with spleen, informed Fulton he had been forced to sell his furniture to buy firewood and shoes. "You now threaten with vengeance a family reduced by your passionate, unthinking & unreflecting treatment," he ranted. "The day of retribution will come for *You. . . . You* will not sleep or rest when you reflect that a lady whose hospitality & friendship was an honor to you is reduced to the performance of the meanest domestic affairs by your fault." [11] Then in a right about face, he admitted that this letter was perhaps imprudent, "in as far as it was dictated by my feelings without reference to yours." [12]

Simultaneously, Latrobe poured out his heart to Delacy, pledging to send copies of Fulton's letters to assist his attack. The only prospect of relief from his "absolute distress"—the result of his own foolish confidence in Fulton—was in Roosevelt's forming a new company, he explained. With a host of ideas to contribute, all he required was capital. "[I]f I could find a partner with a few thousand dollars I should do admirably well," he wrote, "for my character would support me." [13]

Attempting to win another ally, Latrobe sent Edward a parcel of butter and buckwheat meal to enhance his breakfasts together with a letter accusing Fulton of attempting to injure his character. Roosevelt would prevail, he declared, for he—Latrobe—had friends and spies who would testify to Roosevelt's early steamboat experiments with Robert R. Livingston.

More trouble for Fulton was brewing in New Jersey where Aaron Ogden was using his monopoly to put John R. Livingston out of business. Frantic, John R. filed a petition with the New Jersey legislature asking for the repeal of the act. This gave Ogden a splendid opportunity to plead his case in his own territory, for like Ogden's petition to New York, John R.'s would receive a public hearing. With the connivance of Delacy, Ogden drew on Roosevelt with whose experiments from 1795 to 1798 and new patent he intended to destroy Fulton's exclusive claims to steam navigation.

Roosevelt was ecstatic at the thought of garnering "a few fragments of the Loaves and fishes so long feasted on by Mssrs. L. and F." [14] His deposition asserted that in 1781 and 1782, when he fled the British occupation of New York for Esopus, he made "many experiments on the motion and buoyancy of bodies in and through water" and "rigged a small wooden boat with vertical wheels over the sides, each wheel having four paddles made of pieces of Shingles whereby to take the purchase on the water." [15] After the war, he erected an expensive foundry at Belleville, New Jersey, and publicly declared his intention of building an experimental steam engine and boat. To finance this venture he associated with Robert R. Livingston. Had he not been so occupied with making engines for the Philadelphia waterworks and supplying copper to the federal government, he certainly would have pursued his ideas after Livingston left for Paris. Livingston had prevented him from testing the mechanisms later used by Fulton. Therefore, Fulton had obtained them either from Livingston or from his foreman Charles Staudinger.

When Fulton got wind of the assault Ogden, Roosevelt and Delacy were mounting against him, he began a desperate search for clues to Livingston's early relationship with Roosevelt. All Edward P. could find among his collection of papers was a document that said that Livingston had settled his account with Roosevelt, with the exception of the cost of one engine. Later, however, he discovered a letter in Judge Wilson's possession, dated September 6, 1798, in which Roosevelt informed Livingston that his horizontal wheel was impractical and recommended they use side wheels. Still other letters made it clear that Roosevelt's recollections were substantially correct. This was bad news. The documents weakened Fulton's already fragile patent claim. They also cast a shadow on Livingston's right to the state monopoly. Fulton's quavering hope was that Roosevelt had not retained copies of the correspondence, in which case the originals might be suppressed.

Delacy and Roosevelt kept Latrobe informed of developments. Thoroughly enjoying his conspiratorial role, Latrobe demanded more details. "You have sent me so *dashing* an account of your crusade against Fulton with such a variety of incident, perjury, conspiracy, & state prison in perspective," he wrote Delacy, "that I absolutely am as ignorant of what is the real state of the case as if I had never heard of the thing. . . . I have corresponded with [Fulton] till now But it is at an end for in his last he throws dirt on all of us & upon you of whom he says that the officers of justice are after you & you dare not show your face in New York. With this comfort I am with great sympathy yours."[16]

Despite the gathering storm, Fulton traveled to Washington just before Christmas to lobby for a bill authorizing another half-million dollars for the construction of steam frigates. He also signed the lease for the use of his Mississippi boats as troop and ordnance transport. While there he discovered that "that rogue Delacy" had obtained a special permit to sail the just completed *Washington* from New York to the Potomac, but intended to give the permit to a competitor. "I found out in time to get the permit recalled and the boat stopped," Fulton wrote Robert L. on

Christmas Day. "You will please try to find Delacy. If you can, have him arrested for $1174.32 he owes me. . . . Put Delacy in prison. Do not neglect this one moment."[17]

Correctly suspecting Thornton to be an *éminence grise* in the affair, Fulton stepped up his attack on Thornton's abuse of the Patent Office. On December 27 he wrote Monroe: "The case of Dr. Thornton I think is very simple. If he is an inventor, a genius who can live by his talents let him do so, but while he is clerk in the office of the Secretary of State and paid by the public for his services he should be forbidden to deal in patents and thereby torment patentees involving them in vexatious suits. . . . My good sir I expect this justice of you. . . . my rights, my peace of mind and my duty to the arts and to my family demand that this man should be removed from the patent office."[18]

Monroe had long realized that he must take care of this unpleasant business, for he had received irate complaints from other inventors as well. That very day he had written Thornton officially informing him of a new Patent Office regulation that prohibited the officer in charge "from appearing as a party interested, either directly or indirectly in any case of a claim for a Patent right." Specifically to give Thornton time to perfect any rights he might already have, the law would not go into effect until February 1, 1815.[19]

Thornton took a week to formulate his four-page tightly spaced reply, which was in essence an attack on Fulton. Monroe's letter, he said, had caused him as much surprise as regret; it represented a great injustice not only to himself but to his successors. Indeed, the law deprived him of his inherent right as a citizen to exploit the produce of his mind. It was, in fact, his ability to think inventively that made him so effective an administrator of the Patent Office. If Monroe could see the many letters of thanks he had received from patentees during his years of unselfish service and knew of the many valuable presents he had returned—though his meager salary would barely support his small family—he would turn a deaf ear to the enemies who hoped through malicious insinuations to drive him from office. Chief of these, he hissed, was "Robert Fulton, formerly a Chevalier d'Industrie, whose Infamy I shall not fail to publish to the world."[20]

As a call to arms against Fulton's "avaricious desire" to obtain monopolies on all the waters of the Union, Thornton distributed *A Short Account of the Origin of Steamboats*, the pamphlet he had written in 1810 and had recently brushed up and published. In it he referred to the report of Fitch's boat in Jacques Pierre Brissot de Warville's *Travels in America*, the description of side wheels in the *Lexicon Technicum*, and a clockwork fireboat presented in the 1796 issue of the *Repository of Arts*. He also accused Fulton of stealing Bushnell's submarine plans. Finally, the pamphlet nervously attempted to justify his issuing himself a patent just prior to Fulton's in 1809.

Thornton had no difficulty attracting lieutenants to serve his cause. Oliver Evans signed a deposition drafted by Thornton and stating that Thornton had proposed sidewheels to Fitch, that sometime between 1786 and 1788 Fitch had intended to introduce steamboats that could be converted to iceboats on the Great Lakes, and that Fulton claimed a boat could not be driven more than five miles an hour by steam. Fernando Fairfax, a Virginian of prominent family, formed a partnership with Thornton to promote his patent. In a typical fit of hubris, Thornton instructed him to solicit Fulton, Ogden, and Roosevelt as backers. Should they or their associates show no interest, Fairfax was then to persuade John Jacob Astor to enter the steamboat business. This "for a Gentleman of such immense fortune will be perfectly easy . . ." he wrote, "he will not only reap great profits, but benefit the Country by the Competition, and break up Fulton's monopoly."[21] Expecting Thornton's patents to bring in at least $200,000 a year, Fairfax invested in them heavily himself.

Fairfax's diligence in collecting evidence against Fulton was well rewarded. His major coup was in routing out Nathaniel Cutting, who was only too pleased to take revenge for Fulton's shoddy treatment in the matter of the French rope-making patent. Cutting swore that, in September 1805, when he had been talking to Aaron Vail about the cordelier and also about Fulton's ingenious use of jack flies to propel the *Nautilus*, Vail told him he had lent Fulton all Fitch's drawings and specifications and that they had remained in his possession for several months. Since Fitch was dead, Fulton had used Fitch's ideas, undoubtedly believing he would not be suspected of plagiarism. Cutting went on to claim that after he bought the rope-making machine, he found out it was the same, in principle, as one patented in England by Edmund Cartwright. In fact, Cartwright had shown him a model of his invention, and though he did not accuse Fulton of theft, he mentioned that Fulton had also seen it.

Perhaps Fairfax's most remarkable service to Thornton was to prevent him from altering his original patent document. "Let me dissuade you from the addition of anything whatever to your existing Patent or specification and rather erase the addition contemplated," he wrote on the eve of the legislative hearings. "It is too hazardous and it would be folly to risk anything that might tend even by supposition to invalidate the *best right in America*."[22] Fairfax did not identify the transformation Thornton was so anxious to achieve. It was, perhaps, a change of date that would forever quiet the suspicion that Thornton had held back Fulton's 1809 patent application in order to give his own priority. It is curious that Fulton never directly accused him of doing so in writing.

Without prodding, Latrobe supplied any shred of information he imagined might be useful. He was angrier at Fulton than ever, for a letter from Fulton to the former supercargo of the *New Orleans* asking him to examine Latrobe's accounts, vouchers, expenditures, work schedules, and materials had fallen into Latrobe's hands in a shoemaker's–cum–coffee shop. It had the effect, Latrobe rebuked Fulton, of "depriving me of credit for a pair of Overshoes of which I stand in great want."[23] It was, however, Fulton's disparagement of Roosevelt that most enraged him, for he was afraid Fulton's next move would be to deprive Lydia and her children of their settlement. "There is in your late letters especially when speaking of Mr. Roosevelt a diabolical malignity, an upstart pride which disfigures even your handwriting," he railed. "You talk as if you were My Lord Chancellor. . . . You forget that there is even a doubt as to your name. All we know is that you claim an F is the First letter but whether Francis or Fulton or Fletcher remains to be determined."[24] Latrobe was, of course, sarcastically referring to Fulton's use of an alias while working on torpedo warfare in England and Fulton's having allowed one Fletcher to sign his first patent application for him. For Latrobe this was a somewhat eccentric tack, for in their recently concluded libel suit, Thornton had tried to impugn his character by accusing him of hiding the fact that his last name was really Boneval.

On the same day Latrobe wrote Delacy a manic letter beginning with a cartoon captioned "a hop, a skip, and a jump." Afflicted with ravaging headaches, he was in the throes of another nervous collapse. Nevertheless, he was still sufficiently in command of his wits to worry that Delacy's wild strategies might drive Ogden to support Fulton. Upbraiding Roosevelt for managing badly as usual, he warned, "I have but indifferent expectations from Delacy's exertions at Trenton if Ogden is against you. I wish you could enlist both him and Stevens in your cause."[25]

Propelled by his obsessive desire to be in everyone's intimate camp, Latrobe confided in his former enemy Thornton that his sole comfort was Roosevelt's patent for wheels over the side which would certainly invalidate Fulton's patent. Vaunting his own righteousness, Latrobe warned Fulton that although he had previously resisted solicitations for evidence about the steamboat of 1798, he had finally sent Delacy a deposition: "[A]s I will do nothing underhandedly I apprise you of this step."[26]

The hearings before the New Jersey Legislature, centering on Roosevelt's claim to being the originator of "steamboats with vertical wheels," began on January 14, 1815. Fulton went to Trenton the previous week. With so much at stake, he dared not risk staying away from the opening days as he had done at Albany.

Delacy, as counsel for Roosevelt, submitted all the proofs he had so assiduously collected. Emmet, representing Fulton, countered with a certified copy of the affidavit Roosevelt signed for the Albany Company lawsuit in 1811 in which Roosevelt stated unequivocally that Fulton was the inventor of the steamboat. Delacy perceived this maneuver as a ploy to force Roosevelt to perjure himself. In an attempt to prove Roosevelt had signed the document under duress, Delacy exhibited the original in Fulton's handwriting. "[Y]ou stand upon high and triumphant ground . . . already the current is in your favor," he exultantly reported to Roosevelt, who had not seen fit to travel the 47 miles from his home in Shrewsbury to attend the hearing. The "brazen-faced" Fulton was reduced to "making a last desperate effort," he crowed, "like the stag at bay."[27]

Fulton interpreted the events differently. "Roosevelt has completely ruined himself as far as there was anything left to ruin by his own Injustice, tricks & chicanery," he wrote Latrobe.[28] He could hope for nothing more than the proceeds of Lydia's settlement. The legislature merely referred the matter to a select committee and postponed the hearings examining John R.'s petition against Ogden's monopoly until January 24.

Fulton and Emmet returned to New York City. The general public, they found, was strongly behind Fulton, at least as the "establisher" of steamboats. His quick, on-schedule network gave the city the best and most comfortable public transportation system in the United States, indeed, in the world, reinforcing New York State's commercial superiority over New Jersey.

During this intersession, Fulton had the pleasure of banking $40,000 in Treasury notes, advance payment for the government's use of the Mississippi boats as military transports. He also contracted with the secretary of the navy to build two more steam frigates and a prototype *Mute* at the cost of $500,000. These transactions buoyed Fulton's spirits. He now had money to build the new hull for the *New Orleans* and to complete the *Aetna* and the *Buffalo*. His status as a major contributor to the national defense was clearly recognized.

On January 23, Fulton, Emmet, and Colden, whom they had persuaded to serve as auxiliary counsel, journeyed through the bleak, snow covered New Jersey countryside to Trenton. The next morning they were greeted at the State House by a crush of eager spectators. Anticipating high drama, the crowd jostled for places in the lobbies and galleries. Their expectations were more than satisfied. The long, thundering speeches were even more vituperative than those of the previous winter at Albany. The strategies contained more astonishing surprises.

Emmet was in the difficult position of attacking a state monopoly in New Jersey after having defended one in New York. Nevertheless, at the outset, he managed to appear characteristically "bold, loquacious, sententious, eloquent and audaciously dictatorial."[29] He asserted that Ogden had deceived the New Jersey legislature into granting the retaliatory act since he did not in fact possess the ancient right of ferriage that he claimed, but shared it with one Thomas Gibbons, who owned one-half of Elizabeth Town Point. To discredit Delacy, Emmet depicted him as a mysterious nobody and indulged the galleries by poking fun at his "antics" of the previous session.

At the outset Ogden spoke in his own behalf. His presentation was "firm, indignant and refuting."[30] Abundantly quoting from Shakespeare and Roman authors, he stressed that his goal was not monopoly but equity. He drew wild applause when he offered to relinquish all opposition to the Livingston-Fulton Company, if New Jersey citizens were permitted to enjoy free navigation on the Hudson River. In subsequent argument Ogden was represented by the seasoned Joseph Hopkinson and the rising young attorney and republican politician, Samuel L. Southard. Southard submitted extracts from Fitch's journal and letters to intimate friends to refute Emmet's assertion that Fitch utterly failed to conduct a successful experiment and that he ultimately abandoned the steamboat as hopeless and impracticable. Whipping up a great swell of commiseration for Fitch's illness and poverty, Hopkinson and Southard drew a picture of a brave but persecuted genius whose "feelings of pride and abhorrence of Dependence were such as to have made him resolve upon suicide as his only relief."[31]

In contrast, they attacked John R. as an extortionist who required passengers to pay for meals on his boat whether they ate them or not and, if continuing through to Philadelphia or Washington, to take stage-coaches in which he had a financial interest. Moreover, they asserted, the vessels designed by Fulton were inferior to those built by rivals and associates. Ogden's *Seahorse*, they said, achieved a greater speed with less fuel than any one of Fulton's boats. Stevens's son James was brought in to testify that the *Philadelphia* was superior to Fulton's boats "in lightness & cheapness of machinery and economy of fuel" and at least equal to most of them in speed.[32]

On the evening of the second day, Fairfax revealed Cutting's deposition with a flourish. Fulton could no longer sit still. Although he had not been called as a witness, he insisted on speaking. At first Ogden objected on the grounds that Fulton was not a named petitioner, but he finally agreed. It was then, Fulton's enemies later gloated, that the proud monopolist "dug his grave."

On the morning of the third day, Fulton rose—six feet tall, dark eyes burning, bristling with virtue—to protest that he had never claimed the principle of the rope-making machine as his own. He had legally obtained and sold to Cutting a French patent of importation with improvements. It should be obvious, he pointed out, that he never would have sent Cutting to Cartwright with a letter of introduction if he had been guilty of stealing Cartwright's ideas. These statements were both plausible and true. Fulton then denied ever having seen Fitch's plans or drawings, although he admitted to being acquainted with the late Aaron Vail.

Warmed by fine recollections of his accomplishments in Europe and eager to put an end to the matter once and for all, Fulton boldly presented the copy of the letter he claimed to have written to the Earl of Stanhope in November 1793 that had been so effective in Albany. It was, he said, a rough draft of the original letter. The document was passed among the opposing counsel. Ogden held it to the light and with undisguised joy discovered the watermark showed the paper to be of American manufacture, made in 1796. In the electrifying hush that fell over

Robert Fulton

the legislative chamber, Fulton attempted to explain. What he had meant to say was that the document was a true copy of the original draft. Because the tattered copy was too worn to be easily read, he had destroyed it.

Spewing forth "keen and bitter sarcasm," Hopkinson advised Fulton that it would have been "worth more to him than all his Steam-Boats put together" to produce the original letter, if such really existed, and "if any where short of the *North Pole*." [33] He was astonished Fulton had not sent a courier for it, or, better yet, gone for it himself. According to the evidence, it was now clear that not one of the inventions Fulton so arrogantly claimed was his own. Every one of them had been copied from books or the plans of less fortunate—and less avaricious—geniuses.

The session continued late into the night. To establish his scope and erudition, young Southard discredited New York State's claim that the boundry between New York and New Jersey was at the high-water mark on the New Jersey shore. New Jersey's jurisdiction extended over the whole river; otherwise interstate commerce would be destroyed. Southard reiterated Ogden's sensible plan for compromise, which again drew loud applause. Then he struck out at Fulton's invention. His vaunted "novel combination" was naught but a combination "of *gold* and *influence*, of *intrigue* and of *powerful connexions*." [34] Why had Fulton come to a state legislature to reinforce his monopoly, if his federal patent was valid? he scornfully queried. Why did Fulton shrink from a test of his patent's merits in federal court?

Fulton exploded. He was so infuriated, an adversary reported, that he proclaimed he did not care how the question was decided before the Legislature of New Jersey, he would seize Ogden's boat and even shoot him, if Ogden attempted to navigate the river. He then ordered his lawyers to sue both William Thornton and Nathaniel Cutting for libel.

Hopkinson worked the legislators and rapt audience the following Monday. He pleasantly acknowledged that Fulton deserved much merit for sustaining the risk and expense of bringing into active operation the present steamboat system. His merits were, however, "those of a successful and enterprising capitalist, practically bringing into public operation the labours of others—not those of an original inventor." Yet he had "been rewarded with extravagant governmental patronage whereby he has been enabled to live in a state of princely magnificence and to trample on the just rights of others." [35] In a ringing conclusion Hopkinson condemned Fulton for using false names—Francis in England and

Fletcher to sign his patent. The use of Fletcher, he declared, was clearly a case of fraud. The attempt to pass the copied Stanhope letter off as an original draft was, unquestionably, perjury.

For once the great Emmet was at a loss. Derisively he compared Ogden's engine to an old woman's spinning wheel and to a razor grinder's lathe. Proclaiming Fulton a modern-day Christopher Columbus, he let loose a torrent of invective against Thornton for having *"frequently obstructed by his own pretensions"* other inventors seeking patents. Then, exhausted by the strain on his imagination, he became "so vexed and angry that he forgot his Argument; and having spit his spite, became rather vapid," giving the appearance of "a good man in a bad case," or so one of Ogden's men reported.

It was "a proud day for the ghost of old Fitch and one which the man himself would highly have enjoyed," Fairfax wrote Thornton.[36] Still, because the Republicans were in power in New Jersey and Ogden was a Federalist, the outcome of the contest was by no means sure. To keep their record clean, Fairfax cautioned Thornton against patenting any invention for which he could not irrefutably establish a priority. As for himself, he now thought it prudent "not to enter into any Plan of Boat Building, or other expensive undertaking, with individuals or Companies" but "to let others incur the necessary Expenses." Nevertheless, since a general inquiry into patent rights had not been part of the hearing, he was tempted to commence a federal patent suit against Fulton.

On the afternoon of February 4, the legislature announced that John R. Livingston would be granted his petition. The New Jersey monopoly act would be repealed. Without one word of debate, the vote had followed strict party lines.

For Fulton it was a fragile victory. Roosevelt, Thornton, Delacy, and even Cutting had not lost their enmity. In the West, the Ohio and Mississippi were alive with rivals. The cancerous affair with Latrobe was far from contained.

Of all his great works, Fulton could contemplate only the great steam frigate, *Fulton I*, with undisturbed content. Although exhausted by the hearings, he was compulsively drawn to the vessel. On his way back to the city he spent spent three cold, damp hours at his Jersey City shops inspecting the work done in his absence. When he finally attempted to cross the river, the ferries were not running because the river was still partly frozen. Emmet, Colden, and the eminent legal reporter William Sampson, who had stayed on to keep Fulton company commandeered a small boat, which carried them to the edge of the ice mass. From there they continued on foot. The ice broke under Emmet's great weight, plunging him into the water. Fulton grabbed his arm and with great exertion pulled him out. Soaked through, the party trudged on through patches of slush on the ice.

When Fulton at last reached his mansion on Marketfield Street, he was so hoarse he could barely speak. After three days in bed, he felt marginally better and, encouraged by the news that his ferries had resumed service, called for his carriage. Neither Harriet nor his doctors could dissuade him from returning to Jersey City to observe once more the outfitting of the *Fulton I*.

This excursion brought him great joy, but it aggravated his infection. As usual, it settled in his chest. His physicians were again called. They relieved his deep, racking cough with an array of potents and briefly entertained hope of his recovery. Soon, however, the inflammation spread from his lungs and windpipe to the glands of his neck and lower jaw. When the eminent David Hosack was called in for consultation on the evening of February 22, Fulton recognized him and immediately extended his hand, but he could hardly utter a sound. "The feeble state of his pulse," the worthy doctor wrote, "the hurried and labored respiration, his livid and anxious countenance, all announced his approaching dissolution, and that nothing could be added to what already had been done by his medical friends."[37]

At half past nine on Thursday morning, February 23, 1815, Robert Fulton died.

Friends, adversaries, and the general public were stunned. The sudden absence of that powerful, questing, and experienced mind robbed their lives of a vital focus. Although often jarring, his vision had made them participants in an exciting new era, the potential and rules of which they could not faintly grasp on their own.

"While he was mediating plans of mighty import for his future fame and his country's good, he was cut down in the prime of his life and in the midst of his usefulness," DeWitt Clinton proclaimed in a eulogy before the American Academy of Arts. "Like the self-burning tree of Gambia, he was destroyed by the fire of his own genius and the never-ceasing activity of a vigorous mind."[38]

Epilogue

❖

No matter how shocking unexpected death may be, when the drama subsides, the living continue in their mundane ways and eventually ask: What does it mean to me?

To the investors, virtually all Fulton's close acquaintances, it meant rallying together to carry on the steamboat empire for profit. While they gossiped in private about the narrowness of the victory at Trenton and the "very delicate subject" of Fulton's perjury in the matter of the Stanhope letter, in public they glorified his name at every opportunity. After the funeral, mourning bands were worn and eulogies pronounced. Partition Street, the thoroughfare between the East River and Hudson River ferry slips, was improved and renamed Fulton Street.

Harriet and her brother-in-law William Cutting, the executors of Fulton's estate, achieved a surprising degree of harmony with Edward P. and Robert L. Livingston. Their aim was to minimize capital investment without losing income. In October 1815 Harriet and Cutting sold Fulton's share of the aging *Car of Neptune* and *Paragon* and the newer *Firefly* and *Richmond* for $100,000 to a small group of men headed by Cadwallader D. Colden. Prudently, they retained their control of the steam ferry boats in which they each had a special interest. They put the Long Island Sound boat *Fulton* into service to New Haven, offering a sumptuous breakfast and dinner during the eleven-hour journey. In

1816, they launched the *Chancellor Livingston,* the last, most powerful, and most luxurious boat built to Fulton's design. Her running time to Albany was just over twenty-one hours.

In a tour de force intended to protect the New York State monopoly from further assault, John R. Livingston was persuaded to sell Aaron Ogden the right to run steamboats from Elizabeth Town Point to New York City for the low price of $600 and permission to use Ogden's wharf. Ogden also promised not to serve as counsel against the monopoly. No sooner had Ogden changed sides than he was attacked by Thomas Gibbons who had been waiting for just such an opportunity. A tenacious Georgia lawyer with a fortune to spend, Gibbons bought the small *Staudinger* or *Mouse,* built the *Bellona,* hired the ambitious young Cornelius Vanderbilt as his sailing master and, having procured U.S. coasting licenses, ran his boats from New York City to Elizabeth Town Point and New Brunswick in competition with Ogden and John R.'s lines. New York issued an injunction against him on the basis of the 1811 monopoly act, but neither Gibbons nor Vanderbilt was fazed. As if engaged in a game of cops and robbers, they continued running the *Bellona* and, after more jostling in the state courts, appealed the case—now *Gibbons* v. *Ogden*—to the U.S. Supreme Court. Daniel Webster was their chief counsel. Thomas Addis Emmet again represented the Fulton interests. Gibbons won. In his landmark decision handed down in March 1824, Chief Justice John Marshall stated that the Constitution's commerce clause clearly gave Congress the power to regulate navigation among the states and that Congress had chosen the coasting license to implement it—in essence, the argument John Stevens had advanced as early as 1808. The states might govern strictly internal navigation, Marshall conceded, but the prosperity and happiness of the Union depended on free intercourse between its several parts as well as with foreign nations. Marshall dispensed with the patent problem by declaring that state monopoly laws were repugnant to the Constitution because they impeded the progress of science and the useful arts. In any event, Fulton's patent had almost expired. An earlier attempt to extend it for the benefit of Fulton's widow and children dismally failed.

The protracted litigation added to the risk of investing in steamboats. Yet, even while the case was in motion, boats were launched as fast as engines could be built. In 1821, the naval architect Jean Baptiste Marestier, sent by France to study the steamboat phenomenon, reported between thirty and forty boats on the waters of Long Island Sound, the Hudson and Delaware Rivers, and Chesapeake Bay. Steam navigation also flourished in the West. "The invention of the steamboat was intended for us," the press proclaimed. "The puny rivers of the East are only as creeks or convenient waters on which experiments may be made for our advantage."[1] Rivalry was intense, for, despite his considerable political influence Edward Livingston failed to extend the Louisiana monopoly. As soon as news of Fulton's death reached New Orleans, Henry Shreve, the captain of Daniel French's *Enterprise*, brought suit against the Fulton-Livingston company.

In 1818, Moses Rogers, the former captain of Stevens's *Phoenix* and of the *Fulton* steamboat took the *Savannah* from Georgia to Liverpool, England, in 1818. She carried no passengers or cargo—her hold was filled with wood and coal to fire the engine—and she accomplished most of the voyage under sail, although the voyage proved that a steamboat could weather the Atlantic. In 1815 the British ran a steamboat between Liverpool and Glasgow and, in 1820, the British Post Office added steamboats on its runs to Ireland and France.

Charles Staudinger and James P. Allaire bought the Jersey City workshops. By 1820 they were the largest in the country, employing seventy hands and with a capital investment of $100,000. Both Evans and Dod tried high-pressure engines, but they exploded, killing and scalding numerous passengers. In retrospect, it is another of Fulton's remarkable achievements that, as he brought the art of steam navigation through its first years, no passenger or crew member was killed or seriously injured while any of his boats was in operation.

———

Fulton's instruments of war suffered a markedly different fate. As soon as the Treaty of Ghent was signed, ending the War of 1812, work was stopped on the prototype *Mute* and the Baltimore steam frigate. However, funding to complete the *Fulton I* was continued so that the design could be tested. Staudinger installed the engines, and on July 4, 1815, "steering as easily as a sloop" and with no assistance from sails, the *Fulton I* ran from the Jersey City works to Sandy Hook and back in 8 hours and 20 minutes, a distance of 53 miles. With slight modifications to the giant paddle wheel and the boiler room and a full complement of guns— excepting the underwater Columbiads—the steam frigate performed again on September 11. She executed "beautiful maneuvers around the U.S. Frigate *Java*," which was anchored in the lower bay.[2] The guns fired perfectly. Nevertheless, despite the commission's enthusiastic recommendation that she be used as a training ship, she was laid up. In June 1818 she was brought out temporarily to take President James Monroe on a ceremonial excursion to Staten Island. Then, her guns and machinery were removed.

Berthed in the Brooklyn Navy Yard, the *Fulton I* was used to receive transient naval personnel. The timbers rotted as the years went by, and in 1829 she blew up, killing twenty-four men and one woman. The explosion was caused by two barrels of condemned gunpowder, set off by a careless guard who entered the magazine with a lighted candle to get powder to fire the ceremonial evening gun. It was not until 1837 that the United States built a second steam warship, nostalgically named *Fulton the Second*. Still, the naval establishment was reluctant to give up the grandeur of sail, and, in marked contrast to commercial shippers, resisted converting the fleet to steam.

Only a few isolated inventors showed interest in Fulton's submarine devices until late in the nineteenth century. Even then, experimentation was not supported by governments but by private companies who, like Fulton, sold their designs to whatever country would buy. During World War I submarines, torpedoes, and mines became effective weapons, but they were still widely condemned as a cowardly violation of the accepted code of war.

———

If, with the guidance of Cutting, Harriet was at first an able executrix of her husband's estate, she was less successful in managing her private life. As might be expected, she quarreled with Ruth Barlow about the cost of freight, storage, and duties on the fine ornaments and furniture the Barlows had bought in Paris at Fulton's behest. Ruth caustically observed they were unsuitable for the "small rooms" Harriet inhabited at 353 Broadway, and each accused the other of trying to sell them for personal profit.

On November 26, 1816, less than two years after Fulton's death, Harriet married an avaricious English charmer named Charles Augustus Dale. They lived principally in New York City, although, just before her marriage, Harriet bought Teviotdale from her brother John. In 1820 the Dales mortgaged their country property and, leaving the children with a widowed sister-in-law in nearby Claverack, went to England. They were back in America by 1825, for at that time Harriet, with other investors, endeavored unsuccessfully to incorporate a bank. The petition put before the New York State Legislature carried the unusual provision that interest on $70,000 of the capital be set aside for the support of Fulton's children who were claimed to be utterly destitute of support.

Harriet died in 1826. She was not buried in her family's vault at Trinity church, beside Fulton, but in the cemetery of the Claverack Dutch Reformed Church. A handsome white marble obelisk marks her lonely grave; none of her family is buried near her. Though Harriet and Dale had no children, he inherited a life interest in Teviotdale and all her personal possessions. Dale attempted to find a place for Barlow in the navy through Fulton's friends, but otherwise he behaved callously toward his stepchildren. In 1829 Barlow begged his uncle, Robert L. Livingston, to prevent Dale from selling Teviotdale. His sisters were so poor they were forced to live with relatives, he said. "Money have they none, even to buy necessary garments, & what I can save from my small salary is by no means sufficient for even one of them."[3] Robert L. did not, and perhaps could not, intervene, and Dale sent everything he deemed of value to New York and told the servants to make a bonfire of what remained. Only Harriet's harp, a few books, some family portraits and several drawings of machinery were rescued at that time.

Fulton's children continued to seek recompense for their father's government work. In 1836, they submitted a petition to Congress, asking for money owed Fulton for his services during the War of 1812. After extensive hearings, $100,000 was awarded for Fulton's supervising the construction of the steam frigate, for the cost of his torpedo experiments, and for damages suffered by the *Vesuvius* while under government contract. Actual payment was not made until 1847, when the sum was reduced to just over $76,000. By that time Fulton's daughters were well married, and his son, who had remained a bachelor, was dead.

The members of the Livingston clan with whom Fulton was associated lived out their lives following predictable patterns. John was an unlucky speculator, and Robert L. a gentleman of leisure. Edward P. enjoyed a political rebirth. He served in the New York State Senate and in 1830 was elected lieutenant governor. In 1832 he was the president of the Electoral College. John R. lived to age ninety-three, rich and irascible. The most distinguished of the Livingstons was Edward. He reestablished both his fortune and his political influence in Louisiana and then returned to New York. His work in criminal jurisprudence was world-renowned. In the administration of his friend Andrew Jackson he served as secretary of state and as minister plenipotentiary to France.

Of the dramatis personae in the steamboat controversies, the Stevens family's commitment to engineering proved exceptionally enduring. During the canal boom, John Stevens messianically promoted railroads. By way of demonstration, he bought a locomotive in England and ran it on a circular track in his garden at Hoboken. His steamboat enterprises were ably carried foward by his sons who beat Vanderbilt in a fare war giving the Stevens family a virtual monopoly of the Hudson River. John Cox is remembered for forming the syndicate that built the sailboat *America* and organizing the first race against the British in the series that became known as the America's Cup. Edwin founded the Stevens Institute of Technology in Hoboken, which still retains its preeminence in the field of marine engineering. With Robert, Stevens invented and manufactured an elongated shell for the U.S. government. They also developed an iron-clad submersible, which they endeavored to sell to Russia for use against the Turks. Since Stevens's asking price for going to St. Petersburg to supervise construction was $200,000, he aroused no interest. Toward the end of his life Stevens immersed himself in the study of metaphysics and classical literature. He died in 1838, at the age of eighty-nine.

Benjamin Henry Latrobe responded to Fulton's death with a typical mixture of sincere emotion and practicality. It is, he wrote a friend, "unfavorable to me . . . but what is it to the suffering of his poor widow & children. Independently of his insatiable avarice, he had many great and good qualities . . . his courage & perseverance were very useful to the republic. I am on the whole very sorry he is gone. But regret is now vain."[4] Still shaky from his nervous breakdown, Latrobe returned to rebuild the Capitol in Washington, where he lived adjacent to the widow Barlow. Although he was the architect for St. John's Church and received commissions for private residences, he was never clear of financial difficulty. He died at New Orleans of yellow fever in 1820 and today is considered America's first great architect. His son-in-law Nicholas Roosevelt eventually settled in Skaneateles, New York, where he died an honored octogenarian.

William Thornton, vowing to avenge himself for Fulton's cupidity in any way he could, provided material for Gibbons in his suits against Ogden. He remained the superintendent of the Patent Office, and when he died in 1828, he was buried with much pomp in the congressional cemetery beneath a tombstone designed by Latrobe. Aaron Ogden was bankrupted by the crushing expense of his litigation against Gibbons.

After filing a suit for $2,500 in damages against Fulton's estate, John Devereux Delacy abandoned his friends. Many years later in an abortive attempt to capitalize on Roosevelt's patent, he came to the law office of Latrobe's son John, dressed in seedy clothes, but still slim, erect and exuding enthusiasm. The episode ended with Delacy in jail for having bought a coat on credit with no intention of paying for it.

Ruth Barlow was probably the strongest emotional presence in Fulton's life, both because he loved her and because their lives were so long entwined. Shortly after Fulton's death, she returned to Kalorama where, she wrote a friend, she could "recall the *image* I wish to be ever present to my still bleeding heart." With neither Barlow nor Fulton to minister to her frailties she lost spirit and, in 1818, she died.

In the years since Robert Fulton's death, the controversy over whether he was visionary laboring for the benefit of humanity or merely "an adventurer armed with fortitude" serving his own ambitions, has not abated. He was, of course, both. A courageous idealist, he was also an opportunist. Fulton did not invent the steamboat—nor did Fitch, Rumsey, Roosevelt, or Thornton. But he did "sit down among levers, screws, wedges, and wheels like a poet among the letters of the alphabet, and, making a new arrangement, transmit a new idea to the world." Obsessed by his vision of a society harmoniously united by free trade and reliable transportation, he attempted more than he could accomplish. He overreached himself. His ability to do so, however, was the essence of his genius and the foundation of his lasting fame.

SOURCES

The main sources for this life of Robert Fulton are unpublished letters, diaries, contracts, account books, and government records. There are six major collections of Robert Fulton papers. They are to be found at the New-York Historical Society, Clermont State Historic Park, the New York Public Library, the Library of Congress, the Archives Nationales de France, and in the Stanhope Manuscripts deposited at the Kent County (England) Archives. Of almost equal importance are the papers of his friends, associates, and adversaries. The Houghton Library at Harvard contains a large Barlow collection as does the Beineke Library at Yale University. The Stevens family papers are housed at the New Jersey Historical Society, which also possesses the invaluable Stoudinger-Alofsen Collection of engineering drawings. The Livingston papers at the New-York Historical Society inform almost every period. The Benjamin Henry Latrobe papers have been edited and published by the Maryland Historical Society, and the papers of William Thornton are now being collected. In addition to these holdings, documents are scattered in twos and tens in national, state, university, historical society, and special libraries throughout the United States and in England and France.

Important material was also drawn from contemporary printed sources and to a lesser extent from secondary sources on the period. Because these are too numerous to list, I present below a short, but I hope representative, selected bibliography.

Alberts, Robert C. *Benjamin West: A Biography*. Boston, 1978.
The Ambulator; or the Strangers' Companion in a Tour around London. London, 1782.
Ayars, Walter F., III. *Lancaster Diary 1776*. Lancaster, 1976.
Babst, Germain. *Essai sur l'histoire des Panoramas et dioramas*. Paris, 1891.
Barlow, Joel. *The Columbiad: A Poem*. Philadelphia, 1807.
Bathe, Grenville. *An Engineer's Miscellany*. Philadelphia, 1938.

Sources

———— and D. Bathe. *Oliver Evans; a Chronicle of Early American Engineering*. Philadelphia, 1935.

Baynes, Ken and Francis Pugh. *The Art of the Engineer*. Woodstock, N.Y., 1981.

Beckford, William. *Life at Fonthill*. Boyd Alexander, ed. and trans. London, 1957.

Bell, Whitfield, Jr. *Early American Science. Needs and Opportunities for Study*. Williamsburg, Va., 1935.

Bidwell, John. *The Publication of Joel Barlow's "Columbiad"*. Worcester, Mass., 1984.

Bridenbaugh, Carl, and Jessica Bridenbaugh. *Rebels and Gentlemen: Philadelphia in the Age of Franklin*. New York, 1962.

Brissot de Warville, Jacques Pierre. *New Travels in the United States of America Performed in 1788*. Boston, 1797.

Bugge, Thomas. *Science in France in the Revolutionary Era*. Maurice P. Crosland, ed. Cambridge, Eng., 1964.

Burns, James Macgregor. *The American Experiment: The Vineyard of Liberty*. New York, 1982.

Castlereagh, Robert Stewart, Viscount. *Correspondence, Despatches, and Other Papers*. Charles William Vane, ed. London, 1850–53. Vol. 5.

Chapelle, Howard I. *Fulton's "Steam Battery": Blockship and Catamaran*. Washington, 1964.

Chapman, William. *Observations of the Various Systems of Canal Navigation . . .* London, 1797.

Chastellux, Francois Jean, Marquis de. *Travels in North America in the Years 1780, 1781 and 1782*. Howard C. Rice, Jr., ed. Chapel Hill, 1963.

Colden, Cadwallader D. *The Life of Robert Fulton*. New York, 1817.

————*A Vindication by Cadwallader D. Colden of the Steam-Boat Right . . .* Albany, 1818.

Cramer, Zadok. *The Navigator*. Pittsburgh, 1811.

Dangerfield, George. *Chancellor Robert R. Livingston of New York 1746–1813*. New York, 1960.

Dickinson, Henry W. *Robert Fulton, Engineer and Artist, His Life and Works*. London, 1913.

Duane, William, ed. *Extracts from the Diary of Christopher Marshall kept in Philadelphia and Lancaster 1774–1781*. Philadelphia, 1877.

Duer, William Alexander. *A Letter Addressed to Cadwallader C. Colden*. Albany, 1817.

Dunlap, William. *History of the Arts and Design in the United States*. New York, 1834.

Ellis, Franklin, and Samuel Evans. *History of Lancaster County, Pennsylvania*. Philadelphia, 1883.

Evans, Dorinda. *Benjamin West and His American Students*. Washington, 1980.

Farington, Joseph. *The Farington Diary*. James Greig, ed. London, 1923–1928.

Figuier, Louis. *Les Merveilles de la Science*. Paris, 1867.

Flexner, James Thomas. *Steamboats Come True: American Inventors in Action*. Boston, 1978.

Fowler, William M., Jr. *Jack Tars and Commodores, the American Navy 1783–1815*. Boston, 1984.

Fulton, Eleanore J. *Index to the Will Books and Interstate Records of Lancaster County, 1729–1850*. Philadelphia, 1983.

Sources

Fulton, Robert. *Concluding address on The Mechanism, Practice and Effects of Torpedoes*. Washington, 1810.

——— *Letters Principally to the Right Honourable Lord Grenville on Submarine Navigation and Attack . . .* London, 1806.

——— *Memorial and Petition of Robert Fulton and Edward P. Livingston in Behalf of Themselves . . .* New York, 1814.

——— *Plan for Supplying the City of New York with Fuel by the New-York Coal Company*. New York, 1814.

——— *Recherches sur les Moyens de Perfectionner les Canaux de Navigation . . .* F. de Récicourt, trans. Paris, 1800.

——— *Report on the Proposed Canal between the Rivers Heyl and Helford*. London, 1796.

——— *The Right of the State to Grant Exclusive Privileges*. New York, 1811.

———*Torpedo War and Submarine Explosions*. New York, 1810.

——— *Tratado do Melhoramente da Navegacao por canaes . . .* A. C. daSilva, trans. Lisbon, 1800.

——— *A treatise on the Improvement of Canal Navigation . . .* London, 1796.

Gallatin, Albert, *Report of the Secretary of the Treasury on the Subject of Public Roads and Canals*. Philadelphia, 1808.

George, Dorothy. *England in transition*. Baltimore, 1965.

Glover, Richard G. *Britain at Bay: Defence against Bonaparte*. New York, 1973.

Gontaut-Biron, Marie Josephine Louise, Duchesse de. *Memoires*. Mrs. J. W. Davis, trans. New York, 1894.

Hadfield, Charles. *British Canals, an illustrated history*. Newton Abbot, Eng., 1974.

——— and A. W. Skempton. *William Jessop, Engineer*. Newton Abbott, Eng., 1979.

Hamlin, Talbot. *Benjamin Henry Latrobe*. New York, 1955.

Hammond, Bray. *Banks and Politics in America from the Revolution to the Civil War*. Princeton, 1957.

Harris, Helen, and Monica Ellis. *The Bude Canal*. Newton Abbot, Eng., 1972.

Hindle, Brooke. *Emulation and Invention*. New York, 1981.

——— *The Pursuit of Science in Revolutionary America*. New York, 1974.

Holland, Henry Richard Vassall. *Memoirs of the Whig Party during My Time*. Lord Stavordale, ed. London, 1905.

Howath, David. *Trafalgar: The Nelson Touch*. London, 1969.

Hudson Fulton Celebration Commission. *Hudson-Fulton Celebration; a Collection of the Catalogues Issued by the Museums and Institutions in New York City*. New York, 1910.

Hunt, Louis C. *Steamboats on the Western Waters: An Economical and Technological History*. Cambridge, Mass., 1949.

Hutcheon, Wallace, Jr. *Robert Fulton Pioneer of Undersea Warfare*. Annapolis, Md., 1981.

Institut National de la Propriété Industrielle. *Le Brevet de 1791*. Paris, 1966.

Knowles, John. *The Life and Writings of James Fuseli, Esq*. London, 1931.

Lambert, John. *Travels through Canada and the United States of North America in the Years 1806, 1807, and 1808*. London, 1814.

Latrobe, Benjamin Henry. *The Papers of Benjamin Henry Latrobe*. Edward C. Carter, ed. Thomas E. Jeffrey, Microfiche editor. The Maryland Historical Society. Thomas T. White Co., N.J., 1976.

In order to make the sources of passages quoted in my text both brief and clear, I have used the last name of the principal author to designate printed material as it appears in the above bibliography. For the same reason, I have used the initials of frequently cited persons instead of repeating their full names. The libraries in which manuscript material is found are also designated by initials. These abbreviations are as follows:

BHL	Benjamin Henry Latrobe	JS	John Stevens
BW	Benjamin West	JRL	John R. Livingston
CDC	Cadwallader D. Colden	NR	Nicholas Roosevelt
CS	Charles Mahon, 3d Earl of Stanhope	RB	Ruth Barlow
EC	Edmund Cartwright	RF	Robert Fulton
EL	Edward Livingston	RLL	Robert L. Livingston
EPL	Edward P. Livingston	RRL	Robert R. Livingston
JB	Joel Barlow	TJ	Thomas Jefferson
JDD	John Devereaux Delacy	WT	William Thornton
JL	John Livingston		

Manuscript Collections

AI	McKinney Library, Albany Institute of History and Art	HSWP	Historical Society of Western Pennsylvania
APS	American Philosophical Society	JCB	John Carter Brown Library, Brown University
AN	Archives Nationales de France		
CHS	Chicago Historical Society	KCC	Kent County (England) Council
CSHP	Clermont State Historic Park	LC	Library of Congress
HH	Harvard University, Houghton Library	NA	National Archives
		NJHS	New Jersey Historical Society
HL	The Huntington Library	NYHS	New-York Historical Society
HSP	Historical Society of Pennsylvania	NYPL	New York Public Library

NYSL   New York State Library
PBHL   Papers of Benjamin Henry Latrobe

YB   Yale University, Beineke Rare Book
      and Manuscript Library
YU   Yale University, Library

NOTES

Chapter 1
1. RF Sr. to Msrs. West and Swift, 1/13/72, HSP.
2. RF to Samuel Turbitt, 12/1/88, NYHS.
3. RF to Betsy, 10/20/05, NYPL.
4. n.d., YB.
5. Duane, p. 132.
6. Chastellux, p. 181.
7. Rush, *Letters*, p. 357.
8. Bridenbaugh, p. 351.
9. Colden, p. 371.

Chapter 2
1. Silliman, p. 43.
2. Trusler, p. 156.
3. Alberts, p. 181.
4. West, p. 11.
5. *The Gentleman's Magazine*, June 1787.
6. RF to Mary Smith [Fulton], 1/20/92, HSWP.
7. Knowles, p. 174.
8. Alberts, p. 209.
9. RF to Samuel Turbitt, 12/1/88, NYHS.
10. Sutcliffe, *Robert Fulton* p. 44.
11. RF to Mary Fulton, 6/14/90, HSWP.
12. Sutcliffe, *Robert Fulton*, p. 43.
13. Ibid.
14. RF to Mary Smith [Fulton], 1/20/92, HSWP.
15. Ibid.
16. Ibid.
17. Ibid.
18. Beckford, p. 156.
19. RF to David Morris, 5/21/93, CHS.
20. Ibid.
21. White, p. 143.
22. Hindle, Brooke. "The Contriving Mind." Anson G. Stokes Lectures, New York University, 1980.

Chapter 3
1. Holland, p. 34.
2. Stanhope, Lady Hester, p. 33.
3. Stanhope and Gooch, p. 165.
4. RF to CS, 11/27/93, KCC.
5. RF to CS, 11/30/93, KCC.
6. CS to RF, 12/6/93, KCC.
7. RF to CS, 12/11/93, KCC.
8. CS to RF, 12/17/93, KCC.

9. CS to RF, 12/17/93, KCC.
10. RF to CS, 12/22/93, KCC.
11. CS to RF, 12/27/93, KCC.
12. Patent No. 1988.
13. Dickinson, p. 34.
14. Ibid., p. 35.

Chapter 4
1. Fulton, *Treatise*, p. x.
2. Ibid., p. xiii.
3. Ibid., p. xv.
4. Ibid., p. 12.
5. Ibid., p. 29.
6. Ibid., p. 113.
7. Ibid., p. 133.
8. Ibid., p. 110.
9. Ibid., p. 109.
10. Ibid., p. 109.
11. Ibid., p. 113, RF to CS, 5/24/96, KCC.
12. *Monthly Review*, Vol. xxii, 1797, pp. 411–16; Vol. lxii, 1810, pp. 355–56.
13. Chapman. p. 2.
14. CS to RF, 5/24/96, KCC.
15. RF to CS, 4/24/96, KCC.
16. RF to CS, 5/4/96, KCC.
17. Ibid.
18. CS to RF, 5/24/96, KCC.
19. Stanhope and Gooch, p. 167.
20. RF to CS, 5/12/96, KCC.
21. Alberts, p. 213.
22. RF to CS, 12/28/96, KCC.
23. RF to David Morris, 9/12/96, HSWP.
24. RF to George Washington, 9/12/96, HSP.
25. George Washington to RF, 12/14/96, LC.
26. RF to George Washington, 2/5/97, LC.
27. "Thoughts on the Delaware and Raritan Canal Act," 3/29/97, The Pierpont Morgan Library.
28. S[trickland], p. 132.
29. RF to BW, 2/22/96, NYHS.
30. Owen, p. 70.

Chapter 5
1. S[trickland], p. 139.
2. Ibid.
3. M. S. Harris, et al. "The Life of Samuel Miles Hopkins," misc. mss., YU.
4. S[trickland], p. 139.
5. John Vanderlyn to Peter Vanderlyn,

Notes

8/14/97, Senate House Historical Museum, Kingston, N.Y.
6. John Vanderlyn to Peter Vanderlyn, 10/23/97, Senate House Historical Museum, Kingston, N.Y.
7. S[trickland], p. 142.
8. Institut National de la Propriété Industrielle, p. 7.
9. "Thoughts on Free Trade," 10/29/97, Edwin R. A. Seligman Papers, Columbia University Rare Book and Manuscript Library.
10. "To the Friends of Mankind," NYHS.
11. S[trickland], p. 142.
12. RF to the Executive Directory, 12/13/97, AN.
13. RF to Larevellière-Lépeaux, 12/15/97, AN.
14. Note, n.d., AN.
15. RF to CS, 4/14/98, NYPL.
16. RF to General Bonaparte, 5/1/98, NYPL.
17. S[trickland], 142.
18. RF to E. Bruix, 7/23/98, AN.
19. Report of the Commission, 9/5/98, AN.
20. RF to E. Bruix, 10/10/98, Service Historique de la Marine, Paris.
21. RF to Director Merlin [de Douai], 10/27/99, Service Historique de la Marine, Paris.

Chapter 6
1. Woodress, p. 185.
2. JB, Diary, 5/22–9/12/88, HH.
3. M. S. Harris, et al. "Life of Samuel Miles Hopkins," misc. mss., YU.
4. RF to Samuel Miles Hopkins, 4/30/99, HH.
5. Institute National de la Propriété Industrielle, p. 110.
6. Babst, p. 6.
7. RF to Nathaniel Cutting, 7/9/99, NYHS.
8. RF to Samuel Miles Hopkins, 7/3/99, LC.
9. RF to Mary Smith Fulton, 7/2/99, Sutcliffe, *Robert Fulton*, p. 68.
10. RF to Military Committee of the Executive Directory, 7/17/99, Service Historique de la Marine.
11. Dickinson, p. 98.
12. RF to Marine Minister, 10/5/99, AN.
13. RF to Joshua Gilpin, 11/20/98, USNM.
14. RF to Samuel Miles Hopkins, 4/30/99, HH.
15. RF to Marine Minister, 10/13/99, AN.
16. RF to Forfait, 4/10/00, AN.
17. American Historical Review, xxxix, p. 492.
18. RF to Forfait, 4/10/00, AN.
19. JB to RF, 9/6/00, HH.
20. RF to P. Laplace and G. Monge, 11/7/00, AN.

Chapter 7
1. JB to RB, 8/31/02, HH.
2. JB to RB, 8/24/00, 8/29/00, HH.
3. JB to RB, 8/14/00, HH.
4. JB to RB, 8/18/00, HH.
5. JB to Abraham Baldwin, 8/15/00, HH.
6. JB to RB, 8/30/00, HH.
7. JB to RB, 8/20/00, HH.
8. JB to RB, 8/24/00, HH.
9. JB to RB, 8/17/00, HH.
10. JB to RB, 8/31/00, HH.
11. JB to RB, 9/4/00, HH.
12. JB to RB, 8/29/00, HH.
13. JB to RB, 7/28/02, HH.
14. RB to JB, 1/22/97, HH.
15. JB to RB, 5/15/02, HH.
16. RF to Laplace and Monge, 11/7/00, AN.
17. Laplace and Monge to Bonaparte, 11/19/00, AN.
18. Forfait to Bonaparte, 12/4/00, AN.
19. RF to Monge, Laplace, and Volney, 9/9/01, AN.
20. Cafarelli to Forfait, 7/3/01, AN.
21. Villaret de Joyeuse to Forfait, 7/4/01, AN.
22. RF to Monge, Laplace, and Volney, 9/9/01, AN.
23. RF to Monge, Laplace, and Volney, 9/20/01, AN.
24. JB, "The Canal," 1802, YB.

Chapter 8
1. JB, "The Canal," 1802 YB.
2. JB to RB, 8/9/02, HH.
3. RF to William Reynolds, 2/4/02, NYHS.
4. Charles Staudinger to NR, 12/29/97, NYHS.
5. RF to RRL, 3/25/02, CSHP.
6. JB to RB, 5/13/02, 5/21/02, HH.
7. JB to RB, 5/3/02, 5/29/02, HH.
8. JB to RB, 6/6/02, HH.
9. JB to RB, 5/3/02, 5/29/02, HH.
10. JB to RB, 5/15/02, HH.
11. JB to RB, 5/25/02, HH.
12. JB to RB, 5/21/02, HH.
13. JB to RB, 5/31/02, HH.
14. Ibid.
15. JB to RB, 6/4/02, HH.
16. RF to RRL, 6/5/02, CSHP.
17. Fulton later estimated the distance between New York and Albany as 160 miles and finally settled on 150 miles. The measurement for the deep-water ship route from New York to Albany is presently 126 nautical miles or approximately 145 statute miles.
18. RF to RRL, 6/5/02, CSHP.

Notes

19. RF to RRL, 6/13/02, CSHP.
20. JB to RB, 6/14/02, HH.
21. JB to RB, 7/8/02, HH.
22. JB to RB, 7/18/02, HH.
23. RRL to RF, 7/20/02, CSHP.
24. RF to RRL, 7/25/02, CSHP.
25. RRL to Gilbert Livingston, 12/23/02, NYHS.
26. JB to RB, 7/28/02, HH.
27. JB to RB, 7/8/16; 8/1/02; 8/3/02, HH.
28. RF to Fulwar Skipwith, 6/13/02, NYHS.
29. JB to RB, 8/13/02, 8/15/02, HH.

Chapter 9
1. Farington, 9/27/02.
2. RF to RRL, 9/29/02, CSHP.
3. RF to RRL, 10/2/02, CSHP.
4. RF and RRL, 10/10/02. CSHP.
5. RRL to Thomas Tillotson, 11/12/02, NYHS.
6. RF to RRL, 1/19/03, CSHP.
7. RF to Citizens Molar[d], Bardell, and Montgolfier, 1/24/03, Conservatoire Nationale des Arts et Metiers.
8. Dickinson, p. 156.
9. RRL to Alida Armstrong, 7/31/03, NYHS.
10. Marie Joseph Lafayette to RRL, 8/26/03, NYHS.
11. JB to RB, 4/1/03, HH.
12. JB to RB, 7/27/03, HH.
13. Figuier, p. 191.
14. Sutcliffe, p. 155.
15. RF to Daniel Parker, 10/27/03, NYHS.
16. RRL to James Monroe, 4/9/04, NYHS.
17. JB, 4/27/04, HH.
18. RRL to EL, 4/25/04, NYHS.
19. RRL to JS, 4/28/04, NJHS.

Chapter 10
1. RF, "Motives for Inventing Submarine Navigation and Attack," 8/10/06, NYPL.
2. RF to George Hammond, 5/23/04, NYPL.
3. RF to William Pitt, 6/6/04, NYPL.
4. RF to George Hammond, 6/22/04, NYPL.
5. RF to George Hammond, 6/27/04, NYPL.
6. Dickinson, p. 169.
7. RF, 7/20/04, NYPL.
8. Perrin, p. 93.
9. RF to Dear petit mama [Elizabeth West], 10/4/04, NYPL.
10. Dickinson, p. 188.
11. Keith, p. 101.
12. JB to TJ, 3/15/05, LC.
13. Silliman, p. 210.
14. RF to William Pitt, 7/18/05, NYPL.
15. Castlereagh, p. 86.

16. Ibid., p. 96.
17. Ibid., p. 110.
18. Rf to Mamy [Benjamin] West, 10/16/05, NYHS.
19. Castlereagh, p. 111.
20. Ibid., p. 115.
21. Fulton, *Torpedo*, p. 6.
22. Castlereagh, p. 119.
23. RF to Mamy [Benjamin] West, 10/16/05, NYHS.
24. RF to David Morris, 10/15/05, HSWP.
25. RF to Mr. Hoge, 10/20/05, CHS.
26. Castlereagh, p. 124.

Chapter 11
1. RF to Mamy [Benjamin] West, 11/26/05, HL.
2. RF to Lord Castlereagh, 12/13/05, NYPL.
3. RF to William Pitt, 1/16/06, NYPL.
4. RF to Alexander Davison, 4/17/06, NA.
5. RF to Lord Grenville, 5/4/06, NYPL.
6. RF, notes, 8/10/06, NYPL.
7. RF, notes on arbitration, NYPL.
8. RF to Lord Grenville, 9/3/06, NYPL.
9. RF, notes, NYPL.
10. RF to Lord Grenville, 9/3/06, NYPL.
11. RF to Lord Grenville, 9/23/06, NYPL.
12. EC to Lord Grenville, 10/16/06, HL.
13. Dickinson, p. 202.
14. JB to RF, 3/30/06, HH.
15. RF to Daniel Parker, 9/23/06, NYHS.
16. RF to JB, 9/12/06, YB.

Chapter 12
1. Lambert, p. 64.
2. RF to RRL, 12/14/06, CSHP.
3. Reprinted in *National Intelligencer*, 12/22/06.
4. *National Intelligencer*, 1/2/07.
5. Margaret Bayard Smith to Miss Mary Anne Smith, 2/18/07, LC.
6. RF to RRL, 1/12/06, CSHP.
7. RF to RRL, 1/25/07, Franklin Delano Roosevelt Library.
8. RRL to RF, 3/10/07, HSP.
9. RF to RRL, 4/13/07, CSHP.
10. JB to RRL, 5/2/06, NYHS.
11. RF to RRL, 4/13/07, CSHP.
12. Sutcliffe, *Robert Fulton and the Clermont*, p. 217.
13. RF to RRL, 3/6/07, CSHP.
14. RF to RRL, 5/23/07, CSHP.
15. RF to RRL, 7/14/07, CSHP.
16. Colden, p. 73.
17. RF to TJ, 8/28/07, LC.
18. *New York Spectator*, 7/25/07.
19. *Commercial Advertiser*, 7/20/07.

Notes

20. *Salmagundi*, 8/17/07, p. 255.
21. G. C. Berkeley to James Barry, 9/14/07, HSP.

Chapter 13
1. RF to RRL, 8/10/07, CSHP.
2. Sutcliffe, *Robert Fulton and the Clermont*, p. 209.
3. *American Citizen*, 8/17/07.
4. Catherine Mitchill to Margaret Miller, 8/17/07, NYHS.
5. Sutcliffe, *Robert Fulton and the Clermont*, p. 234.
6. *American Citizen*, 8/22/07.
7. *Naval Chronicle*, 1808, Vol. xix, p. 88.
8. RRL to RLL, 9/2/07, NYHS.
9. Sutcliffe, *Robert Fulton and the Clermont*, p. 252.
10. *American Citizen*, 8/22/07.
11. RF to RRL, 8/21/07, CSHP.
12. Sutcliffe, *Robert Fulton and the Clermont*, p. 234.
13. RF to RRL, 8/28/07, CSHP.
14. Sutcliffe, *Robert Fulton and the Clermont*, p. 252.
15. Ibid., p. 251.
16. Ibid., p. 254.
17. RF to RRL, 11/12/07, CSHP.
18. Barlow, iii.
19. Woodress, p. 257.
20. RF to RRL, 11/11/07, CSHP.
21. RF to RRL, 11/21/07, CSHP.
22. RF to RRL, 11/23/07, CSHP.
23. RF to RRL, 11/2/07, 11/11/02, 12/1/07, CHSP.
24. RRL to JS, April 1808, NYHS.
25. RF to RRL, 11/6/07, CSHP.
26. RF to RRL, 12/1/07, CSHP.
27. JS to person unknown, 8/27/07, NJHS.
28. RF to TJ, 12/3/07, LC.
29. JB to TJ, 12/4/07, LC.
30. RF to RRL, 12/1/07, CSHP.
31. Gallatin, p. 121, 114.
32. Charles Wilson Peale to RF, 11/10/07, 11/15/07, APS; RF to Charles Wilson Peale, 11/18/07, HSP.
33. WT to RF, 12/16/07, LC.
34. RF to RRL, 11/2/07, CSHP.
35. RRL to RLL, 1/19/08, NYHS.
36. JRL to RL, 2/10/08, NYHS.

Chapter 14
1. JS to RRL, 12/28/07, NJHS.
2. RF to RRL, 12/28/07, CSHP.
3. RRL to JS, 1/18/08, NJHS.
4. JS to RRL, 2/13/08, NJHS.

5. JS to RS, 1/30/08, NJHS.
6. RF to RRL, 4/5/08, CSHP.
7. Ibid.
8. Rachel Cox Stevens to RRL, 4/16/08, NYHS.
9. RF to JB, 6/5/08, YB.
10. Catherine Mitchill to Margaret Miller, 12/28/08, William L. Clements Library, University of Michigan.
11. BHL to Captain Tingey, 6/22/08, PBHL.
12. RF to RRL, 7/12/08, CSHP.
13. RRL to JS, 7/4/08, NJHS.
14. RRL to JS, 7/12/08, NJHS.
15. Lambert, p. 64.
16. RF to RRL, 10/23/08, NYHS.
17. WT to JS, 10/11/08, NJHS.
18. RF to JS, 10/28/08, NYPL.
19. RRL to Rachel Cox Stevens, 11/19/08, NJHS.
20. RF to JS, 12/6/08, NYPL.
21. RF to RRL, 11/14/08, NYPL.

Chapter 15
1. Margaret Bayard Smith, Diary, 12/4/08, LC.
2. RF to JB, 3/1/09, HL.
3. Catherine Mitchill to Margaret Miller, 12/28/09, William L. Clements Library, University of Michigan.
4. BHL to RN, 2/7/09, PBHL.
5. RF to James Madison, 2/17/09, LC.
6. RF to François de Barbé-Marbois, 3/16/09, NYHS.
7. RF to BW, 3/23/09, HH.
8. RRL to JS, 5/9/09, NJHS.
9. Turnbull, pp. 275 ff.
10. RF to John Vaughn, 6/8/09, APS.
11. WT to RF, 5/18/09, LC.
12. RF to WT, 5/19/09, 6/24/09, LC.
13. JS to WT, 7/28/09, NJHS.
14. RF to JB, 3/1/09, HL.
15. RF to JB, 6/23/09, NYHS.
16. RF and RRL to JS, 11/11/09, NJHS.
17. JS to RF, 11/27/09, NJHS.
18. 12/1/09, NYHS.

Chapter 16
1. Fulton, *Torpedo*, p. 57.
2. Ibid., p. 54.
3. Ibid., p. 55.
4. Ibid., p. 44.
5. Ibid., p. 6.
6. Ibid., p. 25.
7. Ibid., p. 28.
8. Fulton, *Concluding Address.*
9. Samuel Latham Mitchill to Catherine

Mitchill, 3/23/10, Museum of the City of New York.

10. C. W. Goldsborough to Commodore John Rodgers, 2/24/10, NYHS.
11. Commodore John Rodgers to his wife, 3/13/10, NYHS.
12. C. W. Goldsborough to Commodore John Rodgers, 2/24/10, NYHS.
13. TJ to RF, 3/17/10, LC.
14. RF to R. Bradley, 3/5/10, NYHS.
15. *National Intelligencer*, 4/27/10.
16. RF to Volney, Laplace, and Monge, 5/4/10, NYHS.
17. RF to CS, 4/3/10, NYPL.
18. RF to RRL, 1/4/10, NYHS.
19. RF to JB, 7/1/10, HH.
20. "Extract of Commre Rodgers Journal of Observations relative to Mr. Fulton's Torpedo Experiments, September 21st 1810 [to November 1, 1810], NA.
21. Ibid.
22. Mann, p. 127.

Chapter 17
1. JS to RF, 1/11/11, NJHS.
2. RF to RRL, 12/21/11, NYHS.
3. RF to CS, 11/4/93, 4/10/11, KCC.
4. Elihu Whitney to RF, 3/30/11, YU.
5. RF to JB, 6/28/11, HH.
6. JB to RF, 7/20/11, HH.
7. JB to RF, 8/5/11, HH.
8. Andrew Bartholomew to RRL, 8/17/11, NYHS.
9. RRL to EL, 11/9/11, NYHS.
10. Livingston, n.p.
11. *Port Folio*, Vol. II, p. 264.
12. Memorial of Isaiah Townsend and others against the bill extending the term of patents granted to Robert Fulton, 12/27/11, NA.

Chapter 18
1. RRL to Arthur Roorbach, 2/2/12, 2/23/12, NYHS.
2. RF to Thomas Law, 4/4/12, NYPL.
3. RF to James Monroe, 2/13/12, NYSL.
4. WT to J. Ray, 1/31/12, LC.
5. Oliver Evans to JS, 2/2/12, NJHS.
6. RF to EL, 2/25/12, Private Collection.
7. 9 Johns. Rep., pp. 509–90.
8. RF to JB, 4/19/12, HH.
9. RRL to RF, 3/24/12, NYHS.
10. Ibid.
11. RF to RRL, 6/11/12, NYHS.
12. Harriet Fulton to RRL, 7/29/12, NYHS.
13. Hunt, p. 9.

14. RF to RRL, 9/24/12, NYHS.
15. Dr. Nicholas Romayne to RRL, 12/6/12, William L. Clements Library, University of Michigan.
16. RF to BHL, 11/23/12, NYHS.
17. RF to JDD, 11/27/12, JCB.
18. RF to RLL, 12/12/12, NYHS.

Chapter 19
1. RF to TJ, 4/13/13, LC.
2. RF to EL, 3/29/13, private collection.
3. *New-York Evening Post*, 3/16/13.
4. RF to EPL, 5/12/13, NYHS.
5. BHL to RF, 4/13/13, PBHL.
6. *Niles Weekly Register*, 8/9/13.
7. RF to TJ, 6/29/13, APS.
8. Ibid.
9. TJ to RF, 7/21/13, LC.
10. RF to Stephen Decatur, 7/27/13, Princeton University Library.
11. RF to Stephen Decatur, 7/29/13, Princeton University Library.
12. *Niles Weekly Register*, 8/21/13.

Chapter 20
1. RF to RLL, 9/28/13, NYHS.
2. RF to RLL, 10/12/13, NYHS.
3. RLL to EPL, 12/11/13, CSHP.
4. RF to JDD, 11/25/13, JCB.
5. Elihu Whitney to RF, 12/18/13, YS.
6. RF to RLL and EPL, 10/16/13, NYHS.
7. RF to JL, 11/11/13, Engineering Societies Library.
8. BHL to RF, 11/9/13, Engineering Societies Library.
9. Ibid.
10. EL to RF, 11/28/13, AI.
11. Ibid.
12. Fulton, Plan.
13. RF to Peter Jay Munro, 1/7/14, NYHS.
14. RF to Gouverneur Morris, 2/22/14, Fulton, Advantages.
15. RF to JDD, 3/10/14, NYHS.
16. RF to CDC, 3/6/14, CHSP.
17. Ogden, n.p.
18. Colden, pp. 248 ff.
19. RF to JDD, 3/20/14, NYHS.
20. RF to CDC, 4/2/14, NYHS.

Chapter 21
1. EPL to RF, 5/12/14, CSHP.
2. RF to EPL, 5/3/14, CSHP.
3. EPL to RF, 5/5/14, CSHP.
4. RF to JL, 3/9/14, ESL.
5. EL to RF, 5/19/14, AI.
6. BHL to RF, 2/8/14, PBHL.

7. BHL to RF, 6/9/14, PBHL.
8. BHL to RF, 4/20/14, PBHL.
9. BHL to JDD, 6/5/14, PBHL.
10. BHL to RF, 6/5/14, PBHL.
11. Ibid.
12. BHL to JDD, 5/22/14, PBHL.
13. Colden, p. 262.
14. RF to BW, 5/22/14, NYHS.
15. O. H. Perry et al., 1/3/14 NA.
16. William Jones to the Naval Committee of the House of Representatives, NA.
17. Henry Clay to RF, 1/27/14, NYHS.
18. RF to James Madison, 3/23/14, LC.
19. Sutcliffe, *Robert Fulton and the Clermont*, p. 217.
20. RF, EPL, and RLL Agreement, 7/25/84, CSHP.
21. *New York Evening Post*, 10/30/14.
22. David Porter to William Jones, 10/29/14, HSP.
23. RF to Isaac Chauncey, 11/26/14, Boston Public Library.

Chapter 22
1. EL to RF, 5/19/14, AI.
2. RF to Mr. Gales, 8/17/14, NYHS.
3. BHL to RF, 8/30/14, PBHL.
4. BHL to JDD, 8/23/14, PBHL.
5. BHL to RF, 9/24/14, PBHL.
6. RF to BHL, 10/26/14, NYHS.
7. EL to RF, 11/14, AI.
8. RF to James Monroe, 11/4/14, LC.
9. RF to James Madison, 11/5/14, LC.
10. BHL to RF, 11/13/14, PBHL.
11. BHL to RF, 12/5/14, PBHL.

12. Ibid.
13. BHL to JDD, 12/13/14, PBHL.
14. BHL to JDD, 10/18/14, PBHL.
15. NR deposition, 1/14/15, NYSL.
16. BHL to JDD, 12/13/14, PBHL.
17. RF to RLL, 12/25/14, NYHS.
18. RF to James Monroe, 12/27/14, U.S. Naval Academy Museum.
19. James Monroe to WT, 12/27/14, NA.
20. WT to James Monroe, 1/19/15, NA.
21. WT to Fernando Fairfax, 12/20/14, LC.
22. Fernando Fairfax to WT, 1/23/14, LC.
23. BHL to RF, 1/13/15, PBHL.
24. BHL to RF, 1/18/15, PBHL.
25. BHL to NR, 1/23/15, PBHL.
26. BHL to RF, 1/27/15, PBHL.
27. JDD to NR, 1/7/15, NYHS.
28. RF to BHL, 1/24/15, NYPL.
29. Stockton, n.p.
30. Ibid.
31. Ibid.
32. Ibid.
33. Ibid.
34. Ibid.
35. Ibid.
36. Ferdinand Fairfax to WT, 2/1/15, LC.
37. Colden, p. 267.
38. Ibid., p. 371.

Epilogue
1. Hunter, p. 5.
2. Chapelle, p. 175.
3. Robert Barlow Fulton to RLL, 11/19/29, NYHS.
4. BHL to NR, 3/5/15, PBHL.

N.B. To facilitate reading of contemporary documents capital letters have been supplied at the beginning of sentences and periods substituted for dashes when they were obviously intended. Otherwise interior capitalization and original spelling have been retained.

Index

Index